T0354139

War Children

War Children

A Memoir

Michael Tradowsky

iUniverse, Inc.
Bloomington

War Children
A Memoir

Copyright © 2012 by Michael Tradowsky

All rights reserved. No part of this book may be used or reproduced by any means, graphic, electronic, or mechanical, including photocopying, recording, taping or by any information storage retrieval system without the written permission of the publisher except in the case of brief quotations embodied in critical articles and reviews.

iUniverse books may be ordered through booksellers or by contacting:

iUniverse
1663 Liberty Drive
Bloomington, IN 47403
www.iuniverse.com
1-800-Authors (1-800-288-4677)

Because of the dynamic nature of the Internet, any web addresses or links contained in this book may have changed since publication and may no longer be valid. The views expressed in this work are solely those of the author and do not necessarily reflect the views of the publisher, and the publisher hereby disclaims any responsibility for them.

Any people depicted in stock imagery provided by Thinkstock are models, and such images are being used for illustrative purposes only.

Certain stock imagery © Thinkstock.

ISBN: 978-1-4759-5427-2 (sc)
ISBN: 978-1-4759-5426-5 (hc)
ISBN: 978-1-4759-5425-8 (e)

Library of Congress Control Number: 2012918893

Printed in the United States of America

iUniverse rev. date: 12/06/2012

To Laura and our children,
Kim, Christopher, Anna, Kirsten, and Peter,
and the war children of the world

Acknowledgements

This book owes much of its existence to the support of dear friends and family. I can hardly express all my gratitude. My heartfelt thanks to my wife, Laura, for correcting spelling and reducing the complicated syntax of the original, to Rev. Dr. Hazel Partington for proofreading, to Kim Porter for tirelessly editing and to Kirsten Tradowky for creating the oil painting "Children Exploring Ruins" for the cover.

Names and Relationships

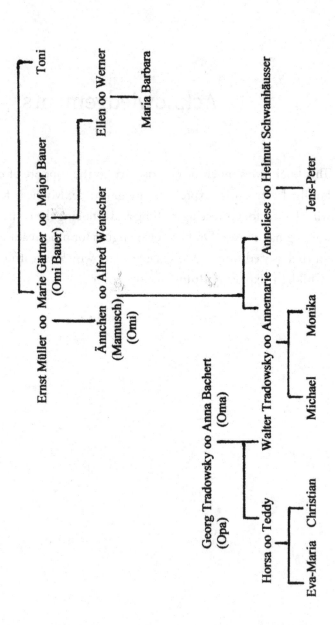

Black Forest

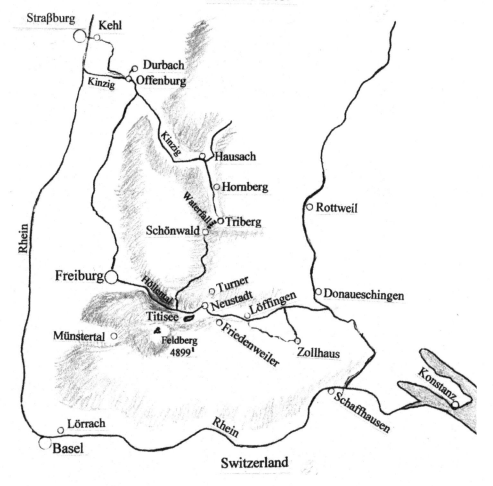

I

Children in the Cellar

1

The day of my life I remember best and try to forget most is Wednesday, April 11, 1945. The morning of this brilliant day in Erfurt, my mother, sister, grandmother, and I, along with all the women and children who lived in our four-story apartment building in the Louisenstrasse 21B, hid in the cellar. Now and then, someone hushed the group, and all listened for any sounds coming from the outside; no matter how we strained our ears, we heard nothing. This was the third day that we'd huddled down there, driven into our dim shelter by the sounds of approaching battle. For two days, the sound of gunfire and tanks had grown ever closer. Then, at last, at midnight, all noises faded to silence. As morning approached, the silence taunted us. Finally, around eleven, my mother stood and declared she would climb to the attic to find out what was going on. Everyone knew that once my mother had made up her mind, she could not be stopped. I begged to come along, thinking she might allow it. The air attacks had ceased for several days now. The bellowing of artillery and the rumbling of tanks from the southern hills of the Steigerwald had died down during the night. Besides, I was almost ten years old. During alerts, out of a strange mixture of fear and competitiveness, I was always the first to reach the cellar. Surely, if we were surprised by an attack, I would be able to make it down here quickly enough. She looked at me with her big eyes, "brown as a doe" as my father described them. I sensed her pleasure with me.

"All right, come," she said, her low voice still deeper with concern, "but if we hear planes, we'll have to get back down immediately."

With that, she started up the concrete cellar stairs, sliding her shoes on each step with those quick *chip-chip* sounds. Curious and proud, I *trip-trapped* behind her up to the basement door, which she flung open resolutely. The blinding light flooded through the tall windows onto the staircase.

The attic was the most dangerous place in the house. I never had been permitted up there before. The roof, our only protection from the sky, was so highly pitched that even my tall mother could walk standing up. The rafters and the clean floor smelled of dry, warm wood. I followed, looking curiously into the far corners, and was surprised to find them totally empty. According to air safety regulations, all rummage had been removed. Only a zinc tub full of sand with a little hand shovel stuck on top had been prepared in the middle of the spacious room. I had learned in school during air safety instructions that this sand was called *Luftschutzsand* (air safety sand). We third graders had been taught, if we saw an incendiary bomb, to cover it with sand, never with water. When unknowing people had carelessly put water on these bombs, the burning phosphorus had floated on top of the water, down the buildings, and along the streets and ignited other houses.

My mother and I took a few creaking steps and then stopped and listened. All was quiet. Over the last weeks, our family had confined ourselves to our first-floor apartment so that we could rush into the cellar quickly enough at each wail of the siren. During the last days, the Americans had moved their airfields very close; attacks came at any time, often before the warning sirens could be sounded, so we had moved into the cellar entirely, putting bunk beds into a small side room. We allowed ourselves only short periods upstairs until the approaching battle sounds kept us below permanently. Only our nagging curiosity could make us disregard all caution and drive us up to the attic.

Following the direction of last night's battle sounds, my mother went to the hatch facing south. She lifted the glass cover, stretched her neck into the open gap, and looked toward the Steigerwald. I observed her scanning the horizon. Two long, vertical wrinkles crossed her brow, starting from the base of her nose and making her most prominent feature look even larger. These furrows meant either concern, anger, and determination or merely deep concentration.

"See anything, Mutti?"

She reached down, boosted me under my arms, and I grabbed hold of the sharp, metal rim of the hatch and chinned myself up. Stretching into the opening, I saw the tile roof, the gutter, and our garden right below me.

A checkerboard of vegetables spread to the white picket fence. Behind the fence was the river, the Walkstrom, a small branch of the Gera. On the other side stood the frayed facade of the neighbor's house that had been hit two weeks ago. From up here, I could follow clearly the path the bomb had taken. It had blasted off half the roof and the exterior walls, ripping off parts of the five floors. Then it had burrowed into the cellar, where it gouged out a dark, bottomless funnel and spewed a wall of white rubble over the backyard.

"Look to the left, to the Steiger," my mother said.

I cranked my neck toward the hills but could not make out anything before my hands hurt too much and I had to drop to the floor. We listened again. Was there a distant hum? We did not wait to determine whether the sound was real or a result of our frightened and worn-out imaginations. We rushed downstairs.

While we were gone, the women in the cellar had busied themselves straightening cots, folding blankets, checking flashlights, replacing candles, and stacking magazines on crates that served as tables. They sent the children into the next room to play their usual cellar games. My mother and I rushed down the flight of concrete stairs into the cool, musty air. Our eyes adjusted to the light of the one naked lightbulb, and we saw the women scramble over the cots to gather around us.

"What's going on up there?"

"Tanks," my mother gasped. "The Steigerwald is full of tanks. There is no shooting. It's totally quiet."

My grandmother, Omi, pushed close while the others made room for the stately old lady. Her lifetime servant, shriveled, little Martchen, followed in her shadow. Omi turned her right ear toward my mother, cupping her hand behind it. My mother raised her voice.

"Tanks, Mamusch, tanks, up in the Steiger."

"What did she say?" said Omi, bending down to Martchen in disbelief.

The maid lifted herself on her toes to shout into Omi's ear. "Tanks, *gnädige Frau* (gracious lady), up in the Steiger."

"Tanks?" Omi repeated. "That close?"

Many years later, I would find out the historical facts of this day. I would read that the tanks belonged to the XX Corps under General Walton H. Walker, who had permission from Patton to take Erfurt, although it was east of the line the troops were expected to reach by this date. That day I understood only that the tanks besieging Erfurt were American, and they would attack.

As if to prove my mother's report, we heard right then the dark, hollow sound of gunfire, like the rumbling of dirt falling on a coffin. Everyone thought the attack was beginning. We waited for the next barrage, but it did not come. Instead, we heard a sound that, after a few moments, could no longer be wished away—the humming of approaching planes. My mother pushed me in front of her into the small side room. She picked up my little sister, Monika, who was sleeping in the lower bunk. She wrapped the thumb-sucking child tightly into her arms and sat down on the edge of a chair. The grinding of the motors bore directly down on us; we sat with lowered heads, prepared to throw ourselves onto the concrete floor with the start of the thuds and the tremors. We held our breath. Every fiber of our beings followed that lowering in pitch as the planes passed over the house. The sound slowly faded. We breathed again. The planes had not dropped any bombs on their first pass. They turned at the northern slope of the valley for a second pass. Here came the approach. This time, one of the planes flew so low that the roar of the motors shook the house. The pitch broke in a glissando. The roar faded away toward the south into silence. We were puzzled. Why did they not drop their bombs?

After a while the adults dared to get up and walk around. My grandmother leaned her elbow on the shelf where the *Volksempfänger* stood. She cupped her ear against the round field of cloth over the loudspeaker. She tuned through the chaos of jamming sounds and Morse signals to find the air safety broadcast. I hated this Volksempfänger (the "people's receiver"), a radio the government expected each household to purchase. Its shape reminded me of a bar of soap standing on end, its corners all washed round. However, in a perverted way, it was black, not white.

I wondered why Omi bothered listening to the radio. With the airfields so close, warning messages came after the attack now or not at all. So, why listen? Perhaps it had become habit. During the last months, we had become accustomed to following the reported routes of the bombers on their approaches and returns. Night after night, following each announcement, I looked up their location on a little square black-and-white map that had been thumbtacked to the cellar door. Remembering this map still makes me shudder. The map showed almost all of Thuringia superimposed by concentric circles of 25-km distances, with Erfurt in the center. The map showed no natural features—no rivers, no valleys, no mountains—just cities as little black round marks like bullet holes. During the raids of the last eight months, the names of the cities on the map had dug themselves into my brain. When the radio announced the locations of the approaching bombers over the cities west of us, each name evoked its specific degree of fear.

There was Eisenach on the extreme western margin. When the bombers were reported over Eisenach, I still hoped that they would follow a more northerly or southerly route. Mülhausen and Nordhausen meant they were close, but there was a chance they would pass us to the north and go on to Halle, Leipzig, or Berlin. If Saalfeld was announced, I prayed they would pass us to the south. However, when Gotha was named, the bombers were heading directly for us, and we would hear the humming within minutes. Gotha made my heart beat in my throat. *Please, God, not Gotha again!* Then the humming would grow into the droning of hundreds of planes that would wear on and on. *Are they circling? Are they continuing to Jena, Chemnitz, or Dresden? Surely they will come back over us on the way out.*

When we first tacked up the map, I studied it with interest, even a slight feeling of appreciation, as if by locating the danger I could control it. But now, after hundreds of nights, it had become a record of dread. I tried to look around the map when I glanced toward the door. Besides, it was useless. Following the concentric circles, the danger closed in on us like the arches between someone's thumbs and index fingers closing around your throat. Finally, it became just as disturbing looking at the map as it was listening to that black bar of soap. Why did my grandmother persist? I did not understand then that she was trying to get information about the imminent occupation of the city, not about the usual air strikes.

That morning, the big news did not come over the airwaves. Disseminated in a unique way, it spread through the city by word of mouth. It would take another hour and a half to make its way to the Louisenstrasse.

I could not stand listening to that radio. I felt compelled to untangle the web of jammed, fragmented words and interpret them on that constricting map on the door. I had to escape this confinement.

I closed my eyes, groped for the door, and rushed into the main room. I almost ran over Martchen, the only adult I knew who was smaller than I. She had gotten down from her chair the same instant, leaving on her seat the black book with the thin golden cross that she'd been reading. She was on the way to do what she felt was her duty even in these perilous days. She had cooked and served all meals for my grandmother and her family for over thirty years.

"Are you hungry, Michael? Surely! We're all hungry."

She stroked her gray hair away from her tiny, round face. My father had compared her face to a small, boiled, and cooled spring potato, its skin smooth but shriveled into a hundred little folds. She refastened the hairpins in her bun and marched up to the kitchen to prepare bread and soup. I turned toward the laughter that was coming from the larger side room where the children were playing their cellar games.

As I entered, the children were sitting on chairs in a circle, facing one another. They were holding hands playing "silent mail." I do not remember the names of the children except for the twins, Hedda and Gerda, who were closest to my age and, therefore, had become my playmates. Not identical, the twins were easy to tell apart. Hedda was pretty, Gerda plain. Having lost their parents, they had found refuge with their aunt, Frau von Reuss, a childless and domineering lady, who abhorred the fuss that children were liable to cause. The twins were twelve. All the other children were younger than I. None of the children were natives of Erfurt. They were all refugees like my sister Monika and I. We all shared the fate of most of Germany's children left in the cellars of the yet unoccupied land. We were children who had fled with their mothers from advancing armies, from the east out of Silesia, Pomerania, and East Prussia, or from the west, from Alsace, like Monika and I. They were children who had fled from devastated cities to other places that had suffered less, like Erfurt. Many were children of large families. Their fathers had been fighting the war for years in every corner of the world. They returned on leave and sired another offspring. The mothers, as obedient citizens, had given birth to five, six, or seven children. For this, they received special privileges from the government. They earned tax exemptions, food allocations, and "mother and child compartments" on the railroads. If they were exceptionally prolific, they received the honor of the "Mother Achievement Cross." The names of the children were Nordic, like Hauke and Frauke, and often from the heroes of the Nibelungen Saga—Brunhilde, Sieglinde, Siegfried, or Gunther. My mother could not suppress an ironic smile when she heard women call their daughters or sons, "Come here, Brunhilde," or "Bring me that, Siegfried," and an undernourished five- or six-year-old with skinny arms and legs protruding from oversized hand-me-downs would appear.

"Brunhilde, Siegfried," she would whisper, rolling her big brown eyes, "oh my."

The husbands, after fathering these children, returned to the front, and would perhaps meet them as toddlers on their next leave. Many fathers would never see their youngest. Someone would find the snapshot of the newborn on their body in the dirt and snow of some distant battleground. The children, separated from their fathers for so long, heard the message that their fathers had "fallen" in silence. They soon understood they would not see them again. By now, their hearts hung on their mothers. Some children had also lost their mothers in air raids. Forlorn and bewildered, they had been shipped to other cities to try to survive with relatives or friends.

Such was the fate of the children in the shrunken land of Germany. It was no different for the hand-holding circle that I now joined. Of all the games we had brought into the cellar months ago, silent mail was one of the three games we still chose to play. The other games we still played were cat's cradle and finger language. We had started out with card games like quartet and *Schwarzer Peter*, a version of old maid, checkers, and even chess. But as the dread of the raids closed in on us night and day, the isolation of winning became as difficult as losing. We favored games that drew us closer. We even made adjustments in the games. Silent mail called for one to stand in the middle of the circle. This child had to intercept the message by noticing the squeeze of the hand that was relaying it around the circle. Toward the end, none of us wanted to let go of the hands and stand alone. We changed the game by sending the message around the opposite side of the circle from where the spotter was sitting. When we played cat's cradle, we did not like it when someone created the suspenders that could not be changed into any other patterns and ended the game. We wanted our warm hands and interweaving fingers to touch forever, while they created rhomboids, parallel lines, interwoven rhomboids, and cat's cradles in silent repetitions.

The three games we still played were silent. In the cellar, all danger announced itself by sounds. The mothers adopted a low voice, always listening with one ear for sirens, planes, and explosions. We children followed their example and kept quiet. But we had our sign language. The twins, Hedda and Gerda, had learned it at camp and taught it to those who were able to spell. They used fingers and hands to form the letters of the alphabet. Over the endless waiting hours, we had become fast and agile in spelling out and responding to messages. The adults gave up trying to decipher what we were signing. This pleased us since it gave us our own code, our way of getting even with our mothers, who kept information about the war from us. My mother was one of the most careful, often sending Monika and me away if someone would start telling of the horrors of the last raid or of the advancing front lines. But we children kept informed. We had raised eavesdropping to an art. Every time we saw a group of adults whispering agitatedly, one of us was in the dark of the cellar listening with open mouth and head cocked toward the scary conversation.

While we were playing silent mail, I left our circle for the main cellar to listen. I had just entered when we heard a hammering of fists on the front door. It was a neighbor, who, rushing into the cellar, pulled a piece of paper out of her coat pocket like it was on fire. Trembling, she held under the light a leaflet. It was one of those she had found in the bushes and drifting in the street.

"Where did this come from?" the women wanted to know.

"They must have been shot over the city by cannon," the neighbor said.

The mothers nodded, recalling that distant rumbling.

"Perhaps they have been dropped by planes," they wondered.

It was obvious the papers had come from the Americans.

The message was an ultimatum. It said that the city was under siege. The mayor had until midnight to come to the Americans with a white flag and surrender Erfurt. If the city would not surrender by this deadline, it would be completely destroyed by bombardment.

The women blurted out their opinions in a tangle of excitement. They eventually calmed down, agreeing that the city government had no choice but to surrender, since there were no troops left in Erfurt to defend it.

The women did not understand what a stranglehold the SS and the party bosses had taken on the city government in order to enforce Hitler's "Total War." The Nazi leaders, who my mother usually referred to as "they" in public, had grabbed complete control. Old men up to age sixty and boys as young as sixteen had been called up as part of the *Volkssturm*, a Nazi-party controlled militia that was to defend each city to the death.

The women expected the Americans to occupy the city that evening or the next day. Their apprehension about soldiers that might come through the houses and into the cellars was swept away by hope of final rescue from the bombardments. The mothers believed there would be no attacks for the next hours. So certain were they that they sent us children into the backyard for a while to take in the sunshine and get the cellar air out of our lungs.

2

On the way out, we heard Martchen clanging in the kitchen and giving off shaky, high-pitched sounds. *"Nun danket alle Gott"* (Now thank we all our God). The old maid had no inkling that she was tone-deaf, and during her work, she loved to sing with confidence and endurance. She sang this hymn and all others she knew all in the same singsong voice. I tried to amuse the other kids by imitating Martchen, but I did not know the words. Her singing faded as we turned into the backyard.

We headed for the spot that attracted us children like magic—a gate in the picket fence that opened directly onto the water. No place in the yard was more exciting or more calming than the gate on the edge of the river. It had become a rule that Hedda, Gerda, and I, as the oldest, sat in the gate, while the smaller ones, who could not swim, had to crowd behind us. As we had done so many times during the last warm days, we took our shoes and socks off and dangled our feet into the water. Again we saw and followed the eddies and currents that streamed by. We threw sticks into the river and watched them race, catch up, and pass one another until they went over the dam at the Walk Mill. It had become a challenge for us to throw the sticks into a particular place on the water where they would wind up under the big, stomping wheel and be churned under. As from a private box, we watched the wheel endlessly dragging the dripping water curtains to the steep gable of the mill. The gray stone building with its blind and dull windows seemed abandoned. However, as I eventually found out, it concealed an angry miller.

Across the river rose the neighbor's bombed-out facade. It looked less threatening from below than from the attic. The wall of rubble hid the crater in the cellar. Parts of the floors were still attached to the walls. The house resembled a macabre version of a Nürnberg dollhouse that looked like it had been demolished by the ax of a madman. The top floor had been whacked off completely. To our amusement, it had left a bathtub hanging by its plumbing, helplessly stretching its little cast-iron legs into the air.

"If we had that tub, we could make a boat out of it."

"Maybe it will fall down in the next raid, and we can drag it into the water."

We all dreamed of having a boat and of going up the river exploring.

"We can fasten it here. This gate will be our landing."

The gate had no reason. No boat was tied there. Water was not being fetched through it. My mother unrolled the hose from the faucet at the house when she drenched the vegetable beds that she had planted. The gate was not provided for bathers. The Walkstrom was too shallow for swimming. Besides, tenants had thrown refuse into the river. Such dumping was forbidden. All those white shards of broken china that shimmered from the bottom must have been dumped in the dark. Indeed, the gate did not serve any purpose. Nevertheless, we were attracted to it. It was as if we sensed that gates leading into water are peculiar places where unusual things are bound to happen.

An accident, which occurred here two weeks before, had reenforced that hunch. I had been sitting in the gate with Gerda, the plain twin. We were telling stories. Then Hedda came by and sat down between us. For once, there seemed to be insufficient room for the three of us. Gerda shoved Hedda, who pushed back, and Gerda plunged into the river. When we helped her scramble out, she had a cut under her ankle that pulsed blood onto the stone. I shuddered. I knew she had severed an artery. Every time she tried lifting her white-knuckled thumb off the wound it squirted again.

The children screamed, "Go to your aunt! Go to your aunt!"

But she did not.

I became afraid that she would bleed to death. The other children understood that she wanted to wait for the bleeding to stop and for her skirt to dry before facing her aunt. However, the blood kept pulsing. She finally hobbled out of the yard with her hand clamped to her ankle, awkwardly supported by her sister. I stayed behind with the others as we lifted water in our cupped hands, carefully washing the blood off the stone.

That seemed long ago. Now, on that day of the ultimatum, we children did not have the heart to start any games. We knew that soon we would be called back down into the cellar. In spite of the brilliance of the sun, grayness, like at the beginning of an eclipse, hung over the scene. We felt as if the flow of the river were coming to a stop and reversing itself.

We were called back into the cellar. The adults were in an uproar. An announcement had emanated from that miserable little Volksempfänger. My mother was so upset that, for once, she could not hide her fury. She was shaking her head and hands violently while spitting out the words, "Defend with what? Those old men from the *Volkssturm*, who can hardly walk? Those children they drafted from the schools? The tanks will just roll over them. There is no one in this whole town but women and children, no one but women and children. But they will not surrender. They would rather have the town wiped out. They have nothing to lose. That's why. They are finished. They want everybody to go down with them."

The city planned to defy the ultimatum. I knew well what that meant. Over the last year the air strikes had come closer and closer. First they'd hit downtown and then our quarter and then houses in the next block. Then had come direct carpet bombing. This time, there would be no stone left on the other.

I recollect the remainder of the day with photographic clarity. While the women continued their uproar, Martchen appeared at the top of the stairs calling my mother, "Frau Annemarie, lunch is ready." The good soul had prepared a meal even now.

My mother calmed. There was nothing to do. There was no escape. Nothing would happen until midnight.

"Let's go up and have something to eat, Mamusch," she shouted into her mother's ear.

I followed Omi and Mother, who led Monika by the hand up the stairs into the dining room. Martchen had prepared potato soup and bread. I had been sick the last days, and the smell of the soup nauseated me. Martchen took my plate away, made me *Pfefferminztee*, and found some *Zwieback*. The sweet twice-baked bread would calm my stomach. Then it was back into the cellar.

I spent most of the rest of the day in the upper bunk, still weak and trying to keep my stomach calm. I watched Monika play with her dolls down in the corner. She was moving them from little beds on top of a chair to the floor underneath and back up, playing air raid. In her little curly, blonde head she had gathered that this was just something mothers and children had to do.

I dozed off now and then. As the day progressed into the evening, I became more and more awake. I realized how close midnight was to coming. Would it all end? How could I get from here to that long and happy life that my young heart had been expecting?

My mother entered the room, settled Monika into the lower bunk, and stroked her until she went to sleep. Then she stood up, asked me how my stomach was, and urged me to go to sleep also.

Her calm was comforting. Haltingly, I asked her the question that weighed on my mind. "Mutti?"

"Yes, Micha."

"What will happen? I mean, how will it go on?"

She stroked my hair and said quietly with her deep voice, "God, he knows how it will go on."

She said it to settle me down. I felt a surge of thanks and love. But I sensed something else from the profound calm in her voice. It told me that my resourceful mother no longer knew a way out. Moreover, it told me that she had submitted her care about our future to God, who knew how the story would go on with us or without us. And I felt that, either way, my mother was resolved to submit.

"How late is it?" I asked.

"It is eight."

Four more hours, I thought.

She turned off the light but left the door slightly ajar when she squeezed out. I could hear the adults in the main room. I knew where my mother was going next. She had done it many evenings when the sky was clear and there was no air raid. Sometimes she took me along. At eight o'clock, she would go up the cellar stairs and step into the open, and be greeted by dead silence. She would look at the sky. With the complete blackout, the stars would be bright. Even the Milky Way would be clearly visible. She would follow the Milky Way north to the familiar constellation, Cassiopeia, the big W.

When my mother had visited my father at the end of boot camp, they had agreed to look at Cassiopeia at eight o'clock whenever they could. It was their way of outwitting the war and holding on to one place in this world where they could meet. Their glances were like huge calipers that would come together in the infinite.

My mother had known for some time where the far end of these calipers was coming back to earth. Even though the soldier's place of deployment was supposed to remain unknown, my parents had devised a secret code. My father spelled out his whereabouts in the first letter of each word in his *Feldpost* letter. And so my mother knew his communications unit had been ordered to the Münstertal in his beloved Black Forest.

Eight o'clock. It fell on me again. Four more hours. Time passed relentlessly with every breath. I lay rigid. The light from the main room cast a triangle across the ceiling directly above my head. I ran my finger along the line where the light met the dark. How strong was this ceiling? Would it hold the three floors and the roof when they came down? Or would the bomb fall into the basement like in our neighbor's house?

I tried to escape to better thoughts. I tried to comfort myself by thinking of my garden in Berlin before the war. Oh, what a secure place of light and wonder that had been. As I went back, I breathed easier for a while. Pictures of my short life appeared. How I had enjoyed life every day for four years of peace. How I had held on to that joy even when the war started and took it away bit by bit up to this night, when it was all gone.

II

The Little Boy and
the Big War

3

I am fortunate to have detailed information about my origin and my parents' circumstances. Two weeks after my birth, my father started a diary for me, which is a little square book with a cover upholstered in beige plaid. The title page reads:

Tagebuch No. 1
Michael Tradowsky
Berlin-Wilmersdorf
Offenbacher Strasse 8
Im Atelier
September 4, 1935

When my father began this diary, he assumed that I would one day like journaling as much as he did. He started journaling at age twelve and accumulated about 180 diaries during his lifetime. I can't be sure of the exact number since he burned some of the books. He bound most of the books himself and numbered the pages continuously until they reached far into the ten thousands. The sheer number filled him with pride.

Though I never shared my father's need for diary writing, I eventually took it up to please him and to try to be more like him. Now, as I record here the story of my tortuous life, I value this wealth of information.

My father's first entry in my first diary reads:

September 5, 1935. 18:00

In the winter of the year 1934, beginning of December to be precise, Walter Tradowsky met with his wife Annemarie (whom he called Anna Maria, Niña, or Murkelchen) in Berlin for a *Wiedersehen* of three days only. Therefore, it is likely that little Michael originated in the night from the second to the third of December …

On the 13th of March, the young father moved into a studio in the Offenbacher Strasse, which was winter-cold and primitively furnished. Perhaps it was on the eleventh already, because two days later he welcomed the arrival of his dear wife and the inch-long son. Given the expectant circumstances, a constant separation with fleeting hour-long or daylong visits had become unbearable.

Perhaps this separation during the first six months of a happy marriage seems surprising. It is explained by the lucrative income of the Erfurt photography studio and the monetary dependency of this fledgling family … The father's theater contract at the Volksbühne was going to terminate on September 1. The prospect for a new one was vague, generally speaking and particularly in its details …

On August 21, 1935, a Wednesday, Herr Walter Tradowsky did not come home until about seven and found his wife in the condition of regular contractions. They accelerated until 9 o'clock. The nurse who had agreed to assist could not be reached by phone.

The scheduled obstetrician was vacationing in the Alps. Finally, my father got a hold of his substitute, Dr. Wilhelm Kaute, who was, no less, the owner of the West Sanatorium in Berlin/ Charlottenburg.

At 10:30 Annemarie descended the 89 steps down to the street.

My father, who had a penchant for counting things, had determined the number of steps long ago and now recorded the figure. Dr. Kaute had sent his private car to take young Annemarie to the clinic. My father's diary entry goes on:

Because of the husband's exceedingly restrained demeanor, he was permitted to be with his wife through her most difficult time until two in the morning. At this early hour the woman in labor was taken into the delivery room, the father-to-be sent home, where, contrary to all expectations, he neglected his diary, read in Roda Roda's Roman, and went to bed around 3:30.

On August 22nd, at eight o'clock in the morning, the young Papa received the message of the just well accomplished delivery of a son and heir. At nine o'clock he had to accept a personal report by the physician. Toward 10:45, armed with a bouquet of red roses, he greeted the weak, happy mother and saw his son, who lay in his crib looking dejected, foreign to the world, unhappy.

Of the three diaries that my father wrote for me, this first one is particularly interesting. Between the lines that tell about my progress (first smile, first turning over, first babblings, and so on), I can get a glimpse of the initial two years of my parents' marriage, which they spent in Bohemian exuberance. There they were in this spacious studio under the roof of a five-story building with hardly any furniture.

Shortly after they had moved in, my grandmother had to check up on her daughter's place. Her curiosity drove her huffing and puffing up all eighty-nine steps. Finally staggering through the door, she sank into the only halfway trustworthy seat, a little corduroy easy chair scrounged from God knows where. In disbelief, she surveyed the studio: the low French double bed moved into the middle of the room under the enormous skylight, a potbellied stove awkwardly away from the wall and obviously causing dust and dirt. No kitchen. A hot plate in the corner. No ventilation for the steam and odors. A sliver of a window looking down on the street, draped with a towel.

Omi was too out of breath and too aghast to say anything. She rummaged through her cavernous purse and found her cigarettes and silver lighter. After a few puffs, she regained her composure and began berating her daughter.

"How could you ever agree to move into this?"

"But, Mamusch, we are happy here."

When my father got home, Omi did not waste any time and made her statement. "If you live in this place, I will not give you the furniture." She did not know my father if she thought she could force his compliance.

"You know where you can stick your furniture," he snapped.

She either did not hear him or did not understand. She could not conceive that someone could resist the power of her wealth. The old lady left, never to climb the eighty-nine steps again.

My parents did not need the furniture for their happiness, as is quite clear from my father's diaries. They managed to get through the winter by firing the little potbellied stove to red-hot at night and clinging to each other under the extra blankets in the cold early mornings.

4

My parents told me that I spent most of the fall and winter of my first six months in the crib between their bed and the potbellied stove. As soon as the March sun got warm, they put me in my carriage on the balcony to soak up the ultraviolet rays. Somewhere from a phonograph below, a tango pulsed over the rooftops, *"Guitarren spielt auf, spielt das Lied meiner Sehnsucht für mich"* (Guitars start strumming, play the song of my longing for me). When I heard this song many years later, the melody brought forth a memory of warmth and light, of being suspended between earth and heaven and resting in complete care.

Then came the summer when the Olympic Games were at the stadium and physical achievements were on everyone's mind. As my father's journal reveals, my parents yielded to the intense heat under the roof, shed their clothes, and lived like Adam and Eve. My father celebrated his young, slender wife by sketching her nude in his diary, standing at the cooking niche, ironing, tuning the radio, or reading curled up in the corduroy chair. They both considered the nude body good and natural.

In the studio, everything was good and driven by the ever-returning desire and fulfillment under the stars. My mother did not yet mind the long hours waiting until my father came home from the theater. Surely, if he spent all these extra hours, he would soon be permitted to direct his own play. He would become one of the famous play directors in Berlin, like Max Reinhardt and Jessner. At night, she moved the chair in front of the sliver of a window and read Storm's short stories until she would hear his steps on the street and then his whistling, "Shine, Moon, Shine!"—the first notes of a song he had written. It was a volley full of energy, as if it announced "Here I come. Be ready." And then another night under the big skylight would lift them above the ominous changes in the streets that worried them about the future of Germany.

———

Ever since Leopold Jessner, my father's mentor and idol, had to leave Germany, my father had considered ways to emigrate. When my parents got married, my mother agreed with his plans.

As he'd grown up, my father had resonated with the Nordic culture by reading Ibsen, Hamsun, Lagerloef, and Gudmundson. He responded by writing Nordic songs himself. Yes, the glimmering fjords of Norway, the little hamlets in the glacier-fed meadows and steep forests would be a good place to rear a boy. He bought books on beekeeping and prepared himself for this contemplative occupation. He studied Norwegian by deciphering novels using his knowledge of Plattdeutsch and a dictionary. A superficial understanding would suffice. He knew full well that he would keep writing in German. He fantasized about my future in this Norwegian setting and wrote in my first diary what he expected for my life.

Sunday, March 22, 1936
You see, my boy, now, on the first day of spring, you have become seven months old.

Perhaps this is why the sun is shining twice as bright and warms twice as much on this summer-like March day. Perhaps this is why your eyes are twice as blue as God's big sky under which crawls this mankind struggling for reason. Perhaps this is why.

Perhaps it is particularly on this day that your parents have on their mind what they want to offer you one of these days. In this aspect, their ambitions are quite different from the conventional.

A judge, a city planning official, a famous theater man—those would be the normal goals—or a mayor (your father was supposed to become one!), a professor, or a Siemens chief engineer!

You, dear heavens, you shall be an altogether different man!

You shall have a house, a meadow, a forest, and the fishing rights for a section of a river nearby. You should have the right to hunt in forest and field; the industrious bees, which fill the summer air with their quiet humming, shall belong to you with their honey. A horse shall carry you on its round and healthy back, and a faithful dog shall accompany you on your wayfaring day and night. You should know the woods and fields, the waters, and the constellations that circle above your head.

This we wish for your life, and I will give you everything I can to make you acquainted and at ease with the wealth of your freedom. Because I had to walk a long way with your mother until we found that place in life, where the first and last values are hidden below the undergrowth of ancient prejudices.

This is a picture of 1956 or even 1960. But it is a tendency of all parents to jump from the future that they hope for themselves into that of their children.

My father and his dreams! My mother was more practical. She started looking in the newspaper ads for houses with gardens in the suburbs. Surely, Michael needed more space, grass, trees, and sunshine. The second winter had been much chillier then the first. Putting me, blue and cold, between my parents in their bed to warm me up in the morning was not a permanent solution. And then the accident happened, when the potbellied stove had been fired to red-hot, and I, being in the crawl-walk stage, had uprighted myself on it. I had screamed for hours while my palms turned into a field of blisters. Then the second accident happened. One morning when my parents were still asleep, I shook my crib to drop the mattress from its pegs. I wedged myself through the crack to freedom and drank my father's India ink from the table where he was writing and illustrating.

My mother found a house advertised for lease in a tract that was being built north of Berlin in the suburb of Glienicke. She convinced my father to forget Norway for a moment and take the double-decker bus with her out to the Oranienburger Chaussee.

My parents got off at the village of Glienicke, which huddled east of the highway around a little gray brick church with a steeple like a freshly sharpened pencil. To their surprise, however, the development was not on the east side of the Chaussee. A thin peninsula of Glienicke reached west across the thoroughfare wedged between the neighboring communities of Hermsdorf and Frohnau. This odd extension of Glienicke was just wide enough for one road and the one-family homes that were being built on both sides. The road was a wide strip of sand furrowed by the tracks of construction vehicles. My parents found the house. It had a temporary address, street A, house 1, the first one on the south side. It was a one-story building of dark brick, with a tile roof, two bedrooms, and one bath. It belonged to the builder of the development. He had designed it with his retirement in mind and offered it for a five-year lease, possibly to be extended. A chain-link fence ran along the 50-foot frontage and extended 150 feet to the rear of the lot. The front fence dipped down to a double gate on the northeast corner. The gate was for a car. The drive continued along the east side of the house and down a ramp from the back into a garage underneath. Since the house was placed close to the front of the lot, it left a wide space of sand in the back. Immediately, my mother imagined a spacious lawn rimmed with flowerbeds of daisies, petunias, sweet peas, and dahlias. The neighboring lot toward the Oranienburger Chaussee was overgrown with a mysterious thicket of trees that pushed their branches over the fence. On the other neighboring lot, on the west side, a similar tract house was being completed. The most imposing feature of the considered property, a gigantic oak, stood close to the back fence. This venerable old man of a tree looked even more dominant because on his right stood the slender woman of a pine. The oak had been planted long ago to mark the border of the village of Glienicke. It had lived up to its importance. Behind the back fence spread the endless community meadow of the neighboring Hermsdorf. The possibility of the garden made my parents decide to rent the property.

My parents moved on June 4, 1937. They gave me the largest and warmest room, which was at the southwest corner with a south window overlooking the backyard. The furniture arrived from Erfurt. My mother placed and polished each piece with great care. It gave her a sense of pride and security to see some of the old splendor of her family in these new rooms.

As more houses went up in the sandy tract, the street was paved and acquired the descriptive name *Am Sandkrug* (At the Sand Mug).

My parents' move and sudden change in surroundings wakened my consciousness. My memory engaged. The house had just been completed and still smelled like lime and paint. In the backyard, close to the house where I started digging in the sand, the masons had left a screen leaning upright against a tall sawhorse draped with a tarp. On the far end of the sawhorse, a shovel stuck in the sand with a pail upturned on top of its handle. This assemblage of tools, which resembled a crouching person, was to give my parents a good scare.

Both my father and mother had grown up in the city. The fringes of the country were, for them, eerily quiet and desolate. Living in the first finished house of the development, they were enclosed by trees and meadows and had no neighbors within shouting distance. At night, they became nervous. This apprehension was stirred by a strange call that woke them one morning around three o'clock. My father staggered drowsily into the hall to answer the phone.

"Hello."

A fever-pitched voice was on the other end. "Walter, Walter, are you there?"

"Yes!" My father's heart jumped into his throat.

"Walter, Walter, where are you?"

"I'm at home."

The voice was desperate. "Walter, I'm at the slaughterhouse, waiting!"

"What?"

Wrong number.

My parents tried to make sense out of the call. Evidently, there was some shady transaction going on where a Walter had to pick up some meat at the slaughterhouse.

Then a few nights later, they thought they heard a strange bump coming from behind the house. What was that? Was somebody there? They put on their bathrobes and, without turning on the lights, tiptoed to the living room window and peeked into the backyard. It was too dark to see much. But there, close to the house, someone was crouching. While my mother barricaded herself in my room, pushing the toy chest in front of the door, my father became heroic. He grabbed the rolling pin, went outside, and approached the intruder by feeling his way along the house toward the back. I'm tempted to write that he snuck up to the crouching man and hit him over the head, so that the metal pail toppled off the shovel with a big bang. In truth, my father discovered his error a few paces before the clash. This odd and troublesome arrangement of tools resembling a crouching man became my first definite memory.

After the builder's equipment had been removed, my mother, with my father's assistance, immediately started to turn the sandy desert into a garden. They left the area close to the house unchanged for me to dig and make mud pies. From there, I watched them seed the backyard. The lawn stretched from the house to the oak and the pine at the south end and to the chain-link fence toward the east and west. Along the west side of the house, my mother planted a continuous bed. She started with a few tomatoes close to my digging area. She went on to dahlias, peonies, and roses and ended in the northwest corner at the street in a rock garden with mosses and phlox.

I was placed in this yard with my blank mind and my thirsty, wide-open senses. My mother thought that the fresh air and sunshine would be healthier than the lime-smelling confines of the house. Every day, she left me in the garden alone for many hours with a shovel and a pail so I could play in the sand.

5

Alone in the garden, my sand plot did not hold me for long. I had to explore. Since there were no older siblings and no parents present to guide me, I had no words for what I saw. I was taught no shortcuts of symbols for comprehending the objects in the garden. I was taught no categories, no prejudices. I made everything my own in its unnamed completeness. Did I ever live more fully than during that first year in the garden before I began to speak? Did I ever again see colors so brilliantly, hear so attentively? Did I ever have more tender hands and feet to feel? Did I ever taste or smell more acutely? Did I ever feel more equal and continuous with anything that grew, crawled, or flew?

I remember the cool and moist sand crunching on my bare feet; the delicate, springy strokes of grass across the lawn toward the pine; the sticky, fragrant, amber tears that oozed from the sun-baked orange scales of the bark; the scraggly stump of a broken-off low limb; and high above, the gnarled and twisted branches that etched tufts of dark green needles into the pale blue sky.

I remember the meadow through the wire windows of the chain-link fence, in it, the buzz of insects, the twitter of birds ascending, the flicker of little yellow and pale blue butterflies, the endless swaying of the tall, silvery grass.

I remember the gigantic oak, the climb over the vigorous roots curving up to the massive trunk, the feel of the cool bark divided into flat ridges, made soft and slightly tacky by a hint of moss.

I remember the branches tossed down into the weeds, the undulating sharp edges of the dry leaves, the polished acorns popping out of little stemmed cups, to be fitted back together, oh so smoothly.

I remember lying under the oak surrounded by the white umbrellas of Queen Anne's lace; looking up along the mammoth trunk into the mighty boughs ever more dividing and twisting and the rush of the wind in the tossing leaves, patches of blue here and there through the branches, clouds drifting slowly into the spaces and sailing on.

I remember the densely wooded wilderness in the neighboring lot and the branches pushing over the fence. *What is hidden in those trees?* Every day, again, *what is hidden in those trees?* Finally, one evening, an enormous disc emerged out of the wilderness, first fractured by branches, slowly rising into the blue-black sky and then hovering over the treetops, smooth, perfectly round, golden, and luminous.

I remember the other side of the garden—the glossy, fire-red tomatoes; the voluptuous dahlias, orange, purple, and yellow, swaying high above; the dry, warm, stone garden, ants hurrying and scrambling along trails in endless procession, carrying loads ten times their size.

I remember resting my cheek on the moss, becoming smaller and smaller, hurrying with the ants through gaping caverns, through the crisscross of grass, through the plush hillocks of pale gray moss, and onward under the towering groves of phlox.

I also remember pain from curious, limp, light green, heart-shaped leaves with sawtooth edges, glossy on the top side, dull with tiny hairs on the bottom. Oh what burn, what fire! I remember the welts on the hands, the run to the door, the screaming, the opening, the consoling embrace, the cold water on the burn.

How good it was always to sense the presence of my mother in the house during all those hours alone in the garden. There was care. There was food. There was the warmth and comfort like it always had been, from my first breath, even before.

I remember the warm tub; the smell of soap; the caring hands over my body; the inside of the white, fuzzy, warm towel; the rubbing through it; the stepping into clean pajamas; the holding on to shoulders; the flight into bed; the kiss; the darkness; the sliding of my soles on the clean sheets.

I remember the warm summer nights, the open window, the moon standing over the land, the firs and the fields exhaling after a hot day and then a train going in the distance, the soft *tap tap, tap tap* on the tracks, the faraway howling of the wind around the wheels, and the feeling of lying outstretched like the land under the night sky.

I remember other nights, climbing out of bed, groping my way through the dark house, crawling into my mother's bed where she was reading until my father would come home from the theater. I remember the snuggly hollow of her back and on the other side, the flower pattern of the wall. I remember playing with a little travel alarm clock in her shadow—the greenish glow of the mysterious ciphers and dots and, when pressed to the ear, the tiny sound of the intricately structured, endlessly hasting mechanism inside.

After my father had come home, long after I had fallen asleep, I remember the slipping from under the sheets away from the warmth, the rise between hands, the lift to the ceiling, the settling on chest and shoulder, and the return through the dark house into the cool bed.

How I cherish the memories of everything that surrounded me during that year—the garden, the house, and my parents. Didn't I have the truest and most complete comprehension of the world in the time before I spoke?

Eventually, my parents became concerned. For long they had not given any thought to my muteness. Since I was the first child of my generation, they had no comparison.

Then my aunt Teddy, my father's sister, came to Glienicke for her first visit. She arrived unannounced, of course, for she liked to surprise. Generous as always, she presented a Melitta coffee machine as a housewarming gift and blue, knit shorts and a striped sweater for me. She also brought along some photographs of baby daughter Eva-Maria. Lying on her naked belly on a polar bear fur, she looked up with huge, astonished, dark eyes.

With the arrival of Eva-Maria in her structured life, Tante Teddy had acquired a library about child care and development. Tante Teddy liked to do things by the book, whether it was as esoteric as choosing a philosophy or as down to earth as cooking, getting pregnant, or rearing children.

"Michael doesn't seem to say much," she observed after a while. "The books say children should start words by one and a half. By two, some say complete sentences. Michael is almost three."

"I think Michael will talk when he's good and ready," my father countered, unconcerned and a little peeved.

After Tante Teddy's visit, my parents talked to me more than before, directing questions at me whether I answered or not.

Why was I so hesitant? As little as I was, I was reluctant for language to unsettle my balanced and complete world. I was apprehensive of language as a disturbance. My fear was, perhaps, exaggerated by the way I saw my parents. I perceived them as belonging together, almost like one person. However, they had episodes when they would split into two, forced apart by those sounds coming from their mouths. What was happening?

It felt right when my father and mother would embrace in the middle of the room for a long time and I would close my arms around their knees, wanting to be part of their union. When they would sit at opposite ends of the dinner table and those sounds would become louder and louder, when the folds would appear on my mother's brow, when my father would bang his fist on the table, this felt very wrong. What were those sounds doing to them? How could these noises be so disruptive?

I felt that my parents were anxious for me to talk. I wanted to please them, and I wanted to be closer to them. Finally I overcame my hesitation. I spoke in clear, full sentences.

"This joker," they said. "He's been listening all along. He just didn't want to speak." Within weeks, I started asking questions with conversational modifiers like *eigentlich* (actually). "Where were you, actually?"

I learned to talk about "Michael" and then about "I." That was when I started to become anxious to watch out for myself. Gone was the year of abundant wonder, of giving all things in creation the time and attention they deserved, and of grasping their essence completely. My thoughts were trapped forever in the barren corridors of language.

6

My parents had their own theory about why I had not talked for so long. "Michael has always been alone in the garden. He didn't need to communicate."

As the lots around us developed and families moved in, my parents looked for children my age to play with me. The Ronnefelds, who lived on the other side of the wooded lot toward the Oranienburger Chaussee, had a yard full of children. Their youngest seemed to be my age. To get acquainted with the parents first, they invited the couple one summer evening after their children and I had been put to bed.

I remember that evening because of the heavenly display that marked it. I was lying awake. I heard strange voices through the window and the slap of a leather handball. I climbed out of bed, and supporting my toes on the ledge of the baseboard, chinned myself above the windowsill. There I saw the adults running back and forth across the lawn, dribbling and passing the ball. In the distance, a dark cloud towered over the meadow. The setting sun selected each leaf of the oak and delineated it with a distinct, radiant, golden border. A few large drops fell, but the play went on. Suddenly, a most amazing arch, in glowing colors, appeared. It curved high in the sky over the oak and the pine and descended into the wilderness of the neighboring lot. My mother stopped the ball and dropped it. She raised both arms and pointed. "Look."

All turned, stood there, and watched silently, so glorious was the spectacle.

After this visit, the Ronnefelds must have decided that the Tradowskys could be entrusted with their son. They brought Jörg over. He had been talking quite nicely for a year. I was intrigued to be together with a person my size for the first time. He looked similar to me, blonde and blue-eyed. He even wore knit shorts, though his were red while mine were blue.

In our play, he followed my lead. He was on my turf. Rarely would we stoop to use the usual toys like sand pail and shovel. We found it much more exciting to subvert the tools on the premises. The garden hose laid out on the lawn on hot days became a wildly writhing snake that the one could try to catch while the other operated the faucet at the house. The metal rod that braced the gate for the car entrance became a piece of gymnastic equipment. It took skill to walk up to the gate and sit on the narrow angle-iron that formed its top without falling into the garden or onto the sidewalk. Walking the gray brick retaining walls of the ramp to the subterranean garage provided another challenge. The wall was a foot high at the far end from the house but man high at the garage door. To walk on it toward the house took more and more courage with every step. Once this feat was mastered, we could climb on the little roof that was shading the garage door. When my mother was working in the garden, the roof was off limits.

"Boys, you want to break your necks?"

We went back to the lawn and turned the rake into a motorcycle. We sat on the broom rake laid flat into the grass and held on to the handle. Off we raced, leaning right and left into the turns, while sounding the appropriate revving of the motor.

Jörg was game for any nonsense I could dream up. Soon, he walked over from his house by himself. If my parents hoped to have him enhance my conversational skills, they succeeded. Resting from our antics, we would lie in the grass or balance on our gate and talk about anything that popped into our heads. One topic that we returned to repeatedly was whose father was stronger. We came up with ever-bigger claims.

"My father can throw your father over that fence."

"Oh yeah? But my father can throw your father over that tree."

"But my father can throw your father with his little finger over the whole sky."

Having no way of settling this question, we both believed that our own father could lick the other. When comparing our own strength, we thought ourselves to be on a par. Having become buddies, we never tested this assumption. The knowledge that Jörg was my equal was important to me. It confirmed my own mental and physical state. We were alike, except for the color of our shorts and, perhaps, for what was hidden beneath. This left an open question that aroused our curiosity. The far side of the oak tree would be a suitable place to find out. When my mother checked what we were doing back there, she found us both with our knit shorts around our ankles.

"No *schweinigeln*" (to mess around sexually), she said. "Pull up your pants. Play something else."

That ended the investigation. However, one short look had been enough to satisfy me. We were, indeed, equal in all parts.

Our curiosity found other targets past the fence in the world outside. Sitting on the front gate, we used to comment on the people who passed on the sidewalk. Men like our fathers came striding; women like our mothers stepped busily. A mother led a child who looked different from us.

"She is a girl," said Jörg as a matter of identification.

I nodded as if I understood. I observed that she moved more carefully. Her skin appeared soft and smooth. Blonde, long curls escaped from the hood of her little rain jacket. She was so unique that I had to give her a name. Because of her long, pointy hood and her flapping coat, I called her *die Vogelspitze* (the bird point).

Soon after seeing this mysterious little person, I actually got acquainted with my first girl. She was one of the many surprises that waited for me in the metropolis.

7

We had two ways to get from Glienicke to Berlin—train or bus. My father took the train to the theater. He rode his bicycle to the station. When he left in the afternoon, I would see him from the garden until he disappeared over the sandy hill in the distance. This rise was the boundary of my world. Returning from work, my father would whistle his "Shine, Moon, Shine" from the hillock.

My mother preferred the bus. She was the one who took me along on her occasional shopping excursions. We would walk one block past the wooded neighboring lot and past the Ronnefeld's house to the cobblestone-paved Oranienburger Chaussee. We boarded the white double-decker that stopped across from Luzi's cigarette stand. I got my mother to ride with me on the upper deck, which was open and passed under the canopy of the oaks that rimmed the road. We usually wound up on the Kurfürsten Damm.

What excitement, to wander at my mother's hand on a sidewalk as wide as our whole street at home, to stroll around the gleaming display cases that rose out of the slab floor, and to turn to the curb and watch the black lacquered automobiles with their whirling, sparkling chrome spokes. Wouldn't it be thrilling to stand on the outside running board of one of those splendid vehicles and glide all the way to the big sandstone church with the bunched towers?

Having been to the city a few times, I was ready to be part of an event in this foreign environment. My parents were taking me to my first party. Tante Teddy and Onkel Horsa had invited us. I was going to meet my cousin, Eva-Maria. My mother outfitted me with a new white shirt, shorts with a real crease, and a striped blue-and-maroon jacket with gold buttons. My father took me to the barber in Glienicke, who, to my great relief, snipped nothing off my substantial ears.

Our travel ended at a classy apartment building on the Hohenzollern Damm. Onkel Horsa's establishment was in the *belle etage* (the second floor). Two entrance doors led inside from the landing. The left one, which led to Onkel Horsa's dental practice, emitted an odor of oil of cloves— unfamiliar and ominous. Fortunately, we were received into the right door, where we were greeted by the smell of fresh-ground coffee. The corridor led past the kitchen, the children's room, the master bedroom, and into the music room, which had a black grand piano like ours. From there, the high and wide double-pocket doors were rolled into the walls, allowing the view into the dining room and finally into the *Berliner Zimmer,* a particularly bright room with high windows on two walls since it occupied the corner of the building.

I did not understand the occasion of the party and felt forlorn standing there in these wide, unknown halls between the towering adults. Then Tante Teddy brought one of those special little creatures over to me that Jörg and I had identified as girls.

"This is your cousin, Eva-Maria. Evi, why don't you take Michael and show him your toys?"

Her hand was warm and soft as she took me to her room. Right away, she hurried around to demonstrate her possessions.

"This is my *Brummkreisel,*" she said, plunging the twisted rod into the many-colored metal top and sending it on its staggering, humming way.

"This is my *Stehaufmännchen,*" she went on, pushing over the little clown with the spherical weighted bottom and letting him stand up time and again, emitting a glugging harmony.

"This is my brother, Christian. He's a baby." She pointed with upturned finger to my cousin, who was sitting in the middle of the toys on his potty. His existence was news to me.

"This is my piano." She turned to a little lacquered grand piano and flexed her fingers on the keys, eliciting a tinkling dissonance.

"These are my dolls," she went on. I was stuck on the piano and tried to play "*Alle Meine Entchen*" ("All My Little Ducks").

By that time, the expected smell spread from Christian's potty. The nurse in her starched, blue-and-white-striped uniform entered to wipe and dress him.

"Let's go somewhere else," suggested Eva-Maria.

I gladly followed. She led me back into the hallway. Rising on her tiptoes, she opened the next door, which led into the master bedroom. The sterile orderliness of this unusually large room in gray and white surprised me. It looked so different from my parents' disheveled, little bedroom, which had large brown roses on the wall. Eva-Maria pointed out a photograph in a silver frame on the glass plate of the nightstand. It was the baby picture that Tante Teddy had shown at our house. I was trying to recognize Eva-Maria in that baby. Yes, these big, brown, wide-set eyes were the same. However, she had short, little curls then. Now her straight, dark brown hair was hanging in bangs onto her wide forehead. As a baby, she'd had a flat nose. As I learned later, my father had called it an electric outlet. Tante Teddy forgave him. She was used to his brotherly candor. Now Eva-Maria's nose was a cute little curve that she would crinkle coquettishly when she was amused. Her cheekbones were higher and her delicate lips more upturned since the earlier days.

When we heard steps close to the door, Eva-Maria remembered that we were not allowed in this room. She quickly put the photograph back in its place and carefully and quietly led me into the hall.

Returning to the living room, we found a number of children, friends, and relatives, who had arrived in the meantime. Tante Teddy had scheduled a few activities for the children. At Tante Teddy's, you went about these amusements in a structured manner.

The planned entertainment started with musical chairs. My father obliged thunderously on the piano. Then we played the golden bridge. Two women standing opposite each other joined hands and raised their arms to form a bridge. We children would keep walking under that bridge and around one of the adults in a circle, while everyone started singing:

> We move through, we move through
> Through the golden bridge.
> What's coming there, what's coming there?
> There comes a golden carriage.
> Who sits in it, who sits in it?
> A man with golden hair.
> What does he does he want, what does he does he want?
> He wants to have the fairest.
> The first comes through, the second comes through,
> The third must be caught.

The women suddenly lowered their hands and caught the child that was under the bridge at that time. Then they would put the captive on their hands and arms and swing the giggling load back and forth and tumble it off one end. The circle went on, and the song started from the beginning until all children had been caught except one, who was the winner.

When I was caught, swung, and ejected from the women's arms, I added a little extra twist by doing a somersault. I thought that I had a special position in this game. Being the only towhead, I was certain I was the man with golden hair. I had no doubt that Eva-Maria was "the fairest" in the rhyme. She had the velvety glow of a ripe peach.

As the rest of the children were captured, swung, and ejected, they caught on to the thrill of shooting somersaults on the thick Persian carpet. They started to roll all over and accidentally strike each other with their flailing arms and legs. It was time for the hostess to call an end to the children's entertainment hour. She did this by having the maid ring a silver bell to call to the table.

I recall how I longed to be seated next to Eva-Maria at the other end of the table. Instead I was wedged between adults and had to quietly listen to their incomprehensible conversation. However, I found a way of entertaining myself. In the proper pause that Tante Teddy interjected between dinner and desserts, I slipped under the table and carefully crawled down the colonnade of legs. If I did not touch any shoes, I could stay undetected for quite some time. It was thrilling to have disappeared and still be in the center of activity. I guessed which pair of legs belonged to what person by the voice that would be sounding above. Searching the timberwork of my table ceiling, I discovered the button to Tante Teddy's secret bell, which was mounted under the ledge at her seat. It answered my question how she had the maid appear when needed without leaving the room to call her. Eventually, I made my way under the table to the other end where Eva-Maria's feet dangled. I pulled on them, but she was too well behaved to join me in my hiding place.

When the dessert was finished and the party repaired to the Berlin room, I was discovered and dragged into the open. Being captured between my parents on the semicircular gray couch and watching the adults settle in easy chairs talking and smoking was the height of boredom. My mind searched for anything interesting to do. Eva-Maria had been whisked away by the nurse. Finally, the cigarette package on the glass coffee table in front of me caught my eye. Onkel Horsa and Tante Teddy smoked Attika, a more expensive brand than the R-6 that my parents bought. Attika had twice as many cigarettes. They were thicker, golden, sweet-smelling, and packed in extra foil in two rows, not one. The most intriguing part of the package was a flap opening diagonally across that could be folded open and shut again with satisfying accuracy. Onkel Horsa had a grand way of opening the glossy cardboard box and offering this expensive brand to his guests. As I saw the number of delicate white cylinders shrink, I hoped that they would all be taken, and I could capture the intriguing package. Indeed, before the party was over, Onkel Horsa took the last cigarette, tapped it on the glass table a few times, put it between his lips, and lit it with a large, silver lighter, holding his head cocked sideways and squinting.

To my delight, I was allowed to keep the empty box when we left. I held it carefully in my hands all the way home. The foil lining was still intact. I kept sniffing its sweet, spicy smell. The box became my treasure chest for my most prized possession—a large coin that my father had given me. It had been minted out of aluminum and depicted a Zeppelin on one side and the world on the other. I understood what a Zeppelin was. Several times, when I had been playing in my sandpit, the silver cigar had appeared and slowly and noiselessly floated over our garden.

I felt rich like a king when I took the coin out of my treasure chest. I rubbed it between my palms and made it blink in the sun like a mirror. I traced my finger over the bas relief of the Zeppelin and, on the flip side, over the world with its raised lines of longitude and latitude. I wondered. What were those places like that the people traveled to in this Zeppelin; what wonders were hidden in all the lands that started outside my chain-link fence?

8

As much as I welcomed my trips into the city, they did not satisfy my curiosity. Every new experience led to new questions. Some events were so far beyond my comprehension that they had me thinking for years.

The second trip to Tante Teddy's brought such a strange event. Our visit started with the usual dinner. However, afterward, Onkel Horsa and Tante Teddy took my parents and me in their Opel to the historic avenue Unter den Linden. On that day, April 20, 1939, all Berlin traffic converged there for the celebration of Adolf Hitler's birthday. Dusk turned into night while we tried to get close. The celebrant himself was expected to stand on the balcony of the chancellery to take in the venerations of the people. Undoubtedly, he was striking the pose that he assumed at such occasions, his right hand stretched out straight, palm at eye level, thumb cramped tight. As Onkel Horsa squeezed into Unter den Linden, the traffic stopped completely. I was wiggling up from between my mother and the armrest in the backseat, trying to get my nose to the window. I had never seen so many people. While we were stuck between vehicles, a thick crowd of pedestrians pressed on the sidewalk past us. Cars were in front of us, behind us, and on our sides. Finally, we moved forward for two seconds and then stood still again.

I sensed from the frustration of the adults in the car that they regretted having come. Now they were captured in the stream of the masses. Then

I saw a flame in the sky ahead. As we inched closer, it turned out to be a torch that burned on top of a giant, gilded column. The flame way above me sent glowing gasses and sparks into the night. It filled me with awe and apprehension. As the flame faded very slowly behind me, another one appeared ahead. The passing of the torches along the road measured our crawling progress. I wished I had stayed at the apartment with Eva-Maria. When we finally approached the balcony where *he* was supposed to be, it had become dead silent in the car. I did not see him. No one pointed him out to me. Somberness and foreboding filled the car as the ominous flames passed above the masses.

I gladly returned to my garden. I was satisfied with having the outside world come to me. Besides Jörg, a number of adults started visiting. Curiously, Jörg's parents were not among them. After the initial meeting, my parents' relationship with the Ronnefelds soon broke up. In retrospect, this does not surprise me. I remember how Jörg once told me proudly that his oldest brother had been accepted to the Adolf Hitler School. The Ronnefelds were evidently so infatuated with the current politics as to make their son apply to this school. They had nothing in common with my parents.

Instead, my parents invited their families and old friends. Hans Wiegener, my father's best friend from the acting school, came out to Glienicke. He revived every time he came out into the garden where he and my father relived the promising times at the acting school and the romantic hikes in the Black Forest.

Onkel Hans was famous for his speaking voice, which was the envy of his fellow actors. Whenever I heard him at our front gate, I rushed to greet him. Onkel Hans always thought of the most entertaining ways to play with me. Even though he was a confirmed bachelor, he liked children. When Onkel Hans spent time with me, he would incite my father to drop being a teaching and guiding parent and turn into a child.

They would flop on the floor in my room with me and set up my train set—two tracks that were connected with switches and intersected in the middle—in ways that promised tremendous excitement. Then each of us would wind up one engine and start the passenger train, the freight train, and the fast commuter at the same time. We would try to avoid a collision by throwing the switches at the last second. The trains would miss at the crossing by a hair. Soon I was so excited at my switch that I screamed at every close miss. Eventually, all our skillful timing would be thwarted. The trains would collide in the middle, and the derailed engines would finish winding down, humming and kicking wildly on their sides.

By this time, I also would be wound up to the snapping point. Knowing I had to get out into the garden and run off the tension, my father and Onkel Hans set up a racecourse. They placed an exercise mat in the middle of the lawn, which served as start and finish. On ready, set, go, we went from the mat around the house, across the lawn, around the oak, and back to the mat. I raced my father first and then Onkel Hans. They gave me stiff competition but always faded on the last stretch from the oak to the mat, which made me win by a step. Onkel Hans would stumble and collapse on the mat, completely exhausted, employing all the dramatic skills of his profession. This made me laugh uproariously and enjoy my hard-earned victory twice as much.

The placing of the mat in the middle of the lawn was deliberate. This spot, halfway between the house and the big oak, was of special importance. It seemed to be the center of our social life. When Tante Teddy visited, my father would bring the wicker chair and table from the garage for lunch and place it right there. This was also the spot where Omi, coming from Erfurt, would eventually settle in a lawn chair and read to me tirelessly from *Max and Moritz*. I would sit next to her in the grass, making sure she would not skip any pages. This was the spot around which the croquet game would be centered. More often, this was the place where my parents set the table when my father had a free morning to enjoy a leisurely breakfast in the sun.

So many pleasurable events occurred on this spot. It became the hub of my realm. I began attributing to it an almost magic quality. Unfortunately, this spell only lasted until one strange occurrence broke it forever.

9

One afternoon, a beautiful lady, accompanied by a much-older husband with a walrus beard, came to our garden. She was Tante Edith, and he was Onkel Paule from Norway.

On the surface, the occurrences of this afternoon did not seem unusual. But many years have taught me about the deeper effects of some seemingly insignificant events. Something horrendous had happened.

My mother knew well Edith's significance in my father's life. He had read his bride-to-be all his diaries before their engagement to be completely honest and open about his past. She learned that he had fallen in love with Edith in tenth grade, and they had gone steady until third semester law school, when she had broken off the relationship.

Tante Edith and Onkel Paule came shortly after lunch. The summer day was scorching. For once, my father set up the garden table back in the shadow of the oak, not in the middle of the sunny lawn. My mother, who expected a short visit, had coffee and cookies but nothing else. Edith and my father's conversation was so animated that the visit stretched into hours. I felt how my mother became more and more annoyed.

The shadow of the oak on the lawn grew longer and longer. My father pointed to the ripe tomatoes that glowed along the fence and suggested my mother serve some. My mother eventually went over to the fence, lifted the ripest tomatoes from the bending vines, and took them into the kitchen to wash them. Having nothing to do at the table, I followed her. I was startled by the manner in which my mother threw the colander into the sink, jerked the faucet open and shut, fetched a bowl from the cupboard and put it on the counter with a bang. When she placed the tomatoes into the bowl, it seemed to be with deliberate restraint not to squash them. Then she stomped out of the house carrying her offering. I jogged next to her. All that my naive mind could comprehend then was that she was agitated. Today, I can imagine so well how my mother felt when she came around the house and surveyed the scene under the oak.

There was the man married to her and Edith looking into each others' eyes. And here she came with the tomatoes, serving these two who were savoring each other's presence. She must have felt forsaken by the man she loved. My mother could not take another step. She turned to me.

"Michael, I am giving you a very important job. Carry this bowl of tomatoes to the table. Serve it to our guests."

I was taken aback and hesitated. I had never been asked to do something so conspicuous and important. What did that mean, "guests"? Would they be pleased with my performance?

With pride and trepidation, I took the bowl and headed for the lawn.

My mother kept looking at the couple at the table. Suddenly, she must have felt ashamed of her jealousy and tried to rein it in. Life has taught me that when jealousy unloads against our will, cataclysmic things can happen, just as when love unloads through learned callousness, miracles can happen.

At that moment, the extraordinary occurred. A rumble came from deep in the ground, and a crack opened up in the middle of the lawn halfway between the house and the oak. It spread across the lot to the fences and beyond. The rumble had been inaudible. The crack was invisible.

Nevertheless, the break in the earth was there to stay. When I returned fifty-four years later, it was still there.

I started across the lawn with my bowl. I began to run. I always ran across the lawn. I came to the middle. I stumbled and fell. The bowl flipped to the ground, and the tomatoes flew in all directions.

I was inconsolable. I blamed myself for the failure. I also felt a twinge of surprise that not everything my mother asked me to do would turn out to be beneficial. Following her wishes also could bring shame. With sorrow, I felt like I had been separated from her by just a nudge.

I could not stop crying until my mother put me to bed early. From that day on, I have been apprehensive whenever guests come. Still today, I am a poor host, strangely embarrassed without reason, tongue-tied, and dreading to serve anything.

A good night's sleep made me forget about the mishap superficially. I resumed enjoying the garden as if nothing had changed. Jörg came over almost daily now. The summer got even hotter toward August.

My father set up the water sprinkler. It spread out its glistening funnel over the lawn. Following the example of my parents, Jörg and I jumped over the sprinkler to cool off. As usual, my father had also placed the table on the lawn, in its designated place in the middle between the house and the oak. Jörg and I decided to have our race around the house, across the lawn, and around the oak. As an added obstacle, we agreed to also jump over the sprinkler. When we came around the house, Jörg was ahead. He closed his eyes, jumped through the water, and ran on. Next, I heard a bang and a crunch. Jörg had run into the table, crashing his mouth into the edge. There he was, lying in the grass, blood streaming from his mouth. For a moment, the vision of tomatoes scattered over the lawn flashed in front of my eyes. How could something so terrible occur in my garden? I was desperate and helpless.

Jörg screamed. My father rushed by. He persuaded him not to run right home. He wet a handkerchief in the sprinkler and pressed it on the cut lip. After a while Jörg's mouth stopped bleeding, and he calmed down. My father took him home to explain what had happened. When he returned, he blamed himself for setting up the table in such a disastrous place and carried it into the garage.

After that incident, Jörg stopped coming. I was alone again. Now that I had known comradeship, the solitude was no longer as blessed as it once had been. One morning, when I was sitting in my sandpit listlessly stoking around with my shovel, my father thought of a special treat for me. He brought out his tent and started setting it up in the middle of the lawn.

He showed me how to feed the four bamboo poles through the loops, how to tap the stakes into the sod and tie the string that erected the A-frame. He opened the snaps on the door, crawled in with me, and taught me how to slide open the celluloid window in the far triangular wall. Then he left me to play alone and started raking leaves. For a while, I enjoyed sitting in the security of the tent, seeing the moving light and shadow patterns from the oak playing on the green canvas or looking through the tiny opening over the endless meadow. Then I needed more excitement. I started investigating the outside of the structure. I climbed on the swaying roof to the ridge, turned around, and slid down the side into the grass. When my father saw this, he stopped me.

"Don't do this. You are going to tear the tent. Once it's torn, it will be ruined. It can't be mended. It would never be watertight."

For as long as my father and mother were in the garden, I resisted the temptation. But when they disappeared into the house, I could no longer contain myself. I climbed up the tent again. Why I had boots on that warm day and was not barefoot like on most summer days, I cannot tell. Two slides went fine. On the third slide, my heel caught and ripped through, leaving a big torn triangle around my knees. At this moment, a shout went out from the living room window. My parents had been watching. I had barely untangled myself when my father came around the house.

"Did I not tell you not to slide down the tent?" His eyes snapped with fury.

Lifted in the back by my belt, I felt my pants stretch taut and the slap of his hand on my buttocks. My reaction was not so much sorrow and remorse but complete astonishment. I knew I had deserved the punishment. Yet, I could not grasp that it was meted out by the one I had learned from birth to trust unreservedly for protection, from the one who only moments earlier had lain next to me in the tent and told me about his hikes. Halfway between the house and the oak, on that very spot where the tomatoes fell and Jörg's mouth crashed into the table, my unbound love for my father became ambivalent. It turned into a mixture of affection, admiration, and fear.

I also lost the trust in the innocence of my own actions. I realized that it was possible to succumb to the temptation of breaking my father's rules. Breaking his rules really had incited his anger. He would have forgiven my ruining the tent if he had not expressly forbidden my sliding on it. I learned that day what all German children have learned through many generations. Breaking their parents' rules and challenging authority would bring wrath and corporal punishment. As most German children, I became a *gutes Kind* (good child) and thus avoided spanking.

Ein gutes Kind
Gehorcht geschwind.
(A good child
Obeys quickly.)

I knew the verse, as did all other children. We were *gut erzogen*, which meant that we were well reared and bent to our parents' will. As we grew up, we were prone to look for people of authority to show us how to behave.

10

We lived under the shadow that the big war was casting. The government was undertaking ominous steps. The Saarland had been appropriated, Austria pushed into joining Germany, and Czechoslovakia occupied. My parents feared that Hitler's megalomania had been stoked by these effortless gains. Now he made claims to have Danzig back as a German city. France and England had made pacts with the threatened Poland. Troops were amassing on all borders. Young German men had been conscripted.

To enjoy peace while it lasted, my parents decided to take an extended bicycle tour through the Black Forest and the Alps that summer. My father had to travel to southern Germany anyway. The Volksbühne was staging a guest production of *Faust* in the Heidelberg Castle, directed by Weichert, who was assisted by my father.

This was my first trip out of Berlin. When my mother started packing, I grew anxious. I was assured that I would not be left behind when she gave me a tiny, leather suitcase all of my own. I fell in love with this Lilliputian luggage. It only held two shorts and two shirts, but it was the one token from home I could cling to.

My memories of this tour lack the cohesiveness and the large sweep adults carry away from such excursions. They are unconnected glimpses triggered by something particularly pleasurable, sad, frightening, or unusual.

I have been told that my parents met my mother's father on the street in front of our hotel in Heidelberg. I am racking my brains for the impression of a gigantic man accompanied by a peroxide-blonde lady—the "Blonde Poison," as my mother called her—for whom her father had left her mother. It was the only time I may have met my Grandfather Wentscher. Perhaps I was not at this encounter but had been put down for my nap. Instead of meeting my grandfather, I probably was eating Kollinor toothpaste, the one with the black-and-yellow-checkered tube and the delicious peppermint taste. Or I was endlessly pushing the springy brass button switch of the little lamp on the nightstand. I was fascinated by the subtle click that alternately triggered light or darkness.

My circle of observation was still as confined as it had been in my garden at home. Anything farther away escaped my notice. I do neither remember the spacious court of the castle with the famous baroque facade of the Old Heinrich Wing or the rehearsals in front of it, which theater lovers from all over Germany thrilled to see. Did it not present the foremost actors in the country, Werner Hinz as Faust and Werner Kraus as Mephistopheles? Instead, I remember the minute wooden train that I guided around the plates and saucers of the sun-drenched breakfast table on the hotel terrace.

After the festival in the Heidelberg Castle, my parents were ready to start their mammoth bicycle tour. To be able to take me, my father had mounted a little extra saddle on his bicycle. According to my father's plans, the trip went through the Black Forest to Lake Constance, cut across the northern corner of Switzerland and through the Arlberg Tunnel to Austria. It proceeded down the River Inn and up the Danube to Franconia and then north to Thuringia and Erfurt as the final destination. In retrospect, this tour had a hint of the restlessness that besets humans when they sense the approach of inevitable disaster. Were my parents trying to forget the dread of the big war by filling their minds with ever-new impressions?

I remember nothing about our train ride from Heidelberg over Offenburg to Triberg. The many-tunneled climb up the Kinzig Valley was an impression reserved for later times. However, I recall when we set out with the bicycles at Triberg to push up to the highlands. Halfway on the endless climb up Main Street, I made the disastrous discovery that my suitcase was missing. I thought my parents had forgotten it on the train. For the next hour, I cried incessantly, *"Mein Koffer, mein Koffer!"*

My parents tried to explain to me that they had sent my suitcase ahead to Erfurt. I did not believe them. How could my little suitcase travel to Erfurt by itself?

All efforts to distract me failed.

When we reached the end of the town where the church with the onion-shaped steeple roof stood in front of the famous waterfall, it was still, *"Mein Koffer, mein Koffer."* I was getting on my parents' nerves. My mother was edgy. My father, longing to get back to his beloved Black Forest, had minimized the climb from Triberg to Schönwald.

When we started up the switchbacks, my mother erupted. "All flat, all flat—the highlands are all flat! I don't see anything all flat. We've been pushing all the way up through this town, and now it's really starting to go up. Where is the flat? I see nothing but mountains. I thought you had been this way before. You shouldn't have claimed that this was easy."

"Now, Niña, don't be like that. I told you, there will be a slight rise from Triberg to Schönwald."

"Slight rise. Slight rise! We've been pushing for an hour."

"Thirty-six minutes."

"I just hope that this is not going on for the next four weeks like this. That will be a wonderful vacation."

My father fell silent. I was used to these loaded silences. Only the rush of the waterfall, now deafening and then fading away, and my occasional sob, *"Mein Koffer,"* could be heard.

Finally, I stopped complaining. The disagreement between my parents began to weigh heavier on me than my loss. Was it not at times when I was yammering that they were most prone to fall into arguments?

When we finally reached the plateau, we rolled effortlessly past the silvery, shingled farmhouses; lush meadows; and chattering brooks toward Schönwald. My mother's mood flipped almost instantly from indignation to joyful appreciation. My father, as usual, needed more time to work through his disagreement and paid back my mother's earlier sarcasm by retreating into a sulky muteness. He did not fully get over this argument until he complained about it in detail in his diary.

I do not remember the highlands from this trip, not The Turner, not the Titisee, and not the precipitous Höllental. The next memorable impression was in Freiburg, where the extraordinarily wide and deep street gutters with clean, rushing water were a unique feature. My father folded paper boats and set them afloat in the channels. I followed them down the speedy current. With apprehension, I watched them disappear under the crossroads, and I clapped with delight when they reappeared on the other side.

The climb up the red sandstone Münster to the narrow balcony also stayed with me. It was marked by the shock of the unexpected toll of a bell as big as our house that I found hanging right behind me.

I remember neither the ride up the Rhine Valley past the falls at Schaffhausen nor Lake Constance. The large body of water was beyond my comprehension. All I carried away was the joy of watching my father roll into the water with a splash off the flat boat that we had rented. At Unteruhldingen, we came upon a restored prehistoric village. When I got off my father's bike and ran across the street, eager to see this curious site, I was blown over by a fast young bicyclist. This made a temporary impression on my body and a lasting one on my mind. I consoled myself with the excitement of walking over the rickety piers to the thatched huts and seeing their crude, wooden cots and tiny, low tables and benches. The inhabitants must have been hardly taller than I, but they were equipped with enormous mouths, judging by the size of the wooden spoons hanging on the walls. Perhaps stimulated by the play with my beloved building blocks, unusual buildings fascinated me even at that age. That was true for the huts on stilts in the lake, as well as the many castles and churches we visited as we continued our trip.

We took the train through the endless Arlberg Tunnel to gain the uppermost reaches of the Inn Valley at Landeck. My father had adjusted our trip so that there were no more long uphill stretches. From Landeck, we traveled down along the mountain river. I sat on the little leather saddle in front of my father, encircled securely by his arms that reached to the handlebars we both held. I had given up wanting my suitcase. Forgotten was the last bond with my home. My parents were all I knew in the foreign surroundings. They were my only security and had my total attention. Knowing my father above me and feeling his force and control on the bike and seeing my mother pedaling close by was all I needed to feel content. Since I had my father as a captive audience, I asked him questions incessantly until he finally complained.

"Michael, *frag mir doch keine Löcher in den Bauch.*" (Michael, please, don't ask holes into my belly.)

He started asking me questions that would occupy me for a while.

"What do you want to be when you grow up?"

The idea that I would grow up to be like my father thrilled me. Indeed, the need to decide on a job became my preoccupation of the tour.

I had several ideas about this subject, some of which I'd considered before the trip and others that this very journey stimulated.

"I want to be a *Baumeister*" (builder), was usually my first answer.

When we rode into a side valley to Zell am See and hiked up to the Erlhofplatte, another profession came to my mind. Since I had never hiked as far, my parents thought of a way to make me want to keep pace up the long switchbacks.

"You can be our mountain guide."

Eagerly I went ahead, looking for the red dots on the trees and making sure my parents would not wander off the trail. So enthralled was I with my assigned job that I gave myself a new name. I became Herr Keschstamm, *Bergführer* (mountain guide). Even though I had no eye for the far vistas of the snow-covered Imbachhorn, I was delighted by the mighty, moss-covered trunks; the log bridges across rushing and foaming melt water; the graceful arches of ferns; the sprinkles of wildflowers; the sun patches on the pine needles; and the smell of warm resin. For the rest of my life, I have rarely been happier than on the trail in the Black Forest, in the Alps and, later, in the States in the High Sierra and the North Cascades.

My parents pedaled down the whole length of the Inn Valley. When they arrived in Linz, they were ready for a break and decided to take the steamer up the river to Passau.

The day of the trip started with complications and excitement. The steamer was to leave at 8:00 a.m. The bank, where my parents had to withdraw money, opened at 8:00 a.m. We tried to make it from the bank to the pier in a wild dash. But the captain had been punctual. The ship had left the dock and was steaming upriver in the distance. Off we went on a wild chase in the hope of overtaking the boat.

At Wilhering, we had indeed caught up, and my parents led their bicycles across the gangway, staggering, panting and completely drenched. I was fascinated with the ship, with the churning water at the stern, the boisterous horn, and the gleaming parts of the stomping steam engine. On deck, I watched the bridge, waiting for the appearance of the imposing bearded man in the dark blue uniform. I admired him as he commanded this wondrous ship, winding upstream and carefully approaching the landing sites. When we debarked in Passau, the job of ship's captain had moved to number one on my list.

Among the possible occupations that occurred to me, I did not discover my true calling—not that there was a lack of stimulation in this direction. My parents never passed up the opportunity to visit the famous churches in the towns they passed. Sometimes, they even added a side loop so as not to miss an illustrious site. They took me to the dome in Salzburg for an organ concert and for another one in the church at Passau. They walked me quietly and full of reverence through the uplifting gothic dome in Regensburg, the stern, romanesque dome in Bamberg, and the glorious rococo church of Vierzehnheiligen. I took in the altar paintings and sculptures with an interest far ahead of my age, even though the cruelty of the subject matter puzzled me occasionally.

"Why are these angels poking this man, Papi?" I whispered during a pause in the Passau organ concert.

"They are not poking him. They are pulling out the arrows. It's St. Sebastian."

There were statues in every niche. There were wise and foolish virgins, prophets, apostles, and angels—the whole host of biblical personages. I took it all in with amazement. It didn't occur to me then that something so permanent could have been made by human hands;

nor did I imagine that my own hands were called to bring forth objects like these.

From Bamberg, we pedaled through the Thuringian Forest to Erfurt, our final destination. Omi embraced us in her usual exuberant way, coming across the room with her arms up in the air and her mouth puckered. She immediately called in Martchen to settle us in the guestrooms. Before doing anything else, my mother led me into the storage to show me my little suitcase. I looked at it with disinterest and did not pick it up. Now I didn't want it anymore.

The next morning, my mother took me to the barber. According to her special demands and under her insistent supervision, he produced a haircut worthy of the Prince of Wales. She decked me out in a new striped polo shirt, a new pair of white shorts, and white kneesocks with tassels. She took my picture by the wrought-iron rose gate in front of the villa of Omi Bauer, my great-grandmother, recording my prim appearance using all her expertise.

I was going to meet Tante Ellen and her daughter, Maria Barbara. Tante Ellen was Omi's half sister. She was so much younger than Omi that Maria Barbara, who was my mother's generation, was one month younger than I. There would be comparisons made between Maria Barbara and me when the family would gather. The party was in the villa and garden of Omi Bauer, Omi's and Ellen's mother.

Indeed, Maria Barbara had also been fitted for the occasion. She wore an expensive white dress, starched and flaring out in impeccable folds. Her brown hair was brushed shiny, her bangs combed even, and her pert little upturned nose and freckled cheeks scrubbed.

What fascinated me most about her was her white, pedal-operated toy convertible. Impatiently, I waited for her to get tired of showing it off. When she finally did, I gladly took over, revving it along the walkways and through my father's legs, which he spread like a highway bridge.

Later, Maria Barbara led me into the villa to show me her Käthe Gruse doll, but I became distracted in the lobby by the polar bear skin in front of the fireplace. I crawled under it, raised the glass-eyed head, and went after Maria Barbara with a growl. She joined in the fun and rode on my back.

Then we spread the yellow-white fur back on the floor, made somersaults on it, and tried to stand on our heads, grabbing hold of the shaggy hair. We were not interested in our mothers' contest—who had the smarter, better-looking, and better-behaved child. Careening around on the big polar bear skin and exploring the far reaches of Omi Bauer's villa from cellar to attic, we became fast friends.

11

Returning to Berlin, my parents tried to enjoy the last weeks before the impending war. They purchased an 8mm Kodak film camera, a projector, and a pearl screen. Within a week, they made four films. It was as if they wanted to hold on to the last days of peace by recording our still untroubled lives. The first film captured our sunny breakfast in the garden with real coffee, fresh rolls, and our fill of marmalades and butter.

The second film, at my fourth birthday, took me running into the backyard to my little table with toys of peacetime quality—a *Kletter Max*, which was a little wooden man most acrobatically swinging down a ladder; a cable car descending on a string from the fence at the edge of the wilderness; and a yellow, lacquered, metal wheelbarrow.

Three days later, my parents had splurged on their first film in color. The occasion was my mother's birthday and my parents' fifth wedding anniversary. This time, the shot of the table with presents in the garden burst with a bouquet of purple gladiolas. It went on to show Omi sitting in a green-and-blue-striped lawn chair, picking from a bowl of purple, glowing plums and intense yellow bananas. The mailman in his very blue uniform handed letters of congratulations over the red gate. My mother shed her deep-blue bathrobe to jump over the sprinkler in her white, red, and maroon-striped bathing suit. The film was a splash of color and joy. A few days later, my parents' next film, also in color, began in our yard. I am watching my mother loosening the soil around the dahlias and my father watering the flowers and also watering me while I am standing next to her unsuspectingly. Then the reel cut to the visit to the Schubert's house.

Hans Schubert had been my father's geography teacher and advisor. When Schubert discerned that his sixteen-year-old student was avoiding spending time at home, he found out about the disturbing situation in my father's family. He heard about the old man's all-night bouts at the *Kneipe* (pub). He heard about his coming home, when he picked fights, hit his wife, and forced himself on her. He learned about the father coming home the next day sober with a huge bouquet of roses. Such a father was a very disturbing example—selfish and abusive on the one hand and lavishly generous, witty, and entertaining on the other, with a light and pure tenor voice. Hans Schubert, who saw my father's pain, invited his young pupil into his loving family. In summer, he and his two teenage boys took my father along on hikes in the Black Forest, which kindled my father's delight in this region. The Schuberts—Hans; his wife, Elisabeth; and their boys, Dieter and Ulrich—became my parents' best friends.

When we watched this film in later years after the war, we were always taken aback by this sudden cut from our garden to theirs. "Oh, this is the one with the Schuberts," one of us would say. Their sad fate during the war would immediately weigh on our minds. Reluctant to stop the projection, we would watch in silence—the Schuberts in their yard; Elisabeth and my mother among the flower beds, bending down here and there among the chrysanthemums, marigolds, and snapdragons. They stroll along the neatly trimmed edges of verbena and point at the trellises laden with roses, obviously sharing their love of gardening. Then the movie shows my father and Hans Schubert sitting at the garden table, chatting and joking. Schubert's nickel-frame glasses glare in the sun now and then. Dieter Schubert, the tall and handsome younger son, walks through the garden in uniform, waving and smiling at the camera. The older son, Ulrich, did not get on the film. As the reel ends, the images of the Schuberts get shot through by empty patches of light, and a series of holes and numbers until the film slips out of its channels and the screen turns glaring white.

The next film, taken only weeks later, turned back to sober black and white. What was my father doing in the living room window? Was he fastening tar paper over the slits in the shutters, and was I handing him nails to get the job done? Indeed, so it was. The government had ordered blackout. The war had begun.

For my parents, the end of peace came like the death of a long-ailing friend, whose demise had been expected but still caused shock. Hitler had succeeded in leading the country into another war. He had triggered it by his aggression toward Poland. Recalling the deprivation and pain as war children of the last war, my parents looked into the future with dread.

I remember the day of the invasion of Poland vividly. My mother had the NORA radio in the dining room turned up so she could hear it in the kitchen. The program caught my attention. It was so different from the Sunday morning broadcasts that my parents listened to when we had our leisurely breakfasts.

I was used to an hour of baroque music on those mornings. I am sure it included Bach's Brandenburg Concertos. Later, when I heard again this characteristic dancing before God, it brought forth the image of my parents in the easy chairs in their bathrobes, drinking coffee.

On the morning of the Poland invasion, the radio assumed an entirely different character. It became triumphant. Marches and songs praised the greatness of Germany and its provinces. The rousing music was interrupted often in midbeat by *Sondermeldungen*—special reports about the advancing army. The marches and reports were of such contagious jubilation that even I, barely four years old, was affected. Something great was happening. I was running back and forth, jumping over the sunlit patterns in the carpet, even turning somersaults. My mother did not share my excitement. She listened to the *Sondermeldungen* with great weariness, waiting for a declaration of war from France and England.

Then the program was interrupted by the announcer, who heralded the speech of someone who seemed of eminent importance. A unique voice came on, which had a tone like I had never heard before. It reverberated with the *Brustton der Überzeugung* (the deep chest tone of conviction) as my mother scornfully characterized it. It reminded me of the sound of coal rumbling down the wooden shoot into our cellar. In the coming years, when I heard this unmistakable voice again, I learned that it belonged to the man whose name I thought was Adolfitler. After but a few sentences my mother rushed in and turned off the radio with such vehemence that I thought the knob would snap off.

Two days later in the evening, my parents and I were sitting in the dining room; the radio was on again. It was past my bedtime, the time when my father or mother asked me to fetch the clock. I always answered by bending deeper over my drawing and stating, "I'm busy. I have to work here." This trick never worked, except this night when my parents were too absorbed in the broadcast to insist. It was dark outside when the announcement came that Germany was at war with France and England. My mother started crying. I wondered about the strangeness of this disaster. My mother was usually furious when she heard upsetting news, rather than breaking down in tears. My father listened in his brooding silence.

My mother's weeping at the beginning of the war at a time when the radio exuded confidence, even triumph, puzzled me. I am now certain of the utter frustration she felt. The calamity that she had so long anticipated had come to pass. Likely, she regretted having been reluctant in our emigration to Norway. Now we were trapped in Germany. My father would probably have to go to war. Moreover, due to her prophetic sense, she must have had a notion of the pain, depravation, hunger, fear, and utter destruction that lay ahead.

The course of the war during the first year contradicted such gloom. Hitler and the disciplined, well-equipped, and thoroughly trained *Wehrmacht* (armed forces) were spectacularly successful. The fall of Poland in twenty-seven days allowed him to coin the word "Blitzkrieg." Denmark and Norway fell in just one month in April 1940. Now, my parents were thankful not to have moved north. The defeat of Holland, Belgium, and France in May and June fostered the belief that the German Army was invincible. My parents stayed apprehensive. They loathed war, whether or not they were on the winning side.

My mother, who was a keener judge of human nature than my father, feared that these new successes would fuel Hitler's *Grössenwahn* (megalomania) and that his conquest would involve ever-mightier

61

adversaries, until he eventually would run his army into the ground. She dreaded a repeat of the developments of the First World War when England drew the United States into the conflict. Moreover, she had not forgotten Hitler's claim that the Germans were a folk without room and that the space they needed would be toward the east.

For me, the first year of the war was bearable. There was enough food, and the few air raids were more interesting than threatening.

The first alert was on September 9 at 3:40 a.m. For the first time, my parents and I were stirred out of our sleep by the hoarse, undulating scream of the siren. *Fliegeralarm* (air alert). We were supposed to go into the *Luftschutzkeller* (air protection cellar). The air had become dangerous. We had to protect ourselves from it. My father wrapped me in the top of his old green sleeping bag and carried me on his back into the garage. He deposited me in my baby bed, the one from the studio that my parents had put there in anticipation. I was wide awake. Since no sound came to us from the outside, my parents left the garage door open. I looked out into the night, up to the paling stars and the narrow sickle of a waning moon. I enjoyed the sparkles in the sky and started singing,

Weisst Du wieviel Sternlein stehen
An dem blauen Himmelszelt?
Weisst Du wieviel Wolken gehen
Weit hinüber alle Welt?
Gott der Herr hat sie gezählet
Dass ihm auch nicht eines fehlet
An der ganzen grossen Zahl.

Do you know how many stars stand
On the blue heaven's tent?
Do you know how many clouds go
Far over the whole world?
God the master has counted them
So he misses not a single one
In the whole great number.

Then I saw how the shape of the oak appeared more and more in the dawning light and the fog rose in the meadow beyond. At 4:20 a.m. came the long, sustained, high-pitched *Entwarnung* (end warning), and my parents and I went back into our beds that were still slightly warm.

During future air alerts, I became bored of the routine and fell asleep in the garage. Not to wake me again, my father would stay with me until morning. When I finally woke up, I would see the light seeping under the double door. I would shake my mattress until it would slip off the frame and open a gap through which I would escape onto the floor. I would push the garage door open and, in the streaming morning light, find my father sound asleep in the easy chair.

Since the reasons for these nightly excursions into the garage were not clear to me, they disturbed me little. During the days, I went on with my life as if nothing was amiss. I expanded my world out of the garden by learning to climb over the gate. Instead of trying to curtail me, my parents taught me safety. They preached to always stay on the sidewalks and to look first left and then right and then left again when crossing a road. Soon they trusted me to run to Luzi's cigarette stand at the bus stop.

I always ran, whether I was with or without my parents. Next to them, I ran so I could keep up with their long and fast strides, and by myself I ran out of an inborn desire to move. Indeed, I was eleven years old before I slowed down and put an occasional walk between my runs.

An exciting incentive compelled me to get R-Sechs cigarette packages. Each contained a coupon for a picture to be collected and pasted into a book that you could buy. The series comprised a book about the German silent movies, another about the sound films, one about the 1936 Berlin Olympiad, and one with German fairy tales. My parents smoked enough to eventually puff up all the pictures. My father would read to me from the fairy tales at bedtime or when I was sick with an earache or an upset stomach. He always read with great dramatic flair. Eager to get to his own writing, he favored the short tales like *Die Goldene Gans* (The Golden Goose) or *Die Kugelrunden Müller* (The Ball-Round Millers).

When Omi came to visit, I could convince her to read all the stories one after another, morning and afternoon, until her shrill voice turned low and completely hoarse. I always joined in the endings, which were always, "*Und wenn sie nicht gestorben sind, dann leben sie heute noch*" (And if they did not die, they are still alive today). Only, I said, "*Wenn sie nicht gestolpert sind*" (If they did not stumble). The concept of dying was still beyond my comprehension.

The fairy tales got hold of my imagination. Soon the mysterious woods in the neighboring lot were filled with princesses, dwarfs, little tailors fighting giants, witches fattening little boys to be baked into cookies, queens spinning straw into gold, and frogs being turned back into princes by the kiss of a maiden. When I was in the yard alone, these characters came over and played with me, and I turned into one of them. One day, I found a wire frame of a small lamp and a strip of gold paper. I cut a zigzag line into the foil, wrapped it around the frame, and put it on my head. I was the King Drosselbart. I ran into the house to show my adornment to my mother. To my surprise, she was not pleased. She made me take it off and disassemble it.

"What do you want to run around like a king for? You are just a little boy."

Sensitized by the political tenor of the day, she was alarmed by any lack of humility.

12

My parents worried that my long, lonely hours in the garden would turn me into a dreamer. They tried to invite Jörg again and at last got the Ronnefelds to consider the possibility. They also spent as much time as feasible with me. In winter, they took me to the hill just a block away and began to teach me how to ski.

When summer came, my parents thought it was time I learned how to swim. They wanted me to get used to water bigger than the sprinkler or the bathtub. We took the bicycles to Sumter See, a lake surrounded by tall pines. My father suggested carrying me across the lake on his shoulders. When he found me trusting and eager, he lifted me on his shoulders and slowly walked into the water, which was dark but comfortably warm. When the water reached his shoulders, he told me to slide down on his back and keep myself above the surface by folding my hands over his forehead. My father did the breaststroke and soon I tried to help him by spreading my legs and kicking them out sideways like he did. When we reached the other shore, my father sat me down onto the warm sand, turned around, and swam full force next to my mother. I keenly observed their moves, determined to figure out how to perform this feat.

I was still excited by the prospect of swimming after we had returned home and I had been put to bed for my usual nap. I was not tired. My skin felt prickly and alive from the water and the warm air. I considered how I could practice the breaststroke. Lying flat on the sheet, I found it difficult to pull up my legs, kick them out and force them together. So I took my pillow and lay on it with my belly and ran one corner between my legs. I did not learn how to swim this way. However, I learned something else. As I continued my strokes a strange new feeling came over me. I pressed my hands into the soft down and turned my legs in and out. The pillow made me feel better and better. What was happening to me? Was this right? Was this dangerous? I became scared and stopped.

The next afternoon I could not resist trying to arouse the curious feeling again. This time, I went beyond the point of no return. I forgot myself and my darkened room, and my whole being converged into one great desire. Then I felt the throbs of incomprehensible delight and then the relaxation. What had I discovered? How could I tell my parents about it? I believed I was the only one in the world who had ever experienced this. How could they understand what I was talking about? Was I normal? Was I bad? Finally I decided to keep it my secret. I did not want my parents to forbid me the most desirable emotion I had ever felt.

It was around the same time that I also experienced the other extreme of the range of human feelings—the fear of death. The realization of my mortality came suddenly during one of the air raids.

The war in the air had been steadily escalating. As chronicled by my father—by date, time, and duration—the first year, from September 1939 to September 1940, brought only sixteen alerts. By September 1941, he had counted sixty-eight. During the second year, the raids not only quadrupled but also became disturbing. The flak started bellowing away so that the garage door shook. Searchlights scrutinized the sky. The fiery balls of flares shot up. Guns chattered as the English bombers fought with the German *Nachtjäger*. The population had long given up on Göring's promise that no enemy plane would ever be permitted over German territory, a declaration that an assembly of women had answered with the unceasing shouts, "Never! Never!" as if their fervent hopes could make it true.

There were other alerts, when the nights stayed quiet because the bombers had flown on to farther targets. On such nights, my parents sometimes took a chance and went back to bed before the Entwarnung. On one occasion, however, the silence had been deceiving. When my father put me back into his sleeping bag and carried me up the ramp from the garage, I suddenly saw the most amazing spectacle over his shoulder. A searchlight streaked up from behind the big oak. It locked onto the gleaming cross of a plane. In the next instant, the plane burst into flames. Then I heard the sound of the flak. The burning plane curved upward in a desperate diversion and then plunged down steeply and disappeared behind the oak. My father let out a shout of surprise and distress. He quickly turned around and carried me back into the garage.

I was agitated. What was going on? Evidently, these nightly trips into the basement were not just an exercise that adults had dreamed up for entertainment. What were those horrendous events in the sky?

"Papi," I asked, "what happened to the man in the plane?"

"He probably jumped down in a parachute."

"What's a parachute?"

"It's like a big umbrella that opens up and lets you down easy."

I tried to imagine how the pilot could have gotten out of the plane in that short instant. I had the vision of the door catching his leg and the plane dragging him down into the deep.

"But, Papi, what if he could not get out?"

"Then he probably died."

That night, I could not fall asleep for a long time. The next morning, I was lying under the grand piano, looking over toward my father at the desk, where he was illustrating the short story he had written for my mother's birthday. The incident in the night still disturbed me.

"What happens to people when they die, Papi?"

"They go to heaven and live *mit dem lieben Gott*" (with the dear God).

"Does everyone have to die?"

"Yes, Michael, everyone has to die, someday."

"But, Papi, I don't want to live *mit dem lieben Gott*. I want to stay here, with you and Mutti."

"You don't have to worry your little head about this. It will not happen for a long, long time. First you'll be a child for many years, then you'll grow up, then you'll have a family and children, then you'll have grandchildren, and then you'll get very, very old. And when you are very, very old and you look back on a long, long life, then you'll be so tired and fulfilled, you won't mind dying anymore."

I pondered, how long was very, very long?

That night, when my mother said my prayer with me, it was no longer just a formula.

> *Lieber Gott, mach mich fromm,*
> *dass ich in den Himmel komm.*

> Dear God, make me good
> So that I get to heaven.

I thought about how I wanted to go to heaven but not just yet. I was surprised to wake up in the morning and find myself still alive and was thankful to have another day. Lying in my bed, cozy, warm, and breathing, I made plans for how I would use my time. I would build a tower out of my blocks higher than ever. As soon as my mother had coaxed me to eat a few bites of my oatmeal, I set to work.

The joy of being still alive in the morning overcame me for several weeks, until the evidence slowly convinced me that my departure to heaven was indeed so far in the future that I could forget about it for a while. Yet, the difficulty of falling asleep after my prayer stayed with me. Eventually, I found a way of taking my mind off the threats that lurked in the dark. I began to sing, first the songs my parents had taught me. Each song brought with it pleasant images that filled the black void around me. There was one about the stars and the moon; one about the woman in the sky, who made it snow by shaking out her feather beds; and one about a train that had a stanza each about the steam engine, coal tender, baggage wagon, diner, and all the others. After I had exhausted my learned songs, I began to invent my own. I spun a story around my fairy tale realm and invented the music for it. Eventually, I would slip from this fantasy world into dreams. Some of the invented songs I liked well enough to remember for the next night. They formed a strand around which I knit the continuation of the story until the whole fantasy took the form of an opera.

My parents, who were listening behind my door, were amused by the concerts that I was sending forth into the dark. My father sensed in me the talent for the performing arts. He had observed my bent to memorize and enact every song I heard. Perhaps I would be joining him on the stage one day as an actor or an opera singer.

13

It so happened at that time that *Wilhelm Tell* was to be performed at the Volksbühne. Weichert, who directed with my father's assistance, was looking for a little boy who could play Tell's son, Walter. My father saw an opportunity to launch my career. He asked me whether I wanted to be on the big stage. All I would have to do is stand there with an apple on my head and say, *"Schiess zu, Vater, ich fürcht mich nicht"* (Go ahead, Father, shoot; I'm not afraid). He proposed this with such excitement in his voice that I thought it would be a special treat for me. I agreed to do it.

"Do you really think he wants to do this?" my mother questioned.

While my father was thinking of the honor and fame of having me perform on one of the foremost stages in Germany, my mother was concerned about the effect the scene would have on me. She feared that after several rehearsals even my naive mind would catch on to the horror. Was I not too young to have to look into the abyss of human evil?

"Oh, yes, he would like to be in this play," my father assured my mother enthusiastically. "Won't you, Michael?"

I nodded.

The next afternoon, my father took me on the U-Bahn to the Volksbühne in order to have Weichert see me and decide whether I was suitable for the part. When we arrived, Weichert was in conference. My father led me into the *Kantine* and ordered me a hot dog. At one of the tables sat one of the greatest "young heroes" of stage and film. My father chatted with him, introduced me, and added that he had brought me for Weichert to consider me for playing Tell's son.

The great actor looked at me as I stood there, tall, blonde, and blue-eyed.

"My son's name is Michael too," he said and added, *"Aus meinem Sohn kann ja nie etwas werden"* (My son can never become anything).

My father was quiet. Any encouraging comment would have been pointless and dishonest.

I finished my hot dog. I made my *Diener*—bowing to the great actor. Diener, which translates as "servant," was the term for the deep bow, which was the epitome of good behavior for a little boy when meeting adults.

We left to meet Weichert, who was emerging from the conference followed by an entourage of eager helpers. He spotted my father and me.

"Ah, Trady."

"This is Michael, remember, for Tell's son?"

My father looked at me like he was thinking, *Isn't he splendid?* After all, a photograph of me that my mother had taken had found its way onto the front page of the *BZ, Berliner Zeitung*. My father had proudly shown it to Weichert at that time.

But soon my father's hopes were shattered. Weichert took my hand and watched me make my Diener. "Who do we have here?" he said. "I'm looking for a red-cheeked, freckled farmer's boy, Trady. You are bringing me a prince."

My father had to admit, as tall as I was, I was not robust. My fair skin was rather transparent, like pastel. I also lacked the boldness for the part. My expression was cautious. There was something knowing in me that made me look more mature than my age. After Weichert had left, my father introduced me to the stagehands. They were friendly to me. They all liked my father because he treated them with jovial consideration in his daily dealings. The men put me on the turntable that was big enough to hold two full sets at a time. That afternoon the sets were pulled up, and the disc was empty. There I was, the only person on that huge, empty surface, being slowly moved full circle. Standing next to the crack along which the floor was curiously shifting, I looked up into the hanging sceneries and rows of lamps that slowly turned way above me.

On the homebound train, my father tried to console me. "You wait; there will be a part that will be made just for you."

I was not disappointed. As my father found out in time, I had not inherited his burning desire to be on the stage.

My mother was secretly relieved. She had seen the gruesome play. Why should her little boy watch Tell's arrest for not greeting the hat on a pole? How could I grasp the political reason and understand that the hat had been placed there to test who among the Swiss was properly subject to the oppressive Austrian regime? How could I follow the twisted reasoning of Gessler, the Landvogt and governor, when he demanded that Tell shoot an apple from his son's head? How outraged had she herself felt at the feigned generosity of the monster when he let Tell shoot from eighty, rather than one hundred paces? How generous, he gave him twenty paces! How had she agonized with Tell at the choice of either shooting an arrow toward his son and going free or facing outright execution together with his son? Should I get a glimpse of what kind of crimes evil men were capable of when put into power over life and death? Should I learn so young how perverted and dehumanized a ruler could become as to enjoy the prospect of having a father shoot an arrow through his son's head?

My mother was glad I had only been grazed by that story and had not understood more than that a man named Tell had shot an apple from his son's head because he was such a great marksman.

Strangely, this was not the only story that fate had woven into my life on that afternoon—another one was more real and disturbing. It did not have the patina of history, nor was it expressed in the moving words of an immortal poet like Schiller. It was the story of the great actor, who had looked at me with such sad eyes and had lamented his own son's future.

The famous actor had a Jewish wife who had been a movie star before the Nazis came to power and forbade her to perform. The actor was so highly acclaimed that he was able to continue his successful career in spite of his marriage. But eventually the Nazis became disturbed by such a famous man's affront to the party line. They called him in.

"Are you still married to that woman?"

For the good of his own career, he was to consider divorcing his wife. They were willing to overlook that he had been married to that woman for so long. They were willing to give him twenty paces.

"But I love my wife," said the famous actor.

In this case, the men in power regretted that they could not help him. They would be forced to ban him from the stage.

The Jewish wife thought of a solution. When the famous actor came home one night, she had taken an overdose of sleeping pills. The famous actor rescued her. Shortly after that, the famous actor's story ended. Since he was resolved that nothing would separate him from his wife and son, he was found with them dead in their home. They had turned on the gas.

When my father came home with the horrible news about Gottschalk, it was probably one of those days when my mother exploded. "Gangsters!" she would shout and lunge into one of her tirades about the government, whereupon my father would caution, "Niña, careful, the walls have ears," or, "Careful, your head is coming loose."

Then my mother would catch herself, turn to me, and implore me to never ever tell anything to anybody about what we were talking about at home.

My father and mother were outraged, but their outrage was stifled in silence. What kept them from a public outcry against those who had killed the man they had admired and applauded? I know that both had the courage and fortitude to speak up. There was only one reason. I was the reason. My mother had a prophetic sense that the regime would lose the war, and my father believed my mother. In their love for me, they joined with an oath-like determination to get me through the war and save my life for better times.

My mere existence cautioned my parents. Without me, they would have been bolder. Given that their attitude during that time had made them suspect and had placed them on the verge of being apprehended, it is clear to me now how a little less restraint would have led to their arrest.

My parents kept me blissfully ignorant of the political dangers. I did not know yet how I figured decisively into the moral equation of their lives.

14

In October 1940, I contracted whooping cough. My mother took me to a pediatrician who practiced in Frohnau, the neighboring community to the north. To get to his office, we had to walk over the Pfingstberg, a slope that started a block from our house. It was the hill on which my parents had taught me to ski. I dreaded my mother dragging me to the doctor. At every appointment, I had to get a shot in my buttocks, which hurt a lot since my muscles contracted like strands of iron. All my struggling and hollering when they pulled down my pants and wrestled me on the table did not help. The doctor, the nurse, and my mother always won.

Because or in spite of the shots, I overcame my choking spells and was allowed in the garden for the last warm days. Lately Jörg had been allowed to visit. Like the good old times, we sat on the gate, watched the pedestrians pass by, and chatted.

Having overcome my illness, I should have been happy. However, something else had begun to worry me. I observed a strange change in my mother. She walked more slowly and carefully. Her belly was swollen, and her concerns seemed to be more directed toward her body than toward me. Even my father took time that he had used for me to serve my mother with extra tenderness. To my great consternation, I was no longer the center of attention.

Jörg, who had three older brothers, one younger, and a two-year-old sister, knew what the problem was.

"I think your mother is going to have a baby," he said.

I did not know how to respond.

"Just make sure you don't get a sister. Sisters are *Heulsusen*" (crybabies). "My sister cries all the time."

I hoped that Jörg was wrong; another child would not come between my mother, father, and me. But my parents soon discouraged my hopes. They started to talk about a happy new arrival that we would be having next March.

"Michael, think, you will have a little brother, Tommy, or a little sister, Monika."

"I don't want a sister," I declared emphatically.

"Why wouldn't you like a sister?"

"I don't want a *Heulsuse*."

Even though my parents tried to convince me all winter of how wonderful it would be to have a little sister to play with, they did not change my mind. No, if I had to have any other child in my house at all, let it be a boy.

I was in the same frame of mind when the snow melted in February and the three of us took our first walk. We went one block and turned up the ski hill. My mother had to walk slowly with a cane. She had nerve pain in her leg.

On the hill, the snow melted. Patches of withered grass covered the slope, except where the ski tracks, some of them mine, had packed a furrowed glossy, gray layer. I followed the incline down to the bottom, where water collected in a big puddle. Who did I spot there but the very first girl I had ever seen and had named die Vogelspitze. She was floating little sticks. I gathered sticks and joined her. After my mother stood there for a while, she had so much pain that she asked my father to take her home. If I wanted, I could stay and play with the Vogelspitze and then come home by myself. They left, but at the corner they stopped and peeked to observe me play with a friend.

As I stepped back and watched the Vogelspitze, I was suddenly overcome by a tempting vision. I felt as if I were growing into a giant. I saw myself grabbing her, swinging her over my head a few times, and flinging her right into the middle of the puddle. In a few moments, the vision became compelling. I grabbed the Vogelspitze from behind under her arms. I was surprised how heavy she was. I could not lift her, much less swing her over my head. It took all my strength to rock her off her feet and push her into the water. She stumbled and fell with a splash.

"Michael!" I heard from the corner.

My mother's eyes burned under the wide, floppy rim of her black hat. Her look turned me to stone. I could not move until my father was upon me and gave me a thorough spanking. Then he wiped off the Vogelspitze's coat, straightened up her pointy hat, and took her to her house to apologize for the inexplicable behavior of his son. My mother led me home, venting her disappointment.

"What's gotten into you? If you act like that, we just can't take you anywhere."

I was banished to my room and put on my little white folding chair all alone. The door was shut. My parents had their lunch without me.

At bedtime they forgave me. My mother always relieved my sorrow the same evening. Calmly she brought up the incident and accepted my promise to be good. After our prayer, I slung my arms around her neck and felt her warm kiss. With a sigh of relief, I would drift off, grateful to be accepted back into our threesome.

I resolved to be a good boy and to be on guard for the dark urges that had taken me out of control. I even stopped complaining about the possibility of having a sister. My parents told me my sister or brother would come very soon, which filled me with trepidation.

Before that event, however, my parents made another, more serious demand on my cooperation. They had to take me to the hospital for an operation. I was to have my adenoids removed to alleviate my tendency to get ear infections.

My mother took me to the West Sanatorium in Charlottenburg. She checked in also for observation of her painful pregnancy.

As my mother was unpacking the suitcases in our sterile white room, I stood at the window and looked into the night. I saw nothing but the high, dark, rear facades with vertical chains of lit windows—no sky, no trees, and no meadow. My mother, who hung up our clothes in the closet behind me, seemed far distant. Why had she been more and more turned away from me and inside herself? What was to become of me? What was this operation going to be like? Would it hurt? My parents said that I would be put to sleep. Would I wake up again? The black building with the lit rectangles looked heartless and unconcerned.

My mother pulled the curtains and put me to bed. She stroked my hair.

"You are all right in this hospital. This is a good hospital. This is where you were born."

I made up my mind to be courageous and willing. Things would not be as bad as I feared.

Early the next morning, a nurse led me into a room all tiled in white. A man in a white coat lifted me on his lap. He held a piece of gauze over my nose and asked me to count while he dripped a strong-smelling, volatile essence from a brown bottle.

"Four, five, six ..."

———

Then I was back in my bed, my mother sitting next to me. She told me the operation was all over. The next day my father took me home while my mother moved to Tante Teddy's to stay in close driving distance to the hospital.

On the second of March, a Sunday, at eight o'clock in the morning, my father and I were awakened by the telephone. My father rushed into the hall, while I trotted along sleepily. He picked up the phone with a mixture of worry and joyful anticipation.

"Hello."

In the quiet, I thought I could hear my mother's faint voice crackling. I couldn't understand the words, but I know what she said from my father's diary.

"Die Monika will ihrem Papi guten Morgen sagen" (Monika wants to say good morning to her papi).

"Well, that is just wonderful!" my father shouted, his voice two pitches higher than normal with excitement. "We'll be coming to see you."

After hearing a few more details about the delivery, he hung up and turned to me. "You have a little sister, Monika!"

He was so elated that I could not express my disappointment. To please my father, I showed a moderate amount of excitement and got dressed quickly. Then we rode his bicycle to the station and took the U-Bahn to see this thing.

We emerged under the big blue U that marked the stairs to the subway station at the Kurfürsten Damm and turned toward the Joachimsthaler Strasse. On this crisp Sunday morning, the wide sidewalks were empty and peaceful. In sight of the red cross that marked the entrance of the sanatorium, we came upon a flower store that displayed the newly arrived spring flowers. To our surprise, the store was open.

"Let's bring our ladies some flowers," my father said. "Do you see something you want to get for Monika?"

In the lower right corner, I saw a little bouquet of *Tausendschönchen* (thousand little beauties)—daisy-like flowers, shaped like plush buttons in blues, purples, and reds. Such a small, rich, and soft bouquet should be right for a little sister.

"And for Mutti?"

"Those violets."

My father felt extravagant for the occasion and chose the branches of an almond tree, studded with light pink blossoms. He liked to be generous but usually restrained himself. He always handed his paycheck to my mother and kept nothing but a little pocket money. She was the trained bookkeeper. He respected the fact that my mother held on tightly to our limited purse and that she frowned on unnecessary expenses.

Clutching the daisies in one hand and the violets in the other, I was eased into the tall, white private room by my father, who followed with his unwieldy bouquet. From the door on, I stretched both hands full of flowers toward my mother, who lay half propped in bed, weak and happy. She closed me into her arms, and her embrace was again as unreserved as it used to be.

There was a crib and, in it, a tiny white bundle with something pink on top. I guessed that this was my new sister. Hesitatingly, I walked over and looked through the white bars. I was relieved. This little round head with the minuscule ears; the tiny, well-formed fingers; and the mess of the finest hair had nothing to do with the Vogelspitze. There was no threat in these delicate and vulnerable features. Monika was something entirely new and different. Even her crying seemed to awaken my pity and consideration instead of alarm. I was relieved to hear how different this cry was from the wailing that the Vogelspitze had sent through the neighborhood when I had pushed her over.

When we left the hospital, I started to proclaim to anyone who would listen that I had a new little sister, Monika. She was no longer a thing. I had accepted her into the circle of my care. Our family's quartet was complete.

15

The last spring in Berlin, 1941, was a season of change. As soon as I had overcome my worries about my sister, several new concerns arose. My first apprehension came from my parents' talk about having my sister and me baptized. The families on both sides had finally been convinced of the stability of my parents' marriage and had become more supportive. A double baptism would acknowledge this favorable turn and would present a show of affirmation from all.

Unsure of the proceedings, I was anxious about the baptism. This apprehension originated when we were invited to dinner at the house of the physician, Dr. Rolf Richter, and his wife. My parents had befriended the Richters through Tante Teddy and Uncle Horsa. Dr. Richter, who was obviously well respected by my parents, told me with dramatic gesticulations how I was going to be submerged in water. This conjured up an unpleasant memory. I had once slipped in the shallow beach of the lake in Bansin. I had been standing in the water up to my chest next to my father. I had dropped under water; had seen, in panic, air bubbles rising in front of me; and had groped in vain to get up until my father missed me, searched, and pulled me up by my blonde shock of hair. I worried how I would keep from drowning during baptism. I told my parents that I would rather not be baptized.

My parents cursed Dr. Richter and set out on a campaign to make me familiar and at ease with the procedure. They insisted there would be only three handfuls of water put on my head, one for the Father, one for the Son, and one for the Holy Ghost. Also I would be getting presents. To do my own part in curbing my fears, I started to play baptism. I asked my mother for an empty beer bottle for my ceremony, and to my delight, she let me have one. This way, the baptism practice had the added benefit of getting one of those intriguing treasures made out of brown glass with the porcelain stopper, red rubber gasket, and the contorted wire mechanism that snapped it into place. I filled the bottle from the garden hose, knelt in my sand play area, and put three short pours on my head, saying, "Father, Son, and Holy Ghost." After I had convinced myself of the harmlessness of the rite, I decided not to return the precious bottle but kept it for another use.

I had heard in the fairy tales about sons leaving home and had often wondered how it would be to strike out alone into the wide, wide world. I knew the young men took provisions for their journey. I got a piece of bread from the kitchen and stuffed it into my pocket. I filled the bottle to the brim and, with all my strength, managed to close the spring mechanism. When I knew my mother was busy straightening up the living room, I climbed over the red gate. I turned, not east toward Luzi's familiar cigarette stand but west in a new direction. After one block, where the ski hill was on the right and the turn toward the station on the left, I dared to go straight, where I had never been. Wandering along between the unknown buildings of the development, I felt like *Hans im Glück* (Lucky Jack). I started singing:

Hänschen klein
ging allein
in die weite Welt hinein ...

Little Jack
went alone
into the wide world ...

At the end of the cul-de-sac, I climbed a steep dune and down the other side into the pine forest. I was completely alone. I had kept my way home to my mother firmly in mind like a red string rolled out behind me.

I sat down in the cool soil, took my shoes off, and shook out the sand. Then I forced the bottle open, set it in the sand, and freed the crust from my pocket. It was hard to suck water out of the bottle, and in the attempt, I got baptized all over again. But finally I managed to get some water into my mouth. The water even had a tinge of beer. Between sips, I munched the bread, savoring the sour taste of rye.

As I looked around through the underbrush of the forest, the end of the song popped into my mind:

> *Aber Mutter weinet sehr*
> *hat ja nun kein Hänschen mehr.*
> *Da besinnt*
> *Sich das Kind*
> *Kehrt nach Haus geschwind.*

> But mother weeps a lot
> Doesn't have little Jack any more.
> There to his senses
> comes the child,
> Returns home quickly.

Strange cackling and fluttering noises came from the underbrush. It was time to retreat. The return trip seemed much shorter. I climbed back into the garden without my mother ever knowing that I had gone. I put the bottle of water back into the cupboard. I had conquered my fear.

It did not alarm me when my father arranged for the big event. He phoned the parsonage and asked to speak to the pastor. His name was Pastor Kopenhagen.

A few days later, unannounced, as was usual for his profession, Pastor Kopenhagen visited to discuss the ceremony that he had been asked to schedule. He rang the bell at the gate. My mother and I looked through the kitchen window and saw the clerical white collar over the black frock.

"Oh my."

My mother was still in her bathrobe, though it was almost noon. She rushed into the living room, whisked two empty champagne glasses and several abandoned articles of clothing into the bedroom, threw herself into a dress, and made it back to the remote button in the kitchen that opened the garden door. The pastor was turning away. After having rung three more times, he was shaking the dust from his shoes. When he heard the buzzing gate, he responded and entered, even though he was probably a little put out to have knocked and not been greeted for so long.

My mother felt awkward. How would this unknown minister take it that one of her children was five years old and not yet baptized? Something needed to be done to break the ice.

"How about a cup of coffee?"

"No, thank you, I just had coffee."

"How about a beer?

"A beer would be fine."

My mother placed the bottle and the glass in front of the pastor and sat down to explain why I was so old. It never seemed to be the right time. The families could not get together on this. We lived in Charlottenburg where we did not know a church. Now her husband usually had to work on Sundays.

She almost got the pastor to nod just once, when he opened the bottle and poured. Miracle of miracles! The beer had turned into water.

Generally, my mother was not beyond telling white lies when it would spare someone's feelings, but to the pastor she considered herself beholden to honesty. So she confessed the truth, and to her great relief, the stern man laughed. Pastor Kopenhagen resolved to play along with this crazy family. He even accepted the outlandish request of having Bach's *Toccata* and *Fugue in D-Minor* played when he heard it had been performed at the wedding. After he had scheduled the baptism for Wednesday, May 14, at 3:30 and a rehearsal on the Monday before, he proffered his hand to my mother and then let it rest on my head for an uncomfortably long period and departed in peace. As she told my father that night, my mother was surprised to have discovered in the minister someone "quite human."

When my parents and I set out for the rehearsal, we had an idea where the Glienicke church was. Yes, it was the one with the pencil-sharp steeple sticking out over the trees behind Luzi's cigarette stand. However, we had never seen it up close. It was a narrow and gray village church, almost completely devoid of adornment and small enough that the baptism party of seventeen people, counting the pastor and the organist, would not look lost in it. Pastor Kopenhagen went through the program of the music, sermon, and the procession in detail and seriousness. I examined the baptismal fountain and noticed, with relief, that it was too small even to drown my little sister. Then we squeezed up a narrow stone staircase onto the loft around the organ. The young woman who played the challenged instrument went through *Toccata and Fugue* for us. My father had timed the piece on our record at home at seven minutes and heard with concern how the young woman needed nine. She kept tripping on the tonal staircases. However, she reassured my parents that she would practice a lot before Wednesday.

Omi and Tante Anneliese, my mother's younger sister, came a day early from Erfurt to help with the preparations. Omi was standing in the way smoking, and was soon relegated to my room to read me stories. Robust Tante Anneliese, on other hand, was a great help. She wielded the vacuum cleaner, mop, and dust cloth with determination and verve. No pot was big enough for mixing the punch. She spotted the diaper kettle, grabbed it, scoured it, and voilà.

"Just keep the guests out of the kitchen, and bring the drinks out in small portions in this fancy glass bowl."

On the day of the celebration, all other guests came from Berlin and went directly to church. My father's parents, Opa and Oma, arrived almost an hour early. Tante Teddy and Onkel Horsa drove up in their Opel and brought the Richters. Hans and Elisabeth Schubert hiked from the train station, accompanied by their future daughter-in-law, Else Konietzko. Her fiancé, Ulrich Schubert, had been drafted as an orderly.

As my mother carrying Monika, my father, and I approached the church, there arrived one guest in a taxi. When he extracted his sizable body from the vehicle, the curious villagers, who had come to see what was happening at their church, called to each other, "Is this Jakob Tiedtke? No, he can't be."

They had their doubts, like everyone who suddenly sees a famous person in his or her own humble surroundings. But he *was* Jakob Tiedtke, the famous character actor, the essence and representative of the old boisterous and witty Berliner. He had become a good friend of my father and had agreed to be one of my godfathers. To me, he looked much like my Opa, bald and potbellied, only bigger.

After my father had settled Tiedtke in the pew, he gave the pastor the nod that everyone was present. The *Toccata and Fugue* came off without any embarrassing gaps, even though it stressed both organist and organ to the breaking point. Pastor Kopenhagen scaled down much of his sermon to my understanding. He talked about little devils, making me think of the red, hairy creatures with tails and tridents that appeared in some of my fairy tales. Other than that, I understood no more about the three handfuls of water than Monika.

After the ceremony, the party proceeded through Glienike to our garden. The day was overcast and almost as cold as the inside of the church. My mother attempted to film the guests; the movie turned out so dark that the faces dawned out of the background like in Rembrandt's *Night Watch*. Grandfather Georg's and Jakob Tiedtke's hairless domes, as well as Pastor Kopenhagen's white collar, provided the only highlights. Yes, the pastor did come. He sipped a glass of punch after he had assured himself that it was, indeed, nothing else. My father introduced the guests to him and pointed out the children's godparents. I had four: Jakob Tiedtke; Tante Teddy; and two men who were away in the service, Ulrich Schubert and Onkel Helmut.

I had specifically requested Onkel Helmut, who was Tante Anneliese's husband and a wing commander in the *Luftwaffe*, airborne. He had visited us recently. He had arrived at night when I was already in bed.

The next morning, my mother woke me up full of excitement. "Your Onkel Helmut has come last night with his plane."

I rushed to my bedroom window and looked into the backyard. The big lawn was empty.

"Where is his plane?" The next morning, my mother wanted to capture Helmut on film. She led him into the backyard to my sandbox. To put some action into the scene, he picked me up like a feather and lifted me over his head onto his broad shoulders, while the sand from my shoes dropped down his uniform. Before he left, he gave me a round, flat tin container with a disc of bittersweet chocolate. It was the kind the air force distributed to flight crews as extra rations. I broke off a little corner to taste it. I saved the rest in my toy cabinet. Every few months when I came across it, I opened the lid and smelled the chocolate. Then I closed the canister carefully and put it back. Eventually, I learned to read the name, "Kalich," on the lid. Considering how I valued Onkel Helmut's present, it is no wonder I wanted him for my godfather.

Monika's godparents were Tante Anneliese, Elisabeth Schubert, and Dr. Rolf Richter. Three of our godparents would not survive the war.

The party went on in the garden for most of the afternoon. When dinner was called, our little house filled to more than capacity. Tables stretched over three rooms, the dining room, the living room, and the hall. Since my sister had been put to bed before the meal, clearly I was the center of the festivities. My mother even had arranged flowers around my plate. I relished the attention, gloried in the congratulations, and suggested that from now on I should be baptized once a month.

16

With the baptism past, one of my concerns vanished. Two others remained. The first worry was my parents' plan to move, the second that I had to go to school.

After several years at the Volksbühne, my father finally admitted that my mother's assessment of his chances for advancement were correct. He had lost hope of ever being given a play to direct and realized how his boss had exploited him shamelessly. He asked his agent, Fritz R. Schultz, to look for a position anywhere in the Reich. The agent found an opening for a play director in Königsberg. For a week, my parents' conversation buzzed with Königsberg, Mountain of the King, as a place of promise and excitement. My father showed me its location on the map. It was in East Prussia, right at the Baltic Sea. I had the vision of a radiant city and a king's castle on a mountain at the edge of a vast expanse of silvery water. It seemed almost worth giving up my home to move to such a place.

The job in Königsberg was awarded to a competitor, and my father accepted a similar position in Straßburg. The move west to Straßburg instead of east probably saved our lives.

Neither my father nor my mother had ever been to Straßburg. Before signing the final contract, my father joined a group of theater administrators who were interested in working there for an exploratory visit. The oddity about the Straßburg Theater was that it was empty. It had been closed for two years. At the declaration of war, France had ordered all Straßburgers to evacuate. Most of the approximately 200,000 citizens complied, leaving behind a dead city. The French military settled in the heavy bunkers along the wooded western banks of the Rhine, resolved to repulse the German onslaught. By June 1940, the Germans captured Straßburg and called on the inhabitants to return. Most Straßburgers willingly came back and rediscovered their German heritage. Since the local dialect had always been German, they switched from French to German with ease. As life normalized during the following year, the cultured and convivial population hungered for theater and opera.

My father liked the artistic freedom that a completely fresh start would offer. He called my mother from Straßburg. He outlined the advantages of the position and praised the beauty of the city. He told her how he had visited and climbed the Münster, and from the high platform, had seen the lands from the Vogesen in the west to the Black Forest in the east. He assured her that he had located a three-bedroom apartment in the newest section of town, which included a modern elementary school, the Gudrun Schule.

"You saw the Black Forest from the Münster?" my mother asked excitedly.

The Black Forest was a strong incentive for the relocation. What a pleasure it would be to reach their favorite area in a few hours by train or even by bicycle. Imagine the hikes in the summer, the ski tours in the winter!

A third consideration made a move desirable—the improbability of air raids, since the English likely considered Straßburg French territory. By now, we had experienced seventy-one Fliegeralarme in Berlin, and they were coming with mounting frequency and destruction. It would be a relief not to have to rush into the basement at night.

Before they hung up, my parents agreed to move. My father rented the apartment and hired plasterers and painters for a complete overhaul.

Returning to Berlin, my father prepared me for the move with the enthusiasm that usually took hold of him when he planned to strike out into the far distance. He felt elated at the prospect of a clean start, of leaving behind all the resentments about unjust treatment that he had stored up. He showed me the pictures of Straßburg, related its location to Berlin on the map, and drew plans of the apartment he had rented. A song about Straßburg appeared in the folk songs he used to sing and pound out on the piano. When this new song came up, he would hush his voice and soften his brisk hammering.

Oh, Straßburg, oh Straßburg, Du wunderschöne Stadt
Darinnen liegt begraben so mancher Soldat.

Oh, Straßburg, oh Straßburg, you wondrously beautiful city
Therein lies buried many a soldier.

I asked, "Papi, what does it mean, therein lies buried many a soldier?"

My father, who never dodged any of my questions by claiming I was too young to understand, explained. "You see, Straßburg is a border city, so when there is a war, it's always right in the middle. In the Franco-Prussian War of 1870–71, there was a long, bitter battle for the city. It's called a siege. Finally, the Germans took Straßburg from the French. That was the war my grandfather Hermann Tradowsky was in. Straßburg was German until the end of the First World War, when the French took it again. I still remember that time. Then it was French until a year ago. Now it's German again. And so, it has been going back and forth for many centuries. When it was German, it was called Straßburg; when it was French, it was called Strasbourg. And in every war, there were many soldiers who died there. So people started singing this song about Straßburg."

My father's explanation filled me with qualms. A beautiful city built on buried soldiers? I was unsure whether I wanted to go there, and yet I was curious.

I became restless and sad when my parents started packing crates. I did not know how to separate from the world I knew. They admitted that this was not like our trip through the Alps, since this time we would not come back. We would never come back here.

I felt a bitter yearning for everything I saw in the garden and the house. How would all this exist without me?

89

When I lay in bed with the fragrant night air fanning through the open window, I listened once again to the train in the distance, the barely audible *tap-tap* on the tracks, the faint whistling of the wind around the wheels. I felt stretched out under the stars, one with the land. How could I ever be lifted from it? And yet, didn't the tapping of the wheels call, *come-come, come-come*, as it was fading in the distance?

During the day, I did not want to play. My blocks, my train, and the garden tools, which I counted among my toys, were packed. I strolled aimlessly outside and through the house. I ducked under the grand piano, where I was hiding the Attika pack on top of the beams that supported the frame. I took the little box from the beam, lifted out the silver Zeppelin coin, and carried it with me through the house. At the door between the hall and the living room was a catch in the frame for the lock, which looked like the slot of a large piggy bank. I wondered whether the slot was large enough for my coin. It was. But there was a cavity in the door frame behind the metal plate, and after I'd fit the coin through the slot a few times, it slipped out of my fingers and disappeared. I was desperate. I tried to pry with a pencil through the slot. The coin was gone. I called my mother to the scene. She looked into the slot with a flashlight but could not see anything. My father could perhaps have unscrewed the plate, but I never had seen him tackle a screwdriver, so I did not ask.

The morning of Tuesday, May 17, we departed. My father was to take my mother, Monika, and me to the Anhalter Bahnhof and put us on the train to Erfurt. We were to visit there while he would supervise the packers and then go to Straßburg to oversee the restoration of our apartment.

We had to get up when it was still dark. While my mother fixed a hurried meal in the kitchen, I wandered through the house one last time. The furniture was still there but awkwardly pulled away from its accustomed locations. The movers were to come later that day. The sober bareness that had spread throughout the rooms disheartened me. The bookshelves were empty; the carpets had been rolled up. Instead of pictures were empty places. I circled the pile of suitcases in the hall. Again I stopped at the door between hall and living room and forced my little finger into the slot in a last attempt to retrieve the coin.

When my mother called me into the kitchen, I had to give up trying. She had set out fried leftover noodles and some grapes. I usually liked fried noodles, but this morning I had trouble swallowing. The curtains had been taken down, the lamp had been packed, and a naked bulb spread its sober light over the bare white walls. How could I tell my parents, who seemed so thrilled about the move, that I did not want to leave—that I wanted the house and garden back the way it had been?

Out of the stillness of the predawn a flash of lightning streaked across the sky, and an immediate clap of thunder sounded close enough to have struck the oak. Gusts rattled the shutters, and rain drove against the windows while continuous claps of thunder rumbled over the commons. My mother worried, "How will we get to the station in this?"

We waited as long as we could. We finally had to leave and stepped outside. The storm had moved on toward the southeast, and only a few large drops were drumming on my rain jacket. From the distance, the storm was spectacular. Lightning branched back and forth between shifting towers of clouds. The flashes backlit the familiar silhouettes of the scraggly pine and the majestic oak. When we went over the sandy hillock, I looked at the house and garden one final time. More lightning flashed, and thunder rolled close and vehement. I felt like I was being torn out of the ground. My parents urged me on. When I turned around again after a few steps, the sandy hill had swallowed my world.

17

O n the train to Erfurt, I consoled myself by anticipating the warmth and affection of my relatives. Since we only stayed for a few days, our hosts dropped their daily pursuits and lavished all their attention on us. Omi Bauer, with the help of Omi and Tante Ellen, gave a garden party, the last of an almost-endless string of celebrations that had enlivened the estate for over four decades. It was like the afterglow of a once brilliant, shining fortune and must have had some melancholic overtones for my mother. I felt no such nostalgia. I jumped right into the garden as it was. The wilderness taking over the fringes made it all the more enchanting. Omi Bauer hired a gardener for a few days to cut the lawn, find the survivors of precious plants under the weeds, and rejuvenate them one more time. The weather helped bring out some of the blossoms, particularly the jasmine along the front fence.

On this sunny afternoon, my mother took an 8mm black-and-white film, "Garten Fest, Juni 1941." The center of attention, Monika, lay, a little bundle in Omi Bauer's arms, squinting and distorting her mouth like she was searching for food. The matriarch, sitting in a wicker chair in front of a juniper tree, bent down over the baby. Her white, loosely pinned-up hair blew gently and glistened in the sun. Then, called by the camerawoman, she raised her wrinkled, refined face with the wise eyes and broke into a smile of great-grandmotherly pleasure and pride. I was in awe of Omi Bauer's age. At seventy-seven, she was the oldest person

I knew. Her slender figure seemed alarmingly fragile. Also, I wondered about her nervous condition of nodding constantly, which made her appear even more delicate. Not far from her sat my Tante Toni, her sister, who was almost as old, a little smaller, and had the same white, pinned-up hair. Tante Toni shook her head from side to side rather than up and down. In a conversation with both old ladies, Omi Bauer approving and Tante Toni denying, it appeared that every word spoken resonated true or untrue at the same time. I moved between and around the two old ladies cautiously. Their age was so pervasive that it did not occur to me they ever might have been young. I listened to them politely and only talked when asked questions. Greeting or leaving them, I took their bony hands and made a deep Diener. I did not like to kiss the old ladies. I was afraid their age might rub off, particularly that startling smell of dead leaves on their gray, wrinkly skin that the cologne could not quite hide. As always, I was relieved when I sensed that my mother thought I had talked to them long enough, and I could go back to play with Maria Barbara.

I spotted my friend in her new white dress that flared out like one of those jasmine blossoms along the fence. She was standing next to her father, my Onkel Werner, who was stretched out on a lawn chair in the fancy part of the garden house. This room with its polished floor and lavishly upholstered garden furniture was usually off limits for us children. We were restricted to the other room of the building, where the wind blew leaves through the open windows and the only furnishings were two hard benches fixed to the far wall. But on this festive afternoon, we kids were freshly scrubbed and dressed in spotless clothes, and the glass doors of the fancy garden room had been opened wide for children as well as adults. I stepped up to Onkel Werner and Maria Barbara, who was begging her father to perform some of his magic tricks.

"Oh, yes, please, Onkel Werner," I joined in.

For a moment, the balding man did not respond but kept watching the family under the trees—the silently nodding and shaking old ladies; the starched nursemaid who had reclaimed Monika; and the younger generation, including his beautiful wife, Ellen, standing in a group on the lawn, smoking and laughing over some inside joke. For some reason, Onkel

Werner did not seem to be quite accepted by the in-laws. Particularly my mother did not trust him. My mother trusted very few people. I, however, liked Onkel Werner because he did these magic tricks with us. Finally, turning to us children, he reached over to pinch Maria Barbara's pert nose between his knuckles, said "abracadabra," and extracted a ladybug wrapped in brightly colored tinfoil. Boy! Then he picked a tiny, green, shimmering frog from behind my ear. He had candy appear, disappear, and multiply, and after circuitous routes through our bodies, it unfailingly wound up in our hands. When we opened the foil and found real chocolate, we considered it an additional treat because chocolate was becoming scarce.

Onkel Werner disappeared like magic out of my life after this sun-drenched afternoon. He and Tante Ellen got a divorce. My mother had known all along that this would happen. She did not even take his picture on the film.

After Onkel Werner had exhausted his magic, Maria Barbara and I left to play ball, and the camera rolled again. There we were on the seething-hot concrete in front of the garages, stepping from one bare foot to the other and throwing the ball over my cousin, Jens-Peter. This sturdy, white-blond two-year-old stood planted in the middle. Oblivious to our shouts that he should try to get the ball, he saw it appear and disappear in our hands and did not much care where it went or came from. Then his mother, Tante Anneliese, stepped in and began a game that was more his speed by calling us to form a circle around him. Maria Barbara and I rushed to the game. Omi joined, abandoning her hearing aid at the garden table and maneuvering her round, stately body through the flower beds with remarkable agility. Tante Ellen, badgered by the others, gave in, crushed her cigarette, and took my hand. My mother moved in and filled the last gap. My mother? Did she agree to have Werner use her camera?

Jens-Peter knew the song about the poor little bunny in the dell that was so sick that it could not hop. He crouched down, put his dimpled hands over his face, and stayed put while the circle started moving around him.

When I see this film now, I realize the cameraman stood too close to the dance. The scene shows serious amateurish flaws. It is a quick sequence of persons with partially cut-off legs and heads, faces suddenly obscured by backs and a whirl of legs moving around the patiently crouching boy. First, Maria Barbara tiptoes through the frame, self-possessed, graceful, and proud of her new dress. Big Tante Anneliese floats footless through the picture, her frank, high forehead and blonde waves cropped by the frame, her large hooked nose, her clear blue eyes and smiling mouth showing a straight row of healthy teeth. And there I am, with gangly legs moving in all directions; light blonde hair bobbing; and new, big, almost unnaturally white teeth flashing. Enter dark-eyed Tante Ellen, measured, dignified, and slightly imposed upon. Then comes Omi exuding friendliness, a big smile pushing her cheeks up and lifting her vibrating double chin, while her large, hooked nose, intelligent eyes, and straight forehead try to maintain respectability. She is suddenly obscured by Tante Anneliese's enormous back. "Tante Anneliese has shoulders like a furniture mover," my father used to say. The shoulders move by, and my mother comes into view, as tall as her sister but slender and of dark complexion. Her hooked nose is actually not much bigger than Omi's or Tante Anneliese's. It appears more prominent in her narrower, more tapered face, and it is elongated by those deep furrows that energy, determination, ambition, and temper have engraved across her forehead. My mother avoids showing her profile. She knows that, from the side, her nose is abandoned by all other features and juts out like the bow of a capsized boat. From the front, it is balanced by her large, dark eyes. The circle turns. Maria Barbara. Tante Anneliese. Arms and legs bounce by. The bunny in the dell is still crouching and waiting patiently. The round continues. Discombobulated me once more, soon covered up by my mother's back. How much more refined are my mother's shoulders than Tante Anneliese's! How they curve gently and delicately like the lowest boughs of a tree. The shoulders move on. The song comes to an end. "Bunny hop, bunny hop." Jens-Peter tries lifting his pudgy little legs off the ground by swinging his round arms up and down futilely. The circle disperses.

My mother rescued her camera. She took the rest of the film with Maria Barbara and me on the gondola behind the juniper tree. The footage turned out dark. Only Maria Barbara's white dress and my shirt were swinging. The sun had dropped behind the villa. The garden was getting cool. Omi Bauer and Tante Toni moved inside, and the party broke up.

The next day, Tante Anneliese invited my mother, Monika, and me to the Fliegerhorst. She lived on base alone with Jens-Peter while Onkel Helmut was in the Balkans.

We must have taken a taxi out late that night because I arrived very tired. I did not notice anything about the room Tante Anneliese put me in before I went to sleep. I was awakened by a humming that went past the window. The morning sun searched for gaps in the drawn curtains. Through my blinking eyes, I noticed photographs in narrow black frames neatly hung on the walls. They depicted airplanes performing all kinds of maneuvers close to the ground and high up against the clouds. The humming approached as if it was going right through the room. Then it faded. I got up and pulled back the curtains. I looked across a narrow strip of grass onto a sun-drenched runway. It was as close as my backyard lawn in Berlin had been. Another plane came down toward me, revving the engine. Then, right opposite my window, the wheels miraculously parted with the ground and the craft rose. I felt like I was taking off into the air. The roar of the prop engines down the runway thrilled me. The war had not touched me much yet. The same sound would later strike terror. Even today, when it wakes me in the night, I have the impulse to run into the cellar. But that morning out at the Erfurt Fliegerhorst, my mother could hardly tear me away from the window, so fascinated was I with watching the practice takeoffs and landings.

I remember this day particularly well because my mother told me a story from her childhood about an unusual event in an unusual place. She recounted it right where it had happened, which made it more real. In retrospect, the whole morning seemed a prelude to this story.

Since it was such a sunny day, my mother decided to walk back to the Louisen Strasse, a hike of several hours. Tante Anneliese offered to bring Monika to the city. My mother and I approached Erfurt from the high plateau in the west. The ripening fields of wheat and rye stretched endlessly, and I was wondering where the city was. Would we be able to reach it before dark? The plateau spread farther and farther, and there was no sign of a settlement except an occasional farmhouse. I was searching the shimmering distance for tall buildings. Finally, we came along a broken fence covered with brambles of wild roses. It was through the arches of those brambles that I first saw the two churches on the horizon. My mother had seen them also.

"Look, way in the distance, there are the Dom and the Severi Kirche. This is where we'll go."

As we approached, I noticed that the two churches stood unusually close, like they were seeking each other's company. The towers grew bigger and bigger until they stretched mightily into the sky. We passed in the shade between them like through a canyon. The churches stood on the last bluff before the land dropped down to the Gera Valley. The passage opened, and there was the city. I found myself on top of a most amazing staircase, issuing like a cascade from between the churches and falling in broad flights, occasionally resting on landings and then plunging on, in new and ever more expansive runs. Fanning wider and wider, it finally flowed into the immense dome square.

My mother explained, "In the Middle Ages, a huge fire burned the center of town. The townspeople did not rebuild but left this big square so people could see the churches on top of these stairs."

At the periphery of the square began the old city. My mother pointed out some landmarks. There was the roof of the Barfüsserkirche along the river and the modest spire of the Augustine Monastery where Luther had been as a young monk; there were the city hall, the railroad station, and the distant hills of the Steigerwald at the south of the valley. As we descended these steps, my mother stopped on the first landing and told me what happened on this square when she was little.

"Each year, on the tenth of November," she began, "all parents in Erfurt bought their children little paper lanterns to celebrate Martin Luther's birthday. I would be excited all day. When it finally got dark, Martchen would bundle me up in the entrance hall. She would fold the lantern to reach the candle and light it and carefully unfold it again. Then she would hand me the stick to carry the lantern before me. As we switched off the electric lamps, the colors and patterns of the paper would glow and reflect on the walls and ceiling. Then we went outside to walk through the city to this dome square. Soon I would spot other lights approaching from the side streets. They would come closer until I could see the faces in the lantern's light and recognize my friends. We would go on together. New rivulets of light would join at every corner. And we children would start singing, '*Herr Martin ist ein guter Mann.*' Our breath would show, but we were warm. More and more lanterns would come from the side alleys. From all over town, these rivers of lights flowed together and onto this square. Martchen would take my hand. Lanterns shone from one end of the square to the other. All children in the city were there, thousands. There was so much warm light. It illuminated these old houses and even these stairs.

"And then the bells from the two churches would start tolling, and a chorus in robes would file onto these stairs from above until every last step was filled. The tolling would slow, and one by one, the bells would fall silent until the big, deep one would give one last swing. Then it was quiet. And then the choir on these stairs, hundreds of voices, would start singing, '*Ein feste Burg ist unser Gott*'" (A Mighty Fortress Is Our God).

"Everyone in the square would join in, all the children and all the adults who had brought them. I would start singing, and even Martchen tried. But I could not hear her. The choir was so strong it sounded loud and mighty above all. This has been a tradition in Erfurt. But since the beginning of the war, we have no longer been allowed to celebrate it because of the blackout."

I took the memory of this day and of what my mother told me with me to Straßburg. During the three years there, whenever a letter came from the Louisen Strasse or when Omi or Martchen visited and brought news from there, the name Erfurt evoked the image of the dome square and the choir on the immense stone steps.

———

On one of the last mornings before our departure, when we visited Omi Bauer once more, she had prepared a special gift for Maria Barbara and me. She gave us scooters of a new and technically highly developed kind, equipped with pedals that propelled the back wheels through a rack-and-pinion mechanism. After we learned to keep our balance, our feet would never have to step on the ground. The two scooters were identical—glossy blue with glittering spokes and a bright-yellow, triangular sign on the handlebars showing a bolt of lightning. How deliberate was it that Omi Bauer gave the same gift to her granddaughter Annemarie's son and her daughter Ellen's daughter? Was it an appeal to end the rivalry between Ellen and Annemarie before it passed on to the next generation? Did the old and wise lady realize how she had perhaps triggered her Ellen's jealousy by having spent so much attention on her favored granddaughter, Annemarie? Maria Barbara and I were oblivious to such possible motives. We rushed into the garden to learn to ride our scooters. We guided them along the straight, stone-plated walks and turned them on the concrete in front of the garages.

At first we wavered, faltered, and jumped off, but we soon became more confident and more stable as we cranked up the speed. If it was Omi Bauer's intent to foster our friendship by having us learn an identical skill, she was successful. We smiled at each other as we circled.

I was thankful for any signs of friendship during this visit in Erfurt. Freshly severed from home, my senses were roaming and searching for stability. I was paying attention to my relatives more than ever. I began to understand them and sensed their character, station, and relationship to each other. I came to comprehend Omi Bauer's gentle wisdom and unquestioned leadership, Tante Ellen's beauty and spoiled idleness, Tante Anneliese's joyful and frank honesty, and Omi's comical sociability.

I even grasped Martchen's position in the family. Since my parents never had a servant, it surprised me to find a person who seemed to listen to everyone's command. She willingly answered my grandmother's every request with "Ja, Gnädige Frau," and even waited on my mother and Tante Anneliese, all with a perpetual smile. I wondered if this servility extended to me. Martchen was hardly taller than I. Perhaps I could summon her also.

One evening, after having been put to bed, I decided to conduct an experiment. I heard her in the kitchen turning the chair into a stepladder to climb up to the cupboard and put away the dishes. I called her. "Martchen, Martchen!"

And, indeed, she responded and came in. "What is it, Michael?"

"I want a glass of water."

She brought it. I drank only half. I was not really thirsty.

Martchen had obeyed my order. I felt powerful. Here was the first adult I could commandeer.

Ten minutes later I called her again. "Martchen, Martchen."

She came immediately. "What do you want, Michael?"

"Come really close. It's a secret; I have to whisper it into your ear."

She bent down putting her little ear, half covered with gray strands, close to my mouth.

"*Kannst wieder gehen*" (You can go again), I whispered.

"Oh, you rascal," she laughed good-naturedly and left.

I was pleased. How witty I had been. I had indeed called her to my side and sent her away at will. Fortunately, any further attempts to test my powers over old Martchen came to a halt. The next day, we moved on.

18

I do not remember the trip to Straßburg, except the last part. As we crossed the Rhein River, the train made a three-quarter circle around the city from east to south and finally up the west side to the station, as if the builders of the railroad had planned to display the beauty of the ancient town. At the beginning of this encirclement, my mother and I pressed to the window.

"There it is!" she shouted when the train turned off the bridge. I knew well what she meant. There stood the Straßburger Münster, in its defiant asymmetry, jutting incredibly high over the tiled rooftops. It had only one complete spire, but what a spire it was. Our eyes remained fixed on the cathedral, as it became the axis of our encirclement. Its astounding features shifted into our view one by one—the apse, the octagonal crown over the crossing, the south portal, the endless nave bolstered by the flying buttresses, the steep roof above it like a mountain ridge, and, finally, the formidable facade of the west side rising to the platform. The single tower ascended from there, like the index finger of a gigantic hand pointing to the sky.

When the train finally drew into the station, my father waited, throwing up his arms when he spotted us. We wound out of the train dragging our baggage. My parents fell into each other's arms and did not care that they were an obstacle to the milling crowd.

My father took us by taxi to the Mason Rouge Hotel at the Karl-Roos-

Platz. He had reserved lodging for a few days until the painters were out of our apartment. We took the streetcar to look at our new place, which he had chosen. It needed my mother's approval. My father seemed apprehensive. He was unusually talkative and cheerful, while my mother was rather quiet. On the trip through the city, I was eagerly absorbing every sight. As we skirted the medieval old center, I caught glimpses up narrow alleys of respectable, ancient, half-timber houses; stepped patrician gables; and the similarly stepped tower of the Münster above. Then the streetcar glided into a long, rectangular square that was planted with severely trimmed sycamore trees and framed by official-looking buildings.

"That building on the far end is my theater," my father said pointing to the Greek facade. "Those statues on the roof over the entrance are the four muses." I was impressed. He was play director in such an illustrious building.

Past the theater, the streetcar took us from the distinctly German Medieval inner city into the eastern part, which had been built in the 1800s by the French.

We got off at Brand Platz. Looking south one block away, we saw the palatial buildings of the university. North, we peered down an avenue with a wide middle strip bearing old maple trees, the Ruprechtsauer Allee. My father mentioned for my mother's benefit that this avenue led to the city park, the Orangerie. He hoped this park, with its famous plantings, would compensate for the loss of her flower garden. He wanted her so much to like Straßburg. This was the place where he hoped to become famous.

We did not follow the wide avenue but the Schweighäuser Strasse, which branched off in a northeasterly direction. After one block of five-story apartment houses with mansarde roofs, we reached the Geiler Platz, a small square on which six streets converged. On the north sidewalk, I spied a *Litfass Säule*, a thick column for advertising. I knew *Litfass Säulen* from Berlin. They had delightful possibilities. While your parents read a poster, you could walk around the column to the far side and disappear. When they would look for you, and you would sense which direction they were coming, you could move away on the other side until they would shout your name as if you had run away. Ideally, you would sneak up on them from behind and scare them with a, "boo." To have a Litfass Säule in my neighborhood was a definite asset.

My father pointed to the corner building on the south side where the Geiler Strasse took off eastward. Right under the blue enamel street sign was the house number.

"This is it," my father said, "Geiler Strasse 18, fifth floor, apartment on the right."

He unlocked the heavy door from the street and pushed into the cool entrance hall. A tile floor bordered by fleur-de-lis patterns led to the first flight of stairs illuminated by a large, stained-glass window above the landing. Our hands slid up the polished rail of elaborate brass work. Never had I been in an apartment building with so much ornamentation. Its venerable patina of age hushed me. It would take weeks to adjust to these high halls from the cozy, modern house in Berlin. On the fifth floor, the door to our future apartment was open, and voices in the local German dialect and French echoed from the empty rooms. We entered a dark hall indirectly lit from the kitchen by an internal window. Through the six open doors, we saw painters ripping off wallpaper, replacing depressing dark greens and maroons with cheerful light yellows and whites. How different had been the taste of those prior occupants, who had fled when the Germans took the city two years earlier.

From the floor plans my father had drawn in Berlin, my mother and I were somewhat familiar with the L-shape layout of the apartment that angled around an inner court. Some unforeseen features troubled my mother. In the children's bedroom facing the street, two high and narrow doors opened onto a petite balcony. We stepped onto the narrow platform that sloped disconcertingly toward the street. Feeling the dizzying pull down five stories to the sidewalk, we soon pushed away from the shaky banister and retreated into the room.

"If this is going to be the children's room, these doors will have to be locked permanently," my mother said emphatically.

In the other two rooms toward the street, the designated dining room and living room, she spotted a similar hazard, windows of unusual vertical stretch that started at knee level. "I don't like these windows."

"Well, we'll have to teach the children to stay away from them," my father retorted.

My mother kept looking dubious. The windows toward the inner court did not concern her. They all opened onto the wide balcony that ran the full length from the kitchen, past the music room, the bath, and the master bedroom.

The rooms were high and spacious. My mother admitted that the antiques would look splendid being displayed here, more like in Omi Bauer's villa.

"But, what about these stoves?" my mother wanted to know. In Glienicke, we'd had central heating. Here were black, cast-iron monsters with stovepipes in every room. My father pointed out that the scrolling feet on their asbestos-insulated metal pads and the ornate silver doors with mica windows were the dernier cri when they had been installed.

"But who is going to fire these?" my mother asked.

"I'll get the anthracite from the basement. Michael will help me with this, won't you?"

What finally convinced my mother were the two mansarde rooms above the apartment. The one could house all her photographic equipment; the other could be for a maid. Yes, my father assured her, we could have a maid now that he was earning over $\mathcal{RM}$1,000 a month.

When we moved in a week later, my mother and I found it easy to accept the wide spaces; we missed the garden. My mother thought of substitutes. She placed vases on tables and shelves and filled them with ever-fresh bouquets. She ordered flower boxes for the banister of the large balcony above the inside court and planted geraniums. The perpetually blooming flowers afforded privacy. We almost felt like we had in our garden when we stretched out in the sun.

My father needed nature just as much as my mother, but instead of trying to pull it into the apartment, he followed the call of the outdoors. Before his season started, he had to visit his Black Forest. He strapped his bag on his bicycle and got ready for a three-day tour. He took me along. My mother had to stay home to nurse Monika.

We went by railroad across the Rhein to Kehl and Offenburg and then took the Schwarzwaldbahn up the Kinzig River Valley like we had two years before. This time I was old enough to get excited when the train went through many straight and curved tunnels, always announced by a short whistle of one of the two steam engines. After the howling ride through the mountains came sudden, blinding vistas from dizzying bridges over white waters. Halfway up, at Hausach, the Kinzig River made a sudden turn east, and the train followed the side valley of the Gutach River south to Hornberg and Triberg. There we got off the train and pushed the bike up main street to the famous waterfall behind the church with the onion-shaped roof on its tower. I was in awe seeing the silvery water drop from somewhere high above, many hundred feet over the wooded precipices.

"Do you remember how you cried about your little suitcase?" my father pointed out.

"I don't remember," I fibbed.

Having reached the plateau, we rode through a valley between rolling hills covered by a surprisingly dark pine forest. We rested at Schönwald. My father marked the town as a future vacation spot for hikes and ski tours. Here we pushed up to the Höhenweg, a path for hikers and bicyclists that ran along the crest of the Black Forest. We turned south toward The Turner, a hamlet at the height of the Black Forest where my father had stayed with Hans Wiegener in 1929.

My father had underestimated both the distance and my weight. I was tall for my five years and, sitting on the little leather saddle in front of my father, completely filled the space between his arms. It became dusky, and attempting a shortcut, we got lost in the forest. The Höhenweg narrowed to a path. The pines were covered by an eerie, fluorescent moss that hung from the branches like ghostly beards and stroked our shoulders. By my father's artificially good mood, humming and whistling, I knew that I was not alone in feeling spooked. Finally, the forest opened and the shingled roofs of The Turner gleamed in the moonlight on a distant rise. When we arrived, the inn had no more vacancy. My father asked the owner about Lydia.

The man thought for a while. "Oh, you mean Frau Herrmann. She lives down in that farmhouse. Follow the brook."

I asked who Lydia was. Lydia had been the proprietor's daughter when my father and Hans Wiegener had lodged there on their hiking trip. She had been beautiful, and both my father and Hans had fallen in love. She had prepared lunches for their daytrips, butter sandwiches and boiled eggs. On the eggs, she used to write Walterleben (Walterlife) for my father and Hänsekin for Hans. They were terms of endearment the three had adopted.

We rolled to the lonely homestead. When the inside light fell on us through the door, Lydia recognized my father instantly. With the sense of hospitality that graced her Alemanni tribe from ancient times, she asked us in to put us up for the night. She lived alone with her two children, who were sleeping. Her husband was away in the war, of course. Lydia scrambled eggs and fried sliced potatoes on the wood stove. She also put bread, cheese, and ham on the table and filled glasses with milk. We ate with great appetite and then went up to the chamber where Lydia had made the beds. She had brought water in the carafe and hung fresh towels on the side of the wash cabinet. My father poured water into the porcelain basin so I could wash. Then, emptying the soapy water into a bowl in the cabinet underneath, he refilled the basin for himself. I had never been in a room upstairs in a Black Forest house. The ceiling was so low that I stood in my bed and ran my hands along the wooden boards. Then I lay down and fell asleep, while my father went back downstairs for a while.

The next morning, Lydia's children were in the kitchen. Her daughter had the most amazing hair I had ever seen. Lydia was brushing the blue-black silkiness, while the girl had to stand on a footstool so that the ends would not touch the floor. Glistening in the morning light that fell in fractured shafts through the windows, her hair got smoother and shinier with every stroke. Finally, Lydia parted six strands and plaited them into a crown. I have treasured the sight of the girl with the beautiful hair forever.

That day, my father and I hiked to the top of the Brent. The sun pulled golden mist from the valleys. When we gained the summit, only some of the highest peaks were rising like islands out of a glaring sea. My father pointed out the most prominent rise.

"Over there is the Feldberg. Onkel Hans and I almost got struck by lightning on that slope. We were hiking in the rain about thirty paces apart. We were cross with each other about Lydia. The lightning hit right between us. The ground was scourged and steaming."

My father and I spent another night in Lydia's care. Going home, my father had the choice of dropping back down the Kinzig Valley or descending the Höllental, heading southwest and ending in Freiburg. He chose the Höllental, which was the more exciting ride with hairpin turns and slopes so steep and long that he had to stop at Hirschsprung to let the brakes cool. There were narrows here between towering cliffs that just allowed the passage of the whitewater and the road. My father pointed out where, according to legend the stag of Hirschsprung (Stagjump), pursued by hunters, had escaped by jumping from the highest tower of rocks over the river and onto the tiny meadow. I shuddered at the thought.

As we rested in the grass, my father unwrapped the lunch Lydia had packed—two buttered rye sandwiches, two hard-boiled eggs, and a tiny wax-paper envelope with salt. The one egg had a delicate pencil inscription, *Walterleben*.

"Don't you think that an egg is the most perfect shape in the world?" my father asked as he held up an egg, top to bottom, between thumb and forefinger.

I shrugged.

Then we rolled on down the deep and narrow Höllental (Valley of Hell) until it opened up to the flat and fertile Himmelreich (Heaven's Realm). Getting to Freiburg, my father circumvented the inner city. He talked me out of wanting to see the water channels and climbing the cathedral. He was eager to catch the last train and return to my mother.

19

While my father and I had taken in the views and fragrances of the highland, my mother had tended her flower boxes. Her geraniums had responded with such growth of leaves and blossoms that they almost blocked out the view into the windowless, brick walls of the back court.

In spite of these rather successful attempts to bring nature into the house, my mother still longed for flowers in their natural setting. As my father had predicted, the Orangerie quickly became her favorite place. The park had two distinct parts, a French garden and an English garden. My mother, as did most Straßburgers, preferred the French garden. Therefore, we found the most direct route to this section, which went past the ominous Gudrun Schule where I was to start in fall. We entered the Orangerie through the south gate. After passing through an alley of old sycamores that joined branches high above, we stepped onto the bright, open walkways. Geometrically trimmed hedges and meticulously manicured lawns with medallions of raised flower beds made precise patterns of various stars and arabesques.

Only once, my mother ventured into the wild and deserted English Garden, when a man exposed himself to us from the distance. Her furious shouts and threats to summon the police made him flee before I had seen him.

My mother, Monika, and I went to the Orangerie every sunny day that summer. I usually rode my scooter. Occasionally, my father would join us. He had a limited capacity for looking at flowers. With him, we would rent one of the flat bottom boats painted in poisonous green and row back under the trees and around the romantically arranged island with the artificial waterfall. Invariably, we would stir up young couples hidden under the overhanging branches who had abandoned the oars for sweeter pursuits. At other times, we would stroll to the Bürehiesle Restaurant, which was a historic half-timber farmhouse moved there from the country. We would settle in its garden for a piece of wasp-attracting fruit pie or safer cake with butter crumbs.

In all the new impressions of the summer of 1941, there was one familiar event that I was looking forward to—my birthday on August 22. This year, the one present that outshone all others was a new bicycle. Eager to follow my father on his tours around the surrounding villages, I wanted to learn to ride the bike that afternoon. It was a small adult bike, and we found out, to my dismay, that I could not reach the pedals. As I expected, my father became ingenious. He got two little wood blocks from the stage workshop and wired them on top of the footrests. Now I could reach. We took the bike to the wide Orangerie Ring along the south border of the park. It was completely devoid of traffic. With the gasoline rationing, the few private cars always took the shortest way on the main roads. I climbed on the saddle, while my father steadied the bike. He promised to hold on to the carrier in the back and run along with me. After a few wobbly swings right and left, my sense of balance that had been trained on my scooter was awakened. Being able to hold a straight line and gain speed, I told my father to let go. He did not answer. A quick glance backward revealed a wide gap between him and me. I swerved, caught myself, and then realized that I could indeed ride my bike.

Next, we men took my mother along to demonstrate what we had accomplished. Proudly, I leaned through U-turns and figure eights and soaked up my mother's astonishment and praise. On the way home, I became overconfident and drove ahead of my parents. I disappeared from their sight around a left turn into the Antwerpener Strasse, which was particularly wide. Halfway down the block, I saw an elderly couple helping each other across the road. Notwithstanding all the space, my bicycle was magically attracted to the pedestrians. Seeing the inevitable coming, I forgot where the brakes were and drove right into them. I apologized profusely. My parents, catching up, joined me. The old Alsatian couple seemed more concerned that I might be hurt than about their own welfare. The shock left me less cocky. I stayed behind my father from then on, taking his cues on speed and braking.

After my birthday, the dreaded enrollment into first grade approached inescapably.

"Now the seriousness of life begins," my father said.

My mother emphasized the positive, namely, the first school day. It was set up as a pleasant occasion and, as I suspected, as a smoke screen for hiding what was coming afterward.

Like all the other neophytes, I got a *Schultüte*, an arm-long cardboard cone decorated with multicolored paper, lace, and glitter and filled with candy and small toys. I proudly carried my *Schultüte* to school at my mother's side. We arrived rather late at the first grade classroom, which was filled with twittering boys. Where did all the boys my age come from? The mothers slid their offspring into the tiny benches two by two and then stepped back and were leaning against the wall. One little boy up front was crying and clinging to his mom, not wanting to let go. *Ridiculous*, I thought. I found an empty place in the second-to-the-last row, next to a small boy with disheveled dark-brown hair and a smile that showed little, decayed teeth. Jakob was his name. I learned this when our teacher, Frau Reiss, read the list of her assigned pupils from the podium.

Frau Reiss was an old, stocky, middle-sized woman, with curly gray hair and a square face. Her expression reflected that mixture of kindness and no-nonsense strictness that good old teachers acquire. Frau Reiss read and edited the class list, told the mothers what supplies we needed, distributed the reading and math primer, and dismissed everyone. No, the mothers were not allowed the next day.

My mother and I went shopping and bought a leather *Schulranzen*, the customary boxy backpack with a big flap. Into it we fitted a *Schiefertafel*, a black slate with a wooden rim inscribed with rows of four red lines on one side and a graph grid on the other. The lines were to practice the letters, the grid to learn the numbers. The wooden rim had a hole through which my mother threaded two strings. On one end she tied a sponge and on the other a linen rag torn from an old bedsheet. "These are for wiping your slate," she said. The sponge and the rag hanging out of the *Ranzen* were the signature equipment of the first graders. She also bought me a wooden pencil box with a sliding cover into which she placed the *Griffel*, a long, thin, gray, and hard slate scriber. The primer completed the contents of my Ranzen.

The next morning, I had to make it to school alone. It always took me a long time to get dressed, for I had the habit of falling into a dream state with my shirt or pants half on. I would have been late that second day, but I was always running. Down the stairs I bounded, out the door and to the next corner of the block with the rag and the wetted sponge flipping. At the corner, a shoemaker had his little workshop, three-legged stool, iron shoe support, canary, and all. In front of that shop, I turned around to see my mother standing on the precarious balcony. I waved, she waved, and then I ran on around the corner. I had to survive the next three hours on my own. On a regular school day, I was going to be a captive for eternity.

Since my attention was locked to the teacher every second, I was tired after one hour. But after the bell, there was another hour and, after recess, still another hour. More and more, I started dreaming about what I would do when I would get out, if ever. After one endless week, I concluded that school was not going to be my favorite occupation. I had to stuff the free hours of the day with things I really wanted to do, and I was annoyed about the homework's intrusion. I sat on the back balcony for hours diddling over the slate. The task was really not daunting—two rows of *i* and two rows of *s*, easy, straight line letters. In an effort to foster the Germanic heritage, the government required us to learn first the *Syterlingsschrift*, the lowercase of which looked like a series of horizontal zigzag lines.

"If you only concentrated, you could have this done in twenty minutes. Then you would be free to play," my mother advised.

But I was distracted by wasps in the geraniums, by the screeching flight of the swallows round and round the back court, by Frau Stoeber beating her rug far down in the yard, and her son, Claude, shooting an arrow up to the third floor on a bow he had made out of the ribs of an umbrella.

"Mutti, do you have an old umbrella?"

"Finish your homework."

Occasionally, something entertaining would happen in school. The way Frau Reiss would cut a piece of paper was interesting. While she was cutting, she would thrust her tongue out with the tip curled behind her lower teeth and bite down on it with every snip of the scissors. I always wondered whether she would bite off her tongue, and it would drop on her desk alongside the cut-off piece of paper. But she disappointed me.

She also investigated the origins of bad odors in the classroom. She singled out several benches that seemed to be the center of the offensive emission, grabbed the little boys who were sitting there by their collars one by one, pulled them forward over their desks and sniffed their backsides until she had found the culprit. Once found, she would not let go of the offender but march him into the far corner, his shirt stretched like a puppy dog's skin, his feet barely touching the floor.

Such unusual actions of Frau Reiss were few and far between. After a few weeks, her lessons basically offered no surprises. Over and over, she pushed the glossy red and green balls on the abacus with a ruler—*smack*, two red ones to the left, *smack*, three green ones to the left.

"Two and three is? Well, count them."

The way she wrote the letters on the blackboard, while reciting mnemonic verses like *"rauf runter rauf, Pünktchen oben drauf"* (up down up, little dot on top) and added a long drawn out "eeeeee," also became routine. We soon could predict how she would go on with other letters and got bored and started whispering behind her back. When the whispering would escalate to talking, perhaps even boxing and smacking, she would turn around and survey the class. Everyone would freeze instantly under her glowering eyes.

Twice a week, I had the welcome change of having different teachers, one for gym and one for religion. The coach was a party member and looked at us boys with pleasure as youngsters who offered the potential to serve their Führer. He favored team competition, particularly climbing the poles, which he perhaps thought was going to help us to overcome enemy obstacles one day. I did not understand such motives then but was busy figuring out how to get to the ceiling on these gleaming pipes. Barefoot worked best, particularly if you rubbed spit on your soles; and the dirtier the hands, the better they grabbed. The teams had to stand in strict lines. Once, one of the boys *tanzte aus der Reihe* (danced out of the row). The coach swung him over his shoulder, pulled down his pants, and gave him three resounding claps on his bare bottom. From then on, the boys queued up perfectly, not so much to avoid the pain as the humiliation.

Our religion teacher was an old, heavyset pastor with a gray goatee and a gray vest stretched over his large belly. I did not like him because of his perpetually benevolent smile. He had been a missionary in Africa and applied certain techniques of evangelization that had worked there. Since he believed that piousness could be measured by the number of prayers per day, he rewarded frequent supplications. Boys who prayed before every meal and at night would receive a sweet little picture with an angel. He would ask, "Who has prayed three times a day?" Hands went up. "You are Johns, Jesus's favored disciple. Here is your picture. Who has prayed twice? You are Thomases; you are doubting. Who prayed just once? You are Peters; you betray Jesus sometimes."

I was one of the Peters. I only prayed at bedtime. After one boy had been called Judas, no one admitted not praying at all. Before long, most boys claimed to have prayed at least three times. They got all these pictures and laughed when the pastor kept calling me Peter, who was obviously someone shameful.

I then started to disappear into my room whenever my parents would call me for lunch or dinner. However, I never received an angel picture. Before the next religion class, my parents came into my room to check what I was doing. There I was, sitting on my bed, hands folded. In tears, I told them about the pictures and being called Peter.

The next day, my father went to the school and had me discontinue my religion class. The principal had no objection. The regime did not favor religious education.

I was thankful that my father had relieved me from this dilemma. How powerful he was! Knowing that, somewhere, my father was in the wings helped my confidence and the budding relationships with my classmates.

There was a soft-spoken boy as tall as I with brown hair, a short military haircut, and erect posture who walked home in the same direction. We began to talk. His name was Hartmut Bauer. He became my best friend. Once our mothers had met, we spent much time at each other's homes. His house was unique. It was the only one-story building in the block and also the only one with a yard and a garage that was separate and had a flat roof. Hartmut's father was in the army. When I came over, we always played soldiers. As mountain troops, we climbed the hazelnut trees up to the garage roof and then turned into paratroopers and swung from the roof that had become a plane, glided down the same trees, hit the ground, and rolled in the grass. Gathering ourselves from the ground, we became infantry and defended the low brick wall with the white, spaced board fence on top against the outside world.

When Hartmut came over to my apartment, he followed my suggestions in everything I wanted to play, be it art gallery, cramming into the big black closet for a flight to the moon, building tents with blankets over chairs, erecting castles out of blocks, or setting up the train set.

In the early stages of my friendship with Hartmut, I got to know another boy in my class. His name was Fischer. In the usual tug and shove in recess and after school, Fischer found out that he was the strongest in class. By and by, he let the confidence in his strength turn him into the class bully. He began entertaining himself by wrestling down his classmates, particularly the bigger kids—those who did not roll over and play dead but tried to resist him. Perhaps because I stood out, tall and blonde, he settled on me as his favored pick. Every day, when I left the schoolyard, he pounced on me. When I would try to run home, he was ready to run after me; if I would linger and leave last, he would wait for me behind the wall of the gate.

One day, when Fischer was still tussling with someone else but had his eyes on me as his next prey, I grabbed Hartmut around his chest and pushed him backward over my outstretched leg, so that he buckled onto the sidewalk. Next I held him pinned down, shouting over to Fischer,

"See." Hartmut was so surprised that he did not resist. When I let him go, he just got up and went home with me as if nothing had happened.

If I thought that my little demonstration would appease Fischer, I was mistaken. On the contrary, it made me an even more attractive challenge.

"I don't want to go to school anymore," I whined to my parents.

"Why?"

"That Fischer, he's always wrestling me down."

"Why don't you just fight back? Tell him to leave you alone."

"But he's stronger. I just don't want to go to school anymore."

I started to dread school from the moment I woke up. The apprehension wore on me as I sat through my three lessons while Fischer would look over every once in a while and gloat in anticipation. Sure enough, as soon as I stepped out of the school gate, Fischer was waiting for his daily sport.

But wait; who was appearing from around the street corner? It was indeed my father, who was entering the scene in long strides. Before my foe could grab me, my father was there.

"Bist Du der Fischer?" (Are you the Fischer?)

Wham. My father smacked him. The Fischer held his cheek and disappeared into the group of milling boys.

"Hello, Hartmut," my father greeted my friend, who was stepping up.

I was uneasy. I felt my own cheek burn.

Fischer never pestered me again. He even left the others alone. He did not want to take the chance that another father would be waiting for him in the wings.

20

The Orangerie was so different from my lost garden that I did not accept it as a replacement. Also, I missed the people I had known in Berlin. I was still a skipper adrift, searching for anchorage.

My parents and I longed to connect with the local population. The Straßburger's attitude toward the Germans varied from person to person and ranged from friendly to hostile. Those forty and older had grown up when Alsace had belonged to Germany. They happily remembered they had been German and easily reverted to the ways of their youth. The younger people, who had grown up under French rule, resented the Germans, considering their presence an occupation rather than liberation. Often the young kept speaking French in private, even though most could speak German. The local dialect of the Alsatians was a variation of the Alemanni across the Rhein. The owners of our building exemplified the Straßburger's behavior. Old Madame Baldenweck, the owner, who lived with her daughter on the second floor, was helpful, friendly, and open. She could frequently be seen on the landing, wiping the rail, ready to engage in a little conversation when we ran up and down. Her daughter, Mademoiselle Baldenweck, hid in the darker recesses of their apartment. When she met us on the stairs, she put her head down. My father, whose warm and innocent charm few women could resist, brushed up his French and greeted her in her preferred language. After a while, he added some amiable chat. When he kept giving them free theater tickets, the daughter finally came around and accepted him. She probably realized that he had nothing to do with the military or the party but was an artist, totally free from national limitations and prejudices. Following the example of the owners, the other Alsatians in the house accepted us.

To say that all young Alsatians were unfriendly toward the Germans would be inaccurate. One exception was the maid, Agnes, whom we hired in September.

When my parents announced that Agnes was moving in, I expected another Martchen. But Agnes was quite different. She was eighteen and sinewy, with a rather drawn face and dull, reddish-brown, wavy hair. She wore horn-rimmed glasses with lenses so thick that her eyes looked small and distorted. A recent graduate, Agnes had not developed Martchen's servant nature. My parents did not expect subordination. They never made her serve at the table. Following their example, I did not think of ordering Agnes around but treated her with respect and consideration. I even liked to help her dry the dishes or set the table. It gave me an opportunity to listen to her and learn her Alsatian dialect. I wanted to understand the Baldenwecks, as well as the woman at the dairy and the people on the street car. Agnes was amused by my clumsy attempts at speaking like a native and corrected my mistakes. She taught me a song in the Straßburg dialect that every child knew.

Der Hons im Schokeloch
Hot olles wos er will.
Und wos er hot dos will er net
Und wos er will dos hot er net
Der Hons im Schnokeloch
Hot alles wos er will.

Jack in the mosquito hole
Has everything he wants.
And what he wants he doesn't have
And what he has he doesn't want.
Jack in the mosquito hole
Has everything he wants.

In later years, I would understand that this song satirized the disgruntled outlook of many Straßburgers. With the way the people had been tossed back and forth between the two countries, they had developed the tendency to remember only the good of the last regime. They said, "If we would only still have the Germans," or, "If we would only still have the French, things would be better." Over the centuries, this longing for what they did not have became part of their psyche.

My mother scolded me when I fell into vernacular.

"You know how to speak beautiful, High German. Don't speak like Agnes."

When Agnes retreated to her mansarde room, my mother corrected my language openly, glad to have me completely under *her* wing for a while.

But Agnes did not use her room much. It was somewhat claustrophobic, with a low, slanted ceiling and a narrow, deep dormer. Besides, she got lonely. She liked to stay downstairs with Monika and me, particularly in the evenings when my parents went to the theater or the artist club, the Kameradschaft.

Agnes would bring along her hobby. She was stitching a wall hanging of the Straßburger Münster, which was a most ambitious undertaking. I watched her past my bedtime, as she was bent way over the white cloth with her thick lenses. She had completed the three portals and was stitching her way around the rose window. The painstaking process filled me with great admiration. How long would it take to just get up to the platform? Going farther up the west tower and the steeple to the cross would surely occupy her for years. What persistence she had to carry through such a project.

I was never to see the completed work. Agnes began another pursuit, which my parents found incompatible with her employment.

The problem started the afternoon that Agnes offered to take Monika and me to the Orangerie. My mother consented. Agnes set out pushing the stroller with a vengeance so that I had to stretch my leisurely trot. We did go to the Orangerie, but after we'd sat on a bench under two enormous copper beeches for five minutes, she suggested going on. We marched through the ominous English garden and out the far side of the park. We crossed the Ill-Rhein Canal and went along the road to Ruprechtsau. I followed Agnes with great curiosity. She seemed to know where she was going.

As we hurried along the empty, open country road, we came upon a kite hanging in the telephone wires. Its wooden frame was broken, its red paper torn, and its tangled tail flipped sadly against the gray sky. It was such a sad image that it stayed with me as the essence of spoiled and abandoned joy.

We were way beyond where my mother expected us to be. Agnes kept going.

Finally, she took a side road that wound up at a sports field, where a thin circle of spectators stood watching a long-distance race. Agnes found a gap for the carriage. One of the runners, a tall young man with wavy blonde hair and a freckled, reddish neck was passing the rest of the field. The spectators clapped and cheered him on, calling his name. Agnes joined in. She had really no eyes for anyone else. When the young man won, she wanted to reach him, but got stuck with the carriage as he disappeared among his admirers at the far end of the field. On the way home, Agnes asked me not to tell my parents where we had been. I did not.

A few weeks later, my mother was looking for Agnes. My father went up to the mansarde to get her. He did not find her alone stitching her cathedral but under a young, athletic-looking, blonde man, a runner perhaps, in his final spurt. The young man did not make it to the finish line but groped for the covers. My father, puffed up with moral indignation, shouted at the man to leave and at Agnes to get dressed and come down. By the time Agnes appeared, red-faced and in tears, my parents had discussed the situation and decided to let her go.

I regretted losing Agnes. I did not understand what crime she had committed. Out of the corner of my eye, I had seen the young man bounding down the stairs, tucking his shirttails into his pants. I sensed that Agnes had done something with him in her room that was forbidden. I heard my father discuss this "something" with my mother. "*Ich habe sie in flagrante ertappt*" (I have caught them in flagrante delicto).

What was it that young men and women could be doing that was bad? From the secretive ways in which my parents discussed this, I sensed that it had something to do with the parts in which boys and girls were different. My mother had the same reluctance to discuss what the man in the raincoat had done, other than that he had shown himself to her without any pants on. The only term I had for such events was *schweinigeln*, which I had heard my mother use with indignation when she had caught Jörg and me behind the big oak. The delightful caressing of my pillow that I was still doing perhaps fell into the same category. I decided to stop. When I succumbed to the urge again, the old questions started weighing on me. Was I the only one in the world doing this? Was I sick? Was I bad?

My curiosity about how girls looked down there had been satisfied. From my mother's changing Monika in our room, I had learned the interesting fact that girls had simply a crack, where boys had their chick. *But how do they pee if they have nothing to hold on to?* I was too shy to ask my mother. I found out a month later.

On that day, Agnes's father appeared at the door and forced himself into our apartment. At first, my mother thought he wanted Agnes to get her job back. She made it clear that we now had Renate. She was sorry, but she could not give Agnes the job back, even if she had wanted to. But Agnes's father kept following her around tenaciously. My mother went into the nursery and started changing Monika. Agnes's father finally came to the point. He claimed that Agnes's activity in our mansarde had not been without consequence. He enumerated the hardships that this was causing his family. My mother was cleaning Monika, lifting her by the ankles with one hand, and powdering her rosy butt with the other. The man was going on and on. It became clear that he held my parents responsible for Agnes's problem and was pleading for compensation. At that point Monika let go with a stream high up in the air that arched right onto my mother's chest. It was as if she had understood the man's demand and let him know what she thought of it. The man stepped back and, seeing that my mother was not going to sympathize with him but was completely absorbed in taking care of the baby, left in disgust.

I thought, *Hmm, that's the way girls do it. They just let go, wherever it goes.*

As my mother folded the fresh diaper into a triangle and gently wrapped it around Monika and fastened the ends with a safety pin, the question fell again on my mind. *What had Agnes done? What did the man mean by consequences?* I was troubled again by my secret. I almost asked my mother about it. But she was agitated. It was not the time.

Things quieted down. My father talked to Agnes's father, categorically refused his demands, and got him to leave us alone. Renate replaced Agnes, and I became attached to her also. She was more padded than Agnes, had a softer voice, and sang when she washed the dishes. I dried. She usually started with the song that all German-speaking maids knew.

Ja, ja, ja, ach ja,
's ist traurig aber wahr.
Nein, nein, nein, ach nein
Von einmal da kann es nicht sein.

Yes, yes, yes, oh yes,
It's sad but true
No, no, no, oh no,
From one time it cannot be.

When I asked her what could not be from one time, she gave me that lusty, guttural laugh. She looked at me with a sparkle in her eyes and said that I was too little to understand but would understand when I was older. What were the adults hiding? She continued singing other songs, hits of the day, expressing the longing of the young women for their men away in the war. She collected cards with the words of the songs that she put smudged and dog-eared into the silverware drawer. These were songs like "Lili Marlene," "*Weit ist der Weg zurück ins Heimatland so weit so weit*" (Far Is the Way Back to the Homeland, So Far, So Far), and "*Hörst Du mein heimliches Rufen?*" (Do You Hear My Secret Calling?).

Over time, the pile of green cards in the silverware drawer became larger, while the supply of silverware seemed to become smaller. When it turned out that some of Omi Bauer's good silver spoons where missing, the maid who had such an appreciation for the finer things in life, like music and silver, had to go.

Renate was my parents' last attempt at having a maid. My mother seemed quite content to be the sole and undisturbed manager of her household. One morning, my mother was in a particularly good and receptive mood and hummed a melody while she changed Monika's diapers. I gathered all my courage to ask her my question. Not long ago, I had succumbed to the temptation again, and my secret was beginning to weigh on me. Did I dare ask her what that was? Would she understand at all what I was talking about?

"Mutti!"

"Yes."

"Sometimes when I lie in bed, I lie on my pillow, and I rub, and it feels real good."

She paused just a little. Then she said calmly, "Just don't do it too often."

She knew what I was talking about. She must have had this feeling herself. It was all right to do, just not too often. I was not sick. I was not bad. I was not the only one in the world doing this. A flood of gratitude overcame me, even something like a feeling of solidarity.

Everything was right again in my little world. I accepted my body and emotions as they were.

My new surroundings became more comfortable. I came to know and like my new apartment. I enjoyed the high ceilings with the stucco ornamentation, the narrow, high windows that sent their rectangles of light on the polished parquet floor, and the wide spaces between the furniture. I felt the safest and coziest in my room when I surveyed it from my bed at night before my mother turned off the light or when I woke up in the morning. The area of the wall that appeared before my eyes when I had my head turned toward it had become more familiar than anything in the apartment. Its irregularities in shapes and colors had become my private archipelago in the sea of the painted surface. According to their outlines, I had given the different islands names, "witch," "hat," and "fish." I navigated between them as if moving through familiar waters and was satisfied time and again to find them in their expected places. From the safe vantage point of my bed, I had become accustomed to Monika's crib across the room, her changing table, the enormous black closet with the mirror, my toy closet with Onkel Helmut's round chocolate tin buried under my toys, and the black cast-iron stove with the glowing mica window. The apartment had become familiar, warm, and safe.

21

During first grade, my teacher asked me my father's profession. Her reaction when I said, "*Oberspielleiter* at the city theater," (explaining that he was the chief play director) did not escape me. She raised her eyebrows and nodded as if she had heard of him. All the children had turned around and looked impressed. Any profession starting with *Ober* sounded important to them, no matter what it was.

Indeed, my father was becoming known in the city. He had entered the most creative year of his career. He was primed to present to the art-deprived Straßburgers shows like they had never seen before. The theater manager, Kuntze, knew him from Berlin as an untiring worker. He assigned him a wide array of plays and gave him free rein in their production. Finally, the assistant years were over.

My father took off like an arrow released from a bow that had been stretched too long. He staged no less than seven plays in the 1941–42 season. He started with Gerhart Hauptmann's *Biberpelz* and ended with Lortzing's opera, *der Wildschütz*. The zenith of his efforts was the production of Hebbel's drama, *Gyges und sein Ring*. In this production, my father harvested everything that Jessner had sown and that, after years, emerged as the essence of my father's dramatic concept. In a visual interpretation of the tragic procession of Gyges's fate, he had covered the whole stage with a gigantic incline, on which the scenes descended. To get the action onto the incline, he used bare staircases conceived by his mentor

124

and known in avant-garde films as *Jessner Treppen*. During the creation of this production, he had befriended the second stage designer, Kurt von Mülmann, who did not shy from the unusual.

With equal care, my father interspersed the season with lighter contemporary plays, *Ein Windstoss, Die vier Gesellen,* and *Sophien Lund*. He had the opportunity to display his craft from high classic drama to comedy to opera and did so to the applause of the audience and the critics. He did not mind when the famous Weichert, who came from Berlin to direct *Kabale und Liebe*, asked him to assist. Weichert saw some of my father's own plays and liked them, which was enough reward for the temporary step down.

As the season ended, my father had outdone the other two play directors both in productivity and acclaim. The others had been able to stage two or three plays and had been partially relegated to productions in the *Kleine Haus* (Small House Theater) in the Blauwolken Gasse. This theater's seating was only about one fourth of the city theater's, had a shallow stage, and blended outside insignificantly into the neighboring buildings. In contrast, the city theater, which had been available for all of my father's productions, had an impressive Greek facade with the statues of the four muses on its roof, a splendidly decorated hall, and all the technical equipment that enhanced the surprise and enchantment of the audience.

In accordance with their newly acquired status, my father and mother began entertaining. They invited the conductor, Kuppelwieser, who needed only little encouragement to thunder on the Ibach grand piano; the chief set designer, Richter; and Kurt von Mülmann. They hosted also some of the star actors, Winfred Hertz; Else Knott; and last but not least, my father's friend, Hans Wiegner, who had transferred from the Königsberg Theater upon my father's urging. "I need a young hero with a voice like yours."

Having become a cultural leader in the city at age thirty-four, my father felt uncomfortably young. He grew a mustache and acquired a walking stick out of polished mahogany that he swung in measured rhythm, tapping every four steps as he walked to and from the theater.

I never was closer to my father than during that first year in Straßburg. I tried to copy him in everything he did. My drawings and paintings mimicked his illustrations for the books he wrote for my mother. I imitated the way he walked and danced. When he made a joke, I had to quickly invent a similar one. When he explained art to me in galleries and around the Münster, I hung on his every word. He responded by spending much of his free time with me. We were the two men of the family who stuck together, yes sir.

Once I became a reliable bicyclist, my father took me on little tours whenever he had a few hours off in the afternoon. Depending on the length of his break, my father chose either the closer villages northeast or the ones farther across the Rhein and to the south. Some of the names of the villages struck me as so funny that I remember them, like Wanzenau (Bedbug meadow), "an itchy place"; Kork, the village made out of bottle stoppers; or Odelshofen (Sewage farms), which to my surprise did not smell worse than other rural places. It was only a few minutes from the ominous Odelsdorf to the resplendent Goldscheuer (Goldbarn).

Our favorite loop became the tour northeast through Ruprechtsau into the forest that stretched along the Rhein. Close to the levee, the dense foliage hid a long line of French fortifications, bunkers of various sizes, trenches, and pillboxes. They showed the scars of combat from two years before, with the proud flesh of moss, ferns, and saplings growing in the cracks and half-fallen doorways. All around were the pockmarks of craters, some filled with green, stagnant water. Bicyclists had worn winding paths through the forest, taking advantage of the roller-coaster ride through the craters. Usually, our excursions would start gently along the smooth dam of the Rhein. We even had the leisure time to watch the tugboats pull the row of freighters up the river. How exciting it would be to live on these long, dark boats. Clotheslines crossed the deck with shirts and diapers fluttering and dogs barking across the waters. I heard with amazement that those skippers came all the way from Holland and were going on to Basel. Sometimes, ships would intersect with others coming downstream on their own power. For a moment, it would look like the freighters would run into each other in the narrow shipping lane. But then they would slide past, the ones going downstream disappearing for a moment behind those going upstream.

Heads up! No more dreaming about living on board and going to faraway countries! My father had found the start of the winding roller-coaster path through the overgrown battlefield from the dam into the woods. I tried to follow him at his wild clip. One time he chose a particularly daring ride, and I lost control and went head over heels into one of those swampy craters. My father dried me off with his handkerchief and straightened my handlebar, clamping the front wheel between his knees and promising to eliminate this trail from our list. He took me to the west edge of the forest where he had discovered a hunting lodge, Fuchs am Buckel (Fox at the Hump). We shared *Landjägerwurst* and *Selterswasser*, and I felt fully restored.

22

Rainy November days discouraged our bicycle tours. My father thought of other ways to spend time with me.

I started searching for a reference point outdoors, like the oak in Berlin. I was eager to learn my way around the old city and get to know the famous buildings that my parents talked about. Agnes's cloth with the Münster had made me curious. I had noticed my father's respect for Agnes's craft, but even much more for the building itself. My father explained that it was the most unusual cathedral ever built. It had been planned as a dome with two towers and finished as a Münster with one steeple. One rainy afternoon he suggested taking me there.

I dropped my toys, ready to go. We walked, which meant he walked and I jogged. We passed the theater and crossed its square under the canopy of the sycamore trees. At the far end, we turned left into the Münstergasse. Eagerly I looked ahead through the narrow turns until they opened. What I saw stopped me in amazement—a wall of gray masonry going up forever. Slowly I lifted my head higher and higher, trying to take in the portals; the windows; pillars; buttresses; groups of figures, the mountain slope of the roof; the platform; the tower; up, up, the spire; and, as I bent way backward, a crown-like outcropping and finally a cross.

My father led me to the north portal. Before he entered, he halted and took off his hat. In a hushed voice, he told me to remove my cap. Then he slowly opened the door as not to disturb the peace inside.

My father had an obvious respect for holy places, which, as I found out later, was not limited to churches. I am sure he would have entered a mosque or a Buddhist temple with the same reverence. It was important to him to teach me his respect for sanctuaries and for the believers who gathered there to pray.

From the example he set for me, I should have been surprised when, at the end of his life, on his death bed even, he claimed that he was an "old heathen." He said this without bitterness, regret, pride, or defiance but simply stating an honest fact. I should have been startled, but I knew him well enough to understand what he meant. It was clear to me that he had an unshakable faith. Throughout the many trials of his life, he had displayed a constant confidence that circumstances eventually would turn for the better. Approaching death, he was without fear. He had faith, yet, he had no beliefs. It was as if his faith harkened back to the dawn of humanity, when the general awe for creation had not yet precipitated specific dogmas. It was this primordial faith of his that he called "heathen."

We stepped into the cathedral. My father closed the door carefully behind us. I stood there aghast. The space was vaster than I had ever seen or dreamed. My astounded eyes followed the ascending columns to where their ribs divided and interlaced in the distant dusk of the pointed vaults. The columns were vital and strong like trunks of gigantic trees. Between them, the walls with their huge glass windows seemed to be made of light and air. Similarly, the rose window that glowed at the far end of the nave was held by ribs of such incredible fragility that they dissolved entirely into the pattern of light and color.

I looked up the steps to the high altar and above to the half-round copula. Bearded old men in robes and with large halos looked down on me from the golden, glowing half dome. I felt little and insignificant and knew that I was not to approach the altar. Turning away to the right, I looked into the high space of the southern side nave and saw in its center a most amazing pillar, so delicately structured that I did not even think of its purpose of carrying the ceiling.

"This is the angels' column," my father breathed voicelessly with his eyebrows raised, indicating that I had before me something extraordinarily precious and famous. The column carried twelve figures on three levels. I could identify those who were angels by their wings. There were four on the middle tiers, lifting their trumpets to their mouths, and there were three on the highest tier, whose instruments I could not identify. I was delighted by the angels being ready to make music. My father kept from me that they were blowing the last trumpet and that, on top, Christ sat on a throne ready to judge the living and the dead. Why disturb a young heart with such a stupendous story?

My father pointed to a gallery where a stone statue of a lone man leaned on the banister, watching the column intently. "When the builder erected the column," he explained still in a hush, "there were people who claimed the column was too fragile to ever support the ceiling. The builder finally put a portrait of the one who doubted the most on the balcony. And here he has been standing for six centuries, waiting for the column to fall."

Behind the column on the east wall of the side nave, I discovered another unique feature of the Straßburger Münster. It was a structure four stories high, ornamented with an overwhelming multitude of paintings and figures.

"This is the astronomical clock," my father whispered. Stacked on different floors were green and golden dials as big as wagon wheels. The bottom dial showed a heaven's calendar, which was tracking the movement of the stars. The one right above was an eternal calendar, indicating the month and day, Sundays, holidays, and fixed and movable feasts. Above that, another dial presented the time of each day, sunrise and sunset, phases of the moon, and eclipses of the moon and the sun. Then there was a church calendar and then another dial showing the movement of the planets and the equinoxes of the sun and moon. Way up above the four dials, in an alcove, was an animated scene, a procession of figures that at first I did not understand.

The splendor of the whole clock should have made a permanent impression on me. However, when I returned to the Münster in 1985, after an absence of forty-one years, I had completely forgotten the clock, even though I remembered the angels' column and the man on the banister down to their poses and expressions. On that later date, when I stood in the crowd of tourists, I asked myself what could have repulsed me so much as a child to be so eager to forget the clock.

What captured the crowd's attention? It was the mechanical procession in the alcove way above the four dials.

There was Death standing between two bells in the center of the half circle. He held his scythe in his left hand and a femur in his right. At the quarter hour, a child rotated out of the door, wound up before Death, and struck the bells with his staff once. At the half hour, a young man, a hunter, struck the bells with his arrow twice. At three quarters, a mature man, a warrior, rotated before Death and struck the bell with his sword three times. At the full hour, the climax came, which the crowd had paid to see. At that time, an old man dragged himself before Death and struck the bell four times with his crutch. Thereupon, Death became alive and slowly tapped the number of the hour with his bone.

Had I been repelled by the depressing spectacle of human impermanence and mortality, which had been compressed here into one single hour? Had it evoked the uneasy feeling from Glienicke, when, after the flaming plane in the sky, I had realized that I would die and wondered every night whether I would wake up in the morning? Or was it the hideous legend that was told by the guide about the fate of the original builder of the clock, a Master Habrecht, who was said to have been blinded by the Straßburg City Council so he could not make another such masterpiece somewhere else?

The more I looked at the figure of Death, though, the more I realized that it was this image that had made me wish to forget the clock. This Death was not the usual bleached skeleton but had muscles connecting his bones. He was a walking cadaver, with strands of sinew and remnants of hair on his skull. The fiend could move. He struck the hours with his bone. He was able to follow you and catch you with his long scythe. After seeing Death just once, I must have avoided looking at the clock. I must have concentrated on the angels' column when passing through until I could follow my father out through the south portal.

Once outside, my father put on his hat and helped straighten my cap. Then, stepping down the flight of stairs, he turned around on the wide sidewalk to point out the two statues that flanked the portal right and left. They were two women in dresses that flowed so freely that they adorned rather than concealed their bodies. As my father explained, the left woman was Ecclesia, the triumphant church. There she stood, erect and self-assured, a crown in her wavy hair, in her right hand a staff with the cross firmly planted on the ground and in her left the chalice of forgiveness. She looked across the portal to the woman on the right. This other figure, the Synagogue, I came to pity and love. A blindfold stretched around her head, thin enough to show the shape of her closed and downcast eyes. Her right held on to a broken lance that followed the directions of her pose. The scroll of the Torah was about to fall out of her tiring left. Who had broken the woman's weapon? Who had blindfolded her? Why did she have to stand there and suffer? My eyes touched the tall, slender woman, the refined arms, down to the tapering hands. This is my mother in stone, I shuddered.

Tearing myself away from this statue, I followed my father along the south side to the west facade to the view of the Münster that I knew from Agnes's cloth. However, my perspective of the real building now would have been like that of an ant on the bottom line of her stitching. I dropped my jaw at the immensity of the wall that rose to the platform from where the tower and the steeple took off into the sky.

"Let's climb this," I begged, jumping up and down with excitement. My father agreed to take me up to the platform. We climbed the narrow, worn staircases until we emerged out of the dark onto the platform, blinked in the sudden brightness, and stepped carefully toward the stone rail. I knew that I had never been lifted so high above the land, not even on the Freiburger Münster.

"Can we see our house from here?" I asked. My father took me to the east balustrade. Beyond the near, steep, tiled roofs of the old city we picked out St. Paul's and the university and the Brandplatz. We agreed that there, somewhere in the quarter between the Brandplatz and the green of the Orangerie, must be the Geiler Strasse with our building. Surprisingly close to the area of our residence, we saw the harbor with its oil storage tanks. Beyond that we made out the wide silver band of the Rhein, the lush plains on the other side of the river, and on the horizon, indeed, the dark blue outlines of the Black Forest. Looking west, I found the Thomas Church, the railroad station, and the suburbs spreading into the plain, and on the horizon, I saw the mountains of the Vogesen. North, the view was obstructed by the tower. South, it went over the Rohan Palace directly below, the crooked, medieval houses following the river Ill and then the suburbs and finally the grounds of the Upper Rhein Valley with villages sprinkled here and there.

I begged my father to take me up the tower. He agreed, but the spiral staircase rose precariously out from the corner of the tower. After several turns, my father stopped and took me back down. The open windows were so large that he feared I might fall through.

I followed him back down to the square. We stayed in front of the three west portals to examine the hundreds of figures tucked into the recesses.

Since my father had thought the better of taking me up the tower, I persuaded my mother on my next visit to climb it with me. I promised I would stay away from the windows and let her be on the outside. However, the precipitous view gave her such a dizzy spell that she could not go on. She was surprised at herself.

"How cautious I have become after having babies. When I was young, nothing bothered me. I climbed any high places, skied any slope, and rode any horse. I had no fear, but now …"

So she did not take me up the tower either. In the three years of our stay, my wish of reaching the top was never fulfilled. This unrealized dream added to the attraction the building had for me. The Münster became my point of orientation. Whenever my parents took me to the city, I begged them to visit the cathedral. Often they obliged. In the second year, they took me to a series of Bach organ recitals. As I sat there for hours, I examined and befriended the stained-glass windows and the statues and columns until they entered into my night and daydreams.

Since my parents noticed how much I was drawn to the Münster, they gave me photographs of the Ecclesia and Synagogue for my birthday. I fastened them on the wall over my bed, where they hung over the familiar archipelago.

When relatives visited, my parents let me be the designated guide. Unfortunately, neither Opa and Oma from Berlin nor Omi from Erfurt had ever climbed such a high building, and I could not persuade them to do it now. Omi had enough trouble making it to our fifth-floor apartment. She had to take extensive breathers on every landing. She remembered how she had once struggled to get up to that impossible studio in Berlin.

"Why do you always, always have to move up to the highest floor?"

With the Münster having become such a presence in my conscience, I could point in its direction quite accurately no matter where I was in the city. One day, when I went shopping with my mother in the Münster Gasse, I suddenly ran out from the sidewalk and was promptly mowed down by a bicyclist.

"What's gotten into you?" my mother wanted to know as she picked me up from the pavement.

"But this is where you can see the Münster," I said apologetically.

"You must watch for the traffic, Michael. You'll get yourself killed."

When she saw how sheepish I was, she waited until the street was clear. We stepped out and admired the tower that was soaring over the rooftops.

My kindled love for buildings spread out from the cathedral to other famous sites around the Münster Square. Across the south portal was the Rohan Palace, a baroque building erected after Versaille for Rohan, Cardinal of Straßburg. The palace was open to the public. My father frequently took me through the halls to see its standing and traveling exhibits of paintings. I felt elevated, important, and privileged when I walked between these precious pieces across the polished parquet floors and looked through the wide windows down to the terraces and the river, as if I were one of the cardinals or princes that had lived here. Inspired by these visits in the Rohan Palace, I asked for a sketchbook and watercolors. I had made up my mind to produce my own gallery.

On the north side of the cathedral stood a corner building, the Kammerzellhaus, that was so precious I tried to memorize its features at first sight. Over the gothic base of a masonry ground floor with wide-arched windows jutted out three slender stories with continuous rows of bull's-eye windows. Every timber around the windows was used for elaborate woodcarvings. These were humans and animals as symbolic figures, personifications of virtues and senses, symbols of the zodiac, and musicians playing their diverse instruments. The steep tile roof was broken up with dormers of varying sizes, so that even this steep and high-stretched surface looked structured and delicate. The whole house could have appeared in my fairy tale book, a place inhabited by dwarfs, sprites, and witches.

By the end of the summer, I knew Straßburg as I had known Berlin. Berlin had been a place of a fresh, cool vitality that thrived in the *"Berliner Luft"* (Berlin air). Straßburg glowed with a heavy, warm, melancholic splendor, like that bouquet of dahlias that my mother placed on the living room bookshelf during late August. The flowers had large and full blossoms, and the mild light of the last days of summer rested on them and reflected on the wall behind in muted reds and yellows. Admiration and sorrow filled me at that sight, and that mixed emotion expressed best how I felt for the city I had learned to love.

23

After a mild, short winter, my father and I resumed our bicycle excursions, discovering the abundance of wildflowers that came up in the Rhein Forest. "Mutti must see this!"

The prospect of picking flowers got my mother onto the saddle right away, with Monika in a wicker seat behind her. Monika was usually jostled to sleep within a few blocks, clutching her doll, Susie, and sucking her thumb. When we dipped into the forest my father always broke into the echosong, "*Im Wald, wo's Echo schallt*" (In the forest, where the echo sounds). My mother and I would sing his echo, our enthusiasm not dampened by the profuse smell of garlic in the first section of the woods, where the floor was covered with its light green twin leaves. When the smell of garlic gave way to the perfume of lilies of the valley, we leaned the bicycles against a tree and picked the delicate, pristine bells for hours. Every so often, we stopped and listened to the cuckoo. Monika toddled along, picked a flower once in a while, and brought it in her little fist to add to the big bunches.

Later in May, the lilies of the valley gave way to a variety of violets, which had dark blue and crumpled blossoms and gave off a sweet fragrance so strong that it promised to fill our whole apartment. On one of those trips, when we left the forest to stop at *Fuchs am Buckel* for lunch, Monika started crying for her Susie. Our search in her wicker chair turned up nothing. She had lost her beloved doll in the forest. Susie was a true war child's toy. She did not have a fancy head out of celluloid, for this material was restricted to the war effort. She had a flat linen head, and her body was made out of rags filled with excelsior. Her painted face showed character though. From underneath her red polka-dot babushka, she peered out of the extreme right corners of her big almond-shaped eyes. We turned around and combed the forest floor, moving systematically back and forth and trying to retrace Monika's steps. We finally gave up. We always hoped that we would one day find this little moon face with the screwed eyes looking up from underneath the flowers. As unhappy as little Monika was, she forgot the missing doll first. For me, it marked the second loss, after the Zeppelin coin in the door frame, also something I hoped to retrieve one day.

The day we lost Susie, we also had another frustration. Behind *Fuchs am Buckel* was a small lake hidden in the woods that reminded us of the one in Sumt. Hot from our search in the woods, we decided to go for a swim. While we frolicked in the water, we did not suspect that all the mosquitoes of the Rhine forest would swarm together for an all-out assault. My father was hitting his legs, thighs, and chest as if he was practicing the Bavarian courtship dance the *Schuhplattler*. No matter how we whacked the towels around our bodies, we were losing the battle. Our retreat into the clothes and onto the bikes was not nearly fast enough to keep our skins from being turned into itchy, welt-riddled messes.

My parents crossed off this pond as a possible swimming site and continued their search. The next time they thought big and decided to swim in the Rhein. As they pushed off the shore, they found it thrilling to be taken up by the powerful current and make thirty yards with every stroke. They approached the bridge. People gathered at the railing, watching them, waving. My parents waved back. How friendly these folks were. My parents floated through the shadow of the bridge. The people crossed over to see whether they would reappear. But were they really waving? Were they not gesticulating? And what were they shouting? Was this so unusual? Was there no one else ever swimming in the Rhein? It was really not that dangerous when you were a good swimmer. When my parents finally got back to the bank, people came running.

"You can't swim there. It's full of mines. Only the shipping lane is cleared."

Some of the people were truly concerned, relieved to see my parents step out of the water unharmed. Others, standing further away, probably wondered whether these fool Germans would get what was coming to them.

So much for finding swimming opportunities in nature. My father inquired where the natives swam and bought a family pass for Bad Weiss. This ancient swimming establishment was built entirely out of weathered boards over the river Aar. It was privately owned by the equally weathered Herr Weiss, who was in his late seventies. In the French time, Bad Weiss had consisted of two compartments separated by the changing cabins and a fifteen-foot-high wooden wall. The one upstream had been for women and the one downstream for men. Aging Weiss had appreciated the arrival of the less prudish Germans, who let the men, women, and children bathe together. It allowed him to close the women's court and cut his maintenance in half. Through the knotholes between the men's and former women's changing cubicles, we could see how Herr Weiss was appropriating the silvery gray doors and boards from the women's side to keep his remaining business in repair.

Every day in summer, my father found time after work to stop at Bad Weiss. My mother, Monika, and I would be waiting there. Walking through the entrance passage that went through the Weiss's tiny house, he would pick up his freshly ironed white, linen bathing suit and a white terry towel that Madame Weiss had ready for him. Descending the open wooden stairs to the dressing rooms, my father would change with the unbelievable alacrity of a professional actor. Soon, he would sit like a fakir in the blasting sun on the hot boards with his legs folded under, knees sticking out, brown and scrawny. The tight food rationing was beginning to show. From there, my father would look across the court and watch Herr Weiss teaching me to swim.

He had a special hoist on which he taught the breaststroke. After a few instructions on the deck about how to move my arms and legs, he strapped a leather belt around my chest. He snapped a rope to a metal loop on my back. The rope went over a pulley high above the little man's head and down into his hands. He would lower me into the river and hold me on the surface. I was scared of the stern taskmaster. At the slightest mistake, like not keeping the fingers together while spreading my arms out when he counted "one" or not pulling my knees under my belly at "two" or not kicking my legs out wide enough at "three," the old man would dunk me shouting *"Pfuscher! Pfuscher!"* which meant "botcher, botcher."

My parents encouraged me to continue the lessons. "Just think, you will be able to dive like us from the board."

I hoped when it came to that, it would be like my mother's elegant dive and not my father's belly-slam.

24

Straßburg had fulfilled all our expectations, except one. We were not relieved from the Fliegeralarm as we had hoped we would be. The assumption that the English bombers would spare French territory that was occupied by Germany proved false. Before two weeks had elapsed, the hoarse, undulating siren stirred us out of our sleep. The alerts continued as they had been in Berlin. We hastened the five flights into the cellar. After a second alert a few days later, my mother, aware that our apartment was the first to go in a hit, filled two suitcases with irreplaceable documents, jewelry, and some essential clothing. My father accused my mother of having packed rocks when he lugged the suitcases down the stairs. The old green sleeping bag that used to wrap me in Berlin was delegated to bundle up the sleeping Monika. I was now old enough to quickly slip on socks, shoes, and a sweat suit over my pajamas and sprint ahead. At the long, flat sounding of the Entwarnung, my father would follow us with the suitcases back up the stairs, rolling his eyes.

"No," my mother insisted, "we cannot leave them down there. Things get musty. Mice will get into the papers, or someone might take our stuff."

I had resigned myself; the air raids would continue here and get worse. Already on the September 16, during the twelfth air alert, we had heard again the familiar sound of the flak and the thuds of bombs.

The next day, the war intruded into our lives even more violently with an afternoon telephone call, at the time when my father often called my mother from the office to invite her for a performance that night or out to the club. My mother picked up the receiver at the table in the hall. I stood on a chair in the kitchen and looked through the internal window. This morning, my mother's reaction on the phone alarmed me. After she had answered and shouted happily, "Oh, Anneliese," there came a long pause. As if having received a blow, she sank in the chair with an, "Oh, no."

I came out of hiding and sat down at her feet. My mother was crying. What terrible thing had happened? After a long conversation, she finally hung up.

"Onkel Helmut is dead. His plane has been shot down."

I went into my room and found the round, flat tin in my chest under the tangle of toys. I pried open the lid and broke off a piece of chocolate. I smelled it, put it in my mouth, and savored the bittersweet taste. The presence of my godfather's gift proved that he was not gone. I did not accept that he had been shot down. I had impressed my classmates, telling them that my Onkel Helmut was flying a Me 110. Whenever we would play planes in recess, stretching out our arms like wings and attacking each other in dogfights, I always flew a Me 110 like my Onkel. It gave me status that I had an Onkel who piloted a Me 110. I maintained for the remaining war years that he was still flying.

It took most of my life to find out the complete truth about Onkel Helmut's death. When my mother returned from Erfurt, where she had tried to comfort her sister during the memorial ceremony, she brought more information. Onkel Helmut had been the leader of a squadron that flew missions in northern Russia. On one of his return trips, he was hit by ground fire and had either been killed at the controls or otherwise unable to deplane. He was thirty years old. Tante Anneliese received a photograph of several thin white crosses standing in the vast, grassy plain. She could not tell which of the crosses marked her husband's grave. She also received a package of personal belongings, including his army knife and a document from the Luftwaffe elevating her husband as a hero who had given his life for the *End Sieg* (final victory) and some posthumous decoration. The assurance that her husband had died bravely and honorably for his country was the only consolation for the twenty-four-year-old Anneliese. I fail to understand why the German government had to inform her, fifty years later, that her husband had been killed by friendly fire.

After my mother received the news that Helmut had fallen, she traveled to Erfurt right away to comfort her sister. She urged her to come with her to Straßburg. But Anneliese could not make a decision. Like all wives of soldiers, she had always tried to brace herself to the possibility of such news. But now that she was faced with the reality of her loss, she was in shock. As the warm and sensitive person she was, she spent the winter and spring grieving. Then she pulled herself together and visited us with Jens-Peter in June and July 1942.

My parents were masterful at consoling and at concentrating on the pleasant things in life. They had shut out the war as much as possible. After the incineration of Lübeck by firebombing, they skipped over the national section of the newspaper. They realized that the trips into the air-raid shelter were all they could do to protect themselves. Reading about the destruction of the cities did nothing but darken their days. They never listened to the *Wehrmachtsbericht* (the Armed Forces Report) on the radio, and I rarely heard the Reichskommentator Fritsche, whom I could identify by the particularly relaxed and oily speech and his signature sign-off, slurring the two words into one *"gutenabend"* (goodevening).

Restricting the bad news about the hated war and the propaganda, my parents tried to hold on to what was still good. This attitude helped Tante Anneliese. My father got her to play recorders with him. They practiced until my mother objected to the sad sound and suggested that they get out in the fresh air. My father borrowed a bike for Tante Anneliese, and we took her along into the Rhein forest and over the Rhein Bridge to Kehl. There my parents had discovered a restaurant that served famous *Dampfnudeln*, steamed yeast dumplings with vanilla sauce. For the feeding of the mind, my parents invited her to the theater to see my father's productions. When my father was off, they played skat through the night. My father was as witty and funny as he could be. Tante Anneliese wore her coat with the black ribbon in the lapel less and took the black veil off her hat. Before long, she caught herself in liberating laughter. She left for Erfurt planning to get nurse's training and to work in a military hospital.

25

Right after Tante Anneliese had left, my father's summer vacation began. My parents had searched for some time for a family vacation spot in the vicinity. Predictably, they were drawn toward the Black Forest. They settled on Offenburg, located at the mouth of the Kinzig River Valley. There they had discovered one of the most elaborate public swimming areas in Germany. With its lawns, wading pools, sandboxes, swings, slides, and the Olympic-size pool, the park was made for Monika and me. Monika would learn how to walk and I how to swim. On cool days, we could take tours into the highlands.

My parents made reservations at the Hotel Sonne, which they had noticed for its bright and splendid exterior. A wrought-iron arm hung a gleaming sun far into the street. Large, golden letters announced "Hotel Sonne" over the solidly built entrance. A wide entryway led through the stately, high-gabled building into the inner courtyard. All this splendor had once convinced even rulers like Napoleon to stop here overnight. Aware of the hotel's historic distinction, the owners had maintained the precious antiques and paintings over the centuries.

As soon as the theater closed and school let out, my parents and I got on our bikes. Little Monika sat in a basket carrier behind my mother, where she sucked her thumb, stroked her earlobe, and soon fell asleep. We rode over the Rhein Bridge to Kehl. We crossed the luscious pasture lands of the upper Rhein plain and pedaled through an endless forest. Just as we got tired of being closed in between the walls of trees, we emerged. There was Offenburg, standing in front of the hazy silhouette of the Black Forest.

We stayed in the Sonne for six weeks. My parents liked it so well that they returned the next two summers. During those three years, they befriended the owners, Karl and Edith Schimpf, and their two daughters. This friendship developed very slowly, since the adults showed the typical German reluctance when it came to making friends. Besides, it was a time when people did not trust those they did not know well.

We children had no such qualms. Within a few days, the younger daughter, Hella, and I were drawn together. Our friendship started with looks between tables. The Schimpfs, who ate in the same dining room, usually entered after all guests had been seated and served. Smitten by her during the first meal, I anticipated Hella. I absentmindedly dipped my spoon into the soup while letting my eyes wander to the round, unoccupied table in front of the gigantic grandfather clock. *When will they come?* I would distract myself with the other interesting features in the room—the painted coat of arms in the lead-fastened windows, the wood-carved lamps above each rustic table with scenes of hunt and harvest. A team of horses pulled a cart with a huge wine barrel.

Stocky grape pickers hovered over vines, buxom maidens bundled grain, others herded cows, and manly hunters surrounded a stag. They had all been made by the same carver out of pine, still showing the facets of the knife but lovingly smoothed and carefully painted in subdued colors. Then my attention would be drawn back to the empty table and the clock.

Finally the Schimpfs would appear, the lady of the house from the kitchen, the others from the lobby. They would take their seats, except Karl Schimpf, who first would make the rounds, nodding his greetings to each table. In his tailor-made suit and with his well-groomed gray hair and mustache and manicured hands, he looked every part the distinguished proprietor.

Some of the old-time guests, full of reverence, would whisper to the newcomers what they knew about the owner. He was a member of the city council and in charge of all cultural events, including the Mardi Gras parade with the famous burning of witches in the town square. Those witches were of his own design. Moreover, they whispered that he was one of Germany's most famous *Krippenbauers* (builders of nativity scenes). Every year at Advent, he displayed a new creation at city hall. People would line up far along the snowy sidewalk in order to get a glimpse.

After his round, Karl Schimpf would sit down with the others—his wife, Edith, a serious and stately beauty; the grandfather, old and deaf; Aunt Ivonne, jolly and chatty; and Brigitte, the older daughter, pudgy and full of good humor. Then, of course, there was Hella.

I looked at those black eyes with the long, curved lashes; the soft, shiny waves of her hair; the evenness of her features; and the delicate, slender limbs. I observed her until she cast a furtive glance to the table with the new guests and caught my look of open adoration.

Using her female ingenuity, she became acquainted with me at the next opportunity. I was watching the kitchen boy wash potatoes in the court, turning them in a water-doused drum out of iron mesh. She must have observed the scene through the window. Some of the small potatoes escaped and rolled on the ground. As if it were her assigned job, Hella appeared with a pail and started gathering the potatoes. Of course, I helped her. Before the pail was full, we knew each other's names.

This chore done, she asked me whether I wanted to see her secret. Surely. She led me into the barn that closed off the far end of the courtyard. She took my hand so I would not stumble in the dark. After feeling her way across the room and opening a shutter, she showed me the newborn kittens the cat had hidden under a staircase. I crowded over her shoulder to touch the furry balls with the shut eyes and pink noses. Oh, what a delightful scent of her hair as I touched her nape. After we had stroked the kittens, she invited me to explore the old barn with her. Soon I could not think of anything better to do than to spend every free minute with Hella.

To both families we looked like a pair. We were the same height, even though I was still six and she was already eleven. Our parents winked at each other when they saw us take off together. They were perhaps reminded of princes and princesses of the past that had been betrothed at such a young age. Only here the children, following their natural attraction, had made the match.

Since I took every free minute to disappear with Hella into the wide and varied premises, my father often had to look for me when the family was ready to go to the pool or on a bicycle trip. My father knew of several places where he could find us. The barn offered dusty ladders from which to jump into big piles of hay. We could be in the mangle room where we enjoyed helping Tante Ivonne run the sheets through the flattening roller. Perhaps we were in Hella and Brigitte's sunny playroom in the family quarters on the third floor.

After a few weeks, my parents brought Hella along to the pool. Soon Brigitte would come also. Then Hella's beauty would shine more than ever in contrast. She would sit at the side of the pool on a towel like a sylph and watch Brigitte go off the diving board, feet first, nose firmly pinched with thumb and forefinger, causing a great, drenching splash.

As documented by my mother's film, my father observed us distractedly from a far bench in the swimming area. He was preparing for the next theater season by working on cuts in *Torquato Tasso* and *Der Arzt am Scheidewege.* Occasionally, he looked up and waved to my mother. She was supervising my swimming progress or Monika's random digs in the sandbox. When one of the freight trains passed on the elevated tracks that formed the boundary of the park, he put down his book and counted the cars.

On cloudy days, when my parents would take me on bicycle excursions into the highland, Hella and I would be separated. Hella neither owned a bicycle nor knew how to ride one. Sadly she would watch me swing onto my saddle and take off after my parents to the station. I would not even look back.

What adventure to check the bikes on the Black Forest train and go up the familiar Kinzig River Valley. The ride through the tunnels never lost its thrill. It gave my father many opportunities to count. He counted the number of tunnels and the number of seconds it would take to get through each one. The short whistle blow before entry gave him the sign to look at his watch and then stare in the direction of his wrist in the dark, while the train rumbled and howled and the lights from the windows hastened over the rough-hewn, black, glistening rocks. When light would dawn on the watch, it was time for the second reading. Meanwhile, my mother would exclaim, "Look," every time the train would emerge above foaming brooks and waterfalls in steep, lush meadows and above dark brown shingled houses tucked into the forest of the mountainsides. Little Monika would toddle between our legs, fascinated by the square aluminum ashtray under the window. She manipulated its mechanism until the container flipped down and dumped butts and ashes on the floor.

"*Pfui baba!* Don't touch that!" my mother said, dragging her off the floor. "We have to get off anyway. Come!"

We reclaimed our bicycles in Triberg and effortlessly rolled down the valley, Hornberg, Hausach, Stainach. We shared the road with minuscule trucks, which showed the inscription "*Uhren Wöhrle*" on the doors. They collected parts for cuckoo clocks up and down the valley. When a train passed high above over the viaducts, we would always stop and wave until it would whistle and disappear into the next dark portal. As the valley deepened, the black pines on the slopes accepted the light green patchwork of deciduous trees until they yielded entirely to the friendlier foliage. The mountains would finally recede, and we would spot Ortenberg and Offenburg encouragingly close.

Back in the Sonne, I would jump off my bike and look for Hella. For once, she was hard to find.

Our vacation flew by. Returning to Straßburg thoroughly replenished, my father threw himself into the second season, anticipating another step up in his career.

26

Unfortunately, things were to turn out differently. Though my father put forth as much effort and enthusiasm as in the first year, he could not help noticing a troubling change.

"There is something rotten in the state of Denmark," he wrote in his diary and then analyzed what was happening. The *Arzt am Scheidewege*, one of the plays he had prepared during the summer, was suddenly called off. The other two play directors envied his good standing with Kuntze. They allied themselves with the chief set designer, Richter, who felt slighted. My father, in his need to get the many productions prepared in a hurry, had worked with the less busy and more congenial second set designer, Mülmann. The disgruntled Richter and the miffed play directors were joined by some actors who felt that my father had not given them the parts they deserved. These colleagues, who could not look my father in the eye, began searching for ways to destroy his good relationship with the boss.

They did not have to wait long before my father gave them the tools.

At the beginning of the season, Herr Johst, the head of the Reich's Theater Chamber, sent his emissary to Straßburg. He wanted to make sure that the theater as a cultural outpost reflected the Aryan values of the regime in the choice of its plays and in the conduct of its employees. Ingolf Kuntze asked my father to pick up Herr Sommer from the railroad station. My father took me along. We spotted Herr Sommer when he came strutting from under the banner, *Räder rollen für den Sieg* (wheels roll for victory), spread wide over the entrance arches.

"Herr Sommer?" my father questioned.

"Ah, Herr Tradowsky!" Herr Sommer shouted, shaking the proffered hand. After looking into my father's face, he immediately glanced to his left lapel where he expected the little party button. A hint of displeasure extinguished his greeting smile.

"This is my son, Michael," my father introduced me.

I had been instructed in school to use the *"Deutsche Gruss"* (German greeting). I never did unless I met those strangers who, like Herr Sommer, wore this little, enameled button—a black swastika on white ground encircled by a red margin. So I stretched out my right arm, the flat hand at eye level, and said, "Heihitler!" All second graders said "heihitler," never mind that it didn't make any sense. This is the way we heard it.

"Ah, this is your son," Herr Sommer said approvingly, "tall and blonde. You must be in the Hitler Jugend." Obviously Herr Sommer gave my father credit for having produced such a son.

"No, he is only seven."

"Only seven and so tall already. Terrific! He will qualify for the SS when he grows up!"

My father conducted Herr Sommer to his hotel by the shortest possible way. On route, he was told about the kind of plays that the man from the Reich's Theater Chamber deemed appropriate for the indoctrination of the Alsatians. He was admonished for not wearing his party button. It was inconceivable to Herr Sommer that a man of such marked position and a father of such a tall, blond son could not belong to the party.

Herr Sommer spent the next morning with Kuntze. In the afternoon, he had a conference with the administration and leaders of the theater. My father had already heard his demands for plays suitable for spreading the Germanic heritage. Herr Sommer's expressed expectation that, of course, all leaders should be active party members did not surprise my father either. Ingolf Kuntze himself accompanied the important official back to the station.

Who was it after that visit that pointed out to Ingolf Kuntze that this

Tradowsky he was promoting so much was still not in the party? Who told him that, in his home, Tradowsky had been expounding to private guests irresponsible comments? He had been overheard saying he could not envision putting on *A Midsummer Night's Dream* without Mendelsohn's music. They had also heard him say it was narrow-minded to forbid the books of Heinrich Heine, who had written the *Lorelei*, among other lyrical verses that ranked with Germany's best. Who reminded Kuntze that this Tradowsky had been a student of the Jew Jessner and that his *Gyges und sein Ring* production was full of Jessner's ideas? Who told him that Walter had ridiculed the Aryan play one of the colleagues had staged as having an inane dialogue and mendacious plot?

My father filled his diary searching for answers and lamenting the assignments of plays to the others. Kuntze never broached the matter. He was able to camouflage the treatment of his once favored director, as he was able to engage famous guest directors from Berlin eager to come to Straßburg for a few weeks in order to escape the grueling air raids in the capital. My father was expected to assist those visitors again, which irked him no end. His own productions were reduced to a Christmas fairy tale, *Peterchen's Mondfahrt* (*Little Peter's Travel to the Moon*), and some comedies bordering on farces. By the time the third season rolled around, 1943–44, my father was totally relegated to a few unimportant productions in the *Kleine Haus* in the Blauwolkengasse. As my mother put it, a blind man could feel with his cane that he had been sidelined.

Now that some of his colleagues, perhaps even some he'd hosted at his house, had turned against my father, he stopped his invitations. He limited his social contacts to good old Hans Wiegner and Kurt von Mülmann. After a while, even Hans came less frequently, not out of political reasons but because he became too busy trying out the girls from the ballet. Mülmann, however, visited more often. The bachelor had a special appreciation for my mother's cooking. He also had been pushed aside and, therefore, could commiserate with my father.

Kurt von Mülmann was a descendent of old nobility. He was tall and slender and had refined hands and a narrow face. His high brow rose to his black hair, which was neatly combed straight back. A vein that crossed his high temple and protruded when he laughed seemed to signify his blue blood. With the tradition of his forefathers, some of whom had assumed high positions in the military and government, he disdained the present rulers as lacking any qualifications. Kurt and my father lamented the enslavement of the arts by the regime. In public, they were careful to be out of everyone's earshot. Discussions like that were dangerous. In spite of such precautions, they almost got caught.

As did my parents, Kurt von Mülmann enjoyed the *Kameradschaft* (Comradeship), a club for artists from the theater and the community. The three shared a bottle of wine while looking out of the windows of the wisteria-covered villa down into the peaceful green waters of the Aar. Their favorite table was close to an open doorway that led into the adjacent dining room. One evening, my mother had to leave the table shortly after they had arrived. On the way back, she noticed a man sitting in the dark corner, not much further from their table than a priest from the penitent in a confessional. He held a newspaper like a screen. My mother, who had never seen the man in the club, returned to her table, sat down, raised her eyebrows above her widened eyes and nodded almost imperceptibly toward the man behind the newspaper. My father and Kurt immediately switched their conversation to the weather. Thanks to my mother's timely call from nature, they left the club without having been arrested.

My father and Kurt did not dwell on the frustrations at the theater. They tried to direct their attention toward constructive and enjoyable thoughts. *"Kinder, geniesst den Krieg, der Friede wird furchtbar"* (Children, enjoy the war, the peace is going to be terrible), they used to say, shrinking from the prospect of a world under a victorious Hitler. This expression, as cynical as it was, nevertheless expressed their sentiment. It was best to enjoy every single day as long as possible until the unpredictable war would intrude.

It had taken my father quite a while to struggle through to this philosophy. When he first felt the rejection at the theater, he filled two whole diaries. He wrote bitter ruminations about the deteriorating relationships with Kuntze and Richter and scathing critiques of his competitors' productions. Having analyzed how he had been wronged from all possible vantage points, he finally pulled himself out of his morose state. He resigned himself to the sad reality that nothing could resurrect his career in Straßburg. He was considering sending his résumé to his agent, Fritz R. Schultz, to look for appropriate positions in the Reich.

However, as soon as the thought crossed his mind, he rejected it. One reason was the fear that, before long, his lack of conformity would be noticed. The riders of the political wave would again advance themselves over him. The other reason was the unrestrained bombardments of the cities in the Reich. So far, Straßburg, except for the Rhein Harbor, had been spared.

27

My second school year was markedly different from the first. The boys were the same: Hartmut Bauer and the subdued Fischer. The little Jacob with the decayed teeth was sitting next to me in the second-to-last bench. But our attitudes had changed. We all were proud that we were old-timers now above the first grader. We started testing our limits, and our teacher, Fräulein Kassel, was poor in establishing discipline. Most children ran out screaming as soon as the bell rang, whether or not she was finished with her sentence. When this happened one too many times, she beat those who had escaped back into the room with a ruler and gave an additional homework assignment to the whole class for punishment.

"Over the weekend you have to write one hundred times, *"Wir sollen uns beim Läuten ruhig verhalten"* (We have to keep quiet when the bell rings).

I was a slow writer, and the task was overwhelming. I assured my father that I had not been screaming and running. He was on the verge of talking to the teacher about the unfairness of collective punishment. Then he thought of a way of making my task easier so that I would not have to spend the whole weekend in the house. He got a poster-size piece of paper, drew a hundred lines using his T-square, and divided them vertically into seven columns. I went down the first column, *"Wir," "Wir," "Wir."* Soon my father dispersed some words into the different columns imitating my labored handwriting. When the whole opus was finished and the pencil lines were erased, his contributions blended in rather nicely.

Somehow, the class's rowdy stance was fostered by a general attitude of toughness that filtered down from the upper grades. Boys from age ten had to be in the Hitler Jugend. This organization had been prolific in coming up with all kinds of games that brainwashed youngsters into enthusiasm for war. Flying around in recess with outstretched arms like wings was just one of them. I preferred to be a Me 110 but often was talked into being an English plane. I did not know much about the war. The concept of "enemy" was foreign to me. My parents never pointed out who was flying over our heads during the nights. My mother probably thought that it could be her first love, Dennis, whom she had met in England when she had visited there after graduation. My father was too cosmopolitan and pacifistic to ever generate the hate necessary to consider a group of fellow humans his enemies. So I was an English pilot in the schoolyard, flying into the others with a "rat-a-tat."

Another game became popular. It was called *Luftkampf* (air combat). You needed a matchbox with one match; twine; a coat button; an empty, wooden thread spool; and a pencil. You poked a hole into the flat side of the matchbox, tied the ends of a double string around a match that held the string inside the box. You put the strings through a hole from the inside. They emerged out of the middle of the box and went through opposite holes of the button, then through the hole of the yarn spool and ended tied around a pencil. The smooth hole of the yarn spool was roughened with a pocketknife. With such a gadget, you could let any of your friends enjoy the sounds of air combat. You made your listener hold the matchbox to his ear and told him to close his eyes to heighten the effect. You turned the button so that it would twist the strings. Then you would grab the pencil and pull. The button would start spinning and, once the strings were untwisted, would wind up in the opposite direction. That powerful hum you heard in the matchbox was the incoming plane. Then you rotated the strings that emerged from the spool over the carved notches and created the "rat-a-tat" of the guns. The air battle was on.

Another activity acquainted the youth with the appropriate heroes.

Boys took copybooks and folded all the pages inward so that they were half as wide. In the folds of the pages, they hid at random pictures of heroes of the Wehrmacht who had received the highest decorations, the *Eiserne Kreuz mit Eichenlaub und Schwertern* (Iron Cross with Oak-Leaves and Swords). They were shown in action in their plane or gunning away on a ship or charging out of a trench with hand grenades. On the back, there was a description of their heroic acts. For *zehn Pfennig* you had the chance of choosing a gap in the folded pages. If there was a picture hidden in that location, it was yours. If the spot was empty, the owner kept the coin to buy more war heroes. I was left out of this gambling. My mother was against it. "I'm not giving you money for that!"

I did not mind being left out this time; but when the subtle brainwashing started to influence the clothing of my classmates, I wished to go along. We little shavers were too young to wear the Hitler Jugend's shirts in light yellow-brown—crap-brown, as my mother called it. We were expected to show our militaristic solidarity in another way. The party promoted the wearing of a certain cap. With the exception of the insignia, it looked like the caps of army privates, gray green with a visor. Patterns were handed out at the school that showed the mothers how to sew such a cap. Soon, every boy wore one. I was teased for my knit cap that covered my ears and came to a point on my forehead. It was considered girlish.

I begged my mother to sew me one of those caps like everyone else wore.

My mother erupted. "I'm not going to make you one of those ugly army caps. You were born handsome. You look good with the caps you have. You can't tell me you like those caps the others wear. Don't run after the crowd, Michael. Let them laugh. Ignore them. Stand up for yourself. If they all jump out of the window, would you jump out of the window, too?"

My solution was that I did not wear a cap. I let my hair blow in the wind. The older boys gave me credit for the way I looked, tall and blonde. They thought I would make a fine Hitler Youth. The younger boys followed the older boys' admiration. My mother hoped the war would be over by the time I turned ten, so I would never have to join that organization.

The Hitler Jugend encouraged war games. This aggressive attitude filtered down to us younger boys. We had street gang wars. One of these conflicts came to a battle around Hartmut Bauer's yard. Our opponents tried to storm the fence. We successfully defended by pulling grass sods out of the yard and peppering the assailants with those instant hand grenades. We then pushed the enemy back down from the top of the fence onto the sidewalk, which was littered with the exploded dirt clods.

One of our enemy thought of a ruse worthy of the Desert Fox. His name was Anselm, and he was on roller skates. While we were distracted by the main assault, he led a small troop around the block. One of his troop pried open the back gate, and Anselm zoomed through. By that time, we had discovered the chink in our defense, and a bunch of our soldiers raced around the corner, dragging a board to prop the gate shut.

Either the board hit Anselm's mouth or Anselm's mouth hit the board. This became a question of law, for Anselm lost his big, new front tooth. His screaming and holding his bloody mouth ended the battle but started a legal dispute initiated by Anselm's parents. They wanted compensation for the injury. Consequently, a curious procession occurred a few weeks later. About ten boys in my class, including me, and many others from higher grades marched behind a teacher to the courthouse located next to the Münster. There we were, all milling in a vast, empty hall in the second story with nothing but a few benches on the polished parquet floor. After I had told the teacher that I had not seen "it" happen, I was excused as a witness. I spent my time looking onto the sunny court between the Rohan Palace and the south portal. I found a window from which I could see my Synagogue statue. I was in my favorite location and did not have to sit in the boring school. I was satisfied with my situation, welcoming any break in the school routine.

28

By the second grade, I had formed the pattern of being either very good or very poor in school. I grasped new concepts quickly but started dreaming when Fräulein Kassel went over the same material again and again until everyone understood. In a class of over fifty students, I was rarely called upon. My teacher heard enough of my verbal abilities to give me acceptable marks, but when we started dictation, it became apparent that my spelling was not progressing. Compared to my classmates, my spelling was atrocious.

My father tried to help with my spelling. He dictated and had me write the misspelled words correctly ten times. In the next dictation, I would misspell them again. He showed me his hundred handwritten diaries and the three that he had written for me. I was impressed. When he suggested I continue the half-written volume III, I agreed to give it a try. He drew lines for me and gave me my mother's old fountain pen. Off I went, starting with introducing myself to my diary:

My name is Michael Tradowsky. I am writing with Mutti's old fountain pen. I am from Berlin. I lived formerly in Glienicke am Sandkrug. We had a big yard. We have an oak and a fir. Over a year ago, we moved to Straßburg. Enough for today. I remember that I could write more. I have many friends here. In Straßburg is a beautiful Münster. I am in school now. Before I got into school,

I got a bicycle. I could do it in one afternoon. It was very nice. I learned at the Orangerie.

These first entries appear without spelling mistakes. My father was sitting with me at his big desk, and I constantly interrupted his work, asking the spelling of almost every word. After that, I filled his drawn lines on my own.

Here is the account of the trip my father and I took to Berlin to be present at Opa's sixty-fifth birthday on February 21, 1943.

Ate dais ago, Mutti sad that Papi was goin to berlin. I beged untill I caim along. The last nyt I cryd a litle. Mutti and Papi pakd the sootcais.

in the moning. Now kwikly anuther Kiss. Mutti cals, pai atenshon, you havto tel it to me. Now we went daun the stares. Enuff for toda. Michael

My father read through the German equivalent of these pages and was horrified. He marked the mistakes with a red pencil and wrote underneath, "27 mistakes, 8." Our grading scale went from 1 to 6, with 6 being rock bottom.

I did not want to write more of the travel log. My father felt sorry and let me write on his desk again while serving as dictionary. He even filled in a few sentences that I dictated when I was tired of writing. He imitated my handwriting very well. I now can only identify what he wrote by the length and complexity of his sentences or by the presence of geographic information he wanted to teach me.

Friday, 26 February 1943
I went with Papi to the Brantplatz. There we boarded the 10 and drove to the station. We asked whether the train was there already. The conductor said, "Yes." We had two seats at the window and in the middle a folding table. Now also a soldier came into the compartment. We talked to him. At eight o'clock and three minutes, the train departed. It was beautiful weather.

Sunday 28 Feb. 1943. First were meadows and woods, villages and fields. Then the beautiful sun rose. Then the train had speed. Shoohoo, shoohoo, it went around me. Papi and I waited for the Rhine. The soldier said the next station is Roschwoog. Then came the Rhine. Then Roschwoog.

Now it is 9:30 already. Now there will be breakfast. I got lemonade and ate rolls. Then came Rastatt. Then came Karlsruhe. The soldier said he had to get off in Frankfurt. Then came Mannheim. That was a terminal station. Papi said, "I believe we will ride across the Neckar." Then the Neckar came already. Then Frankfurt came already. Frankfurt was a terminal station. Now the folding table was raised. Our locomotive was changed. Now our trip went to Bad Nauheim. There stand big, funny buildings. Those are saltworks. Earlier we went through Friedberg. At Giessen we came to a river, Lahn. The tracks went along her until Marburg. This is a beautiful city, which one sees from the train lying on the slope of the mountains. Highest stands the castle, which gave the city its name. For coffee time we were in Kassel, where we ate from our Rundkuchen for which Mutti had cracked the form with a hammer, when it did not want to come out. Here also was half of our journey. But the most beautiful part still came. That was between Kassel and Salzgitter, where we rode through the mountains and where the landscape was beautiful. For there flow two rivers, Fulda and Werra, which form the Weser at Hannoversch Gemünd, which flows into the North Sea. After Göttingen, the high mountains stopped. Then it became slowly dark. I saw the full moon first. Papi saw the first star. Enough for today. Michael.

Sunday, 14 March '43
Now we played a game. It consisted of eight triangles, which have to be made into different patterns. Then came the blackout, and I lay down on the soft bench. Then Papi covered me with his coat and his hat. When I woke up, we were in Brandenburg already, and when I woke up again, we were in Berlin. The train arrived on

the minute. Oma and Opa picked us up. We all were glad. Then we went across the Potzdammer Platz. With the U-Bahn, we rode to the Güntzelstrasse. I ate cauliflower soup and went to bed tired as a dog and fell asleep right away.

Herewith, I had completed my third diary. I had seen the last page in reach, and it had inspired the last flurry. My father immediately presented me with the next diary, complete with title page on which he had written in his best penmanship:

Tagebuch No. 4
Michael Tradowsky
Straβburg/Elsass
Geilerstr. 18
14 März 1943

He also drew lines on the first empty pages for me. He always urged me to make entries, and I wrote them to please him. I made so little progress. The spelling was very difficult and not at all like the way words sounded. I began spelling the words in a particularly complicated way. I added all kinds of letters, thinking that the more complex, the better the chance it might be correct.

On Sunday, April 4, I finally sat down to write about Opa's birthday party. After two sentences, I became so frustrated that my father completed the page. It was a list of the guests and the description of the meal and of the games played afterward. My memories of this feast are less specific than my father's entries; yet they are full of vivid flashes that helped me understand what family parties at the old Tradowskys were like. The highlight of the celebration for the adults was the meal. At the head of the table sat my Opa, the celebrant, who gloried in this day. He twirled his blonde English mustache with satisfaction and looked around the large family with a sparkle in his clear blue eyes. Today he was the *Hauptperson* (chief person). A gold chain was draped over his enormous belly. The chain was attached to a golden watch in his vest pocket. He had shown the watch proudly to everyone. It was a gift from his construction firm for his retirement as bookkeeper. As I looked around the table, I saw so many guests that they blended into a chattering, laughing, eating and drinking group. Only a few stuck out. Uncle Otto was one of Opa's four brothers. His belly was even bigger than Opa's. I watched him put away incredible amounts of roast, while pearls of sweat appeared on his clean-shaven scalp. The other person I remembered was my aunt Else, Oma's sister. She was much younger than my Oma and not as stern, but warm and friendly.

After the table was cleared, we played the card game *Schlesische Lotterie* (Selesian Lotterie). My father explained how it was played. "Buy a card from the first deck. Here are ten Pfennig. Then watch when the second deck is laid out on the table two by two. If your card shows up in the first row, you get your money back; in the second row, you get double and in the third row, triple. Then one more card is turned over. If you match that, you get ten times your money."

As the suspense mounted with every game, I screamed with excitement when my card showed.

———

On the last day of our stay, my father and I visited Frau Schubert.

"You remember Elisabeth Schubert?" my father asked. "The Schuberts were at your baptism. Their son, Ulrich, is your godfather. He was away in the military then. The Schuberts brought his fiancé with the funny name—what was it?—Else Konietzko."

"Yes, I remember her."

On the way to Potsdamm, my father bought flowers. Frau Schubert's garden was rigid with frost, the house dark. Frau Schubert had laughed a lot with my mother at my baptism. Was this the same woman who met us now at the door, so much older, all in black? She thanked my father for the flowers with a smile and tears in her eyes. As I sat on the couch next to my father, I tried to make sense of the conversation. Frau Schubert told what had happened in her family, slowly, quietly, swallowing and pausing often in midsentence. My father listened, sighed, and shook his head. They were talking about disheartening events they both knew. I looked around in the gray room for something interesting and wished it would be time to leave. Then Frau Schubert began talking about Ulrich, and I listened up.

"Ulrich was encamped near Moscow in the dead of winter. He contracted double pneumonia and was in the hospital in Warsaw when Hans was … in the hospital with heart failure. Last I heard, Ulrich has been released and sent back to the Russian front."

"Had Hans been ill long?" my father whispered hoarsely.

"He had been ailing since summer '41. He never got over … over Dietrich."

I was glad when we finally got up, I could make my Diener for Frau Schubert and get out of the sad house.

When we walked back toward the station, I asked, "What happened to Dietrich?"

"Dietrich got killed in action."

But my father walked past the station. "I want to visit the cemetery before we go," he said.

The ground in the cemetery was hard with frost as we wandered between the graves, and the overcast sky glared an indifferent, shadowless light. My father halted in front of a simple, white stone marker and stood for a long while, hands clasped on his back, head bowed, eyes closed. Finally, he stirred, looked at the marker again, and murmured "Hans Schubert."

I was glad to leave the cemetery and return to my grandparents to spend our last evening among life and laughter.

But the misfortune of the Schubert family followed us to Straßburg. Two months later, the feared black-rimmed letter from Elisabeth Schubert arrived. Ulrich had been killed in action. The death of my second godfather jarred me less than Uncle Helmut's had. I did not remember ever meeting him.

My next diary entry after our return from Berlin expressed my delight that the school was closed. *Kohlenferien* (coal vacation)—the war effort left no coal to heat the school. My father was very concerned about this interruption in my education and stepped up the dictations. Every so often, he himself would write into my diary how concerned he was about my spelling:

> If he only would concentrate! I get really sad when I have to read this. I would forgive him mistakes that he may do, but "very" and "before" and "until" he should know by now.

I took my father's comments to heart. I overheard my father mentioning his concern to my mother. "He has to improve; he will never make the entrance exam into the *Oberschule*."

She knew what that meant. If I would not pass into this college preparatory school at the end of the fourth grade, I would have to continue in the *Volksschule* (regular school). I would be excluded from a professional career. My father had been the first of his family to be accepted into the *Oberschule* (preparatory school for the university). He did not want me to accomplish less.

The weather warmed; the school resumed. My father hoped he had prepared me for the next dictation. When Fräulein Kassel returned the copybooks, my attempt was covered with red ink. I had received a 5, the second worst of the three failing grades. I buried the copybook in my satchel.

I settled at the end of my father's desk, resolved to tackle my homework while my father was busy putting edits into a play. My Schulranzen leaned between us on the floor against the desk. My father put his book and pencil down and looked at me.

"Listen, Michael, have you gotten your dictation back?"

"No."

"Are you sure Fräulein Kassel has not returned it to you?"

"No, I haven't gotten it back."

My father opened the big flap on my Ranzen and fingered through the books. He pulled out my copybook, opened it to the failed dictation, and held it under my nose. "What is this?"

I looked at the floor.

My father put the copybook on the desk, pulled me over his knee, stretched my pants taut, and spanked me. Then he told me to get out.

I came crying into the kitchen and told my mother what had happened. She had no sympathy.

Wer einmal lügt, dem glaubt man nicht
Und wenn er auch die Wahrheit spricht.

Who lies once, will not be believed,
Even when he speaks the truth.

"Papi is trying to help you, Michael. You must tell him the truth about what is going on in school."

When we sat down for dinner, I discovered a far more painful consequence of my offense than my burning behind. My father did not see me. He did not answer me. He did not hear anything I said. He looked through me like glass. Toward my mother and Monika, he seemed his friendly, entertaining self, but I no longer existed for him. I had broken his trust, and he had written me off. I silently, listlessly poked around in my food and wished for dinner to be over.

I hoped for reconciliation at bedtime, but only my mother came. This was unusual. At night, my parents always had made up with me with a hug and a kiss after I had been punished. I cried myself to sleep.

The next morning, I did not see my father before I left for school. He still was sleeping, having worked at the theater until 1:30 in the morning.

In the afternoon, I anticipated his return from work. Surely today, he would see me again. He came home, embraced my mother, and picked up Monika, but my hello fell into a deep well. He still did not hear me. He looked through me into the carpet. Dinner came and went. At bedtime, my mother assured me that the next day things would be forgotten. I hoped so with all my heart. I did not know how I could go on with my father considering me dead and gone.

The next day, my father had off. It was warm and sunny enough for a bicycle ride into the Rhine forest. However, at breakfast I was still air. During the day, my father busied himself in the living room while I stayed in the nursery. At lunch and dinner, I forced myself to choke down a few bites. I had lost my appetite. My father kept up his friendly conversation with my mother and Monika, but my mother was becoming more and more quiet.

After dinner, my father played the piano. My mother did the dishes. I came to her in tears.

"How can I make Papi like me again?"

She put her arm around my shoulders. "Why don't you go into the living room and tell him you are sorry."

"But he is playing the piano," I objected.

"You just go ahead," she encouraged, "he will listen to you when you apologize."

I stood in the dark of the hall at the door, listening to my father hammering out one of his Clementi Sonatinas. He stopped. I reached out to press down the door handle. He started the slow movement. I withdrew my hand. I listened. I took a deep breath and went in. I stood at the door. He was playing with his back toward me.

"I am sorry," I said.

My father kept playing.

I walked over to his side.

"I am sorry, Papi, that I lied to you."

My father kept playing. I was convinced he would stop any second and put his arms around me. He kept playing, looking at the music.

I left, closed the door behind me, and walked back into the kitchen.

My mother turned toward me curiously. "And?"

"He did not say anything," I mumbled.

"Did you apologize?"

"I said I was sorry."

I went to bed.

As I lay in bed waiting for sleep, my sorrow slowly exhausted itself. As I replayed the troubling scene, doubts came into my mind about my father's infallibility. How swiftly my father had pulled my copybook out of my Ranzen. He must have gone through my books before and had already discovered my failure. If he knew the answer when he asked whether

Fräulein Kassel had corrected the dictation, was this not dishonest too? I heard my father still playing until he stopped in the middle of the last movement.

What happened then was unknown to me until the day of my mother's funeral twenty-one years later. On a drive along the Pacific Ocean, my father talked with the candor that only bereavement can bring. He recalled moments in my mother's life when her character had broken forth most clearly.

"That night in Straßburg, when you said you were sorry, and I played the piano, do you remember that?"

"I do."

"She came in, and she was furious with me."

Her fury must have been quiet, for I did not hear her; but her indignation must have burned in her eyes, and her deep voice must have been even deeper with reproach. My father promised to make up with me. However, he could not get himself to do it that evening.

The next day, when my father returned from work in the afternoon, he greeted me as if nothing had happened. My "hello" in response was listless. I was surprised that my relief was not greater. Something had changed. Upon awakening that morning to face another day of silent treatment, I suddenly felt strong enough to take it. If he persisted in ignoring me, I would survive.

After that, my father and I never bicycled together alone. We always went with my mother and Monika. The time of feeling identical in our essence, of feeling the warm emotion of complete kinship, this blissful time, was over. Ever after, our relationship was tarnished with a bit of reserve, a tiny remnant of distrust.

29

I continued to love my father, who spent most of his free hours with us. He shared his interesting wealth of knowledge freely and was entertaining enough to make us forget the seriousness of the times. To lift children out of the fear of war, he produced a Christmas fairy tale, "*Peterchen's Mondfahrt*" (*Little Peter's Trip to the Moon*), an adaptation of a book that my mother had given me. She had received it as a child from Omi Bauer.

It tells the story of a *Maikäfer* (may bug) who has lost a leg, which wound up on the moon. The leg had gotten hung up on a tree that the *Mondmann* (Moonman) cut down and took with him. The may bug flies in the bedroom of two children, Peterchen and Anneliese, and convinces them to help him retrieve his leg. He teaches them to fly, and they take off to the meadow of the stars, where *Sandmann* supervises and makes sure that the star children polish their shiny star spotless before they put it on their heads. Sandmann agrees to guide bug and children through the different heavenly halls to the moon. He takes them to the palace of the sun, where *Frau Sonne* (Lady Sun) holds council with the elements, *Regen Max* (Rain Max), *Blitzhexe* (Lightning Witch), *Donnermann* (Thunderman), and others, who promise to help. The journey goes through the Christmas garden, where Santa Claus grows the toys that are sprinkled by his assistant, *Pfefferkuchenmännchen* (Gingerbread Man). It continues to the moon cannon, which Sandmann uses to shoot the three to the moon, one at a time. As soon as they bounce onto the moon in the next act, the Mondmann accosts them. He has not eaten in many months and welcomes the children. Peterchen gives him the presents from Santa Claus out of his basket—apples, gingerbread, and a jumping jack. Anneliese sacrifices her doll. He devours everything. Now he is after the children. In the nick of time, there comes heavenly defense. Regen Max drenches him. Blitzhexe strikes. Storm, Flood, and Thunder appear and subdue him. However, Mondmann keeps coming after the children until the Daughters of the Sun blind him, and he staggers away and gets lost between the craters. The children find the leg on the tree, glue it back on the bug, and the three fly happily back to earth.

In the two seasons in which the fairy tale played, I saw it eleven times.

"*Peterchen's Mondfahrt* is playing this afternoon," my father would mention, grabbing his worn briefcase to go to work. "Would you like to come?"

"Au, ja!"

How happily did I run next to him to the theater and spend the next two hours in his personal loge! As I scrutinized one performance after another, my initial wonder slowly gave way to the knowledge of how the theater tricks were pulled off. I was no longer in awe, like all other children, when Peterchen, Anneliese, and the may bug actually flew up off the stage. At one of the later performances, the right one of the two piano wires that lifted the bug snapped, leaving him hanging awkwardly lopsided. He had to be eased down and flown out the side of the stage instead of through the ceiling. From then on, I noticed the thin wires no matter how dark the night scene was.

Once I had discovered how my father had produced the magic of flying, I became curious about the mechanics of the other marvels. "Papi, tell me, how do you shoot them out of the cannon? How do you make Donnermann thunder?"

One morning, my father took me behind stage and up to the floors above. The first was the weight floor, where the counterweights for lifting the scenery ran in chutes. Here also was a big drum filled with dried peas. My father started cranking it and produced the sound of torrential rain that had accompanied the Regen Maxe's entrances. Then my father had two stagehands pick up a large piece of tin and shake and buckle it, sending those peals of thunder that echoed through the heavens when Donnermann fought Mondmann.

After these demonstrations of meteorological might, we climbed to the *Schnürboden* (ties floor). Here, ropes ascended to the *Rollboden* (roller floor), where they went over pulleys and down to attach to the top of the backdrops. These backdrops were hanging above the stage about an arm's length apart from star meadow to moonscape. Returning to the stage, I looked down into the auditorium, into the rows and rows of yawning velvet seats.

"How can you talk, when this is all full with people?" I asked.

"It just looks like a big cabbage field during a performance. So you just forget about it."

We went through the wings into the back of the scenery. We stepped over the hose that lay there to be attached to the Waterman's mask. Aha, the blast of water that Waterman directed into Moonman's face did not really come from his mouth. The moon cannon stood here, so huge close up that you could not comprehend it with one glance. It was open in the back and showed a chamber where Peterchen, Anneliese, and the may bug hid after Sandmann had stuffed them down the big barrel. In their turn, these puppets on wires were pulled out of the barrel with every firing and were flown on cables to the moon, where, at the beginning of the next act, the real actors landed on the stage.

I noticed a pumpkin in a wheelbarrow. I could not place this giant pumpkin in the story.

"This pumpkin is a prop for the night performance of *The Three-Cornered Hat*," my father said.

After my backstage initiation, I felt like a professional stagehand when I saw further performances. While the children in the audience stared with openmouthed enchantment, I knew what was happening behind and above the stage to produce the miracles.

Besides directing the plays, my father liked to take a small part himself. He was Santa Claus's helper, Pfefferkuchenmännchen. He wore a long dress hung with gingerbread and a high, pointed hat as a symbol of magic power. He tiptoed between the garden beds and sprinkled the toys with a little silver can. Being in the play gave him the chance for some surprising improvisations.

One afternoon, when I saw the play for the umpteenth time, Pfefferkuchenmännchen suddenly appeared with Sandmann at the moon cannon. He had no business being there. He claimed that he wanted to accompany the children and pleaded with Sandmann to blast him to the moon. I was on the edge of my seat. *What will he do next?* In the next act on the moon, after the may bug, Peterchen, and Anneliese had careened onto the stage with a frightful boom, another boom precipitated my father's landing on the stage.

The Moonman devoured the children's gingerbread and toys as usual by stuffing them under his beard into his loose shirt. He was quite skillful in deceiving the audience. But in this performance, he ran into a dilemma. Pfefferkuchemännchen produced a gigantic pumpkin and offered it to the ravenous man.

"Don't you want this pumpkin?"

"No," the Mondmann growled, "I don't eat pumpkin."

Pfefferkuchmännchen pointed out all the advantages of the pumpkin. Mondmann refused desperately.

I felt like an accomplice. "Make him eat it, Papi," I whispered.

Finally, the Pfefferkuchenmännchen took pity. He took his pumpkin back to Santa Claus's toy garden and let the distraught Mondmann ease into his accustomed part.

Having learned the secrets of the theater, I felt I was prepared to stage *Peterchen's Mondfahrt* in my own apartment. Hartmut was game after I told him the storyline, supported by the colorful illustrations in my book. Of course, we would need many actors. We counted twenty-seven in all.

I had never seen my mother more perplexed than when I walked in from school followed by Hartmut and over forty little boys. During recess, I had inspired my classmates. "You will be Sandmann. You will be Donnermann. You will be Peterchen." Soon, not only the selected but everyone except the Fischer followed our big troop through the streets. Who would miss this excitement, whatever it was?

The nursery was so full with aspiring actors that I could hardly move. I screamed for quiet to explain the story but soon gave up. A sizable group had gotten into my chest and torn apart my toys. "No, you can't have that chocolate. Give me that."

Where to begin? Hartmut and I finally settled on making the costumes first. We measured little Jakob's head with a piece of string. He was going to be Pfefferkuchenmännchen. We glued together a piece of cardboard into a pointed hat and painted stars on it with colored pencils. It took us so long that even the devoted actors lost interest. The boys remembered that their mothers were waiting and left in droves.

Before long, Hartmut and I were alone. Oh well, we had made a start in our production. We had Pfefferkuchenmännchen's hat.

My father was delighted to see my interest in the theater. His hopes rose again that I might follow in his footsteps. Besides the children's play, he let me see the comedies he staged. He gave me pages from his watercolor pad so I could paint the sets of the Opera, *Der Wildschütz*, from memory. That rekindled my interest in painting and drawing. When my father took me to another traveling exhibit at the Rohan Palace, I decided to have my own show at home.

Hartmut helped me catalogue the art objects. Some were old; others I was producing for the opening. When we had enough pieces, we thumbtacked them on the walls of the nursery and the adjacent dining room. At least two rooms were required. After all, the exhibit in the Rohan Palace went through more than one hall. We also affixed price tags; the paintings in the real gallery had them. The subjects were mostly impressions from the bicycle tours with my father—Black Forest houses like Lydia's at The Turner, women in traditional Alemanni costumes, cows in pastures, and pine-covered mountains. The skies were always enlivened by several Vs of birds. There were also cityscapes—a watercolor of the view out of my window and a sky-conquering Münster. Several hurried sketches of generic houses and people filled the gaps on the walls.

We installed everything in secret with the doors shut. Hartmut, who could not draw, willingly fell into the roles of curator, accountant, and workman. At the opening, Hartmut became the gallery guard, following my demonstration of how to walk slowly up and down the rooms with a grave face and hands clasped behind his back. My parents, Onkel Hans, and Onkel Mülmann were our visitors. They took their time viewing each opus. They discussed their impressions, drew close to examine the technique, and circled with outstretched thumbs around certain areas that they considered particularly compelling. They stepped back to contemplate the total effect, holding their chins in their hands. They were terrific! Onkel Hans purchased a pastel of the view from the top of the Brent into the fog-shrouded mountains. He never picked up his purchase. I still have the picture today. Onkel Mülmann particularly liked the watercolors of the opera scenes. He said that I had talent to become a stage designer.

It was the contact with a different artist that was ultimately to influence my future. My parents had met in the Kameradschaft a sculptor, Brellox, a man in his twenties with disheveled brown hair. He made busts of children in clay and had them fired to make them permanent. My father decided to have him sculpt me for mother's birthday present. I sat for him half a dozen times. His small studio had room for a tin-lined trunk that held his clay, a stool for him, a chair for me, and the stand for his developing portrait in the middle. I followed his every move from the beginning stage of a generic pear to the bold addition of nose, chin, and cheek masses up to the last refinements with wooden spatulas and wire loops. It was a good likeness, except my hair was parted on the wrong side from what I knew. As a final triumph, he measured the width and height of my head with a pair of calipers and slid it onto the clay. It fit exactly. Brellox's creation looked so lifelike that watching him take a wire and cut the clay horizontally above my ears, lift off the top, and hollow out my head with a knife was painful. I felt relieved when he placed the lid back on and smoothed over the cut. "I hollow it out so that the clay doesn't break in the firing," he explained.

A young woman, who had the most amazing blue-black hair, was in that austere, little room. My father's attempt to set me straight—she is not Frau Brellox, and her hair is dyed—did not distract from my admiration. At the end of each session, Brellox asked the woman to bring him a pan of water to wet the wraps for the sculpture. The faucet was at the end of a long corridor. I went with her, and she let me carry the basin back to the studio. I clamped the basin tightly against my body so as not to drop it like a bowl of tomatoes. She said kindly, "Carry the basin away from your body. Then it will not spill."

To this day, I remember the walk down the corridor next to the beautiful woman. Nothing in my youth has made more lasting impressions than simple skills that girls or women have taught me as an expression of their affection.

When my father took Monika along on one of our sessions, Brellox suggested making a sculpture of her. He waved away any concern that she might be too young and not be able to sit still. "I have to see her from all sides anyway."

Monika, with her big, round cheeks; curls; little, upturned lips; and dipped nose, was as cute as the putto angels populating the staircases and altars of baroque masters. The terra cotta was a good equivalent for the warm tones of her face. Monika's finished and fired head was an overwhelming surprise on my mother's Christmas table. My head, in the meantime, had broken in firing. Brellox made a second head out of gray clay. He had run out of terra cotta. Instead of having it fired, he suddenly brought it to us green. He had been drafted. The bust could dry at our place, and he would take care of having it fired after the war. He never returned.

My unfired head was fragile. The right ear fractured when I crawled on top of the wardrobe where the sculpture was standing and accidentally knocked it over. Over the years, it sustained much additional damage. Trips into the Black Forest, to Hersbruck, to Nürnberg, and finally to America took their toll. Besides the ear, the unfired bust also lost parts of the nose and the neck, until it looked more like a find from a Greek archaeological site than a creation of the twentieth century. Sixty-five years later, I finally restored the clay and cast it in bronze.

30

Focusing on many kinds of artistic endeavors was one of my father's ways of diverting our attention from the ugliness of the war. It took our minds off the trips into the bomb shelter that happened with mounting frequency. They started coming in daytime also. During the prewarning, tethered barrier balloons went up around the Rhein Harbor to interfere with possible attacks. Coming from the cellar one afternoon, we discovered that the balloons were gone, and black billows were rising over the rooftops. The planes had evidently shot down the balloons and set the oil storage tanks ablaze. The fire burned out by nightfall. It did not spread along the streets to our house. I had not yet gathered enough experience to know that a bomb fire would not sweep over several blocks.

The Allies did not spare Straßburg. Air attacks would even happen here. Consequently, the government instituted programs in the schools to teach children how to protect themselves in case their houses were hit by bombs. A man came in and hung new, glossy charts all around our classroom. On them were illustrations of the different kinds of bombs. There were bombs that looked like long, skinny cylinders. The man explained that these were *Brandbomben* (incendiary bombs). They were filled with phosphorus. When they fell into the roof, the phosphorus would run out and ignite and start a fire.

"Don't put water on such a fire," the man cautioned us, "because the burning phosphorus will float on top and run down the street and ignite other houses. Sand—that's what you have to shovel on it."

He turned to another chart of bombs of various sizes that looked like fat cigars with little wings on one end. "These are *Sprengbomben*" (high explosive bombs). He explained, "They fall through the floors and then explode and blast the house apart.

"And these here are *Luftminen*" (aerial mines).

I looked out of the window. I heard the man continue.

"These explode in the air near the houses. They generate such air pressure that the houses collapse. They can destroy several houses at the same time.

"Now this here is a special bomb. It has a timer right here."

I looked again. The man poked at part of the bomb with his pointer. "This bomb won't explode right away when it falls. But then an hour or two later, the timer runs out, and it goes off—*boom*."

Then the man instructed us how to protect ourselves. He showed us how to wind a copper wire around a pencil and make a spring. He demonstrated how this spring was to be used on the windows.

"You open the window a crack and tie the spring between the handle and the latch. Now when there is a high explosive bomb or air mine close by, it will not break the window. The spring will straighten out when the air pressure blasts it open. Make sense?

"Another thing," the man went on, "I want you all to bring a washcloth to school." He showed us a face mask sewn out of black cloth and slid his hand into a pocket inside, where a moistened washcloth went. He tied the mask on Fräulein Kassel. He also placed on her a pair of glasses, with black canvas around the frame that fit tight on her face. We children did not know whether to laugh or be scared.

"Now I want you to wear this mask and these glasses in the bomb shelter. The mask is for the dust, and the goggles are for splinters from glass, wood, or other building materials. You put the mask and glasses on and lay flat on the floor, facedown. Now let's all go in the school yard. I will show you what to do with incendiary bombs."

A truck had dumped a pile of sand close to the entrance. The man laid a model of a bomb on the pile and threw several shovels of sand on it. He handed the shovel around to the kids, and they threw sand until the pipelike thing was covered up.

"Excellent!"

When I came home, I informed my parents about all these safety measures. My mother gave me a white washcloth to take to school. My father bought copper wire. We wound it around pencils until we had enough springs for all the tall windows in our apartment. We only used them once. Opening of the windows and hooking the springs took too long when we had to get into the basement.

Three weeks later at school, each boy received a pair of goggles, a flashlight, and the mask that had been sewn by volunteers. I was disturbed that the washcloth in my mask was not mine. Instead of the white one that my mother had given me, it was one that had all colors of the rainbow and the inscription, "*Marke Negergarn*," woven into it. I thought it would greatly reduce the effectiveness to have a washcloth that came from who knows where instead of from my mother. Only after she had checked it out carefully and said it was all right was I willing to take it into the cellar.

I doubted the validity of these protections. None of the tenants that sat along the narrow cellar hall had masks or goggles. With the repeated alerts, I had hours to examine these people as they waited on their seats along the masonry wall and stared across at the wooden lattice dividers of the storage spaces. The Alsatians seemed little concerned about their safety. They stayed close to the stairs. They came into the shelter reluctantly, sat silently and stone-faced, and left as soon as the menacing sounds ceased. If ever they looked at us, their glances were reproachful. The Schells, an old Alsatian couple on the third floor, refused to go into the shelter altogether.

The only Alsatians who were honestly friendly were the Stoebers. Their apartment was on the ground floor. We credited Monika with getting us acquainted with them.

Once, after Monika had started to walk, we returned with her from the Orangerie tired. She refused to climb the stairs, sat down on the bottom step, and started wailing. Frau Stoeber came out of her apartment; saw the little girl with the blonde curls, tears running down her big red cheeks; and took pity on her. She brought out a lollipop. Monika was so surprised and delighted that she stopped crying immediately and started one-stepping up the stairs, sucking her candy. From then on, the bottom stair became insurmountable for her. No matter how short the excursion, she collapsed, whimpering right there until Frau Stoeber appeared. The good woman invested in a large jar of sweets.

From Monika's theatrics on the Stoeber's doorstep, our relationship evolved. When there was a morning alert, we would meet them in the basement. Quite regularly, these morning alerts would be partially "dewarned" by three extended howls of the siren, meaning that the danger was no longer immediate but still close. When this occurred, the Stoebers would invite us to their apartment. Predictably, the bombers that had flown into Germany over our heads would return soon. It was unsafe to climb all the way to the fifth floor.

The Stoebers invited us for lunch. They prayed before meals. I could have received credit if I had still been in religion. Herr Stoeber knew the Bible so well that he incorporated the stories into his everyday life. I was very impressed when he divided his mashed potatoes into two craters, poured tomato sauce in each, and demonstrated by running his fork through the ditch in between how God led the children of Israel through the Red Sea and how he drowned Pharaoh's army, simulated by breaking the craters and letting the sauce run into the middle.

His son, Claude, interested me in a different way. The only offspring of his old parents, Claude was intelligent, serious, and mature beyond his thirteen years. He represented the scientific counterpart to his father's religious worldview. He had turned his room into a chemistry lab. He demonstrated what sodium would do when dropped into a Petri dish with water. It burst into a yellow flame and turned into a little silver ball that shot back and forth with a hiss as if possessed, until it spent itself and disappeared.

Usually, partial all clears would be followed by another full alert. We would all scramble back into the basement for a second time and return to our usual seats in the deep of the corridor. My father and Herr Weiss from the third floor were positioned right and left at the far wall, where masons had prepared a shelter escape. They had cut a hole into the cellar of the adjacent building big enough for a person to squeeze through and had closed it with a thin, brick wall. My father and Herr Weiss would break this wall with an ax in case our cellar was buried.

My father and Herr Weiss shared the job of *Luftschutzblockwart* (air safety block guard). Their main task was to walk around the block during lulls to check the blackout. If they saw seepage of light, they had to bellow, "*Licht aus*," until the offender killed the light.

Herr Weiss was a Nazi. My father had to be constantly on guard. Herr Weiss considered it treason to doubt in the final victory of the Wehrmacht. The debacle of Stalingrad was merely a temporary retreat for regrouping and successful assault. My father never responded to Herr Weisse's enthusiastic war commentaries. Eventually, the dangerous man wrote him off as an artist, out of touch with reality and politically illiterate.

Our visits in the cellar always ended with the hoped for, sustained siren of the Entwarnung. If it was the end of a night alert, my mother would carry the sleeping Monika and my father the suitcases, and we would start our five-story ascent. Before my instruction about air safety, my anxieties were always relieved as soon as I heard the Entwarnung and I would quickly fall asleep. After the course, however, I first walked through the rooms looking for holes in the ceiling and checking for time bombs that might have rolled under the beds. I did this stealthily, for I did not want my parents to notice that I did not trust them to watch out for our safety.

A nightmare began to disturb my dreams. Death, a walking skeleton with vestiges of muscles, sinew, and hair, followed me through the streets, pushing a flat cart heaped with corpses. I heard the grinding and rumbling of the two large wheels behind me. When Death got close, he set down his cart and came after me to hook me with his scythe. I ran as fast as I could, but he still gained. I hastened upstairs, hid in the large black closet in my room, and tried to hold the door shut. I heard his blade scrape, looking for a catch. When he finally succeeded in prying the door open, I would wake up with a scream.

The continuous alerts conjured the nightmare over and over. I dreamed a curious countermeasure. I offered to be Death's friend and help him collect the dead, so that he would spare me. This trick afforded me enough relief that I could sleep.

As the war progressed I learned what bomb damage really looked like. There would not be a neat, round hole in the ceiling and a quiet bomb rolled under the bed. When a bomb hit, exploding or not, you would know it.

Seeing destruction was a way I learned about the ravages of war. Since I could not get any information from my parents, my only source of information on this subject were reports from classmates and teachers. While my parents tried to shield me from the horror, the school was less considerate.

The gym teacher was so kind as to cancel his drill and tell us stories. He started with a fairy tale about a dwarf. I recognized it from the Grimm's fairy tale book with the cigarette pictures. He told it in a distorted way, trying to make it sound funny. Some children laughed, and some failed to see the humor, but all paid attention. He lunged into the second story, his voice intense. "Now this story that I am telling you next is not a fairy tale. It is true.

"There was a mother and a little boy your age and his little sister. They lived in a small laborer's house in the Eder Valley. The father was away in the war. Upstream from the house was a dam, called the Eder Dam, and behind the dam was a big lake.

"One night, English planes came and threw bombs at the dam. The dam broke, and the flood rushed down the valley. The water burst into the house, and the mother took her children on the roof, but the flood rose and was about to sweep them off. The mother grabbed a door that floated by and put the children on it. The mother held on to the end of the door but could not get out of the water. The door could not carry her. She could not swim. The current got wilder and wilder, and her grip on the door got weaker and weaker. The boy tried to hold on to her sleeve, but when the door hit a pole sticking out of the water, it spun, and the boy couldn't hold on any longer. The children saw their mother drown. Down river, the door hit the bank, and the children were rescued."

My classmates did not like the story. Many wiped their eyes. Little Jakob next to me buried his head in his arms on the desk. The gym teacher was too obtuse to notice that he only generated a feeling of resentment against himself rather than hate of the enemy and hunger for revenge. He saw with satisfaction that he had made some children cry.

He lunged into a third story to touch the rest of us, something about a mother and children buried in a bomb shelter. I tried to look out of the window and held my hands over my ears. Even though I avoided the details, I heard the gist of the story. It lingered in my mind and made me more apprehensive during alerts.

With the disturbed sleep and the dwindling food rations, the war was beginning to show on me. I became skinny and pale.

31

The next summer's visit to Offenburg gave us the longest break in alerts. There, no one paid attention to the occasional howling of the sirens. The town had been considered too small to be placed on the bombing schedule. The peaceful nights and the surprisingly plentiful food in the Hotel Sonne returned us to physical and emotional health.

In summer 1943, we stayed over a month. My parents had reserved a private room for me, probably to be able to enjoy their nap pleasures without restraints. There was quiet time in the hotel from one to three o'clock, when the guests and the employees were expected to whisper and tiptoe, not to disturb those who wanted to rest.

At that age, I considered a nap a waste of time, but I had agreed to at least lie down on my bed for one hour. I looked at the high ceiling in the narrow room in utter boredom and waited for the church bell to toll the next quarter hour. Wide awake, I noticed a tiny rustling and a piece of paper being slid under the door. I picked up the slip and read:

Michael!
Come to my room. It's upstairs across from my playroom. I have something to show you.
Hella

Underneath was a little drawing of the private quarters on the third floor with arrows showing the way. Hella's drawing showed the playroom; the parents' bedroom and bathroom; and farthest, her room through the last door of the corridor.

I knew where the playroom was. On rainy days, Hella had invited me there to play games. It was cozy, smelling of linoleum and *Uhu Alleskleber* glue. A Black Forest clock ticked, and, at every half hour, rattled and cuckooed. Jolly Brigitte occupied her desk under the dormer, making ink drawings.

In stocking feet, I sneaked out of my room, up the stairs into the far, dark end of the corridor, past the playroom, and deeper into the dark, where the hall turned left and ended. Hella stood in the bright sliver of the cracked door, motioning me to come in. She put her finger on her mouth.

"We have to be quiet. My parents are on the other side of the bathroom."

Her room was a triangular chamber showing a bed, a chair, a closet, a door to the shared bathroom, and a window. The closed blinds drew stripes of light on floor and bed. Hella's crumpled dress lay on the chair. She was in her underwear.

"Come, I want to show you my favorite book," she said, hopping in bed and tapping on the sheet next to her, inviting me. I was ready to climb in.

"Oh no," she said. "You have to take off your shorts. You don't lie in bed with your street clothes on."

I took off my blue shorts and my socks. In my underwear, she accepted me under her blanket.

She put her arm around my neck, pulled me close on her pillow, and opened the book over our bellies. It was the story of a squirrel and had colorful illustrations. Here was the squirrel holding a pinecone on a branch in front of a hole in the tree. Its bushy tail was curving up as high as its head. Hella read me the story of the squirrel in a low voice.

I felt the brush of her curls on my cheek; felt the warmth of her body; watched the curved, glistening eyelashes; watched her dark eyes downcast to see the book; watched how they slowly wandered from left to right with sudden jumps back to the left. This I savored until the bell on the tower struck three times. Reluctantly, I put on my shorts and snuck back to my room undetected.

The next day, as soon as the houseguests had settled down for nap time, I heard the slip of paper slide under the door again.

"Michael, come to me. We want to finish the book."

I snuck up again. She was waiting in her bed with the book. We finished the story. Then we started "*Pick reist nach Amerika*" (*Pick Travels to America*). Pick was a boy living in Hamburg. He watched the ships on the Elbe until he could not resist the lure of the great blue yonder and went to New York as a stowaway. The book was smaller, and as we read, the bottom lines were hidden in the folds of the blanket. She pulled the blanket down and placed the book on her tummy. The stripes from the window curved over her undershirt and made the little mounds on her chest stand out like two chocolate kisses. After a page or two, Hella put the book down.

"Let's do gymnastics. Can you do gymnastics? I'll teach you."

She stood on the bed, leaned back and dropped into a bridge. Then she let herself fall and moved to the wall so that I could try. I leaned backward and collapsed.

"Let's try it again. I'll help you," she whispered.

I stood on the foot end with my back toward the bed. Hella crouched behind me on her knees and elbows. I arched backward, and as I tumbled, I felt her support. I arched over her and came down on my hands.

"Hold it," she said and crawled from under me. "See, you can do a bridge," she said just before I crashed.

She did a headstand on her throw rug. "Now you try it." I stood on my head as she held my feet. I suggested doing push-ups as something I could do. I did ten, but she matched that. I suggested we do wheelbarrows. She spread her legs so I could get in between and lift her by her ankles while she was walking on her hands back and forth the short stretch in front of her closet. Then I did a somersault.

"This is too easy," she said, "unless you do it from a stand and come back to a stand like this."

I tried but could not get back up on my feet. Before I could try again, the toll from the tower put an end to our session.

After Pick had reached America, there were no slips under the door for a while. I did not know why and did not ask her. We never mentioned our afternoon rendezvous when we met at other times. Someone might overhear us and uncover our dearest secret.

While my friendship with Hella built fast from where we had left off the year before, my parents' acquaintance with the Schimpfs progressed very slowly. It was the arrival of Kurt von Mülmann, who joined us for a week, that brought them closer. Karl Schimpf had the same aristocratic air about him as Onkel Mülmann. They also had a common profound knowledge of art history and a passion for creating illusions.

Soon, Herr Schimpf offered to show Onkel Mülmann the most venerated room in the hotel, the one that was never rented or shown to the public—the Napoleon room. My parents were also invited, and I tagged along. Indeed, in summer 1805, the emperor had led his army across the Rhein at Straßburg and stayed in the Sonne for one night. Since that day, nothing had been changed in the room he occupied. Everything was as Napoleon had seen it—the empire furniture, the bed with the velvet canopy, and the framed silhouettes hung on the vertically striped walls. Perhaps he had stood at the desk and written a directive with the quill stuck in the inkwell. The same mirror in the door of the walnut closet that reflected us now had once shown his self-assured and brooding image.

Herr Schimpf told us that Hitler also had once lodged in the Sonne, with the expressed purpose and demand to stay in the same room and bed as Napoleon.

"We still call it the Napoleon room," Schimpf said, which comment made it clear to my parents and Onkel Mülmann that they could trust him. Obviously, Schimpf had not capitalized on Hitler's visit—no indication that the Führer ever stayed here was present, not even his ubiquitous picture that had to be displayed in all public places.

After that, the friendship with the Schimpfs developed freely. Toward the end of the vacation, Karl Schimpf invited us to his workroom.

We entered the realm of the famous *Krippenbauer* (builder of nativity scenes) with reverence and expectation. We noticed a peculiar odor, familiar from the theater—the smells of glue, paint, and wood. Our attention was captured by two nativity scenes from previous years that stood on opposite walls. The one was in baroque style. Preciously dressed angels contorting in ecstasy hovered in front of the curved facade of a church. A brilliant shaft of light streaked down on Mary and the child. It took little imagination to hear the angels shout, "Gloria in Excelsis."

The other *Krippe* was set in the Black Forest. Silence overcame the loud triumph we just had experienced. Here were the highlands in deep snow, the shepherds standing in the open barn leaning on their staffs, the oxen, the sheep, and a single star shooting over a black sky. I liked it better to see God come to earth in such quiet humility.

We turned to Schimpf's workstation. The spacious table was loaded with little bits of material, threads, and needles; a small hammer, fine chisels, and files; and nails, glue, little bottles of paints, and brushes. Behind all these tools and supplies was an empty stage. In four months, this emptiness would turn into this year's interpretation and celebration of the Christmas story.

We thought we had seen all. When we turned to leave, we noticed another stage that was placed into the doorway to the adjacent private room. Schimpf explained almost apologetically. "Oh this? Well, Brigitte and I are going to perform *The Magic Flute* on that stage. I don't know whether I should invite professionals to this, but if you can stand such an amateurish production, you are invited."

The Magic Flute was scheduled for the following Saturday at eight. My parents dressed up as if they were going to the opera house. They had me put on my best shorts, a snow-white shirt, knit kneesocks with tassels on the side, and freshly polished shoes. As we entered the little room, we saw that the other invited guests had paid the same respect in putting on formal attire. We sat on straight and uncomfortable antique chairs. Hella, who had been waiting in the corner, scooted next to me. We chatted and looked expectantly at the little red velvet curtain in the panel with the crying and laughing masks.

The three double blasts of fanfares cut the conversations. Brigitte's hand appeared briefly through the entrance door and turned off the light. Then Mozart's overture promised the wonders on the stage until the curtain rose.

After seeing the exquisite figures in the *Krippen*, I was disappointed that the singers were paper cutouts moved in and out of the scenery on paper strips, but the stage was mostly dark, so the music prevailed and moved us into a strange and fascinating land. When the overture and first aria ended, I heard the sound of a steel needle grinding. Someone stumbled behind the stage and lifted the tone arm with a scratch. The spell was broken.

Free from the preconceived idea of what a Mozart opera should look like, I was enchanted by the story and proud to be allowed to stay up with the adults until midnight. I gladly endured the hard, scratchy seat, keeping it from my bare thighs by sitting on my hands. Every now and then, I glanced over to Hella to see her bemused face in the dim light from the stage. In the short breaks between scenes, Hella whispered inside information about how her father and Brigitte were producing the special effects. "The fire is fog from a bowl of dry ice over an orange bulb. The water is cellophane crinkled forward and backward over mirrors. The thunder is a large cookie tin from the kitchen. My dad and Brigitte shake it."

The one adult who enjoyed the production without reservation was Onkel Mülmann. He told Herrn Schimpf repeatedly how the sets, which were his prime interest, showed the same perfect interpretation of mood and meaning as the *Krippen*. Herr Schimpf was encouraged. He invited Onkel Mülmann to his storage room to show him the witches' costumes that he had made for past Mardi Gras parades. As the prankster he was, he got Onkel Mülmann to dress up in the most frightening of all costumes. When he heard Monika and me in the hall, he grabbed a broom and, with a cackle, rode out the door. The witch struck little Monika with panic and sent her down the corridor screaming for Mother. It also frightened me sufficiently to make my heart pound in my throat until I recognized the trousers and polished shoes under the green dress.

"Oh, you are just Onkel Mülmann!" I said, calming down.

My mother burst out of her room and picked up the sobbing Monika.

She lit into Onkel Mülmann, witch costume and all. "Don't frighten the children like that. You want to give them nightmares?"

My father excused his friend. "He's a bachelor and has no experience with children."

My mother insisted it was time to get away from illusions and take us children back to what was best for us—the bicycle tours into the Black Forest and visits to the swimming pool. My parents continued my swimming instructions. They bought me a floatation belt made out of ten rectangular corks strung on two ropes that were tied around my chest. Without fear of my old swimming teacher, I made fast progress. Every day, they removed another cork. When there were only two left, I felt the buoyancy of the water and realized that I could keep myself afloat. I discarded the belt, took a few strokes away from the rim of the pool, and I could swim. My parents could hardly get me out of the water. I floated endlessly, looking down where my shadow was projected amid the circles that the sun wove on the bottom.

Now Hella and I could swim together until we got chilled. Then we would swing on the giant swings, play ball, build castles with Monika in the sandbox, and eat pieces of cheesecake at the terrace café rich as in peacetime. Usually, we did not pay attention to the newspapers left on the tables. But in the later part of July, the headlines became unusually large. July 25, "Terror Attack on Hamburg," July 28, a bigger headline, "Terror Attack on Hamburg," July 30, letters even bigger and fatter, "Another Terror Attack on Hamburg." Then on August 3, monstrously big letters, "Again Attack on Hamburg." The people buzzed around us as we ate our cake. "Fifty thousand killed, forty thousand injured, half the houses gone, a million fleeing the city."

Many years later, I read in a book by an American expert that, in those assaults, 3,095 aircraft dropped some 9,000 tons of bombs, about half of them incendiaries. The account further stated that the result was the most comprehensive and catastrophic devastation and slaughter yet caused from the air and that Hamburg suffered in four nights what all of Britain suffered during the entire war.[1]

My parents did not buy the newspapers and never talked about the war in the presence of us children. We played along and pretended we did not see the headlines and did not hear the comments at the other tables. It seemed strange how people were frolicking in the sun as horrendous things were happening somewhere else. This juxtaposition made me question the permanence of the beautiful days and of the people around me and made me behold life and those I loved vividly.

Shortly before the end of our vacation, there was another slip under the door. "Michael, come to me."

When I snuck into Hella's room, I was surprised that this time she had put on her nightgown. Her shirt and panties were on the chair. She scooted in bed and opened the book about the squirrel. I took my shorts and socks off. "You should take your underpants off too. People do not wear underpants when they go to bed."

I said it was quite all right to leave them on and slipped into bed.

We read awhile. Then she said that she had practiced the handstand, and that she could do it now. She was sure I could do it too if I did it against the closet to support me.

She got out of bed, put her hands on the rug in front of the closet, and prepared to swing up high. As her legs lifted, she hung in midair for a moment, torn between impulse and restraint as her nightgown slowly started sliding, but she lowered her legs back down, stood up, took her panties from the chair, and slipped them on under her nightgown. She planted her hands in front of the closet once more and flipped her torso and legs up until her feet struck the closet.

"Hold my ankles against the closet," she said.

I stood over her, looking. Her nightgown had fallen, baring her belly and her arched back. Her delicate, white cotton panties held by rubber bands hugged her form. My eyes were fixed on the cloth as it stretched

---

[1] Noble Frankland, *Bomber Offensive: The Devastation of Europe* (New York: Ballatine Books, 1970), 69.

over the mount in front and then went flat over a hollow area between the thighs and curved again over the two rounded hillocks of her bottom. How perfectly symmetrical and smooth she was, where I had a mass of bumps in my pants.

"Let me down," she said. Her face was red, and her eyes were glowing. "See, I can do it. Now you try."

I tried, and she held me up until I collapsed. That she could have any interest in my shapes did not occur to me. Though we were the same height, she was twelve, and I was not yet eight. How could I know that she was curious, not having a brother, and that her desires were beginning to churn?

When we returned to Straβburg, longer than a week had passed when I got a letter from Hella. I answered it, describing how I had thought of her when I had been sitting in the bathtub and other funny things that I knew would make her laugh.

When I started to ask my mother how to spell almost every word, she suggested, "Just write it all, and I will correct it."

I did. The letter turned out to be an orthographic disaster. I had to copy it. Writing it the second time, it did not seem nearly as funny. I was reluctant to send it, but my mother sent it for me.

Not a week later, Hella wrote her reply, in neat handwriting, without mistakes. I did not answer. If I wanted to allude to our sweet afternoons, I had to skip my mother's edit, and Hella would see my glaring shortcomings.

Hella wrote another letter. "Dear Michael, why don't you write?" She resigned herself and waited for next summer.

32

Shortly after our return to Straßburg, we went to Bad Weiss. I walked down to the river with the smug feeling of having a surprise for the old man. Herr Weiss was getting his swimming tackle ready. He was taken aback when I walked past him to the diving board, jumped in, and swam by, fingers together and wide kicks out sideways. His wrinkled face showed the conflicting emotion of approval and annoyance. He had been robbed of the one moment of true satisfaction, when he would let go of the line, and his students would not go under but suddenly realize that they could stay afloat and swim to the ladder.

It was the last day of the season. Bad Weiss closed for the winter.

Teaching me different sports was important to my parents. I needed movement so much that I only could sit still after some of my energy had been run off. My parents accomplished this by swimming in summer and hikes and bike rides during the temperate seasons. In the two last winters in Berlin, they had taught me to ski. Straßburg, in the plain of the upper Rhine, is the warmest corner of Germany. It offered scarcely any snow. However, the highlands of the Black Forest were full of famous cross-country ski areas. My father encouraged my mother to take me to Schönwald for a week of winter sports. For him, vacations were out of the question, as he was occupied with the repeat performances of *Peterchen's Mondfahrt*. Besides, his skiing had never quite reached the consistently vertical stage.

The Kinzig Valley in winter was a different experience than in summer. The change from a merely fallow to an honest white winter progressed over a few turns. As we would see the snow mount on the roofs and trees after every tunnel, our excitement became almost unbearable.

Our skis and luggage were driven from Triberg to Schönwald by the delivery truck of the hotel, zum Hirschen. We were free to climb the switchbacks along the famous waterfalls and marvel at the fantastic ice sculptures that the spray built on the rocks.

After checking into the Hirschen, we wasted no time strapping on our skis. We picked up the trail right behind the hotel and herringboned up to the Höhenweg. Following the crest through pines, my mother packed down the powder while I followed in her tracks to where the trail opened to a slope. Here, we stuck our four poles into the snow in a row. She taught me how to slalom freehanded, passing on the skills she had learned from her father in the Thuringian Forest.

I could never get enough skiing. My mother had to remind me how hungry I was in order to interest me in the return trip. The schuss down from the darkening forest was the most thrilling event of the day. It ended with a large turn around an old barn and a sliding skate stop at the back door of the hotel. After a bath, I stuffed myself with rustic food reminiscent of peacetime and played pool with my mother, reveling in her undivided attention.

When we returned to Straßburg that winter of 1943–1944, the military requested donations of skis for the soldiers in Russia. My parents' skis went to Smolensk or Kharkov or some other icy field of carnage. Only my short skis stayed in the attic next to my mother's photographic equipment.

In spring 1944, my mother took Monika and me to Schönwald one more time. The fresh air and the milk and butter there pepped us up. We were spending more and more nights in the cellar and were subject to ever more severe food rationing, but there was another reason for this excursion.

After some searching through the village, my mother found a farmhouse with a large, empty attic. The owner, Frau Fährenbach, had lost her husband in the war and was looking for some extra income. She agreed to rent this space for storage.

Back in Straßburg, my mother started a campaign with the officials to get a permit to send the valuable antiques from her dowry to Schönwald. Irreplaceable art treasures could be *ausgelagert*, removed from the cities to the country to save them from bombs. Her true reason for trying to move the furniture was, however, different. She and my father were convinced that the war was lost, that the Russians in the east and the allies in Italy would keep advancing. They anticipated an invasion from England, which would push Germany out of France and out of the occupied Alsatia. To imply such notions was dangerous. The official line was that Alsatia with its jewel, Straßburg, had been incorporated permanently into the Third Reich and would stay there for a thousand years. My mother's request to move the furniture across the Rhein into the Reich proper, therefore, had the potential to mark her and her family as traitors. My father was already suspect for refusing to join the Nazi party.

It was safe to move those pieces that were fit for a museum. The list of acceptable items included two carved chairs with nymphs, satyrs and gods, and an octagonal inlaid coffee table, also a Renaissance oak trunk that my father said could store the trousseau of a princess, or hide a lover. Schreckengast's "Still Life with Tulips and Lilac" and Askevolt's landscape of the "Hardanger Fjord" could unquestionably go. With her inexhaustible persistence and calculating charm, my mother also obtained permission to move the Persian rugs, the Ibach grand piano, and the architect's desk of her Great-Grandfather Müller. Of course, the Renaissance oak trunk did not hide a lover, but the china and silver and the Chinese vase with the geishas, as well as books, music, records, and photo albums. The lock that resembled that of a church portal must have discouraged any investigation during transport. In the end, my mother was really taking chances. She had my father bring inconspicuous crates, which were old and weathered, from the theater. Some boards had splintered, and my father replaced them in the cellar. He did this during the day when most tenants of the building were away at work. He hammered as quietly as possible and suppressed his screams and curses whenever he hit his thumb. My mother packed clothes for everyone into those crates. She even included her specially made riding boots and did not have the heart to turn me down when I came carrying my favorite toys in my arms. She hid everything under oriental rugs, and my father managed to nail the lids shut. The movers came and went. Before anyone could check the contents, everything was stored safely in Frau Fährenbach's attic. Back in Straßburg, no visitor suspected how much furniture had been removed. The four-bedroom apartment was still fully furnished, and the number of clothes missing was negligible.

33

I got my first male homeroom teacher during that last year in Straßburg. Perhaps Fräulein Kassel had spread the word that our class was rowdy. We were assigned to one of the few men on the faculty, Herrn Bauer. Since he was young, he must have been exempt from service because of a heart condition or another serious physical ailment. However, he looked healthy to us.

Nothing stands out about Herrn Bauer's teaching except that he enjoyed music, surprisingly, since he seemed to be tone-deaf. One of his favorite songs was, *"Ein Jäger aus Kurpfalz, der reitet durch den grünen Wald und schiesst das Wild daher"* (A Hunter from Kurpfalz, He Rides through the Green Forest and Shoots about the Deer). This lusty song, which incited the boys to sing full force, inspired him to have it sung as a round. He divided the class into two groups, right from the aisle and left from the aisle. Since it was not a round, the two voices chased each other over the obstacles of total dissonance like the hunter's horses over hedges and rocks. We loved it.

The other song he never could resist started innocently enough as a folk song,

Grün, grün, grün sind alle meine Kleider
Grün, grün, grün ist alles was ich hab.
Darum lieb ich alles was so grün ist,
Weil mein Schatz ein Jäger, Jäger ist.

194

Green, green, green are all my clothes
Green, green, green is everything I have.
This is why I love everything that is so green,
Because my sweetheart is a hunter.

Then the teacher said, "White," to prompt the next verse:

White, white, white are all my clothes ...
Because my sweetheart is a miller.

"Brown":

Brown, brown, brown are all my clothes ...
Because my sweetheart is an SA man.

"Black":

Because my sweetheart is an SS man.

When it was time to stop singing, Herr Bauer consoled us that we would learn many more beautiful songs when we would get into the Hitler Jugend. I knew that. Had I not run from the Geiler Platz to the Ruprechtsauer Allee when I heard the drums, pipes, and Glockenspiel coming up in the distance? Had I not walked along on the sidewalk with the other boys who were too little to join when the neat troop of Hitlerjungen in their brown shirts and black shorts would come marching? In front strode the standard bearer, holding a pole high with a flag on each side and tufts of horse hair at the end. Then came the drummers, filling the pauses between songs with their *trum* ... *trum* ... *trumtrumtrum*. Then came the piccolos introducing the next song:

Es zittern die morschen Knochen
Der Welt vor dem grossen Krieg
Wir haben den Schrecken gebrochen,
Für uns war's ein grosser Sieg

Wir werden weiter marschieren,
Wenn alles in Scherben fällt
Und heute gehört uns Deutschland
Und morgen die ganze Welt.

The rotten bones of the world
Shake before the great war.
We have broken the fear;
For us it was a great victory.
We will march on
When everything falls to shards.
And today we own Germany
And tomorrow the whole world.

The enthusiasm and the precision of the marching column inspired me. The song built to a single high and shrill note on the word *shards*. It did sound like smashing glass and could be heard for blocks. My mother became quiet when I told her excitedly that I had seen the Hitlerjugend march. The deep folds on her brow appeared. "I hope the war will be over before they make you join."

My parents' attitude and the school's indoctrination differed noticeably. For the holiday of Hitler's birthday, Herr Bauer had us learn a poem. It was about a child asking another where Adolfitler lived. In the first stanza, does he live in the Chancellery in Berlin? No, says the second child. In the second stanza, does he live in his mountain retreat in the Alps? No, says the second child. Then came the clincher:

Wo mag der Führer sonst noch sein,
Fragt's Kind mit ernstem Sinn.
In unsren Herzen, jung und rein,
Wohnt Adolf Hitler drin.

Where might the Führer live other than that?
Asks the child with serious mind.

In our hearts, young and pure,
Lives Adolf Hitler inside.

As I copied the verses from the blackboard, I had my doubts. My mother had taught me the bedtime prayer:

Ich bin klein
Mein Herz ist rein
Soll niemand drin wohnen
Als Jesus allein.

I am little
My heart is pure
Shall no one live in it
But Jesus alone.

Imagining how Jesus could live in my heart was difficult enough, but Adolfitler also or instead?

My father first laughed when he read the poem. Then he became angry, frustrated about the intrusion of the propaganda ministry into the arts. He hated how it pushed atrocious poetry and plays as long as they espoused and glorified the party agenda. "Why do they make the children learn such crap?" He realized with resignation that I could not get out of learning this poem. As he rehearsed it with me, he read every line mockingly. He made sure I knew that the poem was trash and the message nothing to believe.

Then my mother who overheard us cautioned again, "Michael, you must not tell anyone what we say here at home. Do you understand?"

A more disturbing clash between school and home came when my mother saw my copybook. Herr Bauer, instead of teaching arithmetic, often let us draw on the graph paper. He gave us the topics. He told us how we, the Germans, had made a new weapon. It was a plane without pilot that could fly alone to England and crash and explode in London. He showed us newspaper pictures of the plane. He said that this was called V1 and that the *V* stood for *Vergeltungswaffe* (revenge weapon). I did not know how to deal with this assignment. I copied what everyone else drew—a plane with very short wings and the inscription "V1" and, on the ground, a sign with an arrow, "To London." On the opposite page, I started to trace out what the other boys liked to do. By following the proper squares in the graph paper, swastikas would appear. Then I drew some other symbols.

My mother, seeing my creations, blew up. "What is this?"

"It's a V1," I said meekly.

"Michael, you used to draw such nice pictures of Black Forest landscapes."

Then she saw the swastikas.

As she turned the page she gasped, "What is this!"

"These are stars, Mutti. Jakob showed me how to draw them. You put a triangle upright and a triangle over it upside down, and you get a star."

She grabbed my eraser and tried to erase the stars.

"Don't draw any stars, Michael," she pleaded.

I sensed I had done something dangerous.

"But why?"

"Just don't, okay?"

She erased the stars so furiously the paper crumpled. She tore the page out with the stars and the swastikas on the other side.

"Just don't draw anything like that—no swastikas, no stars."

The dangerous star reappeared in another incident that I witnessed soon after.

My mother and I had planned to go downtown. We stepped out of our apartment building onto the Geiler Platz and were just crossing the square when a band of children came out of a side street, swarming around an old woman. They were mocking her, laughing, pulling on her long gray Loden coat. She was white-haired and wrinkled and tried to make her way across the square. There it was again, a star on her chest like I had drawn into my copybook. It was yellow and as big as the palm of my hand.

My mother tore into the youngsters, spitting out the words with such vehemence as I had never heard before. "Leave this woman alone. You should be ashamed of yourself. Get away from here. Go home."

Fury broke out of her eyes like a blowtorch directed at vermin. The children ran away terrified. The old woman straightened up for a moment, turned and looked at my mother. It was only for a second, but I have not forgotten that look—that glimmer of gratitude that floated on the abysmal suffering in those eyes. Without a word, the old woman turned and shuffled on into the side street.

My mother grabbed my hand, turned around, and ran back into the house and upstairs. She bolted the door and went into the nursery. She did not walk onto the precipitous balcony but looked onto the Geiler Square from behind the curtain. None of the people who questioned my parents' political loyalty had observed her.

Soon after that, little Jakob did not come to school any more, and a different boy was seated next to me. It did not disturb me much. Boys moved or were transferred to other classes quite regularly.

My school was increasing our brainwashing to love and support the Nazi effort. My father's question was how to give me an antidote without getting us arrested.

On the first of May, a national holiday, my father took me along for a walk to the theater. On the way home, he led me through the Stefansplan, a claustrophobic square hemmed in by the walls of high houses in the ancient part of town. The only exits were alleys on each corner. They were so narrow that my father could touch opposite walls by spreading his arms. He told me the following story.

"In the middle ages, a lot of Jews lived in the old town. People used to borrow money from them. The Jews loaned money. They were allowed to take interest. The Christians were not allowed to take interest."

My father explained what interest was. "When the Christians needed money, they turned to the Jews. At the same time, they despised and mocked the Jews as the ones who had killed Jesus and had refused to believe in him. After a while, the people owed the Jews more money than they ever could repay. So what did they do? They filled the Stefansplan with a mountain of straw. They rounded up the Jews, drove them into the square, blocked the alleys, and lit the pile."

We walked out of the old city into the French quarter toward our house. All buildings were adorned with the red flags with the white circle holding the swastika. All citizens were expected to hang their flags out of the window. As in previous years, my parents were not going to display the flag. They still had the one that their neighbor, Görig, had given them in Berlin, but when we had gone on our walk, my mother became scared. Informers checked the streets, making lists of those who did not show the colors. They were probably the same informers who populated the polling places and checked in mirrors fixed above the voting booths. This is how the party had gotten, as my father put it, 105 percent of the vote. My mother hung the flag out of the mansarde window above the roofline, invisible from the street. If Herr Weiss on the second floor, for instance, would ask where our flag was, she could honestly respond that we indeed had one out.

Most people responded to the expectation. The streets were red with flags. As my father and I walked along, I was silent, trying to come to terms with the story about the Stefansplan.

"You know, Michael," he said, "things like that are still going on today."

I tried to lead my father and me away from such depressing thoughts. We were walking past a government building. Two gigantic flags, bigger than I had ever seen, were hung perfectly straight as if to show the full spread of the design, not at an angle like all the others. "Look at these flags," I tried to divert my father. "What do you think of these?"

"Michael, the *Hakenkreuzfahne* (swastika) is an ugly flag. It is not the German flag. The German flag is black, white, and red—three horizontal stripes."

I was not conflicted between what I was told in school and what my parents said. I trusted my parents completely. When my teachers made contradictory comments, I considered them lies. I came to distrust any public pronouncement. My parents had canceled their newspaper after having exclaimed, "It's all lies." They would turn off radio reports about the war with the same vehement response and only listen to classical music.

I did not draw any more swastikas or stars in my copybook, and I kept my mouth shut about what my parents said at home. Only once, I endangered them by my thoughtlessness. I played with a classmate in his living room while his father, a Nazi, was listening to the radio.

Suddenly, my friend became silent while I was happily chattering on. The Wehrmachtsbericht had come on. The father looked at me with such suspicion that it sent a chill down my spine. Why is this boy talking? Do his parents not pay the proper respect to our cause? The truth was, they never listened to the Wehrmachtsbericht. Fortunately, I felt instinctively that I was in danger and fell silent in midsentence.

The danger became pervasive. The siren could howl at any time, night or day. Teachers and classmates could prompt you into saying something wrong. But the threat became even more nonspecific, best expressed in the posters that appeared on the *Litfass Säule*. I saw it every time I stepped on the Geiler Square and at many other places in the city. The poster showed the shadow of a man. A black silhouette of a coat and a hat angled disturbingly across the field. The caption was, *"Pst, Feind hört mit!"* (Pst, enemy listens in!) I was confused. Who was the enemy? When or where was this man creeping up on me? What could he hear me say that was dangerous? What would this fiend do to me? My senses searched for potential perils. I developed the ability to smell danger.

Another poster was pasted close to the *"Feind hört mit"*—the rather jolly cartoon of a robber with an eye patch. The other shifty eye was under the visor of his cap. He carried a big sack on his back. The caption told his name, Kohlenklau (coal scrounger). In school, we were told that we should not be Kohlenklau. Herr Bauer distributed little cardboard hand mirrors. Under the reflective surface, it said, *"Halt Dir den Spiegel vor's Gesicht. Bist Du's oder bist Du's nicht?"* (Hold the mirror in front of your face. Are you it, or aren't you?) Then we turned the mirror around and saw Kohlenklau squinting at us. Herr Bauer did not fail his civic duty and told us the meaning of that funny little man. We should turn off as many lights at home as possible and only use coal when absolutely necessary. Just fire one furnace in the house. He raised his index finger. This was very important for the End Sieg.

Germany ran out of almost everything—coal, gasoline, clothing, housing, food. Food rations were reduced from month to month. Since my parents tried to feed Monika and me adequately, they starved themselves.

Many items disappeared completely. Monika did not know what an orange, lemon, or banana was. My mother tried to boost our supplies by traveling to villages. She helped the farmers with the harvest and received some goods in return. She brought back suitcases full of plums and strawberries that she preserved. For long hours in the kitchen, she boiled fruit and poured it into glass jars. After burning out the oxygen with sticks of sulfur, she closed the jars with glass lids and rubber ring gaskets. She would also get eggs; bread; and sometimes, joy of joys, even butter. Once she brought back some leaves of tobacco. The R6 that my parents liked to smoke in Berlin had long been unavailable. Even the abominable local brand, Rothändle, had become scarce. My father borrowed a tobacco-cutting machine—a metal press the size of a shoebox that would advance the tobacco toward one end, where a razor-sharp knife would cut off thin strands. A nauseating, tarry, brown juice collected in the tin underneath. Perhaps my parents did not dry the tobacco sufficiently, or the farmer had laced it with rhubarb. When they lit their first cigarettes that they had rolled into paper, the stink was so alarming that they became afraid of nicotine poisoning. They extinguished their smoke and threw away the rest of the batch.

The word *Ersatz* (substitute) became so ubiquitous on items that it characterized the time. *"Einen Tropfen von dieser Essenz in die Ofenröhre und es riecht im ganzen Hause"* (One drop of this essence into the oven, and it smells in the whole house). This saying made light of the way the government was expected to solve the meat shortage by providing just the smell.

Coffee was substituted by Katreiner, a brew out of roasted grain. My father, in his Berlin vernacular, called it "Muckefucke," pronounced approximately "Mookafooka." It tasted like its name.

By some stroke of luck my father obtained one hundred real coffee beans as late as spring of 1944. Surely, this would be an unsurpassable surprise for my mother on Easter. For several weeks, he locked himself in the living room, cut out paper into one hundred little Easter eggs and watercolored them in all kinds of elaborate patterns, a front and a back. He glued them together to form tiny pockets. On Easter morning, he stuffed them each with a coffee bean and hid them. He made a site plan so that not a single bean would be lost. Then he called in my mother and us kids.

My mother wondered what in the world would be so precious for my father to have been so secretive. Then, she discovered the first egg between books in the shelf. "Where did you get that?!" she exclaimed when she teased out its content.

"The Easter Bunny."

Monika and I had long found our two hard-boiled eggs while my mother was still searching every nook and cranny. We helped her find the last coffee eggs, consulting the map. Then, my father sat down in the kitchen, clamped the coffee mill between his knees and ground a few select beans. Soon, the animating aroma rose and conjured up the warmth and coziness of prewar times.

34

My parents, Monika, and I tried to carry on our peaceful activities as much as possible. We picked flowers in the Rhein Forest, walked in the Orangerie, and swam at Bad Weiss. My father took me to the Münster one more time. A chilling transformation had overcome the holy place. Cruel gray light filled the sanctuary. The stained-glass windows had been removed and replaced by clear glass. The angels' column had been encased in thick, raw walls of concrete that showed the imprints of plywood. The portals had suffered a similar enclosure. I was not relieved to see these protections at the cathedral, but had the vision of the angels and my Synagogue suffocating in their stone encasements.

Seeing the cathedral, my father recalled that it was his responsibility as *Luftschutzblockwart* to secure the bomb-shelter section of our basement by closing the windows with similar blocks of cement or masonry. He borrowed a flat cart with two large wheels that looked like the one Death was pulling in my dreams, and he and I rumbled to a vacant lot where field stones hid among high weeds. We loaded up the cart, and after several trips, heaped a pile in front of the cellar window facing the Geiler Platz. We also carried enough rocks one by one through the lobby into the inner court to cover the window there. Masons came, built rectangular blocks, and painted a fluorescent strip on the upper edge so that pedestrians would not run into them in the blackout. I was intrigued with this paint. I managed to break off a painted piece of mortar the size of a pea. I took it into my bed under the blanket. Indeed, it sent out the most amazing glow, illuminating part of my palm and even the fine web of the sheet that stretched around it. The greenish light had not lost any mystery since the time when I had crawled into my mother's bed in Berlin and stared at the glowing figures of her travel alarm clock. I had to find a safe place for my treasure. I opened the flat metal container of Onkel Helmut's chocolate and ate the last piece. Then I put my glowing chip in the tin next to the folded foil that still smelled like chocolate. Shortly after that, I added another find. On one of our walks, my father picked up a curious piece of metal from the flat top of a pillar that held a garden gate. The fragment was the size of my little finger with sharp, glossy edges. It had enough definition so that I could discern that it had been torn out of a hollow cylinder. My father explained to me that this was a piece of shrapnel. It must have fallen out of the sky during the last air battle and strangely come to rest on top of this pillar. I ran my finger over the jagged edges and rotated the metal in the sun. I observed the difference in reflection between the smooth, machined and the grainy, broken surfaces. I carried this little war sculpture home and added it to my collection.

Then came June 7. My father and I were walking from the Geiler Platz to the Brandplatz down the Schweighäuser Strasse. It was an overcast day around noon. The impact that my father's message made locked the location and time in my mind.

"There is an invasion in France. The English and Americans have come across the channel and have invaded Normandy. Now the war will soon be over."

I felt like jumping for joy. The weight of war had suddenly been lifted.

Now that the Allies were advancing on the continent, my parents were thankful that they had managed to store some of their antiques across the Rhine; yet, most had remained at our apartment. How could any of our belongings still be saved? The authorities would see any attempt at moving more furniture as lack of trust in the Wehrmacht. We would be apprehended as traitors and dealt with accordingly. Our possessions had to stay.

In the summer of 1944, we took one more vacation in the Black Forest. My father was still exempt from the draft. In spite of retreats on all fronts and the nightly bombings, Goebbels and the Propaganda Ministerium had ordered all theaters and concert halls to stay open, to give the illusion of normalcy and to boost the morale of the battered people. As usual, my father had his two months of summer vacation, July and August. My parents decided to spend some time in the highlands of the Black Forest before dropping down to Offenburg. They did not go to the familiar Schönwald, but a day's bicycle ride farther south to a tiny spa near Neustadt. The village, which had the fitting name, Friedenweiler (Peace Hamlet), had been untouched by the war. Drawing from the surrounding farms, the Kurhaus still served adequate food.

Reports from the battlefields were so disastrous that my father expected the notice of his induction any day. Cherbourg had fallen, and thirty thousand troops had been captured. The chance of turning back the invasion vanished. In Italy, the allies had taken Rome and were rapidly moving north. In the east, the Russians were approaching the Polish border.

My parents cherished the quiet days with the bittersweet intensity of those who know that hard times, perhaps even death, wait right around the corner. With a sense of melancholic gratitude, they drew in the smell of fresh-cut hay as they wandered through the meadows to the monastery pond in the valley. A film captured me swimming to a raft or little Monika, naked as in paradise, throwing her red ball up in the air. My parents strived to make every day memorable and precious, even when the weather was inclement. We hiked to the Titisee in the rain. When it cleared, we rented a rowboat. As my father pulled the oars, he told us how, in 1929, he and Hans Wiegener had crossed these waters listening to the echoes of their songs. Now he heard complaints about being cold, getting hungry, or being bored. In spite of all the little irritations, I doubt he would have traded his role as husband and father for the freedom of a wayfarer.

My father drew closer to us with every remaining day. On July 20, we had to say good-bye to Friedenweiler. We biked down the Höllental to Freiburg one more time. On this trip, I drove my own bike, which filled my mother with great trepidation. The summer before, on a tour around Offenburg, I had lost control on a steep hill and had shot past my parents. My mother had jumped off her bike, screaming. Letting Monika roll into the dust, she ran down the hill after me while I raced toward the next village with the speed of a car. To stop myself, I steered over to the side and somersaulted into the ditch. I only cut my little finger. On the hairpin turns in the Höllental, however, such a failure could be fatal. My mother did not enjoy the vistas until I had eased down past the chasm of Hirschsprung, and the valley leveled and opened to the Himmelreich.

Freiburg was already visible in the distance when we came upon an accident. A driver had underestimated the height of his truck and had been trapped halfway under a low bridge. Driving past on the bicycle trail, I impressed my father, suggesting that the driver let the air out of the tires. I had read this solution in a puzzle book. Not long after, my father was to recognize this bridge under entirely different circumstances.

When we rolled into Freiburg and checked into the Bären, we noticed that everyone in the hotel was looking angry or disturbed. My father asked the concierge what had happened. The old man looked at my father as if he had come from the moon.

"Haven't you heard? There has been an assassination attempt on the Führer!"

"We're just coming from Friedenweiler," my father said apologetically.

During dinner, the news came over the loudspeaker. Everyone fell silent instantly and stopped eating. A bomb had exploded during a meeting in the Führer's headquarters; a conspiracy was suspected. The Führer had been injured but not critically.

The tension in the dining room was palpable, as if everyone was a suspect. Any false move, like a clearing of the throat that could be taken for a chuckle, a distracted picking up of a bite, or a whisper to a spouse, could have led to arrest and questioning.

When my father looked back to this day, he would contemplate, "Millions of lives could have been saved if Stauffenberg would have succeeded. But," he would continue and nod slowly, "perhaps the cup of wrath was not yet full."

Perhaps that was why someone in that headquarters moved the briefcase with the bomb away from Hitler's feet and behind a concrete table support. Perhaps that was why the destruction of Germany had to go on ten more months until her final annihilation.

My parents were eager to get home. They could no longer escape the storm of war. My request to climb the Freiburger Münster was denied. I sent one last, longing glance up to the red sandstone steeple on the way to the station.

35

The number of alerts had intensified. In August, they came so frequently that my father stopped counting in his diary. We rushed into the cellar night and day, up to three times in twenty-four hours.

The heaviest attack was on August 11, starting shortly before three o'clock in the afternoon and lasting for forty-five minutes. After the droning and the rumbling, word soon spread that the center of town had been bombed. My father made an exception and bought a newspaper. I stared at the photographs. The Münster had been hit. One bomb destroyed the north portal, the one my father and I used to enter the sanctuary. The other had fallen behind the altar, taking part of the eight-sided east tower on its way. Also the Rohan Palace had been hit. Other bombs had destroyed houses in the old alleys around the cathedral. The paper estimated loss of lives at around four hundred. My parents did not comment on the dead. It was such a small number compared to the usual casualties in the mainland cities. Nor did they comment on the damage. They had no inkling how the pictures of the bombed Münster disturbed me. I could only have been similarly shocked if my oak in Berlin had been split by lightning. What would future air raids do?

Our days in Straßburg were numbered. Onkel Mülmann was drafted and had to depart immediately. Even I considered it grotesque that this stage designer, this delicate artist and nobleman, was inducted into a tank division.

On the twenty-second was my ninth birthday. When I was allowed into the room where my parents had set up the birthday table, it looked just as plentiful as ever. They had been searching all over for presents. There was a paperback collection of jokes and puzzles, drawing paper, pencils, and a fairy tale quartet. The only activity toy they had found was a war game. It was a submarine that could torpedo a cruiser if aimed correctly. In the center of the table was the birthday cake. My mother had saved the ingredients for several weeks. It was the traditional circular pound cake with raisins dusted with powdered sugar. Nine flickering candles were mounted on the margin of the plate. The big candle signifying life burned in the hole in the middle. The warm glow lit a jubilant bouquet of dahlias. The flowers were as perfect as if they had been plucked from the garden in Glienicke.

Two days after my birthday, my father came home telling us that Herr Weiss had died. I knew that Herr Weiss had been ill, for my father had kept visiting him for a while. The day before, he had found the seventy-nine-year-old man sitting in his house propped up on pillows in a lawn chair, not as usual on the deck close to the water. He lay there in a daze for some time. Then he recognized my father with a joyful jolt, reached out to hold his hand, and held on to it for a long time. He was almost silent and just indicated that it was too hot for him down on the decks. His faint good-bye had the special emphasis of finality.

Now my father returned with the news of his parting. He came directly from seeing him dead in his bed laden with flowers. He was clean-shaven and dressed in a black frock, a necktie, and a white, starched collar. A little cross with the crucified savior lay on his chest. My father said that the old man looked so calm and removed from any torment that he radiated eternal peace. The tale about Herr Weiss's death touched me curiously. I remembered how I had feared the old swimming teacher and how I had always watched my form when I swam past him. His death struck me differently than Onkel Helmut's had. The fall of my hero had caused nothing but disbelief. This time, my regret had a disturbing mixture of relief. And yet, a swim at Bad Weiss was unthinkable without the old man. I knew our visits to the river were over, just like our visits to the Rohan Palace and the Münster.

We celebrated my mother's thirty-third birthday on August 25. It was also my parents' *Rosenhochzeit* (rose wedding)—the tenth anniversary. That night, the radio announced the *Totalen Krieg* (total war). As part of the supreme effort, all theaters were to close immediately.

My father's induction notice was already on its way, ordering him to report for boot camp on September 1, in Kornwestheim, near Stuttgart.

On the twenty-ninth, we left Straßburg for Offenburg. My father did not want us to stay behind but to find shelter in the Black Forest until the war ended. He thought we could stay in Schönwald with Frau Fährenbach or with Tante Teddy. At that time, she was also in the Black Forest in Bad Dürrheim. She had taken little Christian there from Berlin. Christian had been struck with polio. She tried to free his paralyzed limbs in the renowned bog baths there.

Before we left our apartment, we carried the antique walnut dining table and the inlaid, round table down to the Stoebers. They had agreed to keep the pieces safe for us. We bid a hasty good-bye. Rain threatened, and we wanted to get going.

We carried our bicycles out of the familiar basement. We took one last look at the benches and seats in the aisle and the emergency passage with the ax leaning on it. How many hours had we lingered in this dark corridor? Then we were out on the Geiler Strasse, heading for the Rhine Bridge. Storm clouds brewed over the city. A bolt of lightning illuminated the Münster; the damaged roof and gouged east tower stood out black in the light. Then rain pulled dense curtains over the dark outline. Rumbles and flashes followed us across the bridge.

My father turned in his saddle. "What a coincidence! Remember Berlin, when we left? The thunderstorm?"

Somewhere in the deep layers of my mind, I sensed I would never see my apartment again. I would never see again my bed and the archipelago on the wall. Gone were the toy chest with the chocolate tin and the big black closet with the hiding place for nightmares. Gone were all the other rooms so familiar that I could have walked through them with my eyes closed.

Our stay in Offenburg was too short and hectic for Hella's and my friendship to grow any further. I set up my war game in her playroom and showed her how I could explode the cruiser by a direct hit from my submarine. She was not impressed.

The next morning, we took my father to the railroad station. My mother embraced him so tightly, as if she wanted to prevent him from going. She wiped off her tears when he followed the conductor's call, "*Einsteigen*" (All aboard). He appeared at a window. My parents held hands until the train got into motion. "Be careful," was my mother's last plea.

We followed his waving handkerchief until the train curled out of sight. My emotions swung between the sorrow of seeing my father leave and the expectation of my mother's undivided attention. I also considered a weighty prospect with pride. I would be the man of the house, responsible for taking care of my mother and Monika.

My extended task was put to the test immediately. The next morning, my mother took the train back to Straßburg to fetch as many valuables as she could carry. She left me in charge of Monika, even though Frau Schimpf had agreed to keep an eye on us children. I had become used to watching out for Monika. At alerts, when my parents had been at the club or the theater, I had bundled her in the old sleeping bag and carried her into the cellar.

My mother returned from Straßburg dragging two suitcases full of important documents, jewelry, and clothing. She had hurried to get out of the city. She had heard the distant, dull thuds of heavy artillery that blew in on the west wind from Nancy. The official explanation for the rumbling was maneuvers.

"Maneuvers! Imagine!" My mother told us about the sounds. "Who needs maneuvers at this time?" She breathed easier when the train crossed the Rhein Bridge.

We never saw the Stoebers again. Any contact was broken until they finally answered a letter many years after the war. The French had confiscated all our belongings, even the tables that we had placed into their custody.

36

After my father left for the army, my mother decided to move to the Black Forest immediately. Our departure from the Sonne and the Schimpfs was made easier when Monika dumped a bottle of red nail polish on the genuine baroque sofa. My mother's attempt to correct the mishap with acetone made it worse, emphasizing the red spot on the green upholstery with a bleached ring. Herr Schimpf was very upset. He declined my mother's offer to pay for the damage, pointing out that this priceless antique could never be repaired or replaced. However, times were too serious to hold grudges. The day we said good-bye, the friendship was patched.

On the trip up the Kinzig Valley my mother was subdued. She let the spectacular views go by, worried whether we would find shelter in Schönwald. She wheeled her bicycle up the switchbacks with Monika in the basket. I followed her, pushing my bike and trying to glimpse the thundering waterfall through the trees. A truck from the hotel zum Hirschen labored up the incline, smoking and stinking. The truck was powered by a *Holzvergaser*, a black, vertical, round iron kettle behind the cabin, in which wood was burned and smothered to generate carbon monoxide for the engine. The dwindling gasoline was reserved for the military. To my mother's satisfaction, the truck carried our luggage and my father's bicycle.

We gained the high plateau and rolled into Schönwald. It was packed with women and children evacuated from cities in the Rhine Valley,

Karlsruhe, Mannheim, and Ludwigshaven. The Hotel Hirschen could only give us a room for three days. Then a new shipment of *Evakuierte* would arrive, and all rooms were requisitioned. My mother immediately started looking for room in one of the farmhouses. First, we visited Frau Fährenbach. We took our bikes there to leave beside our furniture. My mother saw with relief our belongings well stored in a corner of the attic.

If we could only stay here, she could have an eye on the things until the end of the war. She hoped my father would be able to join us then and we could find a home, but one look around the attic told her that we could not stay. Mattresses were laid out for the children of the mothers who were quartered downstairs.

While my mother, leading Monika by the hand, pleaded from house to house for lodging, I ran free. I found trails through the woods that my mother and I had skied. Without the equalizing blanket of snow, the forest was full of surprises, hollow stumps to investigate, rocks to crawl under, and trickles of water to catch in my cupped hands.

Most of the details of our short stay in Schönwald blur in my mind, except for two. On one of the strolls, I followed a rivulet from the mossy spring into a high meadow. The water spread through a lush depression marked by blue-green tufts of rushes. I found a barefoot girl sitting on the side of the dell, absorbed in some handiwork. As I came closer and squatted beside her, I saw that she had gathered rushes in her skirt. She was tying three of them together with a knot on one end and was braiding them. I watched the rhythm of her fingers folding over and over until she joined them into a ring. She held it up to examine it and, with an expression of satisfaction, put it on her head.

"Do you know how to braid?" she asked me. "Get some rushes, and I'll teach you."

I took my shoes off and pulled long rushes out of the sucking ground.

On the rare occasion that I have braided something in my life, I always have thought about this girl who taught me on that warm September afternoon above the valley. Like carrying water without spilling, braiding became another skill I cherished as having been taught to me with female affection.

The second memorable event of my stay in Schönwald was my first full-length movie at a makeshift theater in a community center. The projector in the middle of the room was directed at a bedsheet stretched on the wall. There were pauses when the reels had to be rewound although the reels were many times bigger than the ones from our five-minute home movies.

My young fantasy drew me into the screen as if I were a participant. At the same time, some protective reserve nagged in the back of my mind. Stay back. This is only a movie. This conflict soon gave me a sick headache. How different was the viewing of my home movies when I freely participated in the reruns of my reality.

All the children packed into the room seemed to enjoy the show, so I stayed. First came the *Wochenschau* (newsreel). Soldiers around a cannon concealed by trees fired into the sky. The barrel towered above the steel helmets. The gun flashed and seemed to punch forward and recoil as if it was delivering a blow. The children became quiet, thinking about their fathers still out there somewhere or fallen.

The feature was *Zirkus Renz*. It disturbed me to neither understand the plot nor the motivations of the beautiful trapeze acrobat and the two men who pursued her. When the woman fell off the trapeze, I was troubled that neither I nor anyone else in the audience could help her. When the film was finally over, I ran out of the stuffy darkness into the meadows, looking for the girl who could braid. I decided the movies of the adults were not for me.

While I roamed the fields and woods for three days, my mother went from house to house. In spite of her persistence, she could not find a place for us to stay. Our time in the Hirschen was up. We boarded the Black Forest train again and moved on to Bad Dürrheim. Tante Teddy embraced us at the station.

Next to Tante Teddy stood Eva-Maria. I had not seen her since Berlin. She looked at me with her big, brown, wide-set eyes. Did she remember the man with the golden hair? She had grown and was almost as tall as I. Her glistening, dark hair was still in bangs. It framed her high, Asian cheekbones in straight strands. How familiar were her features—her peach complexion; her little, curved nose; and her delicate, upturned lips. Our hug was awkward, shy, and quick.

We deposited our suitcases in Tante Teddy's room and went to the hospital to see Christian. My mother had prepared me about the polio paralysis. I saw him without shock. My mother could hardly hide her grief when she faced how disabled he was. Tante Teddy had talked about great improvements effected by the famous warm bog baths, comparing Christian's present condition to his desperate state at the height of his illness. He had been paralyzed from the neck down. An iron lung had taken over his breathing. Physical therapy and immersion in the black tubs had improved his six-year-old body. Control of his right side was coming back. My mother, however, was dismayed by the remaining afflictions. Last time she had seen Christian, he had been an athletic boy, running and skipping along on sturdy little legs. Now his left leg was still lame, and his foot hung, drooping and lifeless. He had not regained the use of his hands and had to be spoonfed.

In spite of his paralysis, Christian seemed to be in good spirits. He enjoyed the attention and service he could command. Moreover, with his body so restricted, his brilliant mind took off on wild spins. He had inherited his grandfather's wit along with that sparkle in his clear blue eyes. When we loaded Christian into a stroller, he encouraged me to push him faster and faster along the walkways of the park. The sharp turns on two wheels were the height of his enjoyment. He craved movement. Because of his physical inactivity, he had trouble going to sleep. When lying in bed in the dark, he had developed the nervous habit of twisting his head from side to side for hours until he finally drifted off. If turned on his stomach, he would bounce his forehead on his pillow incessantly. The nurses had no good idea how to stop him other than tying his head down in the bed. Tante Teddy, still plagued by nightmares of seeing Christian in the iron lung, did not permit any such restrictions.

After visiting Christian in the hospital, my mother tried to find a place for us in Bad Dürrheim. Tante Teddy's room was so crammed that we could only impose for a few days. She took my mother into her double bed, where she had slept with Eva-Maria. They found a cot for her. I slept on the couch and Monika on two easy chairs shoved together. During the night, the chairs would separate because of her squirming and let her fall into the crack.

When the room was set up for the night, there was no room left for walking. My mother and Tante Teddy stayed out late in the restaurant, while we children were supposed to go to sleep. Monika was the first to doze off. Once she had fallen asleep, sucking her thumb and twisting her blonde curls, she never woke up. When Eva-Maria and I heard her even, deep snore, we flicked on the night-light and transformed the double bed into a trampoline. Eva-Maria was neither as old nor as agile as Hella, but she could manage a quick somersault. Looking for more excitement, we perfected our vaulting by diving from the headboard. This went on until we synchronized our jumps. An ominous sharp cracking sound in the bed put an end to our romping. Luckily, my mother and Tante Teddy slept so quietly that the bed held for the next two nights.

All my mother's efforts to find a room failed. Bad Dürrheim seemed even more crowded than Schönwald. Besides *Evakuierte*, mainly from Stuttgart, Pforzheim, and Heilbronn, there were the patients and their families. We could not stay here. Tante Teddy was also planning to leave for Hohen Lychen, north of Berlin, where Christian could continue his physical therapy close to their home. Onkel Horsa planned to escape from his dental practice and the raids and take the short trip north to visit his family there.

My mother saw no other possibility than to move in with her mother in Erfurt. The trip was daunting. Stations were hit routinely, and trains were attacked on the tracks. Surprisingly, most trains still ran with the proverbial punctuality.

On the morning of our departure, my mother was folding the makeshift beds and packing our four large suitcases. Eva-Maria and I played ball in the front yard. As I caught the ball she had tossed high in the air, I saw something in the sky that stopped me in amazement. Tiny, silver crosses arranged in triangles moved slowly across the azure sky. More and more appeared from behind the western horizon like a band of sparkles. I could not count them. There were hundreds. We called our mothers out to see this. My mother did not say a word, just shuddered. Tante Teddy analyzed that they were flying in from France and wondered where they were headed—Augsburg? München?

Time for our departure came. Tante Teddy and Eva-Maria took us to the station. The gloom and danger of the future made the good-bye desperate. The usual parting wish of *Alles Gute* (all good things) came from the depth of the women's hearts and meant nothing less than the wish for survival.

On the train, my mother became nervous. We had to transfer in Kork to catch the *Fernzug*, the long-distance train from Basel to Berlin. Since Kork was a hamlet whose only distinction was to be a railroad junction, the *Fernzug* stopped for one minute only. My mother tried to think of ways she could get Monika and me and the four heavy suitcases on the train that quickly. We needed to make it. It was the only train that would take us directly to Erfurt.

We were alone waiting on the platform. The train flew into the station pushing air that pressed us back. A chain of windows flickered by and slowed down. We heard the screech of the stop and then a deceptive quiet punctuated only by the impatient couch of the steam engine. No one got off. We found ourselves close to a door, but the steps up to the narrow passage were dauntingly high. My mother opened the heavy door, shoved Monika and me in, and dragged the suitcases close. The conductor, the man with the fire-red, lacquered belt diagonally across his chest, grabbed the suitcases and hoisted them into the train. He helped my mother up the steps, closed the door behind her, and jumped on the running board of the next car as the train started moving. After we found seats, it took my mother until we left the eastern foothills before she could grasp and comment on what just had happened. An official of the *Reichsbahn* had stepped out of his assigned duties to help a passenger with her children and luggage. Did this really happen?

Night fell, and the details of the compartment faded. The people and the luggage in the nets above disappeared. The window darkened. The evening glow on the rhythmically dipping telephone wires vanished. There was not a single light on the train, which howled through complete darkness, as if it were detached from the earth. Only the *tap tap tap tap* indicated that it was still running on tracks. Somewhere in the middle of the night, the tapping slowed down until it stopped completely. During air raids, trains were to stay in the open field. I don't know how long we stood there, for I nodded off. When I woke up, the tapping had resumed, and gray light filtered through the window. The train was pulling into a station that showed heavy damage. All the glass of the roof was gone, and the steel supports were twisted or missing. Several cars of disturbing appearance sat on a sidetrack. I saw through broken windows into a charred interior illuminated by ragged holes in the ceiling. The outside paint was charred from fire, and the metal was punctured by holes with edges bent inward.

On another track, a gang of prisoners was swinging pickaxes and stuffing gravel under the ties. A soldier with a *Karabiner* (rifle) stood watch in the weeds. I don't know which sight stirred me more, the wrecked train or the stooped humanity under the gun.

The three of us were relieved to get off the train in Erfurt and find Omi yoo-hooing and waving. In the taxi on the way to Omi's apartment, my mother told her about our travels since we'd fled Straßburg. Omi seemed to only get half the story. She interrupted with piercing "*Wie?*" cupping her hand behind her less deaf right ear. She had left her hearing aid at home. She could not get any batteries for it.

At Louisenstrasse 3, Martchen had prepared the bedroom wing for us. She had set up the first room with a double bed and a child's bed for my mother and Monika. The room had a spacious alcove with a desk and chair close to the only window. The window was wide and high and opened over the hazelnut tree in the back court. The second room was smaller. In it, Martchen had put fresh linen on the fancy bed that had high, swinging walnut head- and footboards and turned finials on the corners. It was meant for me. Martchen busied her little hands putting our clothes from the suitcases into the closets. She stepped on a footstool to reach the bar. With satisfaction, I realized that I had grown taller than she. She urged my mother to call on her for anything we needed and pointed out that her room was still the last room in the wing. "Frau Annemarie undoubtedly remembers. It's just past the room set up for Michael."

37

I could not wait to run to Omi Bauer's villa and see Maria Barbara. I bounded downstairs and slipped through the private gate of the picket fence into Omi Bauer's garden. I ran along the path of crunchy river gravel, past the circular fountain, the garden house, the dilapidated carriage building, and the garages. I pushed open the ivy-framed, arched back entrance of the villa. In the far-reaching living room, I found Omi Bauer sitting in a high armchair at the window. Tante Ellen sat on the couch, smoking.

"Michael," Omi Bauer exclaimed shakily, bringing her gnarled hands from underneath her crochet blanket. I ran to her. She took my hand between hers and looked at me, while her head nodded, yes, yes.

"He's taller than Maria Barbara," admitted Tante Ellen. I went over and shook Tante Ellen's hand. She was not one to show much emotion. Nothing wrinkled her beautiful face.

I drew back to Omi Bauer, who urged me to sit on a footstool close to her. I was in awe of the old lady. I knew nothing about her past, nothing about the power she'd once had as the widow of Ernst Müller, the owner of I. C. Schmidt, the largest nursery in Germany. I knew nothing about her socialite status as wife of the dashing Major Bauer. I did sense the afterglow of her wealth and the respect that everyone in the family showed her.

I tried to think of something to say. "You know the scooter you gave me? I rode it a lot, in the Orangerie. But it is in Straßburg now. Then I got a bicycle. That's in the Black Forest."

After a while I asked, "Where is Maria Barbara?"

"She is in school. School started three weeks ago."

I did not stay long but announced I would come back in the afternoon. Returning to Omi's apartment, I could hear Tante Anneliese from the landing. Living with Omi had caused her voice to become shrill and loud. She sat tall and erect in the living room, wearing a nurse's uniform and a starched cap with a red cross clipped into her blonde hair. She drew me into a warm, strong embrace.

"Boy, have you grown!" she shouted.

Orbiting Tante Anneliese and climbing over the furniture was Jens-Peter. He was four now and sturdy as ever. Tante Anneliese was ready to go to work. She brought Jens-Peter over for Omi to watch, which meant Martchen took care of him. Since Tante Anneliese had left us in Straßburg, she'd finished nurse's training. She'd found employment at a hospital and advanced to surgical nurse. It was hard work to put soldiers back together, but it satisfied her to aid the cause for which her husband had died.

In the afternoon, I returned to the villa. Maria Barbara sat in the far corner at the fortress of the I. C. Schmidt company desk, doing homework. If she was pleased to see me, she didn't let it show.

"Mother told me that you would come over."

"Can you come play?" I asked from the door.

"I don't know. I should finish this." Then with an, "Oh, well, I'll do it later," she jumped off the chair. In one elegant movement, she stretched up her arms, arched her back, and turned two perfect cartwheels. As her plaid skirt and her brown hair were flying, she finished right next to me. Then she looked up with her freckled, turned-up nose as if she were thinking, *Try this sometime, Michael. I bet you can't do it.* But she said, "Let's go."

Outside, she picked up a piece of chalk and drew a hopscotch on the rhomboid-patterned concrete in front of the garages. She chose a piece of river gravel from the walkway and threw it into the first field, immediately hopping over it on one leg, and suddenly spreading her legs to hit both fields at the arms and the head. Having played hopscotch for years, she beat me handily, which brought a smile of triumph to her freckled face.

As the afternoon wore on, I was intrigued how winning brought out her air of being special. She was aware of her nimble figure and her pretty dress, of the far-flung dwellings where she lived, and of the past wealth of her family. Above all, she had a touch of the mysterious female, as if she was thinking, *You are a boy, you see, Michael, and you'll never quite understand me.* I played into her hands every time I cast my admiring glances at her.

As we got less into playing hopscotch and more into talking, she pointed out that she was actually my aunt, even though she was a month younger than I. She mentioned what I knew already, that her mother, my Tante Ellen, was my Omi's half sister and no less than seventeen years younger. Her mother was still beautiful. She gathered her rich, chestnut hair in curls on top and dressed in bold colors. In contrast, Omi concealed her imposing figure in opulent but gray or black dresses. She wore her hair in a bun and was deaf.

My mother called from the balcony. Tante Anneliese had invited us for dinner at her apartment, which was diagonally across the street, Louisenstrasse 21B. When we visited there, I was taken with the large building. It was newer and sturdier than Omi's apartment duplex. Tante Anneliese's ground-floor apartment had high, airy, and sunny rooms. Exploring the surroundings, I discovered the most exciting features of Tante Anneliese's place—a river that flowed behind the white picket fence of the backyard and a mill that turned its stomping wheels a short distance downstream. Children's voices coming from the upper floors were an added attraction. Tante Anneliese's apartment, Omi's duplex, Omi Bauer's villa, and the gardens in between provided the stage for the final months of the war.

My mother enrolled me in school. On his last day in Offenburg, my father had pointed out how important this school year was. I had to pass the entrance exam for the Oberschule at its conclusion. I knew he was worried how I would ever make it with such dismal spelling.

I entered the school with apprehension. The Gudrunschule in Straßburg had been modern. The Kasino Schule seemed ancient, like a monastery. We entered the schoolyard through a wrought-iron gate that stretched between the dark stone building and the river Gera. Across the river was a church with a roof that seemed as high and long as that of the Straßburger

Münster. "The Barfüsser Kirche," my mother pointed out. "This is where Omi and my father got married in 1909." For her, these were familiar and safe grounds.

After my mother talked to the principal, I started immediately. We ascended the wide, old, wooden staircase. The sun cast several bright spots on the steps. I heard music from somewhere behind the doors. It was a canon I knew:

Himmel und Erde müssen vergehn.
Aber die Musici, aber die Musici
Aber die Musici bleibet bestehn.

Heaven and earth must go away
But the music, but the music
But the music will always stay.

I have always found encouragement in unexpected patches of sun in a disheartening place, just as I have always found hope in hearing unexpected music in the stillness of desolation. Those encouragements eased this simple walk up the stairs toward the door of uncertainty.

A voice behind the door sounded like an old man. My mother knocked. The voice stopped with, "Just a moment." Then came steps. The door opened, and my future fourth class teacher stood before me. He was very old and hunched but quite tall. His jacket, which hung from his rounded shoulders, seemed permeated with chalk. Indeed, a lifetime of handling chalk seemed to have incorporated itself into his clothes, his hair, and even his skin. He looked at my mother and me and knew immediately what this was about. In these turbulent times, boys came and went continually.

He shook my mother's hand. "I am Herr Klaus." Somewhere behind his stern, old face was a friendly glow that encouraged me. I felt he liked me.

As my mother turned to go, he took me into the class where about fifty boys had been trying to look around him to see the new one. There was a free seat for me in the back third of the room, close to my accustomed location. All boys cranked their heads to eye me up and down. Then the lesson went on.

I looked around. Everything in the room confirmed that this was an old school. The wide floorboards were worn and uneven. The windowsills had lost their varnish. The closet in the corner was gray and peeling. My school bench showed scratches and stains, traces of student boredom, initials, caricatures of teachers, and rivulets of ink that had been let flow into worn cracks.

As the classes progressed, the teachers matched the ancient environment. Since all able-bodied men had been drafted when *Totaler Krieg* began, these substitutes had been called out of retirement. Their style of teaching harkened back forty years. The podium with the rickety table and chair indicated their authority. Enforcing submission was the basis of their methods. Discipline was the students' first duty. Any question about this point was soon clarified when the teacher opened the closet in the corner and selected from an assortment of sticks a suitable one for the punishment.

One student, a large, quiet boy, would bring in sticks, nice and straight and stripped of leaves and branches for the teacher. Hazelnut was preferred. It whistled through the air, and its elasticity imparted a special snap. What was the punishment procedure? The culprit, who had been caught whispering to a neighbor or shooting a paper wad with a rubber band or flicking his finger against the ear of the boy in front was called up by name. "Come forward," commanded the teacher, while going for his rod. The offender had to bend down and put his elbows on the bench. The teacher grabbed the boy's pants at the belt and pulled them taut. Then he meted out a number of strikes commensurate with the offense, usually between two and four.

The frequency with which a teacher availed himself of this method depended on his character. Herr Klaus used it reluctantly with an expressionof regret, only to correct crass, disorderly behavior. Our second teacher, though, an erect, little old man, completely bald, seemed to believe that little boys had a malicious, independent streak that had to be tamed. A faint smile of satisfaction played on his face when he saw the boy's reaction after every hit.

I was naturally well-behaved and was confident I could stay out of trouble. I eagerly learned all the rules. When the teacher entered, we had to stand at attention until he mounted his podium and gave the command, "*Setzen*" (sit down). We had to line up two by two while silently going to recess and had to hold hands while going down the stairs.

Down in the court, we let go and walked to the fence above the river. We watched what floated by or counted the doves on the massive church roof across. Recess was also the designated time for a bathroom visit. The bathroom was in the oldest part of the school, partitioned off in a series of low cross vaults like in the crypt in the Straßburger Münster. A long, low, stainless steel trough extended the length of one wall. A dozen boys could stand in a row with the others waiting behind. I soon caught on to a customary competition, which was who could pee the highest on the wall. To gain heights of my parabolic wet spot on the wall, I did not have to use some of the desperate measures of the smaller boys, like standing on tiptoes or pulling up on their spray guns excessively. I won merely by my size and the force of my bladder. This ability helped me toward acceptance in the group. So far, I had received a moderate amount of admiration for being tall, blonde, and blue-eyed.

The large extent of the crypt behind the bathroom was used for a gym. Here, the bald old man drilled us in push-ups, jumping jacks, knee bends, and running around in circles. I got along with him all right by blending in with the fifty others. I do not think I learned much from him.

He also taught singing, which was my favorite subject. The man was too old to know the Hitlerjugend songs that had made up the bulk of our repertoire at the Gudrun Schule. He had us sing good old *Volkslieder* (folk songs).

One day, he picked "*Ein Jäger aus Kurpfalz.*" I thought, *Hey, I know this song from the Gudrun Schule. I even know how to sing it like a round.* Lustily, I started singing the second voice as if I had to carry the part all by myself.

The bald old man stopped the singing. "Who was that?"

I stood up.

"Come forward."

Trying to explain that I had learned to sing the song as a round, even though it was not a round, would only be taken as further insubordination. I bent over and received my punishment. Three times the hazel rod whistled. After each strike of surprising bite, the bald old man paused and looked down on my pained expression with satisfaction.

When I went back to my bench and sat down on my sore bottom, the boys looked furtively to see how I was taking it. When the teacher turned, I shrugged my shoulder and even managed a smile. This was nothing.

From that hour on, I was accepted by the group. "He didn't cry."

During punishment, a few boys could not help themselves and did cry. However, most avoided this embarrassment and, with repeated beatings, took the stick quite stoically. The students accepted the punishment of anyone who "*tanzte aus der Reihe*" (danced out of the row) as part of the curriculum that would be repeated every few days. They did anything the teacher expected, without questioning. Perhaps I was the only one who knew that lessons could be conducted without beating the children into submission. In this old school in Erfurt, I experienced the primary education of my parents' generation and as it had been for all previous generations back to the Middle Ages.

Another old custom concerned the students' behavior among themselves. It was called *Klassenkeile* (class-thrashing). One morning, during Herr Klaus's eleven o'clock class, a small slip torn out of a copybook was passed secretly from student to student. When the neighbor on my bench put it in front of me, I saw that it had "Konrad" written on it.

I knew Konrad better than any of the others. He lived close to me, and we walked home together. On these strolls, we had had experiences together that were far more interesting than school. One time, we watched a pair of men trying feverishly to cut down a huge tree that stood on the bank of the Gera until two policemen walked on the scene and arrested them. Another time, we climbed over a wall into a park that had been converted from a cemetery and found a human femur in the bushes. I liked Konrad, with his disheveled brown hair and ingenious smile. So why was his name on the slip?

I turned with a questioning look to my neighbor.

"*Klassenkeile*," he whispered. "Pass it on."

When Herr Klaus turned to the blackboard, I passed the slip across the aisle, still not knowing what this was about. When school let out, I was going to find out.

When I entered the school yard, all boys, except Konrad, formed an alley in front of the gate. Konrad stood inside alone. He could only reach the street if he walked through this alley. With an air of resigned acceptance, he entered between the students and was hit by a blow from the first boy. I stood at the end of the row close to the gate, wondering what he had done. He must have offended the class somehow. He must have danced out of the row. As Konrad walked on, I saw that every student was allowed one hit. One boxed his ear. One shoved into his chest. Most whacked their fist onto his back. Konrad looked bewildered. He did not try to protect himself. He came to the end of the line. Every student had hit him. Now they all turned to me. They were curious. *What will the new kid do?*

I hesitated. I had just barely been accepted by the group. So I reached out and hit Konrad. It was a halfhearted tap on the shoulder, barely enough to satisfy the class. Sadly, it was one of the wrongs that I can never undo. But Konrad shrugged it all off. We went home together as always, as if nothing had happened.

38

School let out around noon. Barring any explorations with Konrad, I arrived fifteen minutes later to sit down with my mother, Monika, and Omi for the lunch Martchen had prepared. I convinced my mother to postpone my homework until dark, and I would go out and play.

I joined the gang in the Louisenstrasse, boys and girls of varying ages, none of whom I came to know by name. They congregated at the end of the cul-de-sac in front of the gate to Omi's duplex. The city had dumped a pile of air safety sand, much more than women in the neighborhood were willing to carry into their attics, so most of the mountain stayed there, and the children built tunnels and roads and walls. We older ones climbed the masonry gate column, as high as a man and a child standing on his shoulders, and took an air-whistling jump into the sand. Our gang spread all over the Louisenstrasse. Without gasoline, we had no worry about traffic. We would play tag on the road and the sidewalks until dusk.

I distinguished myself with a special skill when it got dark. With the shoe shortage, I had horseshoe iron nailed to my heels to prevent wear. I had developed a way of striking sparks on the pavement when I ran. "Look at the kid from No. 3!" the boys shouted. "He has fire under his shoes!"

My mother was upset. "Why are you always wearing off your irons?"

Back in Straßburg, I could have used this trick in our war games, like Onkel Helmut in his Me 110 bearing down with his guns blasting. But the children in Erfurt no longer played aerial combat. It had become too scary.

The air attacks in Thuringia had grown more fearsome and frequent than they had been in Straßburg. The first alert came with regularity between 8:00 and 10:00; we did not even try to go to bed. Every evening, my mother, Monika, Omi, and I met with Tante Ellen and Maria Barbara, who had moved into a little room in the former servant's quarters above the garage. The big rooms, except Omi Bauer's, were no longer heated because of the coal shortage. We played *Rommé* in the dim light of a floor lamp. We waited for the hoarse howl of the siren in its three long rises, indicating that the bombers had entered our airspace. Then Tante Ellen and Maria Barbara would go down into the villa and take Omi Bauer with them into the basement. My mother, Monika, and I would walk through the garden into the duplex. If the stars were out, my mother would halt a few seconds and look toward north. "There it is—the big W, Cassiopeia."

In Omi's duplex, we would either go up to her second-floor apartment and wait for the hasty up and down of the main alarm or, if we had heard this alarm on the way, head straight into the cellar. Little Martchen would scamper down also, as well as an elderly lady, Frau Bock, from the third floor. One more tenant lived on our side of the duplex, a man on the first floor. He was a Nazi official and always away on party business. I don't remember ever seeing him. We supposed he spent the air raids in a safe party bunker.

The cellar was much smaller than the one in Straßburg; it was merely a short aisle at the bottom of the stairs. Different storage areas were partitioned off by slats. The coops held all kinds of flammable rummage and the winter's supply of coal. The aisle had just enough room for two little cots for Monika and me and chairs for the adults. As fall progressed and the nights grew cold, Omi brought two electric space heaters. I came to know them so well that I could draw them accurately, even today. The adults would turn off the light so that we children could go to sleep. I would stare into the glow of the coils. The one heater had a red metal casing and reflected the glow off a hollow mirror through vertical wire bars. The other heater was the fancy one, Omi's personal property. It was a white porcelain block with glazed perforations through which I saw two large coils. Lying on my belly, I would stare into these comforting glows. I would see them slowly spread their red light along the dark walls and illuminate the figures and faces eerily from below.

While the red coils mesmerized me, the anxiety with which I listened kept me awake. From the moment the siren of the main alarm ceased, the silence was loaded with tension.

Are they coming tonight? Is the attack on its way?

What is this sound? I hope it is not ... I hope it is not ...

A minute later, the humming can no longer be denied. It grows. The women lower their heads. The sound weighs on them. I fumble my goggles onto my face and the mask with the Marke Negergarn washcloth that isn't mine. *Please, God, please, God, let them move on to somewhere else.* If they fly further east to Jena, Gera, and Chemnitz, they will return. There will be another alert later in the night. *Let them go north to the Leuna Gasoline Works or Halle or Leipzig.* Then, they probably will not come back here.

No, they are not leaving. They're circling. Listen to that droning. A *thud.*

"Quick, lie on the floor."

My mother whisks Monika from the cot, lays her next to me. She spreads herself over both of us.

Deep, hollow thuds—farther, closer, farther. A bomber overhead. *Crash.* The floor shakes. Dust. My heart hammers in my throat. *Lieber Gott, mach mich fromm, dass ich in den Himmel komm (Dear God, make me good so I go to heaven).* Thud ... thud ... *Dear God, make me good so I go to heaven; dear God, make me good so I go to heaven.*

I'm still breathing. Another minute. I'm still breathing. Will I make it another minute? *Please, God, help me make it another minute. Make it stop. Make it stop.*

Boom. Shake. Crashing of broken glass upstairs. *Please, God, let it stop.* Keep breathing ... My heart keeps beating like mad. Keep breathing. The booming slows. The droning overhead eases ... less humming ... less. *Thank you, God, thank you.* I stop holding my breath. My heart slows.

———

After the long, sustained howling of the siren, we would climb up the cellar stairs and step outside. We would walk through the garden to meet Tante Ellen and Maria Barbara as they would come out of the shadow of the villa.

"Are you all right?"

"Yes, we are all right." We would step through the wrought-iron rose gate onto the Wilhelmsstrasse. We would look toward downtown and stop in awe. The sky above the city glowed yellowish white from behind the black silhouettes of the nearest houses and then faded high up into orange and red, carrying tufts of sparks.

Slowly we walked down the Wilhelmstrasse and turned left into the Louisenstrasse. We crunched over broken glass, roof tiles. Louisenstrasse 2, where Tante Toni lived on the second floor, seemed to be all right. Toward Tante Anneliese's house everything was quiet. We turned left into the cul-de-sac of Omi's duplex. We went upstairs, took one more look toward the glow in the city through the shards of the blown-out windows, and went to bed.

Sometime in the night, I would be scared out of my sleep by an explosion. My heart would race again. *This was a time bomb*, I would explain to myself. Then I would lie in bed listening until I drifted off again with the cold air blowing through the broken windows.

The next day in school, the boys would be full of stories from the attack. I could not contribute. My mother never said a word about anything that had happened. Most other parents were not as careful in protecting their children. With a strange mix of curiosity and revulsion, I would listen to some of their reports. They did not talk about the people who had died immediately but about those who had been trapped under the ruins.

"There was this one house that was burning, and the fire department tried very hard to put it out. The fireman's daughter was under it with his grandchildren and the others from the house. They finally got the fire out. But when they opened the cellar it was full of water. They found the baby on top of the closet right under the ceiling. But it had drowned also."

I doubted one detail, namely that the fireman was the father of the daughter. I knew how those who retold stories would try to make tragedies worse. Still, there was no denying that this story had lodged under my skull, and I could never get it out. It infested my dreams. I had the recurring nightmare of being locked in complete darkness with water slowly creeping up my body.

Some told other details about the attacks that I did not believe. One was the claim that those silver strips that we found hanging in the bushes were poison. I had picked them up in our front yard, and they seemed to be nothing but tin foil. What gave me a shudder, though, was the thought of where the bomb-laden planes had been when they dropped these strips.

Another claim was that the planes were dropping fountain pens that would explode when grabbed. I never had seen a fountain pen in our garden.

Much more disturbing were the ruins on my way to school. By the appearance of the destruction, I knew which type of bombs had hit. A pile of charred beams and trusses in the hollow of some remaining walls indicated incendiary bombs. Chalky white ruins were left by high explosives. Piles of white rubble with debris blasted all over the street were the marks of air mines.

Different types of buildings had varying tenacity. The wood-framed buildings of the old part of town were turned into charred heaps by incendiary bombs; however, they were quite tough when hit by high explosives. Under lateral impact from these bombs, the buildings would often open like dollhouses, spilling their contents except for attached plumbing, and the downward-tilted floors would hold on to the sinew of splintered beams. The worst were brick buildings. When hit with explosives, they would completely disintegrate.

Since Straßburg, I had a special appreciation for buildings. As I became familiar with the streets in Erfurt, the buildings turned into friends that would offer me orientation and shelter. When walking along tracts that were still standing, I looked at the houses, estimating their strength. From the distance between bombed-out buildings, I tried to predict which ones of those still standing would fall next. I wondered particularly about the buildings I had to stay in.

My mind tried to burrow into the houses to fathom their life expectancy. *How many more days will you be here?* I would ask, ramming my senses into the future.

My life depended on knowing the answer.

39

As if we tried to hold on to our chores as a vestige of stability in the expanding chaos, everyone went about his or her daily routine. My mother would go to the stores to check what food was still available. I was in school or in the garden or I stayed home with Jens-Peter and Martchen. Martchen would go through her schedule of cooking, cleaning, and washing like she had for the last thirty-five years.

I liked to follow her around and watch how she did her daily tasks with amazing ease. The speed with which she made my bed seemed magic. Several bangs on the pillow, a few tugs here and there and the covers were in place without a single fold and the patterned center perfectly aligned in the middle. Once I looked at the alarm clock to time her. "You did my bed in one minute," I told her.

"Look, Michael, this is easy," she demonstrated the next day. "Just remember that you cannot push cloth. You have to pull it. Get one bottom corner placed perfectly, then pull the other bottom corner perfect and then bring the top corners up, and you're done. You should try to make your own bed. Then you'll learn."

I was not about to try. It was the servant's job.

While Martchen did the chores, she often entertained me with poems and riddles in her Thuringian singsong. One poem told about a little boy who went on the thin ice, broke though, and had to be rescued. The verses had a humorous moral that made her boiled-potato face shrivel in a wistful, little smile.

A riddle occupied me for hours. I had her repeat it over and over:

Osterben, Osterben
Ist des Menschen's Ferderben.

I understood this in the Thuringian vernacular as:

Easterbone, Easterbone
Is Man's Frontbone.

I could not make sense out of this interpretation and kept searching for the true meaning. When I finally gave up, Martchen stressed the words differently, on the second syllable rather than on the first. It now sounded High German:

Oh, Sterben, Oh, Sterben
Ist des Menschen's Verderben

Oh, dying, oh, dying
Is man's undoing.

The cleverness of the two-liner delighted me. I ran around reciting the verse and switching its meaning back and forth by changing the stresses.

After a while, Martchen stopped me. She had become very serious.

"Michael, remember this is really a bad saying!"

"Why?"

"Because it's a lie."

I paused for a while. Then I probed. "Martchen."

"Yes."

"What happens when we die?"

"Well, we certainly don't perish. We become eternal."

"What does it mean, 'we become eternal'?"

"It means … how can I explain it? It means we stop getting older."

I mulled over this conversation and came to the conclusion that, if I would die now, I would always be nine years old. I enjoyed being nine years old.

I returned Martchen's entertaining and wise ways in a shameful and despicable manner. I remembered how I had been able to commandeer her during my last visit. Now that I was indeed taller than she, I succumbed to the temptation to test and expand this delicious power.

I got the idea to entice little Jens-Peter to team up as Max and Moritz, the two little bad boys who played tricks on the adults. All German children knew Max and Moritz, even little Jens-Peter. Omi had read this Wilhelm Busch booklet to him many times.

Jens-Peter tended to be bored. I easily diverted him from his usual pursuits, like twisting out his teddy bear's glass eyes or disassembling his music box. He was willing to be Moritz, as long as I, Max, dreamed up the plots. The first clever trick I devised interfered with Martchen's vacuum cleaning. When she was working around the corner or through a door, we would sneak up and pull the plug and then quickly hide. The first time she thought she had overextended the reach of the cord and plugged it back in. The second time, she suspected us. The third time she got mad and ran after us, but we were both too fast for the old woman. The fourth time, she was near tears. Then we stopped, worried that she would tell my mother, but when my mother returned from the store, Martchen said nothing.

I was surprised. Did the old woman love me so much that she would not complain? This realization motivated me even more than the feeling of physical and social superiority. I thought of ever more annoying mischief to test the boundaries of her affection. We snuck into the kitchen and turned off the gas under the potatoes. For once, dinner was not ready on time. Martchen did not say a word to my mother. We set the kitchen clock backward. We took the broom from the closet and hid it on the balcony. Every time my mother left, we went to work. Our box of our tricks was bottomless.

As a crowning prank, we took her convertible ladder-chair and hid it. We gloated about how this would really set her back. Indeed, the tiny woman could not reach half of what she needed.

"Michael, where is my ladder?"

"I don't know," I answered with a smirk. "If you wouldn't be so small, you wouldn't need it."

She came after me with her little hand raised, but I ran away.

When next I peeked around the corner, she sat there sobbing. She did not even stop when we got her the ladder back.

That night, Martchen told my mother that we had not been behaving. She minimized our offenses, but my mother guessed that we had been pestering her. My mother excused little Jens-Peter and put the blame where it belonged. Her talk was so full of scorn and disappointment that it shook me. She made me apologize to Martchen and promise never to do "such things" again. That stopped the pranks. I did not want to endure my mother's burning eyes again.

My mother forgave me. She always made up with a kiss at night. I was not sure whether Martchen still felt any affection for me.

From that time on, I mostly played in the garden with Maria Barbara. I even stayed when her annoying friend, Inge Natz, came over. Inge always wanted Maria Barbara to play mothers with her. They locked themselves into the elaborately furnished room of the garden house and drew the curtains. I was Onkel Hans, relegated to the other room, which had a wooden bench and piles of leaves that blew in through the windowless openings. "No, you can't be the father," they said. "You don't understand this game." Peeking through a crack, I saw them lying on the couches, writhing and pulling their dolls headfirst from under their skirts.

"Don't think I don't know about mothers and babies," I said when they came out.

The next afternoon, Maria Barbara and I were alone in the garden. She brought two fine china cups and a pot with peppermint tea and set them on the white, painted, cast-iron garden table under the juniper tree to have a tea party together and a conversation like adults. She poured for both of us, and we pulled the heavy chairs through the grass close to the table and sat opposite each other. "Now, tell me," she asked, "what do you know about having babies?"

We were both excited about this topic. I said, "When the baby is ready, the mother's belly splits open, and the baby comes out."

"You are right about the baby in the belly, but where it comes out is not right," she said taking a sip of tea.

"So where do you think it comes out?" I asked.

She blushed.

"It comes out between her legs," she said looking into her cup.

"But the baby is too big to come out there," I objected.

"We are different than you," she said with an enigmatic smile.

"I know you are different," I said.

Neither one of us had a firm understanding what the difference was, but we bathed in the delicious curiosity.

Had we reached the end of what we knew about the subject or of what we were willing to tell each other about ourselves? Maria Barbara seemed to think so.

"I think I'll go and see whether Inge will come over," she said, preparing to get up.

I swung around the table, grabbed her pigtails, and held her back. She stood up and, suddenly, straightening her knees, gave the cast-iron chair such a push backward that it toppled and fell on my foot. I let go of her hair and hobbled around in pain. Maria Barbara was genuinely sorry.

We children had a rule. If one hurt another, either by accident or out of a sudden flare of temper, the injured could hurt the other in return. Then we called it even, shook hands, and the friendship was restored.

"Come, you may hit my butt," Maria Barbara said, putting her hands on her eyes and her elbows on the table. "No stick! With your hand just once," she said, proffering her little, rounded bottom toward me.

I swung to hit her there, but then my hand traveled upward, and I smacked her full force on the side of her head.

"That was not fair," she cried. Her ear and cheek turned fiery red. She buried her head in her arms and cried. I could not believe how hard I had hit her. What had come over me?

"Maria, listen." I stroked over her back, trying to make her look at me. "Hit me again. Come, please, hit me hard." She shook her head and did not look up.

"See, I'll hurt myself. See like this, uh."

She could not help peeking up from her folded arms. Now that I knew she was watching, I smacked myself in the face so that she could hear it. I jumped around in pain, fell on the ground, and smacked myself again and again in more and more ridiculous distortions. I wailed louder and louder until she started laughing and wiped off her tears.

"Stop," she said, "It's enough. We'll call it even. Let's finish the tea."

It started drizzling. Little drops collected on the inside wall of the teacups.

"Look," I said, pointing to the cup. Maria Barbara's eyes widened. "What is that?"

The drops were not clear. They were red. They flowed together and ran down the translucent porcelain.

"The sky is bleeding," Maria Barbara whispered.

"It can't bleed," I said. "These are ashes from another city."

"I know," she said.

We sat and watched how the red rivulets collected in the cup and mixed with the remains of the amber tea. That was the last day we sat in the garden.

40

November 10 came, Martin Luther's birthday. My mother told me again about the children carrying their lanterns to the dome square. I would have liked to go with Maria Barbara, but with the war and the blackout, this celebration would not take place. It was a sign of the perniciousness of those days that my vision of the warm light of the thousands of children's lanterns shifted into the blaze over the city that I saw after attacks.

On December 15, my mother and I visited Omi Bauer, who had mentioned that she had not seen me for a while. That was the day when she gave me the apple. She sat in the living room in her high armchair tucked into her crocheted blanket up to her waist. A mild light lay on her white, pinned-up hair. It caressed her neck and shoulders that curved so delicately, like the lowest boughs of a tree. *How much like my mother's her shoulders are*, I thought. Next to her on a side table was a red, glossy apple on a saucer of fine china. When she saw us, a friendly glow went over her wrinkled face, and she nodded more than usual with excitement. In her quiet, shattered voice she asked about Monika and about my father. Perhaps she also asked about his mother, Anna. She did not talk about the war and seemed untouched by the destruction around her.

When we got up to leave, she brought her old hand from under her blanket and picked up the apple.

"Here, Michael, this apple is for you."

She lifted the apple toward me. I took it from her ancient hand and thanked her. Then she leaned back into her chair and rested.

The next morning must have been a Saturday or Sunday. I was not in school and stood at the window in my mother's bedroom. I looked through the glass, which had been replaced many times. I saw the back court and across the shaky carriage house to Omi Bauer's garden and her villa shrouded in gray, which made everything seem far away.

My mother came into the room and said, "Omi Bauer died this morning."

I looked at her briefly and then turned to the window again. I thought I should be feeling sad, but a liberating joy overcame me, as if I had heard about a bird that had been released from a cellar or from this room, from behind this impermanent glass, a bird that was flying free now over roofs and trees and beyond. I kept looking out of the window, feeling whole and at peace.

The following day, the family assembled in the villa's living room to discuss the funeral arrangements. While we children, Maria Barbara, Monika, and I, were wandering on the widespread carpets, the adults, Omi, Tante Ellen, Tante Anneliese, and my mother, were sitting around the coffee table on the heavy couch and easy chairs. Tante Toni was also there. The delicate old lady sat there shaking her head from side to side as if she wanted to deny that her sister was gone. However, Tante Toni's negating affliction was misleading, for she recounted the details of Omi Bauer's last night with acceptance and gratitude. Omi Bauer had asked her to stay that night and sleep in the next room. Around three or four in the morning, Marie wakened Toni and said, "Toni, I think it is time." Toni sat on Omi Bauer's bed and watched her go back to sleep. After a while she lay down herself. When Toni woke up at eight, her sister had stopped breathing.

"Peacefully slept away," was the term that the group in the living room chose as they tried to put together the obituary.

"Peacefully slept away ... eighty one ... born Gärtner ... married Ernst Müller (owner of I. C. Smith) ... widowed ... married Major Bauer ... survived by ... in deep sadness ... our mother, grandmother, great-grandmother." As everyone tried to doctor the obituary and went over it again and again, Tante Anneliese suddenly got the giggles under her tears. Funny comments that the deceased had made years ago, when she enjoyed life to the fullest, bubbled up irresistibly, and for a while, the women could not stop laughing. They agreed that Omi Bauer was somehow among them or looking down on them and would be laughing also. I doubted this.

Omi Bauer was decked out in her bedroom. I was asked whether I wanted to see her.

"Yes, you can come see her," Maria Barbara urged. "I have already seen her twice." Again she was ahead of me.

I hesitated and looked across the lobby, where it was so dark. I could hardly make out the polar bear skin in front of the cavernous fireplace. Her bedroom door was all the way across where my mother used to have her photo studio.

"Don't be afraid; there is nothing to it. It's easy," Maria Barbara said.

As I took another step forward, she planted her hands in front of the wide door post and flipped into a handstand, her feet supported against the polished frame. "It's just that easy."

I could not go past her. She flipped back down and lifted her hand, offering to lead me. I did not want to see Omi Bauer dead; I wanted to remember her alive, like on her last day when she had given me the apple.

"You don't have to see her if you don't want to," my mother said.

The adults discussed the particulars of the funeral. An emergency law forbade burying the dead in clothes. They had to be buried in provided paper sacks. The government found it unreasonable with so many people dying to waste all these good clothes. It was clear to the family that they had to break this law. Omi Bauer was remembered by the older population as one of the richest women in Erfurt, as a cultural leader, as a philanthropist and a trendsetter in her appearance. She could not embark on her eternal journey stripped naked and stuffed into a paper bag. The family still had enough influence to find an undertaker and a pastor willing to risk their lives by burying her in one of her resplendent dresses.

Two days after Omi Bauer died, my father's mother, Anna, my Oma, also passed away, as if the women were traveling together. During their lifetime, they had only seen each other once, at my parents' wedding. They'd had an immediate affinity. The one was a wealthy socialite in a major city, the other a shoemaker's daughter from provincial Demmin. Had their bond something to do with having the same birthday, albeit in different years?

When my Oma, Anna, had been on her deathbed, my Opa, Georg, had called at the boot camp in Stuttgart. "Walter, if you want to see your mother once more, you have to come quickly."

My father was permitted to take leave and hurried by train diagonally through the convulsed, torn country to Hohen Lychen. His mother had been with Tante Teddy, Eva-Maria, and Christian since they had moved there from the Black Forest.

In Berlin, my father had to transfer to another station. He took the U-Bahn part of the way. Coming up from the subway station, he found himself standing in piles of rubble that lined up along flat aisles, the former streets. He had to ask his way in the city where he had been born and had lived for thirty-three years.

When my father arrived in Hohen Lychen, his mother had died and had been buried in the nearby village of Zehdenick. His father had returned to Berlin. He was needed at the Bezugsamt, an office for rationing clothes and household goods, where he had to continue his bitter task of denying women's purchase requests. Onkel Horsa had also returned to Berlin after the funeral, taking care of his patients as if nothing had happened.

My father stayed with Tante Teddy for a day and visited the grave. Finding his sister resigned, strong, and functional, my father hurried to Erfurt to spend Christmas with us. When we picked him up at the railroad station, he looked so thin in his dull green uniform. The collars of his shirt and jacket stood away from his neck, and his cap seemed too large. Still, seeing his family animated him, and he had many questions for Monika and me. As we went along the pedestrian's tunnel, another soldier who walked past us turned and came after my father.

"You did not greet me."

My dear father, who had always been second in rank to God, became flabbergasted and apologized profusely. "Sorry, I did not see you, sir. I was talking to my children, sir."

He apologized again and thanked the man of higher rank when he let him off the hook!

My esteem for my father was partially restored when he went with us three *spazieren* (going on walks) to the Cyriacsburg. On the way we ran into my gang in the Louisenstrasse. The boys, who had not seen any fathers for a long time, admired my father in his uniform. Some even snapped to it and greeted him with outstretched arm, "Heidler!"

While my father visited, the alerts kept coming. He sat next to my mother in the dark of the cellar. He still had cigarettes from somewhere. Besides the heating coils, I now saw the glow of his cigarette, dimly at his knee level and every once in a while wandering up and briefly illuminating his fleshy mouth and fine, straight nose.

My father seemed to be more nervous than my mother. In boot camp, he was located in the country and relatively safe from bombs. The nearby Stuttgart had fewer casualties than other large cities, even though it had endured heavy bombings. Being built on mountainous terrain, the citizens had burrowed deep *Stollen* (tunnels) into the hillsides for safe shelters. We in our basement had little protection. It was partially above ground with cellar windows, had much wood and stored coal; gas lines went openly through it, and the cellar door above the short flight of stairs seemed flimsy. My father urged my mother to consider getting back to the Black Forest or at least getting out of the city. She agreed that she would try.

On Christmas Eve, we counted on peace and quiet. In the old tradition, my mother, Monika, and I, this time joined by Omi, Martchen, Tante Anneliese, and Jens-Peter, stood in the dark at the door to the *Weihnachtszimmer* (Christmas room). This Christmas room had been off limits for us kids for a day, while the adults had set up the tree and the presents open on tables. My father lit the candles, and more and more light would seep through the crack under the door. We sang Christmas carols in the dark. Then my father opened the door. Since he had no piano, he just started singing, "*Ihr Kinderlein kommet*" (Come Little Children).

My parents said that the *Weihnachtsmann* had had trouble getting around this year. I did get a set of animal stamps that had a zebra, a lion, a giraffe, and a penguin. Monika got a ball sewn by hand out of hexagonal scraps of cloths and filled with sawdust. Jens-Peter got a desperately crude car with pedals made of slats of wood only partially smoothed and with wooden wheels. It was held together with wooden screws, not glue. When Jens-Peter climbed in and started pedaling across the room, it fell apart. A wheel came off and, a little later, the steering column broke. All toys I had known before had been made to perfection with pride and love.

My father had to go back to boot camp. My mother did not leave Erfurt but stayed. She needed the support of the family and of the known surroundings. She had another reason for staying though, which probably was her main one. She did not want to interrupt my education in this critical school year.

The war itself, however, was less understanding.

41

In January, after another attack on downtown, I came to school and found all students in the courtyard. No one was allowed to enter the building. The yard was littered with glass, wood from broken windows, and shingles. My attention, like that of all children, was drawn across the river. The Barfüsser Church was in ruins. The winter sky filled the space where the enormous roof had been. At the east end, there were a few charred rafters. The rest had collapsed into the nave. Scattered doves flew with clapping wings through the empty spaces.

The teachers appeared and tried to establish order in the courtyard. My class flocked around Herr Klaus, who told us that the building was no longer safe. We had to move to another school. He selected about ten students, including me, to help him move and sent the others home. I followed him to our second-story classroom. A cold wind blew through the frameless window openings. The old floor tilted toward the outside. Herr Klaus opened the closet in the corner and loaded a stack of books onto each student's arms as we filed by. He left the hazel sticks behind.

An odd procession crossed the city as the old teacher led his troop of book-carrying students through the ruins, circumventing blocked streets and climbing over rubble. The dust-laden clothes of the teacher looked like they had wiped the remaining walls. Eventually, we crossed the Flutgraben, a flood relief canal that marked the periphery of the old city. We entered the southern part of Erfurt, which had been hit less. Our new school was in the Schiller Strasse. As we approached the building, I scrutinized the walls, the windows, and the roof. It was a brick building. I did not trust it. The double entrance doors opened toward the inside. Behind the door was a small, claustrophobic landing without any other side doors. Almost immediately, it led up a wide staircase. On the next landing was a small door in which stood the custodian watching the newcomers. Another flight of stairs brought us to the second floor and our classroom. We deposited our books up front on the teacher's desk. Herr Klaus had to find storage for them. When I returned the next day for the resuming instruction, we had been consolidated with the regular students of this school. The building was dangerously overcrowded in spite of the fact that some classes had been moved to the afternoon.

The new location offered one advantage. My way home was shorter. I went one block on Schiller Strasse and then through the park along the Flutgraben and across a pedestrian bridge. I continued one block on Wilhelmstrasse and finally through Omi Bauer's garden into the duplex and upstairs to my mother. This way, home was always in the back of my mind when I sat through my classes.

Herr Klaus taught us long division and multiplication. I always had correct homework. My mother helped me. She loved math and enjoyed explaining the principles. However, the timed tests at school became more difficult for me with every trial. The generous time allotment ticked away as I tried to focus on my five problems. I was distracted by the furious pencil scratching of my neighbors, their sighing, their breathing, and their erasing. I kept losing my place, starting over, changing numbers, checking again, and changing them back.

"Five more minutes."

I was still on the first problem. Herr Klaus walked slowly back up the aisle. He looked over my shoulder, watched how I would make a short run of computations, stop, try to recheck, and lose my place. I raised my head. I saw his face in a blur. My eyes were ready to overflow in desperation. He looked surprised, but behind his consternation was a glimmer of understanding and compassion.

I flunked the test. After I failed the makeup also, my mother became alarmed. How would I ever be able to get into the Oberschule? She had a conference with Herr Klaus. She expressed how important it was for her that I would be able to pass the entrance exam. She assured him that I was, indeed, able to solve the problems at home where there were no time limits and distractions. "He cannot concentrate in school."

"I know," said Herr Klaus.

"Could you possibly tutor him?" my mother asked, pleading with her big, doe-brown eyes that hardly any man, young or old, could refuse.

Herr Klaus agreed to give me one lesson a week, on Saturday morning, in his home.

I found his apartment a few blocks past the school, on the second floor of a three-story house out of sandstone masonry that was black from age and faced a bombed-out lot across the street. The narrow staircase seemed unusually dark. I had as much trouble concentrating at his place as I did at school. He drilled me in the large multiplication table, from eleven to twenty. "What's seven times eighteen?"

I could have memorized the table, like the better students. Herr Klaus did not insist on memorization but tried to teach me to figure in my head.

Seven times ten is seventy; no, I have to do it the other way around.

I looked at the dark oak furniture clinging to the dark green walls and heard the grandfather clock ticking. I looked out of the window where the opposite house had been and looked into the empty canyon of brick fire walls.

"What was the question? Seven times eighteen?" I asked.

"Yes, seven times eighteen. Take your time. I'll be back."

Herr Klaus lifted himself out of the worn, green easy chair and left the room, closing the dark brown door behind him.

Seven times eight is fifty-six. Seven times ten is seventy. Why does dark sadness hang in this room? The grandfather clock keeps ticking. It seems to slow down. Could that be? The sun beats into the bricks across the street. The room is getting darker. Seventy plus, what was the first number? Something is wrong with this house. In twenty minutes, I can go home. Concentrate, concentrate; I've got to get this answer.

The door opened. The old man entered slowly and looked at me expectantly.

"A hundred and twenty-six."

I had trouble getting any answer after that. Herr Klaus asked me to do my figuring aloud and prompted me more and more until the old clock struck the hour and I could leave the building.

The following week, we had the closest bombing yet. As I lay trembling under my mother, the floor kept heaving with dull impacts. The worst hits were followed by crashes up in the house. The lights went out. The smell of mortal danger stung my nostrils, like ozone from the sparking wires above moving streetcars, but dusty and astringent. The endless droning of the circling bombers was unbearable. After the attack, the light did not come on. We followed the wandering beams of our flashlights up the staircase to the apartment. The kitchen door was missing. Martchen found it in the back court under the hazelnut tree. It had been blown out the window. In the bedrooms, the air pressure had rolled up the carpet and shoved the blankets on the beds against the wall. I shook the glass from my pillow; got in bed; pulled my blankets tightly around me, leaving only nose and eyes exposed to the cold air that blew from the empty window; and went to sleep.

The next morning, my mother did not wake me for school. I woke up when the window man came. He covered the opening with plywood and put a small pane in the middle for light. This way he could nail the wood back up again next time.

I looked through the opening into the back court and over the neighboring gardens, searching for a crater. I saw nothing unusual except for the white kitchen door, lying glossy with rain under the tree; splintered pieces of wood from the window frames; and strewn bricks from the old wall that closed the east side of the back court. The old carriage house that formed the north side of the court was still standing, though its walls were cracked and bulging more than ever.

The bomb had gone down in the Wilhelmstrasse, the first block on my way to school. It must have been an air mine. It destroyed several buildings in the middle of the block completely, and the air pressure had damaged all houses within the neighboring blocks.

My mother, Monika, and I checked on Tante Ellen and Maria Barbara. They were sitting in bed with umbrellas over their heads, trying to divert the drips from the ceiling into pails on each side and a tin can on the dresser next to the big mirror. The rhythm and pitches of the drops captured my attention until they faded into monotony. Tante Ellen was reading the newspaper, letting Maria Barbara have discarded sections. Tante Ellen followed up on war information in detail and did not care if Maria Barbara read about it or listened in on her discussion. Maria Barbara flaunted the news in front of me. Tante Ellen asked my mother for a cigarette, but she had none left. An article about the loss of historical sites caught her attention.

"Look." She tapped the back of her hand on a picture. "Saint Augustine is destroyed."

I knew this medieval church and monastery as the one that Luther had entered as Brother Martin. The news did not shock me. My Münster had been hit. To war, nothing was holy. As Tante Ellen went on about the raid, my mother suggested that I go out and play.

"Look, the sun is coming through."

"Yes, let's go out and play," I said to Maria Barbara. "You are not going to school either, are you?"

Maria Barbara dropped the newspaper on the bed and sat up high. I had never seen her in her nightgown, with little pink flowers embroidered on the rounded collar and across her chest.

"Turn to the wall, Michael," she said, "so I can get out of bed and get dressed."

I turned obediently, looking at the floor in front of the dresser. I heard the rustling of blankets and sheets behind me and then the slap of her bare feet on the floor. I raised my eyes, and there she was in the mirror, lifting her nightgown over her head and flinging it on the bed. Before I shut my eyes, I had seen her—her arms raised high, her hair falling down her neck, her stretched chest, the deep curve of the small of her back with two dimples above the ample fullness of her rosy bottom. In a second I had taken it all in. In the last instant, our eyes met in the mirror. I waited in the dark of my closed eyes. I heard no comment. Could it be that she did not mind my seeing her?

"Now you can turn round," she said.

I opened my eyes, turned, and saw her fully dressed, looking straight at me. An almost-imperceptible smile, half-embarrassed, half-pleased, faded behind the blush that rose from her neck over her face.

Tante Ellen looked over the top of her newspaper and suggested, "Now that you have the day off, why don't you visit Tante Toni and bring her the things."

Maria Barbara agreed happily. Since her sister's death, Tante Toni had become sick with kidney trouble that hampered her ability to walk. Maria Barbara had been visiting the old lady willingly every few days, bringing her cookies that she had baked and other necessary items that Tante Toni had called Tante Ellen for.

"Why don't you come along?" Maria Barbara suggested.

I nodded. I had walked past the sandstone building, Louisenstrasse 2, many times. I had even seen the brass nameplate, Saniter, at the door, but I had never been in Tante Toni's apartment.

42

My mother had told me Tante Toni's story several times. I knew about the tragedy that had marred her life. That knowledge always had made me a little shy toward her.

In many ways Tante Toni reminded me of Omi Bauer. She had the same refined stature and the white, pinned-up hair, but she appeared smaller and more fragile. She was friendly. However, her friendliness had a tinge of sadness, while Omi Bauer's enjoyment was free from any melancholy. Perhaps it was the difference in the shaking of their heads that gave me the impression of the two women having a slightly different attitude.

As Maria Barbara and I walked down the Wilhelmstrasse and turned into the Louisenstrasse, Tante Toni's story was again on my mind.

Toni, the youngest of the three Gärtner girls, had married a squire by the name of Saniter. Unlike her sister Marie, my Omi Bauer, who came to riches slowly while Ernst Müller amassed them through his ambition and ingenuity, Toni had everything instantly—a mansion teeming with servants, extensive grounds with riding stables, tennis courts, and the obligatory lake with a pair of swans. Within a few years, she moved into the center of society by virtue of her charm and education, put her personal stamp on what she and the squire owned, and easily made friends of all ages.

Toni had everything she could wish for, except the one thing she wanted more than anything—a child of her own. The years went by in disappointing barrenness. She and the squire had almost given up hope, when, after many doctors' consultations and many prayers, she finally conceived and had a son.

No parents cared for their son more than Toni and the squire, but as the boy grew older, he became sickly. He had diabetes. All the money, love, and state-of-the-art medical care could not save him. Toni nursed him through his long decline until he was gone. She did not understand why this had to be. She shook her head, no, no, when a few years later, she heard about the discovery of insulin. Why now? Why not earlier? Her greatest gift was this special understanding for children; why was she not allowed to give it?

Toni lost her husband early. She buried him and sold their estate. She followed Marie's urging and moved close to her, bought the apartment building within walking distance, and occupied the third floor, where she could see her sister's villa over the trees.

———

Maria Barbara rang, waited long, and rang again. The buzzer sounded. We pushed the door open and climbed the stone stairs to the third floor. The tiny old lady was sticking her head through a crack in the door to see who was coming.

"Oh, Maria Barbara and Michael," she exclaimed, and the warm, welcoming smile contrasted with her head shaking, no, no.

"Come in, come in."

She tried to make way for us, pointing toward the living room. She could not walk. She moved by turning her feet on her heels and then, on her toes, scooting sideways, supporting her hand on the wall.

When she caught up with us in the living room, Maria Barbara held her basket toward her.

"Oh, what have you brought me here, cookies again? Thank you."

She immediately gave each of us a cookie and put the basket on the table. She made us sit down on the couch. Over a grand piano hung a large oil painting that I could not see very well. The room was dark, the large window covered with plywood except for a small, glass pane.

"Yes, it's dark in here," she said following my eyes. "When the plywood is not there, you can see the villa over the trees from here. I used to see you play in the garden. Now I can't look out. I'm too small. Is snow out there?"

We told her that there was frost but no snow on the ground.

"When I was your age, I used to go ice-skating with my sister, your Omi Bauer. Yes, we were good—did figure threes and eights and pirouettes and skated in pairs."

How could the shaky, old lady ever have been able to get on the ice? Now, she can hardly move. What is she doing during air raids? She can't get into the cellar. What happens when doors and windows come flying? Does she crawl under her bed?

We did not stay long. Tante Toni twisted behind us to the door, thanking us again profusely for the visit and the cookies.

Shortly after, Tante Toni called my mother with a surprising proposal. She wanted to give a party for children. She wanted to serve cake and hot chocolate, for which she still had the ingredients.

Seeing my puzzled face, my mother tried to explain.

"Tante Toni loves children. She used to give children's parties like that on her estate when her husband was alive."

On the indicated afternoon, we children climbed to Tante Toni's apartment. We wore our best outfits and had freshly washed hands and faces. We sat around the table in the boarded-up living room. A sliver of light fell on the grand piano. The young ones did not say a word, a little scared of the old lady who moved so strangely and could not stop shaking her head. The older children were quiet out of respect and somewhat intimidated by the strange situation. How long had it taken Tante Toni to set the table with the white tablecloth, damask napkins, and porcelain and to carry the cake and the pot of hot chocolate from the kitchen? Trying to control her tremor, she filled each child's cup and put a piece of cake on each plate with a silver spatula. As we started munching and drinking, we relaxed a little. Some even started talking to each other. The old woman rested her eyes on each of us as if we were her own.

We finished our cake and hot chocolate and thought we could go now, but Tante Toni twisted over to the piano. "How about a few songs? What songs do you know?"

"'All My Little Ducks,'" suggested Jens-Peter.

Tante Toni slid onto the piano bench and started playing, but we children listened to her rather than participating. We felt shy and awkward.

Tante Toni tried, "Hänschen klein" and "Häschen in der Grube," satisfied that we could tell her the name of the songs. None of us knew how to leave.

Tante Toni closed the lid over the keyboard, pulled herself up, and said that we could go now and play. She twisted into the hall, opened the lock for us, and saw us squeeze by with hurried thank yous and disappear down the stairs.

That was the last time I saw Tante Toni. The next time Maria Barbara asked me to visit the old aunt with her, I excused myself as having too much homework.

The night after Tante Toni's party, we had another air raid. When I got to school the next morning, Herr Klaus was absent. The substitute did not explain why. Nobody found it necessary to inform us children about the reasons for such puzzling changes. Before school was over, I did find out what had happened.

Gunther, a classmate, told me. He also took tutoring. Gunther was a tall, heavyset boy, whose parents wanted him to be accepted at the Adolf Hitler Schule. Indeed, there were adults so deluded that they still believed in a final victory, while everything was falling into shards.

Gunther told me that Herr Klaus was probably looking for a new home. "I went for my lesson yesterday afternoon, and his house was gone, nothing but a pile of rubble. I did not know what to do, but then I saw him climbing around in there. He was looking for something left from his stuff, but there was nothing."

I was glad my teacher was alive and not surprised that the building had been destroyed. The next day, the old man was back teaching.

The tutoring had helped a little in my performance. Herr Klaus had not been able to teach me much math in such a short time, but his benevolence toward me had become obvious and calmed my anxious mind. Still, I was too nervous in that classroom to concentrate on numbers. To compensate for my poor math grade, I was good in geography.

I was also good in verbal recounting of stories. That helped my German grades, which were being dragged down by my poor spelling. I struggled along and tried to suppress my unease about being in this brick building.

One morning, during geography, my dread suddenly became justified. The siren started howling quickly up and down—a full alert. The children screamed. Before Herr Klaus could get across the room to the door and establish order, they ran out and down the stairs. Waiting for the teacher to take charge, I was one of the last to leave.

In the hall, panicked students poured from all classes. I was taken up by the stream. As I came around the landing and looked down the last flight, my blood froze. A solid mass of children pressed against the doors, those doors that opened inward. Crying, screaming, no teacher yet in sight, more and more children charged down the stairs, pressing and shoving against the mass. Some were falling and others climbed over them, banging their fists on the doors, screaming, "Mama!"

I grabbed the rail with both hands, pulling myself up against the current. I reached the landing. The custodian, in his door, waved at me. "Come this way."

Several boys and I followed him through his apartment and out his narrow back door into the open.

Now home! Before the humming starts. *Do I hear anything?* The children! The screams fade as I run. Just the furious tapping of my feet on the deserted pavement. On. On. Thomas Church. Passed. The rush of the Flutgraben. The bridge. Wilhelmstrasse. The ruined block. Dahlbergweg. The rose gate. The garden. Down the cellar stairs. Mutti, I made it.

I sat panting. After I had caught my breath, I told my mother what had happened, how I had gotten out through the custodian's door. The humming did not come this morning.

That evening, the school secretary called. Erfurt's schools were closed until further notice. With attacks during daytime, the schools could no longer carry the responsibility for the children.

"Was ist aus den Kindern geworden, die nicht rauskonnten, Mutti?" (What happened to the children that couldn't get out?)

"I don't know, Micha. The woman didn't say."

43

All my schooling stopped. My mother was no longer concerned about my entrance exam. Nothing was important except our survival.

In February, the winter turned cold. Maria Barbara and I spent more time together and became closer. Noticing a patch of ice under a dripping faucet on the carriage house, we opened the tap one evening and flooded the concrete drive. The water flowed down the gentle decline past the garages. It froze quickly as it spread and smoothed the unevenness of the rhomboid grooves. The next morning, we had the longest ice slide that Maria Barbara and I had ever seen. It would have been the envy of any child in Erfurt. Everyone would have liked to come *glennern*; that is what they called sliding in Erfurt. But we had this magnificent *Glennerbahn* all for ourselves. In the following days we perfected our skills, taking ever-faster runs, jumping on the ice and sliding farther until we made it to the very end, in front of Omi Bauer's arched back entrance. We added special tricks. We squatted as we slid. We learned that a little spin on takeoff would turn us backward. Finally, we could turn completely. We kept sliding into dusk and stayed as the moon rose in the clear, cold sky. Before we went inside, we opened the faucet and poured another layer of water. The next day, we would start out again on muscle-sore legs. Eventually, we both could slide at the same time. I caught up with her on the way and slung my arms around her until we came to a stop.

It was pure delight until one gloomy evening around the middle of the month. I called up to Maria Barbara's window, but she did not come down. I had to go up to her apartment and remind her that we had planned to *glenner*. Tante Anneliese was visiting Tante Ellen. Newspapers were strewn over the bed. Tante Anneliese paced in the small room. Tante Ellen sat on the bed and shuffled around the disorganized, loose pages, while drawing on a cigarette in furious puffs. Maria Barbara followed me down the dark, narrow staircase.

She started to slide on the ice mechanically.

"What happened?" I asked.

"Haven't you heard?"

"Haven't I heard what?"

"About Dresden?"

"No, what about Dresden?" I slid and turned on the ice past her as she was walking back to the top of the slide. Dresden appeared before my mind's eye. I had seen it once from the train. My mother and Tante Anneliese and I had passed through on a vacation trip from Berlin. I remembered an unbroken row of palaces and churches curving along the terraced shores of the Elbe.

Maria Barbara waited for me so I could catch up with her. "Dresden is completely destroyed. Tante Anneliese has talked to people at the hospital who came from there. The whole city burned like a furnace. The flames were so hot they drew the air around the city and made a firestorm."

"You mean, like in Hamburg and Lübeck?" I asked.

"Yes—no, worse. It was bombed two days ago and is still burning."

Immediately, a thought choked me. How would I get out of a furnace like that? I slid away from Maria Barbara. I did not want to hear the details. But my ears were too keen.

"Before the bombing the city had taken on so many refugees they had to camp in the park. They had to stand around drums with wood fires. The night was clear and ice cold."

I did not want to see this—the women and children standing out in the open around the fires in the park.

"What about blackout?" I asked, trying to cast doubt on her tale.

"They were not worried about attacks. They thought that the city would be spared like Heidelberg. You know, even more palaces, churches, and museums, no factories. They didn't even defend—no flak, no planes."

Maria Barbara went on, even though I slid away again. I did not know how to stop her. Her voice did not have the usual coquettish tone that she assumed when she showed off. She sounded serious and urgent, like she needed to get the story off her chest.

And so the image of ultimate destruction settled indelibly in my mind.

Over the years I learned details. When the first bombs fell, people outside tried to get into the cellars, but as buildings started burning, those who were not trapped in the houses ran into the streets also. Then came the second wave. Now everything started burning. The heat was so intense that buildings exploded in fireballs. The dome that did not suffer a direct hit collapsed from the heat.

The fire sucked up the oxygen. Some of those who did not suffocate made it to the Elbe, driven into the water by the heat. The next morning, a third wave of bombers came and turned over the ruins with high explosives. Low-flying aircraft machine-gunned into those that huddled in the middle of the squares, crazed but still alive. Lions from the zoo wandered through the ruins, not touching anyone, not the living, not the wounded, not the dead.

When the fire had burned down, the dead were hauled out of the ruins on carts and put into mass graves. Others were incinerated by flamethrowers in the cellars right where they had perished. They were covered with rubble, never to be identified or counted. The city had been congested with refugees from the Russian front—hounded, fatigued, desperate refugees—and those who perished were mostly women and children, children, children. Never before in history had fewer soldiers killed more children in such a short time.

In bed, I drifted back and forth between conscious thoughts of horror and nightmares. I saw flashes of my mother, Monika, and me on crowded trains. I saw us standing around fires in a park, hearing sirens, the humming, the thuds. I saw us hammering our fists against doors, running through burning streets, lying in a square in broad daylight. The pictures haunted me until I finally fell asleep.

I had a dreamlike vision. I was lying in my bed asleep and was awakened by a faint singing. I listened. It came from outside. I got out of bed and went to the window. The plywood was gone, and the panes were all restored. I opened the window. I heard it more clearly then, high above, thousands of silvery voices. I looked up, and I saw a stream of lights passing overhead. I strained my eyes further until I made out that the lights were lanterns carried by children. The children were singing. I leaned my elbow on the sill, cupped my chin in my hand, and watched and watched and listened as the thousands and thousands of lights rose from a burning city in the east, streamed over my head, and farther up into the sky where they vanished.

44

Which city would be next? The question weighed on my mother. While she fretted and despaired how we could escape, I fell back into enjoying every hour between the alerts.

I decided to build a fortress in the back court under the hazelnut tree. The materials strewn around were begging to be used. I dug a basement with a pickax through the frozen ground and then switched to a shovel to remove the loosened clods. Maria Barbara came over. She would not stay; she was not interested in construction projects. And, no, I would not come *glennern*. I was doing this now. By dusk, I had finished the excavation.

The next morning, I gathered the bricks that had been blown off the old wall, fitting them in a circular arrangement, leaving small gaps through which I could peek. My plans grew more elaborate. It would take me days to complete this fortress, but that did not deter me. When I had three sides of the tower built, I ran out of bricks. I searched. That back wall of the carriage house had popped off its roughcast here and there, and beautiful bricks were showing through. I took a board from a broken window frame and started pushing against the wall. The masonry was so weak that I could shake it. If I pushed with all my strength, perhaps I could make it collapse, but I thought about Tante Ellen's little carriage inside. I could not destroy the wall without getting into trouble.

The next attack came. As I lay on the floor under my mother, I prayed my evening prayers to God, and then I wondered whether he could perhaps arrange for a bomb not on our house but close enough to collapse the carriage house.

The next morning, the carriage house was still standing. However, another building material offered itself. The back court was covered by a heavy blanket of wet snow, so I rolled several large balls and finished the missing section. The kitchen door, though splintered at one end, made a splendid roof.

Maria Barbara came over and examined my castle. "Shelter," she called it and asked what would happen when the snow melted.

"I will build something else," I said cheerfully.

I invited her into my castle. Enough time had elapsed. She would no longer be talking about Dresden. She crawled in. Since the room was not high enough for her to stand, she had to sit down on the brick floor. I walked around the tower and looked in. We saw eye to eye through the gaps. Then I crawled in myself. There was hardly enough room for both of us. I felt her breath on my cheek. The bricks were cold and hard, and we soon crawled back out, the possibilities of this building exhausted. The real satisfaction had been the planning and the construction. Immediately, new and exciting projects formed in my mind. I hardly noticed when Maria Barbara left.

When the snow melted and my castle collapsed, I was ready to construct another one. I had found a drawer of tools—a hammer, a saw, nails, a screwdrivers, and screws. I could utilize all the broken lumber that had fallen down from the house. I dreamed up new projects for hours. When I set to work, I had the finished structures firmly in my mind, as well as organized plans on how to materialize them.

This pleasant and exciting dreamworld was disrupted routinely by the reality of the air attacks. As a nine-year-old, I had a horrendous fear of dying, much more intense than that experienced by the adults. I had my whole life still before me and did not want to lose it. When the alert sounded, I flew into the cellar, taking two and three steps at a time, and arrived there faster than anyone else. As suddenly as panic grabbed me during the attacks, so quickly it subsided when the planes left. I returned to my play, and enjoyed life, intensified by the lingering awareness of death. I did not worry about danger unless it was immediate. My mother, in contrast, worried constantly about the broader perils of war.

My mother was my security. No matter where I was, a subconscious awareness of my mother connected me to her like the red thread in a labyrinth. I always knew the fastest way to her. The trust in her love and protection spread over me like a sheltering hand.

I never spoke to my mother about my plans and their realization in the back court. Our understanding was almost entirely nonverbal. What I needed was her presence in the house or in the room. It reassured me completely to look up and see those shoulders, like the lower boughs of a tree, traced gracefully against the light or to have her walk over to me and run her hand over my hair. When she was there, peace came over me. In this quieting completeness, I could not think of anything to say to her, as if words would have broken the spell. I knew she understood me and she read my thoughts.

Withdrawal into my own world did not mean that I was unhelpful.

When my mother traveled to Stuttgart to see my father at the end of boot camp, I took care of Monika and led her into the cellar at alerts. Neither did my self-centeredness express itself in greed. I knew that supplies of all kinds were running out, and, consequently, I became a model of self-denial. I did not need anything. I did not want anything. At Christmas, I had not asked for a single present.

Still, I saw the world foremost in relation to me. My friendship with Maria Barbara was best when she played my game. When she played hers, I wandered off. I was not interested in what she did when she was away from me, where her school was, or what her favorite subjects were. When I was with her, I drank her in with my senses—her coquettish face with the freckled, upturned nose; the smell of her hair; her delicate motions; her figure. Besides her, I took in the love of everyone around me and did not feel the need to share my feelings toward them. It would have never occurred to me to visit Tante Toni, like Maria Barbara, who was spontaneously driven to such kindness. If my mother would have suggested such a visit, though, I would have gone.

My understanding of the adult world was rudimentary and

oversimplified. All adults were the same in stature and importance, wandering above me in their own space. I looked up to them, physically, by raising my chin, and mentally, by respecting them. When I met them, I made my Diener, shook their hand, and returned to my own thoughts. I had little inkling of the intricacies with which adults related to each other—how they arranged themselves in social or intellectual order, how they paid heed to the importance of turf, and how much importance they affixed to who were superiors and inferiors, leaders and followers. I was not really interested in the adult world. It was incomprehensible and even suspect. After all, the war was part of it.

The more the projects in my head delighted me and called for my attention, the less attention I paid to my everyday life. I existed on two levels, relegating the everyday tasks like washing myself, getting dressed, eating, and simple errands to automatic control. Meanwhile, I focused my attention on projects in my head. Was it my age or the ever-present fear of death that determined how I acted?

45

In March 1945, my mother, Monika, and I moved from Louisenstrasse 3 to Louisenstrasse 21B, occupying the apartment that Tante Anneliese had vacated.

A week before, Tante Anneliese had returned from the hospital in tears. As usual, she came to Omi's in the late afternoon to pick up Jens-Peter. She sat down in the dining room with my mother and Omi to explain what was the matter. Pulling her white, starched nurse's cap out of her blonde hair, she said that she had quit. She could not handle it anymore. With the front coming closer, the hospital was overfilled with wounded. Besides the soldiers, the hospital was now taking bomb victims. "I can't bear it when they bring in children. I'm no good in the operating room then. I can't forget who is on the table."

A few days later, Tante Anneliese left for the country, heading southwest to the estate Schilfa by Greussen. It belonged to a nobleman, von Haake, whose daughter had become Tante Anneliese's friend while they went to the Königin Louise Stiftung, a private school. My mother urged her to write if there was any room for us, so we could also escape from the city. In the meantime, we moved diagonally across the street, from one cul-de-sac to another.

I was relieved to move to a different cellar. I had heard from Konrad that cellars like ours with wooden dividers and storage of coal were dangerous. Burning bomb phosphorus carried on the water from fire hoses had run into such cellars and ignited the coal and wood. "When they finally dig the people out, they are all charred and only that big." Konrad spread his hands, indicating the size of a shoebox. The building we moved to was newer and sturdier, being constructed out of sandstone masonry. The basement had several rooms without wooden dividers or storage of coal.

A few days after our move, a prewarning sounded early in the evening. We went into the main room in the cellar. It had a glaring lightbulb in a porcelain socket. It threw strong shadows on the wall next to the stairs. As we waited, I climbed up a few steps and enjoyed myself by projecting shadow images on the wall using my hands. I made an Easter Bunny, an old man without teeth, and a snake's head. Every time, I asked my mother what it was. "Look at this, Mutti."

Finally, I projected a devil on the wall, with big horns sticking forward.

My mother said, *"Du willst doch nicht den Teufel an die Wand malen"* (You don't want to paint the devil onto the wall.) This German idiom means, you don't want to predict a terrible thing. Perhaps the prediction will precipitate the event. I quickly changed back to the Easter Bunny and wished I had not made the devil. Entwarnung came, and we went upstairs.

Two hours later, a full alert sent us hurrying into the cellar. When my mother was almost at the bottom of the stairs, she heard wild banging on the entrance door. She went back up and unlocked the door. A young man, a stranger, pushed the door open so violently that it swung against my mother's foot. "Christmas trees. Christmas trees!" he cried as he ran down the stairs.

Before my mother drew the door shut, she saw clusters of lights descending that illuminated the rooftops eerily.

The strange young man who came tumbling down bewildered me. I had never seen a man so young in a shelter. Besides his mere presence, his fear-ridden nervousness was new to me. I only knew the stoic control and acceptance of women.

My mother had hardly limped down to us when the heaviest and longest bombardment yet came down on the city. I breathed the kicked-up cement dust. I had given up wearing my mask and goggles. No one else used them. As the bombs dropped, I said my evening prayers again and again and promised to never paint the devil on the wall. The bombing continued. I was shivering with fear. Where was God? I searched with all my attention above me like a searchlight. Where was God located? Then I suddenly felt where He was, straight above, a little left of the highest point in the sky, way above the circling bombers. I fixed my eye on the Old, Mighty Man with a long beard. He lowered down a swing from endless ropes. I sat on the board. I calmed down. I knew that no matter what would happen I would not fall off that swing, and that the hands that held it would never let go. From that night on through the rest of the war, I would sometimes stop in my play, close my eyes in concentration, and send my searching senses up into the sky until I felt where God was. I would open my eyes and point my finger up at that place. *There He is, I know.*

After that bomb attack of unprecedented severity, my mother just had to get out of the city. She found two old bicycles, and we set out over backcountry roads to Geilsdorf, which was close to Schilfa. Geilsdorf was the village where Martchen's cousin, Lina, lived. Lina had been my mother's and Tante Anneliese's nursemaid. She was married to a man who had a construction business. My mother assured us that Lina would take us in if she could.

Our bicycles were squeaky and rusty and the road full of gravel and chuck holes. The landscape was a continuous series of ridges, like I imagined ocean swells. The many hills slowed our progress. The trip seemed particularly long because I did not know the distance to our destination. My mother had the extra weight of Monika in the basket, and her foot was sore. My bike needed oiling. It resisted my pedaling, even when I stood up off the saddle and gave it all my weight.

The wide-open fields did not offer any cover. The apple trees along the road were tiny and bare, like broomsticks. I was worried about how exposed we were. As if conjured up by my fear, we heard a plane in the distance. My mother yanked Monika off her bicycle. We dropped into the shallow ditch and covered our heads with our hands. I lay a little uphill from my mother, who was covering Monika. The plane flew directly over us. We did not look up. We were like children putting our hands over our eyes, believing that this would make us invisible. The droning faded in the distance. We beat the dead grass off our clothes and went on.

We reached Geilsdorf at dusk. Lina's house was small and surrounded by a stock of drain pipes and piles of stones. She embraced us warmly. When she heard that we were looking for a place to stay, she regretted that the house was already full to the attic with her husband's relatives.

Lina and her husband shared their dinner with us and made their bed for us for the night. My mother objected that we could not possibly displace them from their *Ehebett* (marriage bed), but I knew her resistance was politeness and that we would eventually take the old couple up on the offer.

At breakfast in the crowded living room, the news came from the Volksempfänger that there had been another bomb attack on Erfurt. We felt we had cheated death in this latest assault but worried about those we had left behind.

We got back on our bikes and continued to Schilfa to find Tante Anneliese and beg for shelter in Herr von Haake's estate. His expansive mansion and park teemed with children, milling in the hallways, hanging on the swings like grapes, and running around the pond. They were throwing stones at the swans, which escaped with loud honks, flapping their wings on the water. Finally, we found Tante Anneliese with a group of women scurrying to keep track of the kids.

Tante Anneliese introduced us to Frau von Haake, begging her to let us stay. Frau von Haake made a wide gesture over the premises. "Where?" was all she said.

My mother started pleading, told her that we would only need a little chamber or that we could stay in the hallway.

Frau von Haake eventually agreed to talk to her husband, but she did not see how this could work. "He's already made an exception for Anneliese."

My mother understood the word, *exception*. It was the same type of exception they had made when they admitted Anneliese and her in the Königin Louise Stiftung. It had been a special school reserved for nobility.

Frau von Haake permitted us to have dinner and stay overnight. During the second shift in the crammed dining hall, it became quite clear that the bulk of evacuated people were nobility from all areas of Germany—from Berlin, from the Ruhrgebiet, from Saxony, and from Thuringia. Oblivious to any consideration of class, the government had added a group of war orphans, commoners, who forced everyone to double up in their quarters.

I do not know who we displaced out of the bedroom in the main part of the mansion. Tante Anneliese relayed the message that Herr von Haake had consented to talk to us, personally.

The morning came. Herr von Haake entered after knocking briefly, shook my mother's hand, and positioned himself in front of the large dresser mirror. Looking at my mother through the glass, he listened to her plea, how the bombing in Erfurt had become unbearable, and whether we could please, please stay. Her voice was tight.

Still looking into the mirror, Herr von Haake, straightening his necktie, said that my mother obviously did not understand the situation, that they had been overfilled with evacuated people and refugees and then had to also take orphans. Besides, the country would be just as dangerous as the city. "How are we going to protect the women once the front line arrives here?"

My mother made a last-ditch effort, assuring von Haake how little we would need and how little bother we would be.

Then Herr von Haake made a comment that I did not understand. He said, "Well, after World War I, Germany had no use for nobility any more, even though we had known how to rule for thousands of years. Now we all have to reap the consequences."

"All right, we'll leave," my mother said.

She could barely wait for the man to get away from the mirror and out of the room without venting her indignation.

She stomped around in the room, gathering pajamas, nightgowns, and toothbrushes and snapping the bag shut vehemently. Her brow was furrowed as deeply as I had ever seen. We embraced Tante Anneliese and Jens-Peter and climbed back onto our bikes, heading for the city.

"We can't all leave Erfurt," my mother said, trying to console herself and me. "Omi, Martchen, Tante Ellen, Maria Barbara, Tante Toni—they are all still there. They can't leave."

It was getting dark when we reached Erfurt. A few blocks from our house, we came across a bombed building that had been standing when we had left two days earlier. We picked up our bicycles and carried them over the broken glass and rubble that had spilled over the street. This section of town had not been hit before. We hurried on, worried, and found with relief the buildings in the Louisenstrasse still standing and our loved ones unharmed. They were in the calm stage right after a bombing, when they knew that the alerts in the coming nights would most likely be overflights to and from other targets. Though the probability of another bombing right away was slim, you could never be sure. Many large cities had been annihilated on successive nights. But so far, in Erfurt, there had been a few days after each attack when we were less afraid. We tried to go about our normal lives—going shopping, paying bills, and writing letters. Martchen was the one who kept the busiest, cleaning and cooking. She also went to church regularly, no matter how long it had been since the last attack.

In those lulls, we would walk over to Louisenstrasse 3. My mother had left most of our valuables there, as well as documents, clothes, and the stationary she used for writing to my father. Also, her mail was delivered there. My mother's other reason for visiting was the superb radio that Omi owned. Being wealthy and hard of hearing, she had bought the best Blaupunkt before the war. The radio was so big that it stood on the floor on its own casters like a coffee table and was sophisticated enough to reach all stations in Europe. The strongest station was the Berliner Rundfunk. My mother listened to the Wehrmachtsbericht and followed the advancement of the front line. The reports were still positive, even though the Allies had spilled across the Rhein and advanced along the Main. Frankfurt had been taken. In order to revive the hope for the End Sieg, the commentator extolled the arrival of a new weapon, a *Düsenflugzeug* (jet plane) that could fly twice as fast as the prop planes and would give the German military the decisive edge.

Whenever the army retreated, we were told they had *sich erfolgreich abgesetzt* (successfully distanced themselves). The only way to find out the truth was to listen to the BBC, but death was the penalty for those caught listening to foreign stations. My mother made sure that the Nazi on the first floor was not home. She closed all doors tightly and put her ear to the cloth of the radio. She fine-tuned back and forth around the jamming sounds that covered the BBC until she caught the English words. At the present rate of advancement, Patton's tanks would arrive in Erfurt in the next two or three weeks.

On March 27, my mother sat at the desk in the alcove of our large bedroom, next to the boarded-up window. She wrote what would be her last *Feldpost Brief* (field-post letter) to my father. I was in the back court, rebuilding my fortress. The carriage house still had not collapsed. My mother opened the tiny window in the plywood and called me up to add my greeting to the letter.

The constant dread had made me speechless. I was incapable of telling anyone how I felt, not even my father. I found the stamps of the animals, which I'd received at Christmas, on the desk. I chose the penguin, wiggled it on the ink pad, and stamped it upside down under my mother's signature. Then I wrote "Tradowsky" upside down next to it and dragged the downstroke of the "y" back as an underline. My mother did not ask me to write something personal.

I did not want to know what my mother had written. It belonged in the adult domain. Many years later, after my mother had died, my father read his war diaries once more. He found the letter and showed it to me. As I read it, I remembered the afternoon vividly, my mother hunched over the desk in the alcove with the large boarded-up window. She took many pauses and stared into the distance as she wrote.

Erfurt, 27th of March '45

My dear Papilein!

As I am writing to you now, I don't know at all, whether this letter will still get through to you. And therefore my heart is very sad.

Times are getting more serious and more critical from day to day. I couldn't find out from today's armed forces report how far along the Main River the enemy tanks have advanced. But if places like Hanau, Offenbach, and Aschaffenburg are already occupied, then one only asks, where is this going to lead? I had firmly intended to go further south with the children before the division, and if I would know where to stay, I would still try. However, I talked to some people, also soldiers, who described to me the misery of the refugees on the roads and trains, which must be simply terrible, and everyone has only discouraged me from getting myself into even more danger. So we are still here, and I don't know what to do. For days I have been waiting for news from you. Perhaps I could find some advice in your letters, and I am waiting for an answer to my room inquiry. And I am longing for some loving words from you and only hope that you will continue to be all right. Every night, I look at our stars and, through them, send you all my love. And I will never give up hope that we will see each other again and will hold each other in health and will fulfill our lives happily together. And even if the load of worries now becomes greater and greater, this belief always holds me upright.

And I go as you like a dreamer through the days and always have only the longing for our reunion.

Here is now the most glorious spring weather, one day more beautiful than the next. How would we relish this time together, if only mankind would leave us our quiet and peace; but eventually the storm has to subside. I have thought so much now about our beautiful life together. We always have created our happiness all by ourselves. Happily, I would go back into our studio with you and the children, where I was just as happy with you as later in the beautiful little house in Glienicke or in the big apartment in Straßburg. For me, it means happiness just to live with you together, never mind where and how. For the children, however,

I would wish our life like in Glienicke. That would be the best for them now. We two know, my Papi, how we can arrange our life happily, and after all that we have experienced now, we know even more what is most important. Let us just hope that time will soon give us the opportunity, so that our love and our happiness can blossom anew.

Stay healthy, my dear Papilein, and let yourself be embraced and lovingly kissed.

Always and eternally,
your
Niñafrau

46

As I retreated completely into myself, my mother found her own way of coping. She planted flowers. She went to the Benari Nursery and bought two dozen red roses in bloom. In the lawn in front of Omi's duplex, the stone walks formed a *V.* My mother dug a triangular flower bed right in the middle. I climbed into the pear tree that stood in the corner of the front yard, my favored observation post. I could watch Omi and Martchen in the second-floor dining room. I could also look in the opposite direction past the tall poplar tree into Inge's window.

I watched my mother dig the sod vigorously. She turned the earth, shook out the grass tufts, and raked the surface into smooth, fine crumbs. She measured the spacing of the plants with her resolute strides and dug holes. Then she started putting the roses into the ground in her characteristic stance. She squatted, working around her like the Arab women in my *Thousand and One Nights* book. The bloodred buds were fading into the dark when she carefully watered each plant.

Night fell, and we braced ourselves for the next alert. We had not been bombed for several days and were due for another attack, and our apprehension peaked. The alert that night was a flyover, but the next morning around eleven was different from any bombardment we had endured so far. We had hardly reached the cellar and thrown ourselves onto the floor when the destruction sounded. The planes flew so low that the slide of the Doppler effect was more ominous than ever. The roaring of the motors shook the house. The earth heaved under the impact of bombs that came closer and closer. Then a scream started—thin, high up in the air, and growing ever more intense and hoarse—and ended in a shattering crash that made the ground quake violently. I thought our house had been hit. We heard another big crash close by and more thuds farther away.

The siren had hardly finished, and we were still getting up and dusting ourselves off when someone shouted down the stairs that a bomb had gone into the neighbor's house. We went out on the street. Women were running back and forth, relaying which houses had been hit in the block. Before we could go into the backyard to see the damage to the neighbors' house, another woman came yelling, "A bomb has gone down at Louisenstrasse 3!"

We hurried over there.

To our relief, the bomb had missed the duplex and landed in the front yard. The whole lawn between the forking pathways was a crater. The stone plates of the walks were sticking out of the dirt at odd angles. The poplar tree had been felled by the blast; the bizarre disc of the root system stuck sideways, high in the air, and the top of the tree had smashed into Inge's window. The crater smelled like fresh, upturned earth; spent explosives; and gas. Severed pipes were twisted in the depth. We scrambled around the crater and ran into the house to find Omi and Martchen. They were already starting the cleanup. The bulk of the earth had been thrown against the second story. Martchen and even Omi went to work in the dining room in coats, boots, and babushkas, shoveling the earth through the windowless openings back out into the yard. The dirt in the room was a foot deep. My mother relieved Omi. She was working to find the edge of the Oriental rug when she came upon something bloodred. Shaking it free, she unearthed a blooming rose plant. The bomb had hit the bed of roses like a target.

Before we left, I took a quick hopeful look into the back court. The carriage house was still standing.

I could expand my building projects anyway. The alerts came so frequently and unpredictably that my mother wanted Monika and me to stay close to Louisenstrasse 21B. Omi and Martchen moved in with us.

With the windows blown out, part of the roof gone, and the lines cut, Louisenstrasse 3 had become uninhabitable.

My new playground had plenty of excitement. The river Walkstrom ran behind the white picket fence at the edge of the garden to the mill downstream. There was also the ominous house of the neighbor. The bomb had ripped it open with nothing but narrow remnants of floors and plumbing hanging in the air. Here I made friends with the twins, Hedda and Gerda, the pretty and the plain, and we and the other children spent our time sitting in the gate, throwing sticks into the water, and watching them being churned under by the big wheel.

Often we glanced over to the ruined building with apprehension. What had happened to the people in the cellar? How little change it would have taken for the bomb to have hit our house—a puff of tailwind, the tiny hesitation of a hand? I owed my life to the timing of a split second. How long would my good fortune last?

Our visits in the garden grew shorter and shorter. By the beginning of April, our runs in and out of the cellar became constant. One morning we walked up the stairs after Entwarnung. Before we could reach the landing, a new alert sent us back down. My mother erupted in frustration.

"This is the trouble with war," she hissed. "It's such good business. They have made all these wonderful bombs. Now they have to throw them."

This comment startled me. It was the only time I'd ever heard her complain.

I became sick. I had no appetite, and when I ate, I threw up. I ran in my pajamas from my bed into the cellar and back. The fighting lines moved so close that the planes were upon us while or even before the sirens sounded. My mother decided to place bunk beds in the small room in the cellar and move down there.

On April 10, our anxious ears discerned sounds different from bombers and the dull thuds from their discharge. Now there were explosions with a punch, first faint and deep and far away and then ever closer and more vehement and, finally, underscored with the grating roar of motors and the grinding of chains. It was the sound of Patton's tanks fighting through the Steigerwald toward the city. At midnight, all sounds stopped. A silence ensued that filled the early hours of April 11 with tension and dread.

My story returns to the most consequential day in my life. I hear again the cannons and then the low-flying planes moving back and forth over the city. I see the woman burst into the cellar with the leaflet. The mayor must come out of the city with a white flag before midnight, or the city would be bombed into oblivion. The mothers felt certain surrender was eminent. No military was left inside Erfurt. They sent us into the garden.

But soon we were called back in. We found out the inconceivable news. Erfurt was to be defended at all cost. The ultimatum was rejected. The city would be bombed shortly after midnight, not a stone left on the other.

I spent the afternoon in my upper bunk, still weak from my illness. At eight, my mother came in and put Monika to bed in the lower bunk. She turned off the light. As she left, she kept the door ajar. She went outside and looked at Cassiopeia.

Four more hours. I shivered with fear. I distracted my mind by clinging to better memories of my life. That helped me to drift off into dreams for short periods. My mother came in several times to check on Monika and me. I pretended to be asleep. She would like that.

The voices in the main cellar became loud. Some of the women had found wine. I heard Frau von Reuss starting a song. She was drunk and repeated the same refrain, *"Komm zu Papa"* (Come to Papa), over and over. Other women joined.

My mother came in and saw me awake.

"Go to sleep, Michael. Those women are loud, I know. I'll close the door."

"How late is it, Mutti?"

"Es ist halb zwölf" (half past eleven), she replied. "It is really time to go to sleep."

She ran her hand over my hair and left, pulling the door shut behind her.

The minutes advanced relentlessly. I thought about what my father had told me about dying. I should not worry because it would not happen for a long time. I would have a family and children and grandchildren. I would get very old and look back on a fulfilled life and would not mind dying. Now the end would come as soon as I heard the humming.

I thought about what Martchen had told me about dying, of becoming eternal and of stopping from growing older. *I will always be nine.*

Images accosted me. Not long ago, I had seen a picture in a magazine that someone had left in the basement, too catching to avert my eyes and make it unseen. It was a photograph of a bomb shelter into which a bomb had fallen. It showed the wall into which the people had been blasted. They were flat like a relief.

I stared at the ceiling, holding my hands tight on my chest under my blanket. Where was the swing that my God let down for me? Time was running out. Time was getting less and less, like the air in a cellar where the water was rising. I could not get out. I was trapped like children behind a door that did not open outward. I expected the end from moment to moment.

My mother opened the door. The noise from the main room had died down. The women were listening. My mother walked to our bunk bed in the dark. She spread her arms over me and rested her head on my chest. I knew it was midnight.

I listened and listened with extreme intensity. One minute. Five minutes. *Is there a distant hum?* Ten minutes past midnight. Still no sound in the air. *When are they coming?*

After an eternity, my mother sat down. I asked how long after midnight it was. Half an hour. All was silent. One o'clock. All quiet. Two o'clock. I fell asleep.

Around seven in the morning, I was awakened by the sound of gunfire. My mother explained that it was artillery shooting into the city.

Just that, I thought relieved. The bombers had not come. Think! The bombers had not come!

At midmorning, the shelling stopped. We heard the grinding and grating of tanks, the smacking of rifles, and the *rat-a-tat-tat* of machine guns. The Americans were occupying Erfurt.

The next day, we still had to stay in the cellar. We heard explosions and gunfire as the army was mopping up. The sounds became more and more sporadic and eventually died. As silence settled down on us, the cellar became oppressive, no longer the place of protection during bombardments. Quite suddenly, I became aware of the musty, cool air; the gray, chalky dust; the burdensome, low ceiling; and the pitiful light seeping into the general darkness.

A most amazing spectacle took place in our cellar that day to make me feel even more trapped. A middle-aged man who none of us had ever seen came down into the cellar. He was stocky with a shock of graying curls and carried a metal folding bed and blankets. Not speaking a word to anyone, he hastily set up his bed in the main room opposite the stairs. He pulled a babushka out of his jacket pocket and tied it around his head. He lay down in the bed fully dressed, pulled a lock of hair into his face, and covered himself with blankets up to his chin. Why was this man hiding in our cellar and disguising himself as a poor, little, sick, old woman?

"Look at this," my mother said to me, "one of the big shots that everyone was afraid of. Just look at him now." Her expression of utter disgust told me clearly what I had to think of him.

I spent another night in the bunk and was awakened by the crackling of the radio—translated ordinance from the Americans about the curfew that specified what hours we were allowed on the street. On the morning of the third day after the occupation, I was allowed to get out of the cellar and go into the backyard. My mother would call me when it was time to return into the house.

I walked slowly up the cellar stairs, opened the door, and stepped outside. The light flooded over me. For a moment, I stood as my eyes adjusted to the brilliance. I lifted my head and greeted the blue dome above that was now free, endless, and purged from all danger. I saw the sun again!

I walked—no, I strode, deliberately, like one coming from the grave. I felt the pressure of the good earth against my soles. I proceeded around the house into the little vegetable garden that my mother had planted. The leaves breaking through the soil were of a radiant green like I had never seen before. I lay down between the beds, resting on my back, my arms beside me, in the direct sunlight. I looked into the red of my closed eyelids.

I breathed in slowly and deeply, felt my chest rise, savored the tension, and then relaxed. *I am alive! Just think. I am alive! I can lie here unprotected under the open sky.*

I picked a leaf of chives from where I lay and slowly passed the point over my lips and my tongue, feeling the tingle. I chewed it very slowly, savoring how my teeth pressed and sheared through the hollow, smooth stalk and released bits of tangy taste and sharp odor. What a jubilation to be alive and to know that I would be alive tomorrow and alive the day after and on and on.

What had happened? Was it that something had died in me in the night of fear? Had a part of me become eternal?

I was different. All I needed now were a roof; a bed; a meal; and peace, peace, peace—no more bombing, no more burning, no more shooting. This was all I required to fully enjoy my days. Everything else was nonessential. This attitude would stay with me for life and would not be shaken by any turbulence or misfortune. I am always and fundamentally grateful and joyful for simply being alive.

47

That evening, women who had been in the street during the short lifting of the curfew spread the news about what had happened in the night of the ultimatum. The mayor had known that defending the city was insane. Suspecting the mayor's intent to surrender, the SS put him under house arrest. As night fell and time was running out, the assistant mayor got away, dodged the German patrol by some tortuous route, and arrived in the Steiger, holding the white flag out of his window.

Taken to the command post, he'd pleaded that the city was full of women and children and that there was no one except some old men and boys forced by the SS to resist. The tanks could just roll in and take the city. This, he said, was the message of the mayor of Erfurt, who wanted to surrender but was detained by the SS. General Walker accepted the surrender and called off the airborne.

In the morning, Walker had the city shelled. I read much later that Patton had his generals shell each city before they took it to leave a signature that the XX Corps had come that way. I wondered how Patton found the signature in all the devastation that had preceded. Perhaps he had given that order before he realized that the bombing of the German cities had been, as he described it, "barbaric."[2]

---

2 George S. Patton Jr., *War as I Knew It* (New York: Bantam, 1947), 272.

My mother and I felt such gratitude toward the man who had risked his life to save the city that we wanted to know more about him, but since all communication was defunct, we never even learned his name. The only news we could get from the radio were translated ordinances from the American headquarters concerning curfews. All government agencies in Erfurt, including the police department, had been dissolved. Anarchy descended on the city.

On the way through Thuringia, the army had liberated the survivors of prison camps. The freed prisoners swarmed the city looking for their tormentors. On their list were Nazis who they remembered as causing their arrests or those for whom they had been forced to labor.

Woe to those they found. The tortured and embittered men broke into the offenders' apartments. Their rage fired to unbearable intensity by the Nazi paraphernalia on the walls, they choked, clubbed, and stabbed whomever they found; broke everything into kindling; and set the house on fire. If the man had a business, they trampled his supplies, threw them out of the window, or torched them. Soon the rampage deteriorated into general looting.

Courageous women left hiding during the short times between the curfews to find food and benefited from the lawless situation. My mother braved the chaos in the ruins and returned with five boxes of vanilla wafers and three jars of pickles. She had found them thrown onto the street in cracked crates. Struggling for a while about whether or not she should take them, she saw other women helping themselves and the supplies dwindling. Her concern for our survival overruled her qualms.

The hunt for the Nazi bigwigs went on. Some of them tried to run; some tried to hide.

The next day, when I came downstairs after enjoying my first night back in my bed, the "sick, old woman" was gone—bed, blankets, gray lock, babushka, and all. The adults concealed what had happened, but there was no doubt in my mind. The avengers had found their man.

Seeing the fury of the freed prisoners in the streets and even in our cellar, Omi worried about the fact that a Nazi functionary was living in her house.

"What are we going to do? Right on the ground floor! It's just full with all the party things. If they find it, they'll burn the house down, and if they find anyone in this apartment, oh, my God!"

Still, Omi overcame her apprehension, and she and Martchen moved back to her patched apartment building. My mother followed to help them get settled, taking Monika and me along on their walk across the Louisenstrasse. After skirting the bomb crater, I left the others. I snuck into the back court while they went upstairs. I gathered the newly fallen bricks to start another fortress. To my surprise, my mother appeared with a spade and a gunnysack and started digging a hole that could have been big enough for a child's grave. She lifted the gunnysack, which emitted a metallic tingling; lowered it into the hole; and covered it with dirt.

"What's in that sack, Mutti?" I asked.

"Our silver. Don't tell anybody."

Then she went back upstairs. I wondered, who would break in and steal silver?

When I was going inside for lunch, I noticed that the door to the Nazi's apartment was ajar, and someone was in it. I peeked through the crack and saw a cast-iron stove with the top rings and plates removed. Flames were shooting out of the opening. The stove pipe was red hot. In front of the stove, Martchen stood on a footstool, stretching on her toes, and stoking the fire with a poker. Behind her was a bookshelf that she had almost emptied, and above, Hitler's picture and a draped swastika flag. I walked in just as she put a crap-brown uniform jacket on her poker and lowered it into the fire. "Brown, brown, brown are all my clothes because my sweetheart is an SA man."

At that moment, Martchen noticed that I was standing there. She quickly pushed the jacket into the fire and waved her poker at me. "You get out of here, immediately. Go upstairs. You must not be here."

Her wrinkled potato face was covered with sweat. Smudges of soot and strands of hair stuck to it. She spoke so vehemently and gesticulated so desperately that I retreated, closed the door, and went upstairs as she had ordered.

Omi was pacing the floor. "I told her not to go down there."

Martchen stayed until the last scrap of evidence was scoured. Last, she pried the sign with the name off the door.

The next morning, I made my bed like I had observed Martchen do it. I have made my bed ever since.

Not twenty-four hours later, the avengers broke into the apartment. They destroyed nothing. They did not torch the place. Only several bottles from Omi's wine cellar were missing.

After a few weeks, the MP started patrolling the streets and stopped the looting during the day. The break-ins shifted to the nights. Since the women could not call the police, they came upon a curious solution. As soon as they noticed an entry, they would grab a pot or pan, open the window, and start banging on it with a spoon. Neighbors would join in with their pots, pans, and whistles. Someone even sounded a horn. Soon the whole quarter would erupt into such a din that the military police arrived at the scene and dispersed the intruders. I enjoyed rushing to the window at night and making such an infernal racket, since at all other times, the adults reminded me to keep it down.

48

Days after Erfurt had been occupied, something I had dreamed of appeared on the river. An empty wooden boat, the length of an outstretched man and painted white as snow, hovered above its shimmering reflection. It drifted into the morning sun from underneath the branches of the overhanging lilac and floated along the picket fence toward the gate. I ran through the garden and searched frantically for anything long to extend my reach, grabbed a rake, ran to the gate, and hung over the water from the post as far as I could. The boat floated close, but my arm was too short. The metal spikes splashed into the water a foot from the stern. I almost jumped into the river but thought of Gerda's cut. The boat went on slowly and irrevocably until it tumbled over the mill dam out of my sight. I was about to throw the rake down, when I saw another boat coming down the river and right behind it another. They were just as white and ethereal as the first, but, unfortunately, also both far out of my reach.

"Mutti! Mutti!" I yelled and ran into the house, "there are boats coming down the river. Mutti, I want one of those boats."

She came but the boats had disappeared.

Later when my mother and I went for a walk to the fork where the Walkstrom branches off from the wide and slow-flowing Gera, we saw about a dozen children in boats like the one that I'd had to let pass. They had put seats into them and painted them in bright colors and designs.

Maneuvering the boats with their homemade paddles, they hid under the overhanging willows playing pirates, raced down the river, collided, splashed, shouted, and laughed.

My mother asked bystanders where these boats had come from. They had been thrown into the water from a factory upstream. The owner had produced these boats for the military, to serve as sleds in Russia for transporting the wounded over the snow. He had obtained and assured his army contract by becoming an active party member and an informant and had manufactured these boats with prison laborers. When the German Army had been swept back from Russia, he'd cut back his production, stored the surplus boats, and dismissed his prison laborers, who were herded into a camp in the Thuringian Forest. The free prisoners, returning for revenge, searched for this Nazi and, not finding him, demolished his factory. Out came the wall to the river in a blast and down flew the stacks of boats from the second and third floors, splashing, dunking, and then drifting down the Gera and its branches through the city. Children snagged the boats and dragged them ashore.

I wanted such a boat more than anything in the world. But all the boats had gone downstream now and found their new owners. The only remaining opportunity was that one of them had been caught on the bank somewhere undetected and would be blown free. And so I kept my eyes open. As days passed, I had less and less hope.

The morning I had given up, Gerda came, breathless. "There is another one in the lilac branches."

This one was not going to escape. It was pressed against the retaining wall and tipped by the branches so that it had filled with water. I took an old prop from underneath a washing line, and reaching over the fence, I eased the boat along the wall. I did not let myself be hastened by the shouts of the twins and the other kids. The boat was so submerged that it was hard to maneuver and the slat kept slipping out of the stern. The rim shone white as snow, and the hull shimmered under the water.

"We'll pull it out at the gate and dump the water. This will be our boat, our boat!" the kids shouted.

The gate came. I needed help stopping the boat against the current.

Gerda helped push on the stake and then Hedda. The stern started moving toward our hands and then, *snap*, the notched tip of the old slat broke off. Under our screams of protest, our boat went on. Filled with water, it hung up on the mill dam rather than going over the top. For a long time, we watched the white rim shining without movement, while the water was streaming, eddying, and tumbling around it. We finally turned away from the sad sight.

When I looked for the boat later, around noon, it was no longer in the water. Instead it was leaning vertically and slender against the mill with its bow propped onto the wide deck. This deck extended along the mill and across the river above the dam all the way to our side. I could not take my eyes off the elegant white curves of the hull. I noticed the blinking of the metal ring fastened to the bow. I was all alone. The other children had gone for lunch. Nobody was at the mill.

I considered ways of getting from our yard over to the deck. It was difficult but not impossible. I looked at the boat again. If the slat wouldn't have broken, it would belong to us now. The noon hour was ticking away.

Papi would not approve of this plan, I thought as I was untying a washing line and cutting off a piece by rubbing it over the edge of a stone. I stuffed the rope into my shorts pocket.

The main thing is not to get caught, I thought, climbing the last post of the picket fence and, from there, onto the neighbor's retaining wall. I eased myself along the ledge on the outside of the fence high above the rushing water. The door into the mill remained closed and the deck empty. *What if I fall in and get spilled over the dam or sucked under the wheel?* I inched toward the mill.

Look at the boat; how close it is. I dropped onto the deck. There was no need to sneak across to the boat. Any noise was drowned out by the turmoil of the falling water and the stomping of the wheel. I eased the hull from its upright position down onto the deck and turned it so the bow was heading over the edge. I fastened the rope to the ring on the bow and tightened the other end around my waist. I hastened across the deck and hoisted myself back onto the ledge for the home trip. When I dropped down into our yard, the rope had become taut. I untied the rope and started to tug on it. The boat on the deck moved. I pulled further and it slid toward the tipping point. Then I gave it a hard yank and off it flew, landing right side up in the water. I walked to the gate, pulling the boat and reeling in the line hand over hand until I could reach the ring.

A surge of strength flowed into me when I finally grabbed hold of this most coveted possession. I lifted the bow up into the gate and started dragging the boat out of the water.

It may be a good idea to hide it behind the house for a while, I thought.

However, it was too late for that. Just then, the miller appeared on the deck; he looked puzzled at the empty wall and then up the river. He spotted me pulling desperately on the boat while the stern was still wiggling in the gate. He shouted something that drowned in the noise of the mill and shook his fist. I was certain this miller would come to our house and raise hell. Only one thing could calm him down. I untied my line and shoved the boat back into the water. The miller lifted it out professionally with a hook and pulled it into the mill, not giving me another look. I felt so discouraged that I kept the story from my friends, but I lamented to my mother about the loss.

"Now, you can't just go and steal a boat from the miller," my mother said. "There will be another one coming down the river."

I resigned myself. A boat was not written into my stars.

And then, that afternoon, the incredible happened. I wandered into the yard when I heard the shouts of my friends and splashes and plunges in the water. They were trying to move a boat toward the edge by throwing rocks and clumps to the far side. I grabbed the rake and leaned over the fence, but again the boat was out of my reach.

Suddenly the rake was taken from my hand with a firm pull. My mother, dressed to go downtown with stockings, high heels, and hat, had heard the commotion. But even she, with her long arm, could not reach the boat. It came to the gate. She made one last attempt. She touched the hull but, falling short, pushed it further out. The kids let out a cry of disappointment, which, an instant later, turned into a shout of utter amazement and disbelief.

There was my mother, kicking off her shoes, jumping into the river and walking after the boat. Water up to her thighs, she snagged it with one determined throw of the rake, dragged it back to the gate, and climbed out, water splashing from her skirt. Her feet were unharmed. Jubilant, we all helped lift the boat into the yard. We danced and jumped around like mad, while she went into the house to change.

All my friends agreed, "This is Michael's boat because his mother pulled it out."

Once we started paddling on the river, I was glad to take turns with Hedda and Gerda. They had received permission from Frau von Reuss to get onto the water. "Keeps them busy."

The boat quickly revealed a serious flaw that made it necessary to have two or three children handle it, even though it could carry only one person at a time. Destined for the snow, it leaked like a sieve. After a ten-minute cruise, I was sitting in water up to my belly button and had to come to the gate where the twins helped me pull up the boat, turn it upside down and dump it. Our trips were bound to be short anyway because they were limited downstream by the mill and upstream by a bridge that was too low to pass under.

In spite of these limits we relished the rides. It was like sitting in the middle of life itself—sensing the water glide smoothly under seat and heels and feeling the tipping, the drifting with the current, and the response to the push of the homemade paddle. Occasionally, when I saw the water seeping in between the boards, I thought of the boats with wounded being dragged across the Russian plains but not for long. Shaking my thoughts off like a wet dog does water, I would push from the shadows of the lilac into the glare of the sun. I would dig in my paddle right and left and race between our yard and the bombed-out building. Right before the dam and the big wheel, I would make a turn and, if luck would have him there, send a salute to the angry miller.

Did I thank my mother? I don't remember that I did. It is not likely. I was so certain that she could see and feel how grateful I was that expressing it in words did not occur to me.

49

On one of my trips upstream to the bridge, I saw my first American half sitting, half leaning on the rail. The jacket and the cap of his yellow-green uniform seemed too small. I knew that he was American by his stance. He was relaxed, loose in the joints, while German soldiers were all tight.

Little children were approaching the strange man, some apprehensively looking around the corner, others cautiously venturing forward. The soldier was coaxing them to come closer until they dared pick one of the colorful, glossy loops from the many-striped paper roll he extended toward them.

He called something to me that sounded guttural and slurred, not clipped and pronounced between the teeth like German. I did not understand him and turned my boat downstream.

So satisfied was I with guiding my boat ever faster in front of the admiring horde of children that I seldom did anything else. For a few days, I appropriated the gleaming new ax that leaned against a woodpile in the back of the house. Obviously, the wood needed to be split, but there were no men to do it. I lit into the pile with my vigor of newfound life. I let the ax swing through the air and down into the block. I felt the delicious strain in my back as I swung the ax with the wood stuck on it high into the sky. I turned it and brought it back down on the chopping block with a crash. As the pieces fell clean on both sides of the block, my strained body relaxed in a feeling of joy and satisfaction.

Now and then, I heard a splattering noise high above me. I looked up freely. My war was over. The noise came from a strange plane shaped like a window streaking across the sky with incredible speed. *This must be the new* Düsenflugzeug *(jet plane)*, I thought. I was confused about the weapons. I did not care to know anything about them other than that all had ceased to threaten me.

One remarkable day that early May, I joined Tante Anneliese and my mother for an unusual excursion, a hike designed to take their minds off their many worries. While my mother's unease was general, Tante Anneliese's fear was specific. She had returned from Schilfa and, on her first day back in Erfurt, had broken the law. While she had been away, there had been an edict from the occupational forces that all weapons had to be turned in by a certain deadline, after which noncompliant citizens would be prosecuted. The deadline had past. She had in her possession a dagger that had been sent to her after Onkel Helmut's death with some other of his belongings. The fancy weapon had a mother-of-pearl handle with his name and the Luftwaffe insignia inlaid. She was afraid to hand the weapon in late and decided to throw it into the river. Being concerned that children might cut their feet while swimming, she wrapped the dagger in newspaper and tied string around it. Then in the evening, when the streets were empty, she nonchalantly strolled to the bridge with the package in her purse. Glancing left and right, she quickly tossed the bundle over the rail. To her surprise and dismay, the package did not sink but floated down the river.

For days she was haunted by the vision of the package hanging up on the dam or washing ashore somewhere else and being handed to the authorities. To my mother, this was a far-fetched concern. There were discarded weapons in every ditch.

My mother's worries were more realistic—finding food and whether her husband had made it through the war alive and uninjured. She had not heard from my father since the beginning of March. The last communication had been the letter that had revealed his address in their prearranged code. If he was still as far away as the Black Forest, she could not expect any message. Telephone and mail services were defunct.

But the spring weather became jubilant, and my mother and Tante Anneliese decided to take us children on a walk into the Steigerwald to pick *Himmelschlüsselchen* (little heaven's key) daffodils, like they used to do in peacetime. I had not been outside my block for months. As we walked through the southern suburbs, I curiously observed any changes. Approaching the main thoroughfare, we heard the roar of engines in the distance. We reached the highway, turned south, and continued through the park along the road, while convoys passed us without pause—big trucks loaded with soldiers and then little short and boxy vehicles with four passengers sitting so high and exposed I thought they would fly out in the turns. Tanks came, grinding and groping around, shaking the pavement with their clunking weight and deafening noise. My mother looked at this endless train of gray-green vehicles marked with stubby white stars and shook her head at such abundance of weaponry and gasoline.

"And our men tried to fight this?"

The armed soldiers on the trucks looked determined and formidable. They had a mission.

Suddenly, I saw on several trucks black glistening faces with incredibly white teeth. *Were there actually people from Africa in America?* I asked myself.

One truck had a net that was stretched from the cabin over its load and tied down firmly on sides and back. As it passed by, I saw a mass of men crouched underneath. I looked questioningly at my mother.

"*Deutsche Kriegsgefangene*," she said.

I felt sorry for these German prisoners of war. A shadow crossed my mind. Could my Papi be on such a truck?

When the roar of the motors had faded, we had another unusual encounter. A young man walked down the hill. I had not seen a young German man since that night of the foreboding Christmas trees in the sky, when the panicked stranger had forced the door into my mother's foot. The young man, who now came toward us on the other side of the road, walked with the slow and automatic stride of a hiker. He wore a tattered jacket that had obviously been given to him by someone much larger. It hung open and far down over his uniform pants. His belt and buckle were gone.

This was not the first soldier coming home that my mother had seen. She had observed others in similar ill disguises. Martchen had seen them also. German soldiers were walking home all over. They were walking down the middle strip of the Autobahn in broad daylight, while the American convoys were overtaking them. The Americans probably thought, why stop and pick up those who had thrown away their arms when there was a pressing need for fighters at the front?

"How nice to be close enough to be able to walk home," my mother said enviously. She realized that our Papi did not have this option if he had stayed in the Black Forest.

We finally left all reminders of war behind and stepped into the halls of the beech forests. The light streamed through the unfolding light green foliage. The daffodils flashed in full bloom. Even Jens-Peter and Monika could find enough for a handful. We came to a clearing and rested. Tante Anneliese gave everyone a vanilla wafer. Then we went on to pick more *Himmelschlüsselchen*. My mother could not resist gathering all she could hold from what the warm, sprouting ground offered. These were, indeed, keys for the escape from misery and worry.

We were combing through the underbrush along a forest dirt road when Tante Anneliese gave a little yell and stopped dead. She waved my mother over and told us children to walk down to the road and stay there.

My mother and Tante Anneliese looked down among the ferns for a while, then joined us saying, "Let us go straight down this road. We have enough *Himmelsschlüsselchen*. Let's not look for more."

They were upset, their curved noses elongated with the familiar furrows.

It was not until we left the Steigerwald and descended into the Gera Valley toward Hochheim that the women slowed their pace.

"What was it, Mutti?" I kept asking.

She did not answer. I insisted until finally, she fell behind the others, lowered her voice, and told me.

"There was a dead soldier in the ferns. Did you see him?"

"No," I said, "I did not see him."

What was going to happen to this dead man? Was my mother going to report him? Where would she go? The police department was defunct. I added these questions to the many unanswered ones I had about the war. A dead soldier was lying in the Steigerwald. Could we do nothing about it?

The forest opened to the lush grounds of the valley. We walked right into the resurrecting nature, the sprouting, the blooming, the humming of insects, and the gleaming of the river behind the trees along the banks.

I noticed long, narrow basins that stretched across the valley floor from the foothills to the river. My mother told me proudly that my Great-Grandfather Müller had built those basins as expansion of his nursery, I. C. Schmidt, to supply Berlin with watercress. But then she added with a hint of bitterness that I. C. Schmidt had to be sold during the Depression, and all this now belonged to Benari.

We returned home, and my mother and Tante Anneliese distributed the bouquets of golden flowers on tables and shelves. There were enough for my mother to give a bunch to Omi, who said they were terribly nice and handed them to Martchen to take care of. Tante Anneliese brought some of her flowers to Tante Ellen. My mother had no such inclination.

We did not venture out into nature any more after that. The day we picked *Himmelschlüsselchen* remained locked in my memory as a curious mix of spring's glory and mortal suffering, of life's blend of elation and sorrow.

50

I was in my boat when Hedda came running. "Michael, Michael, your father! He is home!"

I jumped in the river, swam to the gate, and ran past Hedda, hearing her shout, "You are crying! Are you scared?"

I ran through the garden. *Where is he? Where is he?*

There he was, standing in the narrow passage between the house and the back shed, hugging my mother, Monika's arms around his leg. They turned to me. I leaped into Papi's arms wet as a dog. When I let him go, he picked up Monika, hugged and kissed her, stroked her blonde curls, and set her down gently. He embraced my mother again. We went on hugging for a while, incapable of words.

My mother eventually asked, "But where did you come from?"

"From the Black Forest. I was stationed in the Münstertal until the end of April. I walked."

"No! You walked from the Black Forest?"

My father nodded. "I got some of my clothes at Frau Fährenbach's."

"But where did you get this hideous coat?"

"I traded my winter coat."

"Your beautiful winter coat?"

For a moment, the folds on her forehead appeared. "It doesn't matter. You are here."

"I exchanged it for a present for all of you. I left it at Mamusch's on the porch. I looked for you over there."

Soon Martchen brought the present, a paper bag with a dozen eggs. We had an early supper of delicious *Eierkuchen*. Then we settled in the living room.

"Now tell us what happened," we urged my father. He got up and fumbled his diary out of the shabby coat. He opened it, and a blue field-post letter slipped from under the cover.

"Which one is that?" my mother asked.

"Let's see." My father unfolded the flimsy blue paper. "The twenty-seventh of March."

"Really?" My mother picked up the letter and turned it back and forth. I glimpsed my "Tradowsky" signature and the imprint of the penguin upside down. She shook her head. "This is the last letter I wrote. It still got through?"

"Our unit stayed in the Münstertal." My father flipped through the small pages filled with miniscule pencil writing to find a drawing for which he had used a whole page. "Here, this is where I was lodged." A farmhouse under the hood of its massive, shingled roof stood in a pine-covered slope. A flume from the creek behind the house passed along the shingled wall under a tiny upstairs window and dropped its stream in front into a cattle trough carved out of a log. "My chamber was here. At first I thought I could not sleep with the splatter directly under my window, but I became used to it."

My mother said, "When I got your message, I thought how fortunate that you were assigned to the Black Forest."

"Hear how incredibly fortunate this really was. After you visited me, we were digging fortification around Stuttgart waiting for our marching orders. Half of us worked outside. Half stayed in the barracks. We switched on alternate days. Middle of February, it got very cold. One morning, my roommate, who was on the opposite shift, complained about having to go out in this terrible cold. So I volunteered to take his place. You know me. I like the fresh air much better than a stuffy room.

"When I returned, the barracks were empty. The troops had left. They had received orders that morning to move out immediately."

"What happened to them?" my mother asked.

"They were sent to reinforce against the Russians. Most of them fell or were captured and sent to Siberia. A week later, the rest of us were assigned to the Black Forest.

"Fate," my mother whispered.

My father nodded. "It was really peaceful there. Once a day, I walked down to the valley and did my shift in the communication truck. We *Funker* were able to follow how the Allies advanced, cutting through the middle of Germany in a pincer to meet the Russians at the Elbe. I knew they'd come through Erfurt. You wrote you didn't want to go south. I heard they took Erfurt on April 11 or 12. I was worried. The bombardments, the occupation. How would you get through it?

"We finally received orders on April 26. We were to join an armored column in Freiburg the next morning, move up the Höllental and over the top of the Black Forest, Titisee, Neustadt, as close to the Swiss border as possible, along the north shore of Lake Constance to Bavaria; join forces there; and squeeze through before the French could seal off the Black Forest. They were moving south on the east side, from Freudenstadt, over Rottweil, Donaueschingen to Neuhaus."

I interrupted my father. "So you started where we rode our bicycles last July."

"Only this time we went in the opposite direction, from the Himmelreich to the Höllental."

"Did you see the bridge, where the truck got stuck?"

"Let the air out of the tires. I thought of that when we crossed under.

"At noon we reached the high plateau, past Titisee. It was the same road we walked from Friedenweiler. We came through Neustadt. Our officer, Trabold, was from Neustadt. He looked out of the truck to see his family but did not see them.

"In Löffingen, we turned south on a side road, winding and hilly. We crawled. An hour before sunset, we approached Zollhaus. It was 15 kilometers from the Swiss border, the farthest point south were we could cross the main road on which the French were coming. If we could make it through, we had a chance to reach Bavaria.

"Our convoy moved up a small valley toward a pass. We came to a bridge that was so narrow the first armored car stripped off the rails. Under our truck, large chunks of pavement fell into the creek. Past the bridge, the left side of the road dropped to the creek. The right side rose into the woods.

"Suddenly I heard an explosion. We were under fire. The French had blocked the pass. The rounds from our guns fell short. The French range was so superior, no sense returning fire. The French artillery adjusted its aim. One grenade destroyed the bridge. Another blasted the leading armored car on its side and blocked the road. We were stuck. The French trained on the convoy like a shooting gallery. Trabold ordered us to seek cover. We grabbed our rifles and backpacks and scrambled up the hill into the forest. With every explosion, I threw myself onto the ground. Trees splintered. Dirt fell on me. I thought, is this it? The shooting went on until dark. When it stopped, I went down to the road."

My father paused, pressed his eyes shut among folds of pain, and shuddered. "The vehicles, twisted and burning; the dead; the injured, moaning and screaming for help; the confusion—oh, it was horrible.

"The communications truck was destroyed. The vehicle ahead was still burning. Officer Trabold and my two enlisted *Funker* buddies, Fritz and Herbert, were looking at the wreckage. All the equipment had been blown to pieces. For a while, we stood there. We had the same thought. No one wanted to come out with it. Finally I said, real quietly, 'I know this area like the back of my hand.'

"Trabold looked each of us in the eyes. He had a violinist, a singer, and a play director here; all had families. In a low voice he asked, 'Who wants to stay?' Silence. 'Then follow me!'

"Trabold jumped into the ditch and struggled uphill into the forest. We followed, quietly and cautiously. When we heard branches breaking in the dark, we stopped dead. Hush! We realized other soldiers were leaving also, and we relaxed. We felt our way up between pines, in the pitch-dark, slowly. After about an hour, walking became lighter and easier. We made it over the ridge and came to the edge of the forest. The full moon was up. A meadow sloped to a creek under trees. On the other side, the meadow went up to the forest again. We had to cross here."

I said, "It's a good thing that you had a full moon, so you could find your way."

"In the woods, it was good. In the open, it was dangerous. If the SS would have seen us, they would have hung us or shot us. If the French would have found us, they would have shot us or taken us prisoner.

"We waited until a cloud began to drift across the moon. Then we dashed down the meadow and made it to the creek and the trees. The creek was high because of the snow melt. We had to jump. One by one, we took a run-up and jumped across. No one got their feet wet. This was important. We still had to expect frost at night and snow on the ridges. We waited for another cloud and ran uphill to the trees.

"We decided to head for Neustadt. I knew the direction. We followed the forested ridge northwest for several kilometers until the trees opened on a field. There was a homestead on the distant slope, windows dark. We approached in the shadow of the trees and came upon a shed. The door was open, farm equipment inside.

"'Let's get rid of our rifles,' said Trabold. We dumped our ammunition into the creek behind and leaned the secured weapons against the workbench. I was glad I never had to shoot it once."

Hearing my father say this, I was relieved. I did not want to think of him killing someone.

"We observed the house for a while. Since we saw no vehicles the place was probably not occupied by the French. We wondered, would they have something to eat? One of us should go and knock.

"I volunteered. I snuck over to the house and knocked on a window. Nothing. Another window. Nothing. I'd turned to leave when a window upstairs cracked open and a woman's voice whispered, '*Wer ist da?*'

"'*Wir sind Lanzer*' (We are soldiers), I told her. 'Do you have anything to eat?'

"'Wait,' came the whisper, and the window was drawn shut.

"I waited so long I thought the woman had changed her mind. Finally, a window next to me opened, and a hand appeared with something wrapped in paper.

"'Here, God bless you. My husband is out there somewhere too. Take care of yourselves.'

"Trabold opened the package with his pocketknife; it had half a loaf and a blood sausage. He divided the provisions into four equal parts. I split my portions into two, wrapped one part into paper, and stuffed it in my backpack. We chewed looking out the door. The trees began to show details. It was time to hide for the day. We went back to the ridge, crawled into the underbrush, covered ourselves with branches, and went to sleep."

My father thumbed through his diary until he found two pages, covered with a list of dates and addresses. "These are the places where I stayed each night," he said. The first line showed April 27 and a tiny row of pine trees.

"As soon as the moon rose, we started moving again. We followed the same ridge, west-northwest. I knew we had to cross the main highway, the one our convoy had used. It was now in French hands. We heard motorcades from far away. Coming closer, we saw the headlights flicker through the trees. We halted at the edge of the forest and waited for a break. When it became quiet and dark, we beat through the brush down to the road, but before we could get across, another convoy came through the turn. We hid in the ditch. As soon as the last vehicle had disappeared, we made a run for the other side and scrambled into the forest.

"For the next hour, we climbed. We came to an opening and caught our breath. From here, we saw the highest ridges of the Black Forest. On the northern slopes, snow gleamed in the moonlight. Before dawn, we reached the area of Oberbrand, about 10 kilometers from Neustadt. It became so light that we had to hide again. I tried to doze but woke often. I was hungry and cold.

"In the afternoon, Trabold called us together. 'I am going to leave you now. It's only two hours home from here. I'll go through the woods. By the time I get to Neustadt, it will be dark.'

"He opened his knapsack and pulled out some forms and a fountain pen. To our surprise, they were army documents. Trabold signed. We were honorably discharged. 'Here, this may help you out of trouble. My advice is, don't get caught.' He paused. 'So, where do you go from here?'

"'We three will go to Switzerland,' Fritz said.

"Trabold cautioned, 'Be careful at the border; lots of SS.'

"Trabold shook hands with us and disappeared into the forest. We three were too nervous and hungry to wait for the dark. We had become used to the danger and less cautious.

"'Let's go through the woods,' Herbert suggested. 'Walter, you'll come with us to Switzerland, won't you?'

"'No, I don't think so.'

"'So, where are you going?'

"'I'm going home. I'm going to my wife and kids. I'm going to Erfurt.'

"'Halfway through Germany with a war going on? You're crazy. You will be caught. Come with us. We'll be in Switzerland tomorrow. We'll wait there until this is over.'

"'No,' I said, 'I'm going to Erfurt.'

"They shook their heads and said no more.

"We walked together for a while. The forest thinned out, and we got into a snowfield. The ridge toward the south became visible through the trees. Herbert and Fritz decided they had to get over to the other side and follow the valley toward Schaffhausen. We shook hands, and I watched them climb the ridge and disappear.

"I went west toward the hamlet of Schwarzenbach. The pine grove suddenly stopped, and I found myself on a wide, open snowfield that sloped down to the valley. I saw a homestead, quiet and desolate. I considered waiting for the dark, but I was very hungry and went on.

"I was about one kilometer from the building when a door opened and a French soldier came out."

My mother drew her breath through her teeth.

"He looked around and disappeared again. Had he seen me? I turned and scrambled uphill toward the tree line. Moments later, the soldier reappeared, followed by another. They had rifles over their shoulders and went up the hill after me. I tried to run but slipped in the heavy snow. When I reached the grove, they were almost in shooting distance. I knew they had no trouble following my tracks through the trees. I came to the clearing where I had said good-bye to Fritz and Herbert. Here the snow was trampled in many directions. Quickly I used the tracks that we had made when we approached this spot and crawled in the hollow under a pine.

"Within minutes, the Frenchmen stepped into the clearing, rifles in hand. They came to the trampled area, examined the tracks, and talked over which way to go. Finally, they followed the tracks up the ridge."

"Did they get the other soldiers?" I asked.

"No, they were too far ahead. I stayed under the tree until it was dark. I heard them come back down alone.

"Then I waited a long time. I thought, boy, I want to walk to Erfurt, and I almost got caught the first day. I promised myself to be more careful. I had a plan that would make it possible to get through. I was in walking distance of The Turner. If I would make it to Lydia this night, I could get food and a hiding place. The next night, I could make it over Neukirch and Brent to Schönwald. At Frau Fährenbach's house was a crate with my clothes and my bicycle. As a civilian on a bike, I could reach Erfurt in a week. It didn't turn out that easy.

"I walked to the edge of the grove and observed the homestead. When the lights went off, I moved on. The first kilometers were slow walking in the dark. When the moon rose, the Titisee glimmered in the distance. I turned north and reached The Turner and Lydia's farm at dawn. I halted under the trees and looked at the house. Was it safe to approach? An old man came out and went to the barn. I stepped out from under the trees. He grabbed me by the arm and pulled me inside the barn.

"'I am a friend of Frau Hermann's. Can you hide me for the day? Can you get me some food?'

"The old man did not say a word but waved me to follow him. He led me up a ladder to the loft, scrambled over a pile of loose straw to where the roof met the floor, and made a deep dell. He motioned me to lie down in it and covered me.

"I said, 'Tell Frau Hermann Walter is here, Walter Tradowsky.'

"He did not answer and left the barn. Had he heard me? I drifted off. When the ladder creaked again I woke, and the man reached a hunk of bread and a sausage up to me. I ate and covered myself deeper and slept like in Abraham's bosom.

"A shuffling sound woke me. I scrambled out of the straw. The old man struggled up the ladder, holding a flashlight. 'Come. It is safe now.'

"At the door he gave me a bag with sandwiches. 'From Frau Hermann.'

"I headed up the hill for the Höhenweg. I knew the way so well, I found it even in the dark. I passed Neukirch, saw the lights shining in the distance. This is where we sat when we climbed the Brent, Michael, on our first bicycle tour from Straßburg, when you went on and on about the miraculous hair of Lydia's daughter."

"Oh, yes, I remember," I nodded.

"The stars were fading when I dropped down to Schönwald. You know how the Fährenbach's house is built into the hillside. I ducked to the backdoor on the second floor and knocked, waited, knocked again, and heard steps.

"Frau Fährenbach opened the door a crack. 'Walter Tradowsky.' She recognized me and pulled me in the door.

"'Can you hide me?'

"'Not like that; the French go in and out downstairs. Wait here.' She came with a bundle of civilian clothes. 'Go up into the woods and change. Get rid of your uniform and backpack.'

"I climbed back to the woods and changed and then stuffed my uniform and pack in a hole under a tree. The pants were way too short and big. I had to hold them in my hands.

"'I have some of my own clothes in one of the crates,' I said.

"We went into the attic. The furniture and the crates were in one corner, neatly, all there."

"Oh, that's good," my mother said, relieved.

"But I could not find the bicycles. 'Where are the bicycles?' I asked.

"She confessed. 'Yesterday, there came other German soldiers going home. I gave them civilian clothes. They saw the bicycles and took them. They didn't listen to me. I'm sorry.'

"I thought, bicycle or no bicycle, I'll make it to Erfurt.

"I opened crates to find my clothes. It was difficult. She only had a hammer and a little screwdriver, no crowbar. I had to yank the boards off with my hands. I found my clothes in the second crate."

"See, how good it was I put some clothes in. You were concerned about putting things in that were not antiques," my mother said.

"You were right," my father admitted. "I was glad to have something that was warm. The weather was still cold. The coat was hard to get from under the boards. I got a splinter in the back of my hand. I pulled it out, sucked the wound, and did not pay any more attention to it.

"By now it was noon. Curfew was at five. I decided to stay overnight. Frau Fährenbach hid me in an upstairs bedchamber and brought me lunch and dinner. In the morning, I woke up around seven. I stretched and hit my hand on the headboard, and that hurt. Could it be that some of the splinter was still in there? I washed and examined the wound carefully but did not see anything except a slight redness.

"At the end of the curfew at eight, I stepped out on the road with Frau Fährenbach's blessing and sandwich, a civilian, blending into the pedestrians. I snuck past Hotel Hirschen, teeming with French military. They did not pay attention to me; there were other Germans walking. I thought that once I got out alone on the open road, the likelihood that I would be stopped would increase. I resolved to always memorize the name of the next village. You were allowed to walk to the next village. I took the switchbacks down along the waterfall. Every time I crossed the stream, I stuck my hand into the cold water. When the onion-shaped roof of the church showed through the trees, I knew I had made it to Triberg. My plan was to walk down the Gutach-Kinzig Valley to Offenburg to the Schimpfs. Boy, I thought, if I only had my bicycle, I would roll down there in two hours, like we used to. Walking it would probably take me two days. The highway through Hornberg was very busy, one French convoy after another coming up the valley. They were occupying the highlands."

"Were the trains going?" I asked.

"No trains. The bridge over the Kinzig had been blown up.

"After I almost got run off the road twice, I went on smaller side roads, slower but safer. It was almost curfew when I reached Hausach.

You remember where the Gutach flows into the Kinzig and where the road from Freudenstadt joins. Well, the traffic tripled, and I had to stay off the highway. I found a path through the woods to Stainach. Now it was past five o'clock. If I would drop down to there, I would be arrested. I had no choice but to spend another night outdoors."

My father ran his finger on the line that said, Tuesday, followed by a tiny row of pine trees. "I shored up some pine needles and broke off branches, lay down, and covered myself. It started to drizzle. An icy wind blew up the valley. I folded up my coat collar over my ears. My hand hurt and was swollen. The drizzle changed to rain and then to big, wet flakes. I watched the snow being tossed out of the dark sky until white covered as far as I could see. Oh, I was really cold, hungry, and discouraged. How would I make it to the Sonne the next day? And to Erfurt?

"I slept badly, waking every time I turned and leaned on my hand. At six, I got up. I felt nauseated and dizzy. The swelling was worse; my arm was painful and sore under the armpit. I went down to the stream and held my hand in the cold water till the pain numbed.

"At eight, I was back on the road down the Kinzig Valley, through Biberach and Gengenbach, and then I reached the spot where the valley opens into the Rhein Valley, you know, Ortenberg and Offenburg in the distance. I did not pay attention to the French military on the road but drudged right down Main Street to the Hotel Sonne. Now I can get help, I thought. There was the gilded sun swinging out into the street. But what was that? In front of the iron gate in the courtyard stood two Moroccan guards with rifles and mounted bayonets."

"Oh no!" my mother shouted. "They are terrible!"

"An old man saw me standing there and looking. 'That's French headquarters, not a good place to get close to.'

"What to do? The hospital was under French control. Who could help me?

"That's when I remembered Baronin Steffi de Neveau."

"Oh ja," mother said, "In Durbach. She invited us to coffee and cake once. The Schimpfs' friend. You gave her tickets for the Wildschütz."

"Yes, she was my only hope. So I went on and reached Durbach right at curfew. I pulled the doorbell. An old woman with snow-white hair opened. I explained to her that I was a friend of the Baronin, Walter Tradowsky, play director at the Straßburg Theater, and friend of the Schimpfs.

"'Just a minute, please,' she said.

"The Baronin appeared. 'Herr Tradowsky.' She wanted to shake my hand.

"'Sorry, I can't.'

"'For heaven's sake, what happened?'

"'A splinter.'

"'We have to do something right away,' she said. 'Lie down and let us treat this. We can talk later. Marie, take Herr Tradowsky to my room.'

"I lay down and drifted off. The white-haired woman came in with a bowl with a warm infusion that had a strong fragrance and put my hand in it. I called her Grandmother. I was confused. She looked like my grandma to me. She put a yellow ointment on a bandage and wrapped my hand. The next morning, she came with another infusion. When she opened the bandage, the boil had opened and the rest of the splinter had come out. She soaked the hand and bandaged it again.

"The baroness was so happy that I was better. We had breakfast in the kitchen. When she heard that I was walking to Erfurt, she wanted me to stay till the war was over. I saw that every room was occupied by evacuated families. I think she had put me in her own bed and slept in a chair.

"'No,' I said. 'Thank you, but I must keep going.'

"I took the country road out of Durbach. I had no map. As long as I kept the Rhein Valley on my left and the sun in my back, I had to head north. I estimated how far it was to Erfurt—500 kilometers. I had come 150 kilometers already in six days. In two to three weeks, I should be able to make it. If my stride was 80 cm, it would take 625,000 steps to get home. I had to make sure to soak my feet every night."

My Papi, I thought. *He always likes to count things.*

"My way went along a ridge. The sun was already over the Rhein Valley, when the road turned west. I saw a highway in the valley on the east side of the ridge that went north. I took a shortcut through the fields down to that road and went on north. After a while, I thought, *nanu*, there is something *komish*" (funny) "about this road. Why is it totally desolate? No oxcarts here, no farmers on the fields, no pedestrians. There were also strange patches in the road. After a few kilometers, the road met another in a *T*. My road had been barricaded. I walked around the white and red boards. A sign on the other side warned, '*Durchgang verboten, Lebensgefahr, Nicht entmint*' (Off limits, Danger, Not demined).

"*Um Himmels Willen* (For heaven's sake), I thought. How did I survive this? I felt like I had when I returned to the barracks and learned that the others had been sent to the Russian front."

"You must have had a guardian angel," my mother said.

"After my heart had calmed down, I went on. From then on, I felt sure I would make it to Erfurt. At the next village, it was curfew, and I found a place for the night." Papi ran his finger over the line and read, "Thursday, third of May, Frau Müller in Waldulm.

"I felt strong the next morning and got an early start, hoping to make it all the way to Neuweiher. I took a small road that wound through the foothills.

"Around ten thirty, I came to a valley that I had to cross to keep my direction. The valley opened into the plain of the upper Rhein. I sat down and searched for the Straßburger Münster. But Straßburg was in a haze. I saw the outline of the Vogesen, though, above the haze.

"Then I looked closer and I thought, *Mich laust der Affe*" (The monkey is lousing me).

Papi explained, "Right at the foot of my hill, there were rows of wooden one-story barracks, observation towers. Barbed-wire fence surrounded the area, and hundreds of people were between the buildings. I had come upon a *Kriegsgefangenen Lager* (POW camp)—something to get away from quickly. I walked fast until the whole Rhein Valley was out of sight.

"I found a road that was heading north and followed it. It was a winding road in a side valley, and you could not see far ahead. Much too late, I saw what was coming around the turn—a troop of *Kriegsgefangene*, guarded by two French soldiers, one in front and one in the rear. I quickly went through the ditch, stood at a tree, and peed, waiting for them to pass. They stopped behind me and waited. When I turned around, the front guard crooked his finger at me to come closer. I walked up to the guard and showed my slip of discharge. 'Je suis civil.'

"The guard looked at it, shook his head, and put it in his pocket. He raised the butt of his rifle and pushed me into the first row. Then he stepped to the side and bellowed, 'Marchez au pas!'

"When we entered the gate, I saw what the camp was really like— prisoners sitting and lying around in the grass or standing in groups, their insignia ripped off, their uniforms tattered, their faces hopeless and hollow. One or another looked at me, puzzled. The guard called me out of the group, crooking his finger again. The others were herded into one of the barracks.

"The guard took me to the only two-story building in the compound and walked me into the commander's office. The commander stood talking to two of his officers. He looked over at us. 'Qu'est-ce que c'est?'

"'Arrested this man on the road. He claims to be a civilian,' the guard said and handed him my paper. 'What should we do with him?'

"The commander pointed over to a bench on the wall, 'Un moment,' and went on in his conversation. I had to wait quite a while and planned what to say. When he had dismissed his staff, he sat down behind his desk and motioned me to sit across.

"He unfolded my paper and looked puzzled. He probably wondered who would walk on the road with this expensive coat. 'Where are you from?' he asked.

"'Strasbourg. I am play director at the city theater.'

"Suddenly he became interested and friendly. 'Vraiment? Dramaturge au théâtre? C'est magnifique!'

"It turned out the man loved the theater. He dreamed of going to acting school one of these years. So we talked about Molière and Rostand. He seemed to forget the war and the prison camp."

My mother added, "How good that you are fluent in French."

"Yes, it made the difference. Maybe he thought I was Alsatian.

"Finally he came back to business. He took a form from the top drawer and picked up a pen to fill it out. He copied my name from the discharge paper and asked, 'Where do you want to go?'

"'I'm going to meet my wife and children. I want to go to Neuweiher.'

I spelled it, and the man put it down. He signed the form, stamped it, and handed it to me, voilà. I took a quick glance and saw the words 'laissez passer.' It was a passport to the next town.

"I suppressed my surprise and joy and simply thanked the officer. 'Merci beaucoup, monsieur.'

"The officer shook my hand. 'Perhaps I will see you at the theater in Strasbourg one day, no?'

"I left the building. At the gate, I showed my new passport. The guard stepped back and saluted.

"It was three o'clock already when I took the road toward the hills again. Neuweiher was out of reach. I made it to the first village in the foothills. Aspich, farmer Joseph Mug.

"The next morning, I took the direct country road, *frech wie Oskar*" (fresh like Oskar), he smiled. "I had my passport. A patrol stopped me before noon and released me immediately when I showed my paper. This day, I made it to my destination. Saturday the fifth of May, Neuweiher, Herr Seiler.

"The next day I went over Gernsbach and Loffenau to Herrenalb, in the northernmost part of the Black Forest. I stayed on small back roads in the heights. Walking away from Neuweiher, my passport could have made me look suspicious.

"I reached Herrenalb by curfew."

My father looked at his list. "Got dinner and a bed in two different houses. Sunday, sixth of May, Frau Kubler, *Abendbrot*, Frau Stohr, *Bett*.

"On the seventh of May, I walked from Herrenalb over Maarkzell to Spielberg. In the early afternoon, I rested on the last high point of the Black Forest. It was a splendid view west over the Rhein Valley and north over the hilly lands of the Neckar River and beyond to the blue mountains of the Odenwald. I knew I had to hike through the gap between the Schwarzwald and the Odenwald and hold myself on the east side of the Odenwald to reach the Main River valley. I sat there quite a while. The warmth of the last days had brought out the fresh, lush greens. Spring had finally arrived after this long, snowy winter.

"Going on north into the lowlands, I saw in the distance a wide road with lots of traffic. This was the highway from Karlsruhe to Pforzheim, a *Verkehrsarterie*" (traffic artery). "There was no way around. I had to cross it. When I reached the road, an endless convoy was dashing by. I stood there at the edge, but no one had the time to check on me or even notice me. It was the single patrol cars I had to fear. When there was a break in the traffic, I crossed without problem and went on a small side road to Wilferdingen. An old farmer, Christian Daub, took me in.

"While I was eating my *Abendbrot*, several friends of the Daubs came in, all exited with rumors. The one said the Führer was dead. He had died in his bunker in Berlin, and Berlin had fallen to the Russians a week ago.

"'No,' another said. This one claimed Berlin had fallen just two or three days ago, and Borman was now in charge.

"'All wrong,' said another; the Führer had escaped Berlin and flown to the Obersalzberg.

"All of them were sure that, sometime during last week, Berlin had fallen. I was worried. What happened to my father? What happened to Elisabeth Schubert? We all know how ruthless the Russian fighters are, don't we—looting and *vergewaltigen Frauen und Mädchen*" (raping women and girls).

I listened to my father so attentively; no word escaped me. *What is* vergewaltigen? I wondered. *Something about Gewalt* (force). The prefix *ver* told me that the force was used in a bad way. What was the terrible thing the soldiers did to the women? I did not ask and listened as my father went on.

"I could not shake my worries all next day. I went on to Gochheim. A farmer, Huysgen, took me in.

"The following day, I walked through the hilly lands of the Neckar River. I remembered the landscape from my first hike with Schubert and Ulrich and Dieter. It made me very sad to think about the Schuberts, how Dietrich and Ulrich had fallen in Russia and how Schubert had died, and now, how Elisabeth was alone in the Russian occupation.

"That night, I reached Neckarbischhofsheim. I found a place with Frau Albrecht in the Hauptstrasse. She told me there was a cease-fire in effect. It had started at midnight. The fighting was over.

"I struck out confidently the next morning. I could no longer be taken prisoner. I took the straightest highways toward my goal. I could still be arrested by military police. Anyone on the road needed special permission, particularly when crossing county lines. I was at the level of Heidelberg, perhaps 50 kilometers east. I had come about halfway to Erfurt. The first half had taken me thirteen days. The second half, on straighter roads, should take me several days fewer. I was thinking about coming home. You three would be in the garden on a sunny day. I would get in the house, quietly, not seen by any one, and go to the piano and play 'Shine Moon, Shine.' You would listen up in the garden. *There's only one person who can play this song.*"

My father, I thought. *He always thinks of surprises.*

"I am glad you came right to us, even when it was between the stairs and the garbage cans," my mother laughed.

My father went on. "That day, I reached Eberbach on the Neckar River and found shelter with Vitus Kellner in the Stoess Strasse.

"On Friday May 11, I accomplished the farthest hike yet, from Eberbach along the eastern slopes of the Odenwald, to Amorbach. In the afternoon, close to the village of Ernstthal, I heard a car slowing down behind me. I turned and saw a jeep, that boxy little open military vehicle with a white star on the door. Two soldiers with a white MP painted on the helmets sat in it. I wondered, was it good or bad that I had passed into the American Zone? The officer in the passenger seat got out, stopped me, and said something I did not understand. I pulled out my laissez passer. The officer studied it, turning the paper back and forth. Then he looked me straight in the eyes. 'Is it good?'

"I nodded seriously. 'It is very good.'

"The MP returned the document and jumped into his seat. The jeep gunned out of sight in a cloud of dust. I showed this paper every time the MP stopped me and never got arrested. The stamp, the signature, and the unintelligible language worked like magic. That night, I stayed with the teamster, Trabold, in Amorbach.

"I was looking forward to the next day's hike. I expected to reach the Main River. Before noon, the landscape opened up to the wide, lush valley;

the gently flowing, wide river; rows of poplar trees on the banks; and the town of Miltenberg. I had reached the southernmost point, where the river makes a triangle around the Spessard Mountains. I could follow the Main upstream, to Gemünden, in an almost-perfect direction toward Erfurt. In Gemünden, the Main picks up the Saale River, and I could follow the Saale in the same direction into the Thuringian Forest. The bridge at Miltenberg had been blown up, so I walked along the south bank to find a way to cross. Finally, at Dorfprozelten, I found a bridge that had not been destroyed. I crossed over and continued to Hasloch. I stayed in an inn called the Lamm that had been opened to soldiers walking home.

"On Saturday the thirteenth, I made good progress along the Main from Hasloch over Marktheidenfeld and Lohr to Steinbach. That morning, I moved so lightly and freely. A change had come over me. I had now come two-thirds of the hike. So far, I had counted my progress from my starting point, and the distance had become longer every day, until it weighed on me. Now I started to count my progress to Erfurt, and that became shorter every day. And then I thought, isn't it always like this with work that has a beginning and an end? It becomes harder and harder, till you sometimes think you can't go on. Then suddenly, after you have accomplished two-thirds, you hit the magic point. Suddenly you feel encouraged, and things get easier to the end. I walked so long that day that I had missed the curfew when I got to Steinbach. The town was crowded with soldiers walking home. I could not find lodging. I needed to get off the street. I gladly took a farmer's offer to let me sleep in his barn.

"As soon as the curfew was lifted, I was back on the road along the Main again. I saw in the distance where the river turned south, and I had to continue north along the Saale.

"A horse-drawn wagon slowly pulled up to me. A farmer sat in the box, the hood of his rain jacket pulled far over his head, though it was not raining. He had a long, black, full beard. The wagon was open. A tarp had slipped off two bales of hay and some sacks. The road rose up a long incline. The old, tired gelding pulled so slowly, I walked alongside. The stranger examined me.

"I said, 'Guten Morgen.'

"The farmer nodded. After a while, he asked, 'Where to?'

"I said, 'Gmünden.' I thought that up the Saale River would be farther than the farmer would go.

"The farmer pulled the reins and stopped the wagon. 'Get on.' While I climbed on, the farmer got off, went to the old gelding, felt his pasterns, and adjusted the harness. Then he climbed back up next to me, and the wagon ground on. For several kilometers, the farmer did not say a word. When I saw Gmünden in the distance, I asked, 'Where're you headed?'

"'North,' he said, without turning his head.

"Hoping he would go north along the Saale, I said, 'I really have to go to Neustadt an der Saale.'

"The farmer nodded. 'I'm going to Hameln.'

"I looked at him. Was he serious? Hameln? This was much farther than Erfurt.

"'You are a Lanzer too, aren't you?' he said.

"'Yes,' I said. 'I'm going to Erfurt to my wife and kids.'

"The man went on silently. He seemed so absentminded. The horse found the way through Gmüden by himself. He pulled up the Saale River. Good, I thought. Then he turned into the field close to the river and stopped. He got a bucket from under the tarp and fetched water from the river for the horse. He filled a feedbag with oats and hung it around the horse's muzzle. He felt the pasterns again. Then he sat down in the grass next to me. 'Old Hektor has gotten sore feet. He has come all the way from Tyrol,' he said. 'Started out with him in Italy, after all was lost.'

"In Neustadt, I thanked the man and got off. He was turning north. As I watched his wagon disappear, I thought, what an incredible actor! He bet his life on playing a farmer right through the retreating armies, and nobody questioned his part. Nothing would stop him now.

"I went on along the Saale to Heustreu. Because of the lift, I had accomplished two days' distance in one. I figured I was within five days of Erfurt. I found shelter at the farm of Ludwig Greb, house number 186."

My mother asked, "Why did you write down all these names and addresses?"

"You know why? I thought, when it is peace again, we could all take a bicycle tour one day and you could see which way I came. We could visit these people and thank them, maybe bring them a little present."

Papi ran his finger along the next line in his diary. "Tuesday, Fuchsstadt, City Hall. The mayor had orderd to convert city hall into a shelter for soldiers walking home.

"The next day it got warm. My winter coat became a burden. I took it off, carried it over my arm, and then carried it over my shoulder. It slowed me down, but I had an almost-superstitious feeling about holding on to it. It had served me so well in playing the affluent civilian.

"At curfew, I had only made it to Grimmenthal. I found a bed in a nursery.

"On Thursday I climbed into the Thuringian Forest. I reached Zella-Mehlis before lunch already, but I did not stop; I ate while walking ahead. In the afternoon, I reached Oberhof. The hotel was occupied by the Americans. There were trucks and jeeps parked on the golf course. I had to think that, in the twenties, the resort had been your parents' pampering place, how they'd summered there, hobnobbing with their friends from industry and nobility."

"Oh, not only summer," my mother added, "weekends. What money they poured into Oberhof—the sumptuous dinners, golf, tennis, horseback riding, the balls, balloon chases in the convertible, picnics at the end, on and on."

"Well, you should see it now," my father picked up again. "It will never be the same.

"I walked on, and when I stopped in Cräwinkel for the night, I had walked more than 50 kilometers in one day. I knew I would reach Erfurt tomorrow, perhaps as early as afternoon. I stayed at the forester Mathesi's house. He was amazed how long I had been on the road and how far I had come.

"I got up at sunrise. I could hardly wait for the end of the curfew and was on the road on the minute for the final stretch. I descended into the Gera Valley, and it turned warm, like summer. My winter coat became oppressive. No matter how I carried it, it slowed me down. Past Wandersleben, I stopped at a farm. I did not want to come home empty-handed. I thought, how welcome it would be if I brought food for Abendbrot.

"I saw an old woman coming from the barnyard. I told her I had walked from the Black Forest and was going into Erfurt to my family. I wanted to bring them some food, but I had no money. I offered to trade my coat. She fingered my coat and asked me to come into the house. All she had to give me was a dozen eggs. A dozen eggs for my good winter coat seemed unfair, but I could bring them home, and we could have our favored *Eierkuchen*.

"'I have a raincoat I could give you too,' said the woman.

"So I traded my coat for a dozen eggs and the raincoat that she had gotten from the devil knows where. While she was lowering the eggs into the bag, I tried on the raincoat, and it fit surprisingly well.

"I came down through the Steiger Forest. It opened up, and there was Erfurt; the Dom and the Severi Kirche were both standing.

"I hurried on. Suddenly, I heard shouts. Three men came running on a side path across a field. 'Halt, Halt.' What now? The men came and stood around me. 'That's him—beige raincoat, 1 meter 82.'"

My father's voice became deep and fell into the Berlin vernacular. How upset he was just thinking of the situation.

"'I don't know who you are looking for,' I said. 'I am not your man. I am a Lanzer. I have walked here from the Black Forest. I have to go into this city to my wife and children.'"

"'What's in this bag?' they wanted to know.

"'A dozen eggs, so we can make *Eierkuchen* tonight.'

"'Let us see.'

"I opened the bag. They all looked in. They stepped away a bit and consulted in Polish. Finally, they ran along without saying another word, and I went down into our quarter. I noticed from the even spacing of the ruins that the area had been carpet bombed. I turned into Louisenstrasse 3 and saw the crater in the front yard—missed the house by 20 meters. Put my eggs on the front porch, ran up the stairs, and rang the bell. Steps in the hall; the bolt slid. There stood Martchen. She couldn't get a word out. I just hugged the good, old soul. She wiped her eyes on her apron and then called to the living room, 'Gnädige Frau, your son-in-law. He's come home. He's here.'

"Mamusch came, embraced me.

"'Where are Annemarie and the children?' I asked. 'Are they all right?'

"'They are across the street, in the back building, 21B. We are all alive.'

"And so I came over here. And here I am."

When my father had finished, I felt I had taken the trip myself.

Then it was mother's turn to tell what had happened to us after Christmas. She was not a born storyteller like my father. She skipped around and left out many details, and I eagerly filled in whenever I could.

I went to bed feeling warm, secure, and thankful.

My Papi was home.

The next morning, I walked into the garden, determined not to mourn the loss of my boat. To my surprise, there was the boat leaning against the wall. Even the paddle was there. Gerda, who had suffered the bad cut, had jumped into the river and dragged it ashore.

III

Refugees

51

As the Americans eased the curfew, we resumed our habit of spazieren. On one of our evening strolls, we saw a Russian officer, a sign that the Americans would hand over Thuringia to the Russians, according to the division of Germany planned at Yalta.

"Let's get out of here before the Communists move in."

We just had survived one totalitarian regime. We dreaded getting caught under another. We hoped that our belongings in the Black Forest were still intact. My parents talked about moving somewhere close to the southwest corner of Germany, to Heidelberg perhaps. The immediate objective was to escape to Bavaria before the border closed.

On the morning of Friday, June 22, Omi, Tante Anneliese, and Tante Ellen bid us farewell at Omi Bauer's rose gate. Maria Barbara was not there. Would I have gone in the villa to find her if I had known that I would never see her again? I was anxious to get going on this adventure and had no use for long good-byes. Mutti, loosening from her embrace with Tante Anneliese, urged her sister to pack up Jens-Peter and head west also.

"You don't want to live under Communism. You have the Schwanhäussers in Nürnberg."

"I'll think about it," Tante Anneliese said indecisively.

Omi mentioned, "Well, I can't leave the houses," and, with that comment, weighed into her daughter's decision.

"You stop at the Schwanhäussers," Tante Anneliese said. "You can't make it to Heidelberg in one day."

My parents knew Onkel Helmut's brothers, Herbert and Gustav, from the post-wedding celebration, the dance in the parklike garden, the tour through the pencil factory, and the ancient town. They decided to make Nürnberg their immediate destination.

We untangled from our loved ones and headed for the Steiger, where the highway to Arnstadt crossed the forest. When we reached the foothills, it suddenly started to rain. We looked for shelter and found it under the porch of a half-finished building bearing marks of the Reich of a thousand years. It was a colonnade of square pillars and stylized eagles holding in their talons swastikas in wreaths. The rain became torrential, bringing branching flashes and thunder over the city.

"We will not come back here," we agreed.

The storm stopped as suddenly as it had started, and we went on uphill.

We reached the highway where the hill plateaued. We drew up to a group of people waiting to hitch rides.

"Where to?" a woman asked.

"Heidelberg."

"Too late. The border is closed. You won't get out of Thuringia."

"No," contradicted another woman, "the border is still open."

Two trucks came struggling up the hill. The first one was midsize with a curious pale blue, boxy structure made out of plywood mounted onto its bed. The box had a crude window on the passenger side and an opening without a door in the back. The second truck was loaded with coal, on which sat a crowd of hitchhikers. The first truck passed us by and stopped; the second halted in front of us.

"Where are you going?" my father shouted into the driver's cab.

"Arnstadt."

It was the next town in the right direction.

"Here! Arnstadt!" my father urged. "Let's get on!"

I started climbing the tire in order to reach the rail and hoist myself on.

"Wait," my mother shouted, running to the first truck ahead. "Where is this truck going?

"Nürnberg. We are full."

"Here, let's go on this one!" my mother shouted back to us. "This one is going to Nürnberg."

Just then, a man pulled himself into the door in front of her.

He hung half outside. My mother pulled his arm.

"Where are you going? You say Arnstadt? The truck behind us is going to Arnstadt. This one is going to Nürnberg. We have to go to Nürnberg. Could you please go on the other truck?"

My mother was so vehement and pleading. The man jumped off. My mother lifted Monika in, pushed me in after her, and squeezed herself in, but, even with her pushing, there was no room for my father. He held on the door frame and, conquering two handbreadths of space on the threshold, pulled himself up. Until Arnstadt, he and his rucksack were hanging out of the back door.

The driver went through Arnstadt, ignoring the people waiting along the road. He obviously could not take any one else. After Arnstadt, the travelers inside the car started assimilating us, moving an inch here, an inch there, until Monika, I, and even my mother could sit down. That made enough room for my father to press inside and take off his rucksack.

Our progress was disturbingly slow. Every bridge had been blown up. Time and again, the truck had to get off the highway and sway over dirt detours, through stony fords, or over hollow-sounding, temporary wooden crossings. At dinner time we reached a town and stopped in front of a *Gasthaus*.

"What town is this?" my father asked.

"Kronach," the driver said. "We've just crossed the border."

"Thank God, we have made it! We are in Bavaria!" my mother exclaimed.

Relieved, we consumed our meager meal, climbed back into the box, and drove on. The last strip of red sky was fading ahead over the highway when the truck drove into a farmyard and stopped. The farmer led us to a big barn in the back, and we dug into a pile of straw for the night. Burrowed in between my parents and my sister, I felt warm, secure, and elated by the adventure, until I was overcome by sleep.

Two unusual events occurred on the remaining trip to Nürnberg. Over the many hours of being crammed together on the narrow benches, the travelers had become downright friendly. They asked whether I would like the seat at the window. I gladly accepted. We were driving along a river, perhaps the upper Main. I was looking, half dozing, through the rhythmically passing poplars onto the water, when I noticed something perplexing on the road. A truck tire was following us, completely unattended and fancy free. As our truck slowed and stopped, the tire caught up, passed right under my window, overtook us, parted with the road, turned into the grassy spot toward the river, wound itself into a narrowing spiral, and, with a last wobble, came to rest on its side.

We all scrambled out off the box, walked around the truck, and discovered that the renegade tire belonged to our rear right side. *Man*, I thought, *what terrific excitement is in store for us out on the road.*

After the driver had captured the tire and pressed it back into service, we went on to the next unbelievable experience, which foreshadowed what was waiting for us in Nürnberg.

Turning away from the river, we reached a village where the retreating troops had tried to make a stand. As we proceeded through the streets, the driver slowed down. Inside our box, the conversation stopped. Not a single house was standing. An occasional wall held up its empty window openings, or a chimney obstinately stuck out of the rubble, making the devastation even more complete. Utter silence lay over this testimony to past explosions, crashes, and screams. The place had been abandoned by all life. Nothing stirred, not even a dog or cat, not even the air. A great emptiness crept out from the ruins. This emptiness wanted to surround and penetrate my heart and make it stop.

Around eleven in the morning, we reached the northern outskirts of Nürnberg. We got off the truck in the Pirkheimerstrasse and stepped into blinding sunshine. My father shouldered our rucksack, and we walked the few blocks to where my parents remembered Schwanhäusser's house, garden, and factory. The house was burned out. The pencil factory was damaged but still recognizable. There was no one at either place. While we were still looking up to the blackened balconies of the apartment house, a neighbor walked by and pointed down the street to where the Schwanhäussers had moved. Here we found Herbert and Liesel Schwanhäusser; their apartment was crammed with relatives who had been bombed out.

Herbert scratched his head when he saw us. "Where can I put you?"

But he would not turn away the sister-in-law of his dead little brother. Even though he knew my parents only from Helmut's post-wedding celebration, he used his organizational skills to move his homeless charges even tighter. He freed a small room for us next to the bathroom. "For a few days," he said.

At lunch, we were amazed how many people of all ages where trying to fit around the tables, which had been shoved together in a *U* and filled the large dining room from wall to wall. We squeezed in somehow.

I had my spoon in the soup already when it became quiet. Everyone folded their hands in their laps and bowed their heads. Herb started. "*Vater unser,*" and all the adults joined, "*Geheiliget werde Dein Name.*" The group reflected on every word and rested in the moment, without urgency to get to the meal. What had happened to these people? How could they pray so with all their hearts? The daily bread that the Lord was giving us was meager, and the soup had been stretched.

All the relatives were foreign to my parents. Herbert's brothers and his mother were missing. My parents inquired apprehensively and heard with relief that they were all alive. The mighty matriarch had been evacuated by her sons to Hersbruck, a small town east of Nürnberg.

"And Gustav?" my mother asked about Helmut's oldest brother.

"Gustav is all right," Herbert said, "a little singed, perhaps, but all right. You should have seen him when the bombs went into our house. He was on the fourth-floor balcony, letting furniture down on a clothesline. He was all surrounded with flames, still letting things down.

"We shouted, 'Gustav, get down! Let the stuff go.'

"Then the staircase collapsed. We thought, 'My God, how will he get out?' He beat his beard that was catching on fire. Then he swung himself over the rail and let himself down on the line."

Gustav had moved to his summer house in Erlenstegen and had become a little strange since his wife had died. "He has planted vegetables on her grave," Herbert said, raising his eyebrows. "Do I need to say more?"

After lunch, my parents took us children on a stroll into the garden.

"This is where Onkel Helmut and Tante Anneliese's wedding party was," my mother explained. "Let's find the place where they had the dance. They had lanterns strung between these trees."

We went through a grove of tall oaks toward a clearing. Some of the children whom we had seen at the table joined us.

"Do you want to see where the bomb went in?" a little girl asked.

The lawn where the dance floor had been had been transformed into a gigantic crater. We climbed the wall of dirt that had been thrown up all around it and looked down into a funnel so deep and wide that our house in Glienicke could have been buried in it. The earth was nothing but clay to the dizzying depth of the very bottom.

"It's a good thing this bomb fell here," my father said. "It would have wiped out a block."

We stepped back and scraped the clay off our shoes on the exposed roots of the oaks. A group of boys demonstrated what great projectiles this clay made. They shaped it into balls and stuck the balls onto flexible sticks. Then they bent those sticks to the breaking point and released them. They watched the clay soar in the air, hang there for a moment, and drop ever faster into the crater, following the path the bomb had taken. I was permitted to stay with the children while my parents went on with Monika.

The shooting of clay balls lost its novelty. I went back toward the entrance where I had spied a swing set with three swings. A boy and a girl were swinging. I climbed on the third swing. As we passed each other in the air, stretching and pushing forward and bending our knees on the way back, we started talking. They were sister and brother. The sister was eight, the brother seven.

"Where are you from?" the sister asked.

"Erfurt."

"Is that far?" she wanted to know. "We are from Königsberg."

Königsberg, I thought, and the mountain of the king appeared before my eyes. I saw the castle and the city above the gleaming Baltic Sea, as I had visualized them when my father had considered moving there from Berlin.

"We had to flee from the Russians. That was in winter. We couldn't get out on the roads. We had to walk on a sandbar through the ocean."

The girl's eyes were far away. We sat upright with our arms around the chains, swinging less and less.

"So we walked and walked through the water. The water ran into our boots. My mother was carrying our little brother. He was sick. We got to the land. Then we got to a house."

Our swings had stopped. We sat there hanging. The sister fell silent. Then the brother spoke. He looked straight forward as if he was talking to himself.

"My little brother and I were sleeping in the same bed. In the morning, when I woke up, he was dead."

The sister confirmed it. "He died in my brother's bed." She said it in the matter-of-fact way that victims adopt after they have recounted the same tragedy over and over. But there was also a tinge of pride in her voice. She was certain she and her brother had suffered more than I could ever match. I was thankful that we had not moved to Königsberg.

52

The next morning, we were awakened by disconcerting sounds from the bathroom. Herbert, who was evidently suffering from a severe case of hay fever, was clearing his sinuses, blowing, coughing, and sputtering. We got dressed and were greeted in the hall by him and his wife, Liesel, who were ready to go to church. His impeccable, dark blue, striped suit; serious tie; and polished black shoes made it almost inconceivable that he was the same person we had heard ridding himself of his congestion.

To dispel the thought that we might join them, my father said, "We want to take a walk through the city."

"Go take a look," was all Herbert said.

We had to climb the Burgberg in order to get to the old town. We passed the deserted Schwan pencil factory. No sound came from the hollow window openings and no odor of lacquer, only the smell of chalky dust. We entered the fortifications of the Burg through the tunnel. I noticed grated shafts in the ceiling. My father told me that in the Middle Ages, the Nürnbergers would pour burning pitch down on the intruding enemy. I shuddered at the familiar image of fire falling from above.

Stepping from the cool, dark passage into the court of the castle, we had to shield our eyes from the brilliance that burned down from a cloudless sky. We walked to the high ground, where the whole city opened up beneath us.

What we saw stopped us speechless. Only children of wars, who have seen complete destruction with their impressionable eyes, can fully understand how the panorama slammed into my mind.

What had been the city was now nothing but blinding white heaps of rubble in rows along dusty walkways. The searing whiteness was punctuated with the flashes of broken glass that blinked here and there, close and far into the distance. The slope down to the river lay in the glare of the sun. The far side was shrouded in the gray of shadow. The whole valley was a gigantic cemetery, reduced to grave mounds on which remnants of masonry rose like monuments, a wall here, a chimney there.

We stood a long time, tied to the ground like Lot's wife. How could we set foot into a valley where such incomprehensible destruction and suffering had been exacted?

We searched left and right. To the far right, there were four houses still somehow standing. The one in the middle showed us by the outline of its bare roof beams that it must have had a peculiar, hooded shape. With this roofline and the squatted dimensions of its walls, it, even now, looked like a hen trying to gather the neighboring houses like chicks under its wings.

My father pointed. "The Dürer house. It's still standing."

We turned back to the desert of chalk and ashes, searching for more points of orientation. We found the massive sandstone masonry of St. Sebald, roofless below us, and St. Lorenz in the distance on the far side of the valley.

Hesitatingly, as if the grounds had been sanctified by sorrow, we walked down through the flat places between the white mounds. Up close, the gigantic graves were unattended. Weeds grew. We could tell how long the buildings had been destroyed by the amount of growth.

We came to a round, cleared place and stood before the ruins of a building that indicated by its curved facade and curled, swinging roofline that it had been a baroque church. In front of it, a tree thrust its charred remains into the sky like a burned hand reaching out of the ground.

"This must have been were the wedding was, you know, Papi, where the bride and groom came out and got into the carriage under the walnut tree."

We walked through the open portal and advanced to the middle of the ruins. Four pairs of columns reached up into the blue sky. The floor between them was filled with a pile of rubble and ashes, out of which stuck the black and gray shafts of charred beams. The columns had the most amazing shape. They must have been marble. On the bottom, they showed their original color and form, mottled pink and yellow in a bulging spiral. The higher they reached, the more they looked like glass, and the more they lost their shape. A few were melted into bizarre spikes. Others looked rounded like the stumps of amputated legs. What an inferno must have been here when the dome had collapsed into their midst. This church had been no refuge for those fleeing from their burning houses.

We went on and picked our way toward St. Sebald. As we passed one mound that was full of fresh, chalky rubble and barren of any growth, we walked into a nauseating, sweet odor. My mother and father looked at each other. Some of those buried had been forgotten. There had been too many to dig out. No relatives had survived to keep searching. We hurried on.

We entered St. Sebald. Since there were no charred remains, it must have been hit by high explosives. We walked down the middle of the nave. The rubble had been shoveled to the sides. A fluttering above us made us look up to where the raw, massive walls ended in the glaring blue. Doves flew between the high ledges. When one dove knocked down some loose masonry that crashed on the rubble next to us, we left the threatening enclosure.

On we went, picking our way through rubble, ashes, and chalk; rubble, ashes, and chalk. We came onto a clear, rectangular area delineated by white mounds around it.

"This must have been the Market Place," my father said. "Look there, the Frauenkirche."

At the east end of the cleared square was the facade of a church, all the adornments torn off. The empty portal and gothic window holes led to nothing but a pile of rubble and weeds.

I was parched with the heat and the chalky dust. I searched for water, but there was not a drop in this hot devastation.

As we walked toward the church facade, we perked up our ears. Was there a sign of life? So far we had not met a soul. Indeed, coming closer, we made out the whimpering of a Hammond organ. A group of people stood among the rubble to the left of the facade, old people in black, the women wearing black babushkas. The organ stopped, and the group bent down in prayer. The words of the minister faded into the vast distance. The Hammond organ started again, and then—we could barely hear it—the old people were singing.

We kept our distance, sat down on the stones of a foundation, and listened. My father's eyes started overflowing. It was the only time I had ever seen my father cry, and it would remain the only time.

The picture of those old people who had crawled out of the ruins to worship stayed with me—one of the impressions of war that demands an explanation most persistently. Life has taught me why my father was touched to tears. To this day, when I think of how many groups of survivors, like these, in how many destroyed cities, like this one, had come together on that Sunday to pray and worship, I am overcome by incomprehensible sorrow that it took the lives of hundreds of thousands of children to lead these people back to such humility.

Silently, we went on across the bridge and up toward St. Lorenz. This cathedral still had a roof, even though the grounds around it had been plowed by high explosives. Herbert told us later how the bombs had opened an ancient and forgotten graveyard around the church. In a paradox of a premature resurrection, the bombs heaved the dead onto the streets while the living had met an early burial under the houses around.

We drew near the northwest tower, where debris was piled man-high against the foundation. My father searched the wall above the rubble for something. Suddenly he waved us over. "Guess what I have found?"

He had discovered the sandstone relief of a winged and horned devil grabbing a little boy by the neck. My father explained the story to Monika and me.

"This is the *Schusser*, who cheated his friends in playing marbles. When he was found out, he told them, 'I didn't cheat. I swear. If I did cheat, the devil may come and take me.' And here is the devil grabbing him by his neck."

We walked back toward the Burgberg. My mother suddenly wondered whether we could find the Bratwurst Glöckle. She told us children that this had been the best place in Germany for bratwurst. We went up one alley between the ruins.

"It must have been around here," she guessed. "No, perhaps it was the next street over."

While my parents searched, I looked at the weeds on the ruins and found to my surprise that some of them were blooming. One plant outdid all others vigorously and in amazing numbers. It rose up out of the ruins to a man's height in resplendent stacks of rich yellow bells. The plants had the appropriate name, *Königskerzen* (king's candles; mullein in English).

When I inherited my father's desk, I found in it two verses he must have written after this walk. When I read those lines, I envied my father's gift for pouring his sorrows into poetry. In contrast, how mute do I become when disturbed and how much trouble do I have to deal with my past! My father remembered that morning in these words:

Königskerzen
Nicht zu kennen, was gewesen,
Von des Krieges Hand zerrissen,
Bombentrichter, Minenschlund,
Nichts mehr als das Leid zu lesen,
Das nur wir verstehen, wissen,
Hinter unsrem stummen Mund.

Auf dem Grab der tausend Herzen,
Aus den längst verhallten Qualen
In der Städte Massengrab,
Blühen goldne Königskerzen,
Und ihr sonnentrunknes Strahlen
Malet Gottes Allmacht ab!

Mullein Blooms
Not to make out, what was here,
Torn apart by battle's hand,
Bombing craters, air mine rips,
But to see the grief and fear,
Only we know, understand,
Tucked behind our silent lips.

From the tombs of thousand dooms,
From extinguished sighs below,
Out of mass grave's rubbled mess
Rise up golden mullein blooms,
And their sun-drenched radiant glow
Mirrors God's almightiness.

53

Upon our return to the overcrowded apartment, Herbert announced that the illustrious mother Schwanhäusser was returning from Hersbruck on Tuesday. She would need her room, the one where we were staying. Seeing our forlorn faces, he came up with a suggestion.

"When I have my mother picked up on Tuesday, the truck driver can tell her to maintain her room so that *you* can move in. Her landlady, Frau Pastor Kraus, wouldn't mind. This will give you a roof over your heads, at least. Unfortunately, you have to get out there by yourself. The truck is loaded full on the way back."

We packed our rucksack and went on the road again. According to Herbert, Hersbruck was 28 kilometers due east on Highway 14. We hiked to Erlenstegen and farther on. We searched for the group of people who could be found at any highway out of any city, ready to jump on the only means of transportation. Indeed, we came upon the place that, for some reason, had been deemed to be a good get-on point.

Almost every vehicle stopped. We scrambled onto a truck with many others. It was loaded with a disconcerting mess of scattered crates and tangled farm equipment. Before we had found a stable place, the truck pulled off in a mad rush and everyone fell and lay on the heap, helter-skelter. My father became half buried under tumbling people and luggage. Something was wedged on him. He groaned all the way to Lauf that his leg was going to break. We were so stuck in our places that we could not help him. My mother had her hands full holding Monika and keeping her from falling into the cracks.

In Lauf, the truck came to a jolting halt. People got off and freed my father, who limped to the pavement and examined his leg. Fortunately, he discovered no permanent damage and was able to walk off his soreness. How far had we come on our trip? We asked a man who was about to climb into his miniscule vehicle, a tricycle, one wheel in front under the motor and two wheels under the tiny truck bed. In spite of the man's heavy Frankish dialect, we understood that we were still more than one-third short of our goal. He said he was going to Hersbruck himself.

"Could we hitch a ride?" my father asked.

"No way," the man said putting himself protectively in front of the little vehicle. We hung our heads.

"Perhaps, one person, no more," he allowed.

"You go on with the kids," my father said. "I'll walk."

"But it's too far," my mother said.

"It's nothing. I just walked through half of Germany."

Over the driver's objection, my mother dragged us onto the tricycle and made my father hand her the rucksack. The driver shrugged his shoulders, defenseless against such determination. He ducked into his cabin and put his curious vehicle into motion.

"We'll meet at the castle!" my father shouted, while falling into his long-legged hiking trot after us.

The overloaded vehicle struggled up the Pegnitz valley. The hills north and south rose and finally joined, blocking the east in a massive plateau, thus forming a wide basin. A small town arose in the middle. Hersbruck, we guessed correctly, relieved that our tricycle had made it without tipping or breaking down. It went through the narrow, dark passage of a gothic tower gate and onto the glossy cobblestones of an L-shaped marketplace. The car's strained, high-pitched motor echoed from the ancient half-timber houses that stood shoulder to shoulder around a bombed-out city hall. With a last effort, our contraption came to a halt at a fountain in front of the ruined building. We stepped off and looked around.

In the center of the fountain rose a washed-out, sandstone sculpture I recognized as a jumping stag, representing the important *Hirsch* (stag) that had jumped over the *Brücke* (bridge), thereby giving Hersbruck its name.

We estimated it would take my father at least an hour and a half to catch up with us, enough time to acquaint ourselves with the town. The curved streets and nooks stirred our curiosity. My mother shouldered the rucksack and took Monika by the hand. In the haphazard way of building in the Middle Ages, the town had been assembled in a series of passages that widened to squares. Beyond the squares, the streets jutted back and contracted in odd angles into narrow, curved alleys that soon opened again unexpectedly. We ambled down a wide side street. High up on a house corner, we saw the sign of the street's name in white letters on blue enamel. "Martin Luther Strasse," my mother read with a smile. It made her feel at home to see the name of the Erfurt Augustine monk and to be assured of Protestant territory.

The houses, in all their individuality, were quite uniform in size and style. They appeared good and healthy to me, promising to live several hundred years more. The two bottom floors were plaster in pastel colors. Above these wide and stately fronts rose many more floors in the brown, geometric patterns of half-timber construction under a wide and high tile roof. At the peak, each house projected a small, covered overhang with a pulley to hoist the hops to be spread out for drying on the attic floors.

We noticed the rural character of the town in other ways. Cattle lowed behind some of the walls. Bouncy steel plates in the sidewalks covered odorous septic pits. Here and there, the age-warped ground floors of some of these respectable farmhouses had been altered for businesses. Crass, angular shop windows accommodated the butcher shop Sörgel and the soap shop of the Seifen Loos across the street. Some commercial establishments seemed to have been designed as part of the original buildings. These were mostly the *Gasthäuser* (restaurants), like the Schwarzer Adler next to the soap shop. Up a side street called Spital Gasse, we saw what must have been the *Spital* (hospital) in ancient times and a second tower gate, probably the Spital Tor. Continuing on the Martin Luther Strasse, we came to a third tower gate. Through its dark passage, we could see a stone bridge across the

Pegnitz River. I imagined how, in bygone days, this water gate had been closed by drawing a wooden bridge at the approach of enemies.

The old town consisted of a few blocks between the walls, the three towers, and the river that hugged it on the south side. We stayed inside the water gate, turned right, and followed the Schulgasse uphill, which soon led us in front of the *Schloss* (castle).

We were supposed to wait here for my father. It should have struck me as strange that my father assumed there was a castle in Hersbruck. He had never been there. But when he said it, I had known somehow that he was correct. Indeed, the U-shaped building with the one complete tower on the left and the truncated tower on the right looked familiar to me. It was not only that this strange arrangement of the towers echoed a building that I had loved in Straßburg. It was also that the moat and fortification walls and the bridge with the sandstone pillars at the corners lacked the feel of foreignness. The big building across the square—had I not seen it before? Those giant doors on the ground floor that the children now used as a soccer goal—did I not sense that the fire engine was behind them? Or that the second and third floor housed the elementary school?

The gray building on the right that rose directly out of the moat had been sliced by a bomb on the side toward the school. It all looked as if it had to be like that.

I only had to fill in the details, like the sign next to the main entrance in the center of the castle that said "*Landratsamt*" (county office) and the other sign at the side door in the truncated tower that read "*Vermessungsamt*" (office of land survey). I hardly needed the sign on the sturdy building next to the castle with the small, deep-grated windows upstairs. It had to be the county jail.

My mother and I were leaning on the sandstone banister of the bridge, looking down into the moat. Unkempt grass spread between elderberry bushes and hazelnut trees. Sooner than expected, my father arrived between us. He picked up the rucksack, and we went on in order to find Frau Pfarrer Kraus's house.

On the way, we stopped at the Schwarze Adler. Our constant hunger was becoming unbearable. The restaurant was packed with evacuated citizens and refugees who lived in rooms without cooking facilities. The waitress in a sweat could hardly wind herself through the crowd. She held her loads high above her head and called out for gangway in a local dialect that I could hardly understand. When it finally was our turn to sit down, we pried our chairs back against the waiting people. A while later, we received the only dish offered, which the waitress reached to us over dodging heads. The food looked isolated and forlorn in the compartments of the thick, porcelain plates. A matchbox-sized piece of meat hid under a little gravy in one section, a midsize potato in the second, and four strands of string beans in the third. Nevertheless, it was real meat and called for a major allotment of food rationing stamps. My mother carefully tore these out of the sheet for the month and handed them to the waitress with the required amount of our dwindling money. My father's salary in March had been our last income.

With blunted hunger and some advice about how to get to our destination, we extricated ourselves from the restaurant. We asked the waitress how to get to Frau Pfarrer Kraus's house. She explained, trying to speak High German for us foreigners, "Go through the Spitaltor, out the Ambergerstrasse. Turn left at the old folks' home and go up the hill. Pfarrer Kraus's house is halfway before you get to the hospital on the same side."

Once we walked through the Spital Gate, the medieval character of the town changed. Its modern expansion had mainly occurred along the Amberger Strasse, buildings from the turn of the century that expressed the citizen's urban aspirations. These larger buildings were occupied by the American troops and buzzed with activities in the loud, uninhibited, and cheerful manner in which the victors conduct themselves among the vanquished. The headquarters were in the respectable high school, the officers in the solid Hotel Post across the street, and the mess hall was further out in the swanky Teehaus. We could not miss the Altersheim because of the white-haired, little, bent figures following their canes to the stone benches in its front yard. Left we went, through the railroad underpass and steeply uphill.

The house with the sign "Kraus" on its yard gate was a one-story building of beige stucco with dormers in the high-pitched roof. From the backyard, the loaded branches of a cherry tree hung over the roof. To my excitement, I saw a ladder leading right into the glossy, dark red fruits. Inside the house, we met Frau Pastor Kraus, a little, shriveled widow, who had expected us for a while. She drew close below us with her nearly blind eyes and squinted at us through her thick and distorting lenses. She delivered us into the guidance of a younger, robust woman, Frau Pirner, who took care of the fragile widow in Christian love. Frau Pirner led us up a narrow staircase to our room. It was under the roof and had little more furniture than two beds. We were relieved to have found shelter.

It did not take much encouragement from Frau Pastor Kraus to send me up the ladder in the backyard. She said that God had blessed her this year with so many cherries that Frau Pirner could not pick them all to can them. The hunger years had taught me to eat as much as I could on the rare occasion that I was offered abundance. I stored up for the coming days, carefree in the swaying branches.

In contrast, my parents were sitting on the bed in our tiny room becoming more and more worried about our situation; I found them there upon returning from the tree. They were going over the copybook where my mother accounted our finances in neatly aligned columns. Even with extreme frugality, our money was going to run out by the end of September. My father had to find work quickly. But where? My parents reconsidered trying to move on to Heidelberg. However, the trip would add days, and they were tired of scrambling on trucks with us children. Nürnberg's theater was bombed out, as were most theaters in the cities. An exception was Fürth, Nürnberg's sister city. It seemed reachable in one day. The streetcars between Nürnberg and Fürth were running again.

My father remembered that Lya lived in Fürth. Lya, a ballet dancer, had been one of Hans Wiegener's flames in Straßburg until she moved on to the Fürth Theater. My parents decided to go to Fürth the next day to find Lya. Perhaps she would have suggestions about how to approach the theater director for employment. Once my parents had decided on a plan, they relaxed and were ready to enjoy the warm evening by taking a walk up the hill.

We passed the hospital and reached the ridge, which offered a lofty view in all directions. A tarnished plate was mounted on a stone block, on which arrows pointed out landmarks on the horizon. Due north was a castle on a rock with one thick, square tower and a second tiny one on the other end. The plate indicated it was Hohenstein. It looked medieval and partially in ruins. I wondered how to get there, perhaps through the side valley of the Pegnitz that spread north below us with villages strung along a dusty road, or through the forests on the valley's eastern ridges. Turning south, we saw below us the wide Pegnitz valley, and across, a symmetrical, wooded mountain with an observation tower.

"This must be the Arzberg," my father decided, aligning his arm with the arrow on the plate. "The massive, flat mountain over there to the east must be the Houbirg."

The Houbirg closed off the wide basin around Hersbruck. We could make out the Pegnitz entering from the north and meandering between alders and willows down the wide, juicy meadows. As the river approached the eastern extension of the town, it passed a fenced territory that looked suspiciously like a prison camp. Then it flowed past a swimming area on its right bank with an Olympic-size pool and diving boards.

Approaching the old town, the Pegnitz divided into several branches. The farther ones passed several mills. The close ones became part of the southern fortifications of the town around the water gate. Once we identified the *Wassertor*, our eyes skipped to the other towers that characterized Hersbruck. There were the Spital Gate, the Nürnberger Gate, the half-destroyed tower of the city hall, the one complete tower of the castle, and the tower of the city church. We kept hearing its bells toll the hours.

My parents remembered the romantic and contemplative life that they so often had dreamed of in the Black Forest. They loved the gentle mountains, the peaceful villages strewn into the valleys, the gracefully winding river, and the ancient little town. I was anxious to explore. In this hospitable landscape, there was no village and no mountaintop that I could not reach in my usual jogging gait.

We continued our walk up the hill until the forest gave way to the high plateau. A village identified by the yellow street sign as Grossviehberg hid among fields of strangely organized vines that wound upward on wires.

Above the wires were held up by a network of cables stretched over the field by long stakes like telephone poles, only thinner. The outside poles leaned out toward the road to give the construction the proper tension. The fruits of these vines had the shape of tiny pinecones, but they were light green and fluffy. We had discovered the crop that had contributed most to the prosperity of the region in this beer-loving county.

On the way back, we passed an abandoned quarry that showed the almost-white limestone used for the town walls. We descended the steep and stony road. Against my parents' advice, I started running. I tripped, fell, and knocked my head on the ground. The wound bled profusely. We were only steps away from the hospital. I talked my parents out of taking me to have the wound sutured. I stopped the bleeding by pressing a handkerchief on it and went on to my bed in our room.

"No, he's not sick from the cherries," my mother assured Frau Pfarrer Kraus.

A little later, Frau Pirner brought me a bowl of chicken soup that was worth the injury and which, together with a long sleep, restored me completely.

54

We hitchhiked to Nürnberg, took the streetcar to Fürth, and found Tante Lya in her apartment close to the theater. Any shelter that had more than one room qualified as an apartment. Tante Lya's consisted of a small kitchen and a bedroom. The bed was disheveled. On the nightstand lay a glossy pack with a red circle and bold black lettering, which I deciphered as "Lucky Strike." Tante Lya fetched this treasure that my parents had spotted instantly and offered them, imagine, real cigarettes!

She also had a little package for me. It had beige, rubbery strips in it that smelled like peppermint. "Chewing gum," she explained. "You don't swallow it. You chew it and then spit it out."

To top it all, Tante Lya set out to brew a pot of real coffee, not Katreiner, but real coffee. Tante Lya "had an Ami." This is how the Germans referred to the early fraternization of unattached women with the enlisted victors. It was usually a matter of survival, which occasionally transformed into love.

"Have you heard from Hans Wiegener?" was my father's first question.

Tante Lya had heard through a mutual friend that Hans had been hit by a bullet in his right arm. He had been in a military hospital until "the end," as the collapse of the Reich of a Thousand Years was commonly referred to. "His arm is permanently paralyzed," Tante Lya said, distorting her mouth regretfully. "What will an actor do when he can't move his arm? I mean, his career is finished. He went back to Berlin."

My father shook his head and clicked his tongue, shocked by the bad news. After a while he said, trying to cling to something positive, "Perhaps he will find something where he can use his voice."

His prediction was to prove correct. Hans Wiegener became a radio announcer at RIAS. He also dubbed movies. We were surprised and amused when, in the coming years, his sonorous voice would sound out of Hollywood stars like José Ferrer as Long John Silver.

My father's second question concerned where we could find a place for the night. We could not stay with her, given her present relationship. Her life depended on it. As long as she could get cigarettes, she could barter for food. Cigarettes were becoming the valid currency. Fortunately, Tante Lya knew two women, mother and daughter, who perhaps could take us in. She called and sweet-talked her friends into agreeing to rent us a room for a day or two. It would give my father time for an interview with the theater director.

Tante Lya took a slip of paper, wrote down the theater director's telephone number and the address and name of our hosts, and sent us on our way. We found the building in the Max Strasse undamaged. We were received on the third floor by Frau Käte Eisenbeis and her old mother, Frau Reker. Frau Eisenbeis's husband had been missing in action. She was letting us move into the master bedroom, which she had not used. She seemed friendly and helpful, but her expression changed when she turned away from my parents. Her old mother, though, was genuinely sympathetic.

In my clamoring for stability in that vagabond time, I absorbed all places and people with a curiosity and alertness, as if I was to stay wherever we currently were for the rest of my life. I was particularly receptive to anything encouraging. I was uplifted by such diverse impressions as the white-haired Frau Reker, who sat smilingly all day, hunched over her amazingly intricate embroidery; the *Wilhelm Busch Albums* with its forerunners of comic strips that she let me read; the pile of Luftschutzsand crawling with children in the back court; the river swimming area that we visited at the fast-flowing Rednitz; or the mechanical piano at the Gasthaus Blauer Stern, with its ghost-operated keyboard.

My father was able to arrange an appointment with theater director Menke. He returned encouraged. Menke's former play director had been a party member and was prohibited from working. It was questionable whether he would be able to return. Menke just did not know what would happen to these people. He had to admit it was an asset to my father not to have belonged. He also allowed that my father's résumé was impressive. Menke had to make several arrangements and would let him know for sure in three days.

My mother pleaded with Frau Eisenbeis to let us stay an extra day, and as usual, she got her way. As soon as my father would get a job, she was determined to find us a permanent place. She wondered whether he would have to wait for another month to get paid. Perhaps he could ask for an advance.

The promising meeting came. My father returned earlier than expected. My mother, who had cooked some potatoes and soup, was setting the table in our bedroom. From my father's beaten look, I knew that things had not gone well. What went wrong? Menke had hemmed and hawed that he was really not able to make any decision yet. He had heard a rumor that lower-echelon party members, like his play director, would be put through a denazification process and, if they were classified as *Mitläufer* (followers), would be allowed to work again. Menke pointed out that my father certainly would not want to start here, when the other man might come back in the foreseeable future. My father, not having belonged, should consider how many opportunities he would have at other theaters. Better start where he would be assured to be able to stay, and on and on. Menke continued trying to give the impression that he had my father's best interest at heart and closed by stating that, as a *Mensch* (man), he would certainly like to help him but, as administrator, his hands were tied.

"Well, didn't you tell him that he promised you the job?" my mother grumbled.

"He did not totally promise it," my father said trying to be accurate. "He still had to check out a few things."

"Check out a few things," my mother echoed contemptuously. "What is this denazification anyway? *Entnazifizierung* sounds like disinfection. They just go through this *Entnazifizieruns* process, and then they will be white as snow?"

My mother's folds across her forehead grew deep. She spit with indignation. "All through the war, these opportunists have passed you by. Now was going to be your turn. And now what do they do? They get through this *Entnazifizierung*, and then they will be back in their jobs. Those stool pigeons. They were dangerous as hell, and now they just get classified as nothing more than *Mitläufer*? They are getting back in their cozy jobs, and you let yourself be pushed aside again."

My father did not find the words to answer. I knew how distressed he was by the way his hands shook as he picked up his silverware from the shelf to bring to the table.

"What are we going to do?" my mother asked in exasperation.

"I'll try different theaters," my father started with a raised and pressed voice.

"Different theaters—which different theaters? They are all bombed out."

"I'll go to Darmstadt. I'll go to München."

"How will you get there? We're out of money! Besides, they will push you aside again. It's always the same thing with you. It was the same with Weichert in Berlin; it was the same with Kunze in Straßburg. Now was going to be your big chance. And now you let yourself be pushed aside again."

My father's could not take it anymore. His head turned purple. His hair stood on end. He raised the silverware high above his head and, letting out an inarticulate roar that sounded close to, "I can't stand this," slammed it on the floor.

This stopped my mother.

In the quiet of the room, we heard my father take a few deep breaths. His smashing and roaring like lightning and thunder had taken the pernicious tension out of the air. After he had steadied himself, he picked up the silverware—the spoon, the knife, but where was the fork?

"Come children, let us all look for the fork," my mother said. "It's Frau Eisenbeis's fork. We must return it."

At first, we looked perfunctorily around the spot where the silverware had hit the floor. Then we searched the room systematically from wall to wall. Nothing.

"Perhaps it bounced off the floor and got stuck under the mattress," my father surmised.

We removed the mattresses and took the bed apart. Nothing. We moved the table, the chairs, and the nightstands and looked behind the pictures on the wall.

After about an hour of intense searching, we came to the conclusion that the fork had disappeared from the room. This was the first time that I had an inkling of the strange phenomenon that inanimate objects may, on rare occasions, behave outside the laws of physics when placed in the path of our most desperate emotions. We confessed to Frau Eisenbeis that we had lost the fork. We told her that we had searched and searched to no avail and that the fork was somewhere in this room and probably would turn up, but deep down, we were convinced the fork was gone and would never be found. Frau Eisenbeis understood. Why make a fuss when we were leaving the next morning?

Where were we to go? We needed a place to stay. With the employment possibilities in the city exhausted, my parents decided to move back to Frau Pfarrer Kraus. Once more, we hitchhiked to Hersbruck. But when we arrived, the almighty mother Schwanhäusser had moved back in. She had found life around the dilapidated pencil factory too depressing and Herbert's house too crammed.

As we stood there not knowing where to turn, Frau Pirner came up with a possible solution. She had heard that a Frau Kolb wanted to rent a room. Frau Kolb's husband, who had been a leading Nazi, was *im Lager* (in the prison camp). She had two children and no income. Perhaps the room was still available.

We followed Frau Pirner's directions. "Frau Kolb lives on the third floor of contractor Muggentaler's house in the Amberger Strasse."

With the blessings of old Frau Pastor Kraus, we headed for the eastern outskirts. We passed the Finanz Amt, the only large building on the street that was not occupied by the armed forces. We found the Muggentaler's house. It was a young and healthy building. The third floor was under the roof and had large dormers. Frau Muggentaler, the owner, sent us from her ground floor up to the roof apartment. Upon our ringing, a little, lean, dark-complected woman opened. Her straight black hair was gathered tightly in a bun. She looked at us questioningly.

"Frau Kolb?" my father verified. "Frau Pfarrer Kraus sent us. You have a room for rent?"

"Yes, but it is only big enough for one person."

"Please, let us have a look." My mother came forward. "We don't need much. We are refugees. We have nothing."

"All right." Frau Kolb turned around and opened a door across the hallway. "Look yourselves."

The room was still smaller than the one we had left at the home of Frau Pfarrer Kraus. The roofline cut in deep into the opposite wall, except for the dormer, which was filled with a desk and a chair. On the right wall was a short couch, with a small table and two chairs. Along the left wall stood a single bed. As the door opened, it hit something in the right corner, which turned out to be a cast-iron stove. It was the smallest stove I had ever seen, merely twice as wide as its pipe. A narrow, tall, walnut closet stood on the left side of the door. That was it.

My father measured the size of the walls with his eyes. "How can we fit another bed in here? We can't move this bed over to make room for another one. The headboard is too high for the knee wall. What if we take the bed out and replace it with two mattresses on the floor, one shoved all the way into the far corner under the inclined ceiling and the other into the inside corner up to the closet? We would have to move the closet as close to the door as we can. If the mattresses aren't too long, they'll fit."

Frau Kolb needed the rent, so she tried to cooperate. While we started shuffling furniture, Frau Kolb's children peeked curiously from the hallway. There was an eight-year-old redhead and a seven-year-old boy. The boy had his mother's olive skin but was thin and pale and had dark circles under his eyes. The two mattresses did fit. The one, from the daughter's bed, smelled a little like urine. The other, from a storage room, had two escaped springs in the middle that made their presence known. My parents whispered among themselves that they had no choice but to stay here until they would find something better. Then they confirmed openly with Frau Kolb that they would definitely want to rent here.

Before we went to the Schwarze Adler to compete for some dinner, my parents reached over the desk and opened the window to air out the chamber. We looked down onto the neighbor's lot, which had been struck by a direct hit and was a pile of rubble. In a hole in the middle, we saw with a shudder some steps going down into the cellar. My parents turned away from the window and surveyed the room with a resigned smile. Then they embraced.

"At least we are all alive," my mother said. "Let's be thankful for that."

55

After a few nights, we learned to sleep in our new put-up. My mother curved her body around one side of the poking springs and kept Monika on the other side. My father pulled up his knees to make himself short enough so he would neither hit his head against the wall nor his feet against the closet—except sometimes, when he dreamed and struck the closet with a thump. I pressed myself against the back rest of the narrow couch. The length was acceptable for a nine-year-old, even one as tall as I.

We had a bed and a roof and four walls. We felt almost fortunate when we heard at the restaurant how some of the other refugees had to live. Five families were crammed together in one room of a warehouse, separated by a few sheets and blankets on lines. How would you maintain human dignity? How would you dress, wash, or make love? To make the situation worse, many of the natives looked down on us refugees because we lived so deplorably and had nothing, calling us *Zugereiste* ("people that traveled here"), mere vagabonds. They laughed when the unfortunate ones talked about the positions and possessions they were forced to leave behind.

In the Schwarze Adler, we refugees gathered and found compassion and understanding among ourselves and exchanged news and rumors. We tuned in on the mention of any possibilities because our situation was desperate. Ideas for sources of food or income circulated. With the first rent payment, our money was going to be depleted; we would not even be able to obtain food apportioned to us by rationing stamps.

Instead of meat, the Schwarze Adler now served roasted blood. It tasted salty, like a nosebleed, and only the hunger drove us to eat it.

A rumor circulated that a man in the United States had proposed to turn the German country into one large camp and starve the population down to half its number. They called it the Morgenthau Plan. I had no doubt that this plan had been put into effect.

My father was searching desperately for a way to earn money. One steady guest in the Schwarze Adler, whom we called Kasperle (Punch) because he had the large curved nose and chin of the main character in German puppet theaters, would usually come wandering in early, before dinner, and put his walking stick in the umbrella stand and his rucksack under his chair. While he was waiting for his food, he would take a drawing pad and a tin box with colored pencils out of his backpack and work on a little persnickety landscape from the surroundings. Each evening, he had a different one. This gave my father an idea. Why couldn't he use his talent for income, since evidently Kasperle was able to sell his creations?

The countless romantic motifs of the town had begged my father from the start. He hoped to combine the pleasure with practicality and started sketching. He did this while waiting in line. When word got out that a store had received a shipment, people hurried to stand in a long line in front; you needed to get to the counter before the supplies ran out. When the dairy would open at two o'clock in the afternoon, my father and I would line up at 12:30 p.m. People would be waiting already. My father would then leave me for an hour to hold his place, and he would walk down a block to sketch the gothic entrance and windows of the Spital with the fountain in front. He would return before the store opened, for in the wild shoving for the counter, the adults would push children aside. The fight for survival had made people selfish and callous, so I was glad when my tall father came; handed me his sketchbook; and, having both arms free, stood his ground. When we lined up for bread, my father sketched the castle around the corner, for milk, the Nürnberg gate, and so on. Back in our chamber, my father transferred his pencil sketches into finished pen-and-ink drawings and even cut mats for them.

When he had about a dozen completed, he and I took them to a framing store in the Spitalgasse, whose display window showed pictures of Hersbruck between the samples of frames and moldings. The old glazier master lowered his spectacles from his forehead and examined my father's work. Undoubtedly, he sensed from the tight, laborious renderings and the uneven scissor cuts of the mats that these were amateur works produced under pressure.

"You know," he said pushing his glasses back on his forehead, "in these times you can't sell art. People don't have enough to eat. Since the end, I have not sold a single painting—not even a professional oil."

However, when he saw our disappointed faces, he agreed to keep the drawings and display them.

While my father and I were trying to grab the few foodstuffs available in town, my mother was after other necessities. We needed fuel for the minuscule stove before we could cook anything. There was neither coal nor wood to be bought. My mother teamed up with Frau Kolb to scour the forests for fallen branches. A few times I went along to lead Monika by the hand over the steep, slippery stretches or to help pull the wooden handcart. The woods had been picked over by others. Unless there had been a recent storm, we had to move far away to find any twigs. The law forbade the taking of any wood that was alive. Frau Kolb had a little hatchet hidden in a burlap sack in the bottom of the cart. When we were in the deepest part of the forest, she would peer furtively through the underbrush all around. She hushed us and listened carefully. Then she hastily hacked off a few saplings. We helped her cover the cut stumps with dirt. "Put a cap on," she called it. Likewise, we covered the ends of the cut pieces with dirt and hid the poached green logs in the bottom of the cart under the legitimate dry branches.

Frau Kolb was eager for my mother to come along on her hauls. Where would she ever find a woman more energetic and untiring to pull the cart through the boggy, hollowed-out mountain lanes? My mother also would come in handy for sharing the blame in case a warden would examine their load. Fortunately, we never got caught.

Not once did the women take my father. My mother knew he would rather not cook or have heat than break the law in order to obtain wood. However, on Sundays, when the stores were closed, he joined our hike to Happurg to gather apples that had dropped from the trees along the road. He had no qualms about that. In his two semesters in law school, he had learned that fruit along highways fall into the public domain.

At other times, we gathered mushrooms. Following the advice of the natives, we hiked across the valley through Ellenbach and searched in the forest around the Arzberg. In the stony, moss-covered ground, we spotted rich, brown, velvety Steinpilze and the bright yellow chalices of chanterelles. We picked our way uphill until we found ourselves in front of the rough fieldstone walls of the observation tower. We stomped up the resounding wooden staircase, stepped into the light of the platform, and looked out over the treetops to the horizon, from the highest point in the Frankenalb.

A couple of about my parents' age stood on the platform. They expressed to each other their delight in the clearness of the August afternoon and tried to trace the way through the forests and fields to their home. We perked up our ears, hearing the familiar Prussian accent. No doubt, they were fellow refugees. We started talking to them. The usual German reserve in approaching strangers had disappeared among those who had been displaced by a common fate. After a few comments about the beautiful view, our conversation soon switched to sharing the stories about where we had come from. Herr Schimmelpfenning had been a judge of the state of Prussia and, as we, had fled from the Russian occupation. He had applied to the Bavarian State for a permit to work at the courthouse in Hersbruck. He was confident that, as soon as approval would be issued, he would be back on the bench. His wife shared his optimism. They were both grateful to be reunited after the long separation of the war and were dreaming of their rosy future together. He made a curious impression, standing there confidently in his trench coat, his air force trousers, and his hobnailed boots. He outlined his plans while his intelligent brown eyes seemed far away in an unreal world.

The Schimmelpfennigs had been gathering mushrooms too. They

opened their rucksack, and we compared. They had found more because they also collected another variety, *Birkenpilze*. They recommended those as being almost as good as *Steinpilze*.

When we all left the tower and went our separate ways, my parents had formed an acquaintance that lasted. Whenever my mother or father would meet the judge or his wife in the streets, they always stopped and talked about the changes in their lives.

On our way home, our ardor for looking for mushrooms was rekindled. We now could include *Birkenpilze*, or what we thought looked like *Birkenpilze*. The later the afternoon and the hungrier we became, the more edible we deemed our finds, until we discovered that my mother was sneaking back to the bag and throwing out most of our new treasures.

We survived the meal. My mother used her pair of silver scissors out of her precious sewing kit that Omi Bauer had given her for confirmation. The scissors had to be boiled with the mushrooms because we had no silver spoon. It did not turn black, so we ate with some confidence. While the stove was still hot and the pilfered wood lasted, my mother turned the highway apples into sauce. Not having any butter, cheese, or meat to put on our bread, we used apple sauce. If we had milk, our topping became more elaborate. We made quark, spread it on the bread, and covered that with the apple sauce. How did we make quark? Inventive as my parents had to be under the extreme restrictions, they thought of a makeshift way of processing the milk. At night, they put the chair upside down with its seat on the desk and tied a bandanna between the legs like a hammock. Then they poured the milk into the bandanna and put a pot underneath to catch the whey. The *drip-drip* in the dark lulled me to sleep with the assuring thought that there would be a nice lump of curd to eat in the morning.

Hunger perhaps overshadowed all other worries of our living conditions. These other concerns, however, were considerable. Our room was so small that we spent most of the time outside. What would we do when winter came? How long was the wood going to last? In the first days, we had followed Frau Kolb's halfhearted invitation to use her kitchen and living room. My father, in an attempt at congeniality, played Frau Kolb's piano once. He gave up quickly, finding it painfully out of tune. The redheaded daughter wet her bed nightly. Frau Kolb hung the sheets unwashed in her room to dry. The transparent son wandered up and down the hall, coughing incessantly and pitifully. Frau Kolb's interest in my mother was strictly as a workhorse to pull wood out of the forest. Frau Kolb's attitude toward my father was one of suspicion since he had no job. "Where is my rent going to come from?"

Cooped up in our room between decrepit furniture, only my father's wit and vitality lifted us out of our despair. It could have become exasperating to have the only lamp turn off when stepping on the floor or to have the chairs give way under you when you counted on them being there or to have the high, narrow closet fall over on its wobbly feet and wake me in the middle of the night when it crashed on the desk. My father had hit it with his foot. My mother was also in his bed. My father turned these deficiencies into jokes. He came up with advertising slogans that he pronounced to us in a radio announcer's voice.

"Kolb's magic lamp—one breath and you stand in the dark.

"Kolb's stove—works according to the principle, all heat through the chimney.

"Kolb's patented furniture—reach once, a chair; reach twice, a heap of rubble."

He invented others about the collapsible closet and the spring-activated mattress. We started laughing.

This gallows humor deceived us only sometimes about our true state, which became more dismal from week to week. When we were about at our wits' end, we received a boost—two of our suitcases trucked from Erfurt containing personal items we could trade for food. For some time, the refugees at the Adler had been hiking to the surrounding villages to barter for anything edible. Now that we had something to offer, we resolved to try ourselves.

With a selection of tradable things in the rucksack, we set out through the fairy tale forest toward the Hohenstein. We came upon the hamlet Kleedorf in a side valley. My parents halted and looked down on the farmhouses. It took them quite a while before they nudged themselves to hike down and knock on the doors. Perhaps it helped that Monika and I stood behind them. One of the farmer's women refrained from shrugging and closing the door and actually looked into our satchel and selected a roll of bandages. For it, she gave us one egg and about one pound of bread. Our solicitations in the next villages became progressively easier, albeit not any more productive.

This bartering with the farmers would come to an end with the dwindling number of things we could sacrifice. My father needed to find a job. None of his drawings had sold. The glazer master was not going to display any of them in his window. My father thanked the man dejectedly and took his creations home. Encouraged by my mother, my father resolved to make another attempt at finding a position as play director.

56

In the early morning of August 21, my father hitchhiked to München to find some of the theater administrators who had moved there from Berlin. He only found one of his acquaintances, who told him the theaters had all been damaged or destroyed with no telling when any of them would open again. It was too early to think of positions. There would be nothing a play director could do at this time but sit back and wait.

Hopeless and defeated, my father hitchhiked homeward, but he did not make it far. He was arrested for not having a permit to cross the border of the München district, imprisoned for the night, and fined one hundred marks. When I learned what had happened that day, it became the distinguishing fact of my tenth birthday that my father had spent that night in the Landshut jail. I resigned myself that I would have to do without celebration, presents, cake, or candles. To my surprise, my mother revealed a real *Rundkuchen* (a birthday cake). How many weeks did she save the flour, the egg, the milk, the sugar, and the fat to grease the pan? We each ate a small piece and saved the rest for my father's return.

My father made it back on the August 25, my mother's thirty-fourth birthday and my parents' eleventh anniversary. He arrived without present, without flowers, only with the receipt for his one-hundred-mark fine, but how happy we all were to have him back safely. Also, he seemed to be relieved that his attempts at getting back into the theater were premature and that his failure to do so did not result from a lack of talent.

From then on, my father looked for any kind of job. From our daily walks past the different army installations, it was obvious that those Germans who made connections here were tapping into a source of plenty. There was excess food, and there were cigarettes.

Most of those who swarmed around the soldiers' quarters were young females, who jumped the language barrier with ease and soon were able to bring some relief to their parents and siblings. We observed one such relationship up close.

Two regulars who squeezed around the tables with us in the Schwarze Adler were a woman and her daughter. They lived in a tiny room around the corner in the Schulgasse. The woman's husband had been missing in action since Stalingrad. She had little hope of ever seeing him again. The daughter had just turned fifteen. The gloss and abundance of her unfolding femininity was particularly striking in contrast to the outgrown clothes she had to wear. It was less obvious that the mother also had to keep wearing the tattered few pieces she had rescued through the war. They matched the haggard and haunted face and skinny body that marked all adult refugees.

When the daughter appeared with a new skirt, everyone in the restaurant knew where the cloth had come from. The skirt was bright red and showed the circular stitching marks where the white circle had been removed. The mother, like many other women in that desperate time, had taken the banner of a thousand years and sewn it into something useful.

Having outfitted the daughter with this skirt, the mother trolled her past the Teehaus. On the second pass, she had a bite, and her worries about food were over. The GI brought along chocolate, coffee, and cigarettes every time he visited the second-floor room in the Schulgasse.

When we passed through that alley after that, my mother always looked up to that window with regret. The woman never came to the Adler again. She did not need to, and she did not want to.

Besides the Fräulein, other Germans were finding connections with the occupational forces regularly employed in the kitchen or in the motor pool. My father got the idea that he could also work for the "Amis" by utilizing his high school English.

My father hitchhiked to Lauf to the local employment office for the Armed Forces and was referred to the regional office in Fürth. He hitchhiked to Fürth, was told that there were no openings at the time, but got his name on the waiting list. Then he waited, hopeful as always.

He filled his days with trips to town to stand in line wherever milk, bread, and vegetables were offered. He yielded again to the urge of capturing the picturesque corners of the inner town. Now that he no longer produced for sale, he was freed from the concern of getting it right. His unrestrained, fresh pencil sketches and watercolors reflected his joy of seeing. At home, he brought his sketches to completion or he wrote in his diary.

My mother, Monika, and I kept walking through the villages, offering our wares. On a day that tried to gather the warmth of late summer under its clear, dark blue dome, we hiked once more through the forest to Kleedorf, the favorite path for Monika and me. Its many hidden creeks and fern-covered rocks, all animated by the flicker of the filtered light, reminded us of *Grimm's Fairy Tales*. Surely those squirrels and birds were trying to lead us to dwarfs under hollow trees or nixies bathing in springs.

At Kleedorf, we emerged out of the deep woods into the blinding light. We descended into the hamlet and knocked on the doors of the houses. There was no response. We followed the dusty road north to Aspertshofen. In the middle of the village was a curious little house that had neither windows nor doors. A steep tile roof covered thick whitewashed walls. The front gable side was constructed in a Roman arch. Recessed in this arch was a wall with a large cast-iron flap about waist high. The rear gable side was fitted with a domineering chimney. The curious building was one of the communal *Backofen* (baker's ovens), where the women from the surrounding farms gathered to bake their round, black, crusty loaves. Monika and I realized how Hansel and Gretel could have pushed the witch into such an oven. No smoke curled from the chimney. The walls were cold.

Aspertshofen seemed desolate. Were the farmers all in the fields? At the houses where we knocked, no one was home. Or did I notice a curtain move at a window?

We left the village and headed south again toward Hersbruck. Before we

356

got to Kühnhofen, which hid under the northern slope of the Michelsberg, we spotted a single farmhouse standing in the middle of fields that rose toward the wooded, twin peaks of the Grosse and Kleine Hansgörgel.

My mother decided to go to the farmhouse. The farmer's woman let us into her kitchen where she was preparing lunch.

"I have something I would give for food," my mother said, reaching into the pack hesitatingly. I recognized her little black sewing kit with the flower embroidery. She unhitched the latch, unfolded the lid, slid the pair of scissors out of its loop, and offered it to the farmer's woman.

"These scissors are real sterling silver."

The farmer's woman wiped her hands on her apron. She took the pair of scissors from my mother's hand, forced her thumb and finger into the handles, snapped it a few times, and ran her left thumb over the blade.

"Wish they were bigger and sharper," she said. "I can give you half a loaf for this."

To my surprise, my mother did not argue. Usually, she was able to get an additional egg or piece of bacon thanks to her persistence and her pleading eyes. This time, she just nodded.

My mother did not start sobbing until we had walked back to the street and had sat down in the ditch to eat the bread. "I got those scissors from Omi Bauer. They were real silver. And now they are gone too, and we have nothing any more. It was the last thing we had."

Monika climbed on my mother's lap, slung her arms round her neck, and leaned her head on her shoulder. I did not know what to do or say. I chewed my bread and looked over to the gentle wooded summits. How could such a day full of warmth and light and fairy tale wonder hold so much sorrow? Even many years later, I never passed that spot without seeing us in the ditch, eating that last piece of bread, while my mother, all her energy and resourcefulness exhausted, wept in despair.

That evening, when my mother gave my father the rest of the bread, she told him in a deep and quiet voice that this was the last food we could get from the farmers. We were out of things to trade. Her calm seemed to disturb him more than one of her explosions. She did not hint at his failure to find a job or sell any of his pictures; she didn't even allude to the misfortune of losing one hundred marks in fines. He tried to pace the floor, two steps this way, two steps that way. Then he left the room and went for a walk.

The next morning, still half-asleep, I heard my father getting dressed and leaving. I pulled my blanket tighter and dug myself into the backrest. One technique we learned for combating hunger was to sleep more.

Around ten o'clock, my father burst into the room, carrying a cardboard lid, and in it, he had food! He had a plate with a stack of flat yellow disks, which he called "pancakes"—six of them—and a can of condensed milk with a red carnation on its label.

What had happened? My father had walked down the Amberger Strasse past the army installations. The kitchen in the Teehaus blew a mouth-watering smell of bacon, roasting potatoes, onions, and scrambled eggs onto the sidewalk. At the Hotel Post, garbled voices came from the windows. My father noticed that he could understand quite a bit. He went a few steps farther to the occupied high school. He read the big white sign fastened to the venerable building. It said in the sober, chopped-up, sprayed-on letters of the army, "Headquarters 16th A.F.A. Bn."

He walked through the schoolyard, through the main door, and into the first office. He stopped in the middle of the room and said, "I need work."

The officers looked up from their desks in surprise and stared at the gaunt man. He looked like one who would not be denied. They conversed among themselves about what he could possibly do for them, until one had the idea that he could empty the ashtrays and the wastepaper baskets. Was he willing to take this job? They could not pay him, but he would be permitted to eat in the cafeteria in the Teehaus.

"That is all right," my father said and started emptying the ashtrays. At 9:30, he took a break, went over to the Teehaus, and had breakfast. Most GIs had eaten. The food that they had left on their plates seemed enough to feed the people at the Schwarze Adler for several days. Once he had eaten, my father followed the bus trays into the kitchen and rescued a stack of pancakes and the can of milk before they went into the garbage. He rushed home with the food and ran back to his second round of ashtray cleaning.

The pancakes were cold and soggy, but how delicious! The can of evaporated milk was almost full. My mother gave it to me, and over the next hour, still lying on the couch, I sucked the whole can empty, savoring every swallow. For once, I had the almost-forgotten feeling of wanting no more.

In the coming days, my father put himself on a furious program in order to expand his English vocabulary. At work, he asked the meaning of each unknown word that he encountered and noted it in a blue book. At night, he wrote the words on cards that he cut out of his sketchpad and stacked into an empty cigarette carton. He memorized a hundred words a day. The speed with which he would respond when he had me question him filled me with awe.

Two weeks later and 1,400 practical words richer, my father was asked to put down his cleaning rag and help as interpreter. The officers found they could not take care of sudden needs in repairs and supplies without contacting the local tradesmen. They put my father on the payroll. His salary was skimpy but better than nothing, and the fringe benefit of meals was invaluable.

57

I was making the new surroundings my own in a hurry. In my usual jog-trot, I fanned out across the valley, orienting myself to the towers of the town as my hub. With one of the mountaintops as my goal, I would run cross-country through harvested fields, rows of potato plants, and up the pasture slopes into the woods. The tolling of the church bell kept track of my time. I always returned before my mother could get worried. She had no idea how far I had been and that only an hour ago, I had been surveying the valley from one of the overlooks—the Arzberg, the Deckersberg, the Grossviehberg, the Michelsberg, or the Hansgörgel.

Between my excursions, I would join the throng of children roaming all over the lumberyard behind the house, making the most of their long break from school. There was no word yet from the occupational forces when school would resume.

The leader of our gang was Mugge, short for Muggentaler, a sturdy twelve-year-old. He had the unrestrained run of the place. His old man, the contractor Muggentaler, was in the prison camp with Herr Kolb and the other local Nazi leaders. As the primary proponent of the Nazi cause in town, he was probably not going to be released for years. Indeed, he had been so dedicated that he and two other same-spirited men had holed up in the church tower of Altensittenbach, determined to stop the tanks coming up the valley from Nürnberg. After a few of their bullets had ricochet from the armored vehicles that rumbled around the church, the Americans climbed the tower and stopped this nuisance.

There was no evidence that the son, Mugge, missed his father much. While the construction business was down, Mugge felt free to help himself to the building materials and tools for the many interesting projects that popped in his head. He had a perpetually dusty face, into which he licked a clean pink semicircle on his lower lip and chin. The other kids who followed Mugge around to watch or participate in the projects had no such distinguishing characteristics. I have forgotten them except for a few. There was Sand, a boy only a little older than I but unusually mature, tall, and very quiet. He never laughed, but his few comments showed how intelligent he was. The other children looked up to him. Was it because of his mental capacity or the fact that his grandparents had perished under the rubble of the neighboring lot?

The only person I mentioned in my diary, which I dutifully kept during that extended vacation, was Helga Rossner. The entry says:

I want to make a new secret language.

I then recorded a classified alphabet. I continued:

The secret language I want to learn together with Helga. Helga Rossner is a nice girl. She is as old as I and lives under us.

Helga Rossner had a brother, Heinzi, and a cat, Mitzi. Heinzi was four years old, white blonde, and tiny. He looked and behaved like a little old man. Heinzi was curious and always wound up in the middle of our construction. When we made ourselves stilts, we had to maneuver the appropriated poles around his little person while sawing and nailing. When we built a boat, Heinzi was again right in the middle of the action. Of course, he was too little to help bend the boards that formed the side of the boat, a job that took our combined supreme effort since we had been too impatient to soak them. Was it our fault that Heinzi stood next to the bow when the boards popped off, flipped him into the boat, and gave him a big goose egg? Frau Rossner blamed us when she came running to retrieve the screaming Heinzi. She insisted that he and Helga were to stay away from us wild boys. That relieved us from Heinzi.

Helga returned after a few days, just when I was becoming the hero of the gang by rolling out my most prized possession. My mother had stashed my inflatable handball in the suitcase from Erfurt. She had not traded it for food, even though it had a real leather cover. None of the others had a ball, not even one filled with sawdust, and here I came with one that actually bounced. We drew two fields, dragging our heels in the dust, and started a battle of *Völkerball*, a game where players of two teams try to get each other out by hitting them with a pitch they cannot catch. Our battles raged for days. Helga was particularly effective because she threw like a girl, swinging from the side. She let go of the ball at unexpected angles and hit players when they least expected it. I liked to be on the same team with her. When I was upstairs, the boys would send Helga to ask whether I would come down with my ball for another game. How satisfying to have her see me so wanted!

My popularity with the boys declined when my ball sailed into a thicket of brush in the neighbor's backyard. As I mournfully noted in my diary, Frau Pemsel, the neighbor, could not find the ball. With my attraction gone, Mugge seized the opportunity to gather the gang around himself again for another one of his projects, the building of a shelter. This construction was, perhaps, inspired by two strange boys who wandered in about that time.

This pair was much older than the rest of us, thirteen or fourteen. Their voices had already changed. They spent much time around the Teehaus and the Hotel Post. They chewed gum and chocolate bars and had, concealed deep in their pockets, imagine, real packs of cigarettes—Camel and Chesterfield. They embellished their language with English words they had picked up from the soldiers. The GIs, having proven themselves as victorious and being away from the social constraints of their families, expressed their manliness in particularly colorful and inventive expletives. It was a common joke to address native female pedestrians in the dirtiest way imaginable and to do it with a gentle smile. The German

girls would smile back as if having been complimented, whereupon the
GI would break out in bawdy laughter. Things became a little confusing
when the officers brought over their dependents from the States. No matter
how friendly the passing GI smiled at the major's wife, the comment, "Oh,
that hot pussy, baby, how about I give you a good fuck," did not make a
favorable impression. Such occurrences were so common that the offended
women resorted to fastening little American flags into their hairdos.

The two boys, who had won the favor of some GIs, parroted whatever
names they heard themselves called. "Cocksucker" must have been the
most frequent one. They used it a lot and bestowed it on other boys if they
deemed them worthy.

Mugge was taken by those boys, and he organized our gang to build
the hideout they suggested. We dragged boards and tarpaper to the remote
end of the equipment barn. At this hidden corner, there was already a
shelter that Mugge had built and claimed to have slept in one night. It
was no bigger than a large doghouse. The big boys said it was too small
for a club house, and consequently, we built a bigger shelter and included
the doghouse as an extra room. Our finished establishment had a real,
watertight roof and a door that could be locked from the inside but no
windows. The most significant furniture was a bench out of the back of a
car. We had unbolted it with great difficulty from this DKW that sat on
blocks behind the main house. The car's wheels and motor were gone, and,
with the owner in prison, the rest was fair game.

We arranged the bench against the longest wall. It was reserved for
the big boys. We ordinary members sat on boards on bricks. For wall
decoration, the big boys thumb-tacked pictures ripped out of American
magazines and calendars of women busting out of their clothes.

One of the big boys was quite handy with the accordion. He played
the melodies by ear that he had heard at the post—"Give Me Five Minutes
More," "Don't Fence Me In," and "Hey, Good-Looking." For some pieces,
we sang the lyrics, which the local dialect had concocted. The words for
"Sentimental Journey" started, *Meine Frau, die hat en Ami*" (My wife,
she has an Ami.)

I enjoyed the music so well that I regretted when the player unburdened himself from the straps and fished a pack of cigarettes out of his pocket. He also pulled out an American lighter, a longish cylinder with a little metal cap on the wick. It was operated by pushing a metal skin on the shaft up and down. Generously, this beneficiary of the GIs offered his friend and Mugge each a whole cigarette, while he suggested that the others could share one. I declined. My father had let me have a few puffs once, and I had not liked it. In later years, when thinking back on the scene, I became suspicious as to what favors these boys had done to get these invaluable gifts.

When the smoking session came to an end, the older boys starting something that at first looked like mock wrestling but soon changed. Their hands wandered more and more into each other's crotches until they unbuttoned each others' flies, plunged their hand in, and manipulated in there like they were milking an upside down cow. I sat amid all this activity without anyone touching me. From my befuddled and bemused expression, they must have gathered that I was too young to respond. Finally, the big boys crawled into the doghouse, and after some grunting and moaning, emerged rather subdued and calmed.

Then the one played the accordion some more. That was when Helga appeared at the door, looking for her cat. The boys said they had not seen Mitzi. "Don't worry. She is probably catching mice in the woodpiles. Come on in and join the club."

Helga hesitatingly came in to stay a while, but the pictures on the wall made her decide to look for Mitzi some more.

That night, my father asked me what we were doing back there in that house we had built. I suspected he had investigated our hideout and drawn some conclusions.

"Oh, the one boy plays the accordion, and we sing songs," I said. I was not about to tell him that the boys were rummaging around in each other's pants.

"I believe you," he said.

I calmed myself by rationalizing that I really had not told a lie. We did sing. It was not like the time I'd lied about my failed dictation. Nevertheless, I had told my father a half-truth while he believed me, and that never stopped bothering me. The harsh punishment for the lie I had told in Straβburg did not permit such moral deficit.

My father did not probe any further. He had heard by word of mouth, the way you heard any news at that time, that school was to resume on the first of October. I had to report to the Volksschule. "You know, the one over the fire department across from the castle. There is no telling when they will open the real Oberrealschule building. Headquarters is in there. Anyway, they probably will make you repeat the fourth grade since you missed about half of it."

I was determined to make the most out of my last two days of freedom. I decided to take a trip in the DKW that was sitting on the blocks. It still had a steering wheel, gas pedal, clutch, a gearshift on the floor, and the front seats, which had not been pilfered. As I opened the door to climb into the driver's seat, I noticed that the plywood body on the outside of the door was coming loose. With hardly any help, it fell off. I tested the rounded piece by flinging it in the air, and it sailed beautifully. Helga, who came through the yard, was impressed with my new aircraft. She was still looking for Mitzi, who had not turned up for days. Just then, we saw the cat sitting crouched next to the stack of boards, looking at a hole in the ground. Helga, relieved, joined me in tossing my novel projectile back and forth. Farther and farther, we let the sheet sail, until it became dangerous when it landed on us. We found two poles left over from our stilts and learned to protect ourselves with our lances.

As we perfected our technique, I became confident I had invented a game that would regain that popularity that I had lost when my ball flew into Pemsel's yard. Sure enough, when Mugge and the gang emerged, they could not wait to take over the new sport. Mugge raised the rhetorical question, whose are the poles anyway? Helga and I took a break. We got into the DKW to rest. The cat was still sitting at the same spot in the grass next to the woodpile, motionless, only the tip of her tail twitching.

When I pretended to start the car, Helga wanted me to take her to Nürnberg. It was the only big city she knew. She had moved away from there three years ago and remembered how it had been then. I had no wish to revisit the rubble that I had seen. Instead, I suggested we travel to

Straßburg, Erfurt, and Berlin. And so turning the steering wheel, letting out the clutch, and shifting, we made it through the different cities as I described them in travel commentary. When we returned from our trip through Germany, the cat was still sitting.

I tried to interest Helga in my secret language, but, since my code was way too complicated, her attention wandered back to the cat. Suddenly she yelled, "Look!"

I had seen it too. The cat had taken a giant leap and caught a mouse. In true feline fashion, she squeezed it some between her teeth, let it go, followed it as it crawled along the woodpile, grabbed it, tossed it in the air, let it go, and caught it again.

"Would you believe it?" said Helga, "The cat has been sitting there for hours to catch that mouse. I would never have so much patience. What if the mouse would not have come out?"

A curious shudder crept up my back and showered my mind with an unusual sense of clarity.

"The cat is not patient at all," I said. "The cat knew that the mouse would come out and that she would catch it. She saw that all along."

Helga laughed. "How could she have known the future? The future has not happened yet."

I tried to explain. "Maybe the future has already happened just like the past, and we have just forgotten it. But some animals may still see it."

Helga looked at me sideways. "Michael, *Du bist aber eigenartig*" (you are strange).

I did not like her to look at me like that. So I did not tell her about other things I had learned in the war, things you never learn in school.

Once school started and the weather became colder, I did not see Helga much. Mugge's gang was also dispersed.

58

On October 1, my mother and I went to the Volksschule to register. What occurred there was so surprising that I could hardly wait for my father to come home from work to tell him.

"Guess what happened at the school?" I blurted out. "When we walked in, there was a woman at the desk. She asked us whether I was going to be in the Volksschule or Oberschule. We said, 'erste Klasse Oberschule.' Then she said, 'Volkschule, second floor, Oberschule, third floor.' So I went to the third floor."

My father was perplexed. He had passed many hours studying for his entrance exam in the dingy apartment of an old spinster, Fräulein Zengler. For me, it had been a matter of going to a different floor. He mused in his diary how war children these days had special privileges. They slip into college preparatory school without effort but, alas, also without fanfare. He reminisced about his own exam. The principal of the Oberschule had personally complimented him on his performance, resting his big hand on my father's head and saying, "Continue like that, my son."

My class was huge, sixty students perhaps. Some must have wandered in by mistake. My teacher was Herr Rapold. I had difficulty understanding the "Old Rapold," as my mother referred to him. His language was distorted by the local dialect. Also, a curved, smelly pipe, a permanent fixture on his mouth, interfered with his speech. To hamper communications even more, his lips were hidden in a gray, unkempt beard and, thus, hard to read.

The shortage of teachers was even worse than during the war. Many teachers had not returned from the war, and all Nazis were prohibited from working, so we were taught by relics, like Old Rapold, who had been called back from retirement, or by inexperienced Fräulein, who had been assigned to student teaching from college. Some teachers had no qualification other than the reputation that they were good in math or history or whatever subject that had to be taught.

Old Rapold did not like me; it was a mutual sentiment. He favored the homegrown youth over the *Zugereiste* (the refugees) and had a particular disdain for *Saupreussen* ("Pig-Prussians").

One of the marks of our elevated curriculum was the instruction in a foreign language, English. From Old Rapold's abuse of the German language, I can gather that his English must have been atrocious. His efforts were totally wasted. I spelled my own mother tongue like a foreign language. I did not need the vagaries of English orthography to confuse me further.

Once Old Rapold had discovered my weakness, he enjoyed calling me forward to the blackboard to write spelling words, a complete embarrassment since even my appearance at that time was ridiculous. I wore a blue *Training's Anzug* (warm-up suit). Since it was all I had owned for cool weather for the last year, it had become baggy in the seat and around my thin legs, yet was too short around my ankles and wrists.

I stood in front of the big black surface trying to catch and spell the words that Old Rapold demanded from me between puffs. I hesitated. He gently poked my baggy pants with his pointer. "Come on, lame ass," he said. So I wrote something down, whereupon Old Rapold rolled his eyes as if to ask the class to witness such unbelievable ineptitude. After a few more attempts at other words, he called a halt to the performance and made the categorical statement about my prospects of learning English.

"Tradowsky, you'll never learn it."

Old Rapold's English knowledge soon must have come to its limits, for Fräulein Erhart took over. Since she neither had a pipe nor a beard, my skills improved. My father gave me an empty cigarette carton and helped me make a catalog of English words like his. With his patient coaching and questioning and his inexhaustible inventiveness of *Eselsbrücken* (donkey's bridges)—mnemonic devices—he managed to make me learn my daily assigned eight or ten words.

Some words I absorbed from the things that my father brought from the Amis, like "carnation" or "cornflakes." Also, I picked up words from magazines, which my father began to bring home from the wastepaper baskets, like *Saturday Evening Post, Look, Life,* and *Esquire.* I was eager to learn the captions that went along with this world of plenty and perpetual happiness. Every person in these ads was smiling—smiling while getting in their new, larger cars, smiling opening their new, more cavernous refrigerators stocked with food for a year, smiling moving into their new, more rambling houses. I could understand well why, now and then, my parents would bring up the idea of moving to this dreamland.

Occasionally, documentary from Europe was interspersed in the journals. These reports were illustrated with black-and-white, unretouched photographs and stood in shocking contrast with the glossy depictions of America. The pictures from the devastation of the cities reminded me of the reality I had to live in. However, they did not disturb me anymore. It was no news. I had seen it.

Then one day, I hit upon the article that jarred me like an accident. Suddenly, men like skeletons in striped suits lying in bunks looked at me with eyes like holes burned into the paper. A pile of bodies loomed with enormous knee and elbow joints sticking out here and there. They were connected to long bones, thin like kindling, rib cages protruding, and shaved heads with smiling grimaces hanging down from rodlike necks. A black-and-white-striped body hung riddled and grotesquely distorted in a barbed-wire fence. I felt nauseated. I put the article down. I had come upon another inexplicable horror of the adult world.

Later, when my mother picked up the magazine, I watched her reaction. I knew when she hit the article by the way her eyes widened and the folds furrowed across her brow. As she turned the pages, she slowly shook her head. "Terrible," she muttered, "terrible, unbelievably terrible." She put the magazine aside, but the images stayed before her eyes; I could see it in their desperation.

I did not hear what my parents said to each other about the article. I only remember one comment my mother made that evening when she looked at Monika and me. "There will never be a time when the Jews will forget this. They will hold it against every German. They will hold it against our children and our children's children. There will never be any forgiveness. Forgiveness is not in their religion."

I wondered about this religion without forgiveness. I thought how often my mother had forgiven me with a kiss before I went to sleep. She had always made things right between us, and I always had breathed this big sigh of relief. I thought how Martchen had forgiven me. What if people could not forgive each other? How unbearable life would become on this earth.

I remembered the Morgenthau Plan. Was it going to turn the whole of Germany into such a prison camp? After hearing my mother's comments, I feared even more that this was going to happen. Were not the food rations becoming less by each month? Without my father snatching leftovers, we would starve.

In spite of desperate shortages of food, clothing, and household goods, life did normalize in some ways. School had reopened. Traffic started running on the tracks behind the lumberyard—first freight trains and then an occasional passenger train. On October 29, the mail service was reinstated. A few days later, a letter arrived from Berlin. With great relief, we saw the impeccable penmanship and the name of the sender, Georg Tradowsky. My Opa had made it through the war. He was renting a room because his apartment building had burned down. He had maintained his job at the *Bezugsamt* (the office for the apportionment of goods).

A second letter came from a place in Ostfriesland we had never heard of, Remels, near Aurich. We knew it was close to the North Sea. The letter was from Tante Teddy. She had left Hohen Lychen in February and fled west, away from the approaching Russians. She recounted the ordeal of the ride with Eva-Maria and the paralyzed Christian on the desperately overcrowded and attack-prone trains. She told how she'd finally made it to Stiekelkamp, which was the estate of her cousin, Mully. She was so exhausted that Mully did not recognize her. Mully had thought, *Look, here comes another poor refugee family.* And only when they came close she had said, "Teddy?"

Tante Teddy further wrote that Onkel Horsa had continued his dental practice until March, when the part of the building with the office was neatly taken down by a bomb. Standing in the door frame, he looked down a precipice where his state-of-the-art practice was lying under a pile of white rubble. He had nothing more to hold him in Berlin and made his way to his family in Ostfriesland. After the capitulation, they had found an apartment in a near hamlet, Remels. Onkel Horsa had rounded up a barber's chair and an antique, foot pedal–operated drill. He was treating scraggly toothed farmers, who paid, thank God, with eggs, bread, and bacon. The Hengstenbergs were surviving.

My father wrote to Elisabeth Schubert, and when he did not receive answer, asked his father to enquire about her whereabouts. Opa was able to find out from a neighbor what had happened and prepared my parents for the news by alluding to the horrors of the Russian occupation. Elisabeth Schubert and some of her women friends had been hiding in her cellar. Russian soldiers broke into the Haus, found them, forced them into the bedrooms, and raped them all. A few days later, the woman gathered around Elisabeth's kitchen, stuffed towels under the door, and turned on the gas. The neighbor found them around the table. They probably had held hands.

My father filled a whole diary trying to come to terms about the demise of his foster family. Still, whenever we made the mistake of viewing the 8mm film with the part of the Schuberts in their garden before the war, the sudden silence showed my parents' sorrow was unabated.

59

With the trains passing by more regularly behind the house, my mother considered the possibility of traveling to the Black Forest. She hoped to find our furniture still at Frau Fährenbach's. In case we had not lost it, she planned to arrange for its transport to Hersbruck. Within weeks, her urge to retrieve those precious belongings from her family's proud past became irresistible. On Thursday, November 8, she started on her mission.

When I returned from school, my mother had left. I expected her round-trip to Schönwald to take two days and that she would return Friday night. My parents had warned me that it probably would take longer since many of the tracks were still broken. The weekend came and went. My mother was still gone.

My father stayed calm. "If the furniture is still there, she will have to arrange to ship it. That takes time."

Monday evening, we sat on the sofa and sang folk songs as the room turned dark, stopping and listening when something stirred on the stairway.

My mother returned Tuesday night, exhausted. "Traveling is insane. I can't tell you how glad I am to be home. The furniture is all there and in good shape. It will be shipped by freight. How long this will take, nobody knows."

We settled in our room, and my mother told us about her trip. The trains were dangerously overcrowded, people hanging out of the windows and clinging to the sideboards, the bumpers, and the roofs. Everyone was trying to get somewhere; soldiers coming from the war were looking for their families, evacuated women and children were trying to get back to their cities, and refugees were looking for a place to stay.

My mother had to squeeze through a window to get on. Getting to Offenburg had taken two days. Since there was only one restored track, the train stood on sidetracks for hours to let others pass. For two days, my mother stood wedged between people. Getting to the WC was nearly impossible.

She went to the Sonne, still French Headquarters. The two Moroccan guards stood at the door. My mother was afraid of them. "They scared me. I did not want to go past them. You know, my father told me how he fought the Moroccans at the Marne. They wiped out his company. If they see blood, they get into a *Blutrausch* (blood frenzy). If they are wounded, they turn fierce. Fortunately, Herr Schimpf came along. Was he surprised to see me! He took me in."

The Schimpfs were restricted to a small room behind the kitchen and to one room on the second floor. The cook and the maids had to serve the French. The kitchen boy brought leftovers to the back room. Herr Schimpf called their food "*Quer durch die Küche*" (diagonally through the kitchen). They did have enough to eat.

The next morning, my mother took the train to Triberg. She had to hike to Schönwald. The *Hauptstrasse* was teeming with French military, some of them Moroccan. Close to the end of the street, in sight of the church tower with the onion-shaped roof, she noticed that a Moroccan on the other side of the street was keeping up with her. She sped up and headed for the waterfall. Looking back at the switchback, she caught the red on his uniform and the white flash of his teeth. He was following her on the deserted path. Frightened, she climbed as fast as she could, but he was gaining. She started running, crazy with fear. She reached the top of the waterfall where the trail joins the road and fell to the ground. Her heart was out of rhythm. It raced and beat exceedingly faintly. She was fighting for air, dizzy, and felt like throwing up but was too weak.

"I was afraid I would die. I don't know how long I lay there but slowly, slowly I calmed down. And then, from one beat to the next, my heart stopped the fluttering and fell back in the normal rhythm."

My mother continued, but I no longer listened. Disturbed and distracted by her story, my mind tried to fathom that she could have died. She was no longer immortal.

My mother never forgot the story either. Nineteen years later, she prepared me days before she died, saying I should not expect her to be around much longer. She believed she damaged her heart when she outran the Moroccan.

———

Back in Hersbruck, my mother started her campaign at the *Wohnungsamt* (housing department).

"We need more space. Our furniture is coming."

The prospects were dismal.

"Your family should be thankful you have a room for yourself," said the smug official. "Have a look at the warehouse where the other refugees are." As she left she heard him muttering, "Furniture!"

My mother was not put off by the haughty official. She was used to the *Beamten* wielding their power. She purposefully started making a nuisance of herself by inquiring every time she went to town.

As the colder season forced us indoors, our room was becoming unbearable. On top of our physical restriction, Frau Kolb had become hostile. It had not taken her long to find out that my father had started working for the Amis. On her daily walk with Frau Muggentaler down the road, they talked to their husbands through the barbed-wire fence. She felt ashamed to admit that she had rented her room to a traitor who was fraternizing with the enemy. She kept swinging her broom in the hall in front of our door, muttering with every stroke, "*Kommunisten Pack, Kommunisten Pack*" (Communist rabble), as if she wanted to sweep us out the door. We kept our door closed tightly to shut out her insults, together with the smell of urine and the boy's incessant coughing. Even his affliction, which at first had roused our pity, had become an irritation.

Christmas arrived, and we were still at the Kolbs'. I doubted whether we would have a Christmas tree this year, but when it became dusky on Christmas Eve, my father took Monika and me spazieren until nightfall, while my mother had the room for herself. Upon our return, my father left Monika and me in the dark hall and squeezed through the crack into the room. The Kolbs had retreated into the kitchen. With Herr Kolb in prison, they did not celebrate. It was as quiet as if they had gone away, but we could feel them listening. Monika and I were too embarrassed to start Christmas carols. Then my parents began singing inside and slowly opened the door. Lo and behold, a Christmas tree reached from the table to the ceiling, spreading its warm, flickering light. My mother had discovered real candles somewhere. Silver stars and snowflakes hung on the branches. The ornaments revealed by their jagged edges that my father had cut them out of tin cans. As we sang "Stille Nacht," we let the mild radiance calm our hearts. We contemplated. A year ago, we had sung like this in Erfurt. So far we had survived. What was the coming year to bring?

We did not have to wait long for a big change. Right after the holiday, my mother stopped by at the *Wohnungsamt* again.

The smug official was exasperated. "I wish you would get it through your head that there is nothing available." To get this woman off his back he added, "There are two empty rooms that you can look at. You won't want them. Nobody does."

My mother perked her ears. "Why? What's wrong with those rooms?"

"They are way too big and too high. You can't heat them. Besides, there is no bathroom."

"Where are they?" my mother asked.

"They are in the castle, second floor, above the *Vermessungsamt*" (office of land survey).

My mother went to the castle in her fastest marching step, looked, and returned to the office.

"We'll take it."

We all explored our potential residence. We agreed that, by some providence, we were offered rooms in the only building that had spaces designed for furniture like ours. The two rooms were palatial. The smaller was four times as big and twice as high as the chamber at the Kolbs'. The larger one was even a third bigger.

I walked into these rooms with that strange feeling of familiarity I'd had when I had first seen the castle. Their unusual features did not surprise me. These extraordinarily wide doors that were, nevertheless, so low that my father brushed his hair on the lintel had been built for the noblemen and women who lived here hundreds of years ago. They might have been corpulent but had been much smaller. Unusual also were the windows that were as large as doors and revealed the thick, sandstone masonry. With a sense of recognition, I glanced out of these windows—it all looked familiar—and took in the view across the moat and the wall directly below and through a gap in the houses onto the church and beyond into the meadows, where the gleam of the setting sun lay on the river. Turning back into the rooms, I beheld the green tile stoves that were so high that my father had to stretch to touch their top. They threatened by their sheer size to be gluttons of wood or coal. At the moment, we did not consider that we had no fuel to heat these century-old edifices. The only other object that should have struck me as odd was a ceiling lamp made out of antlers. The landlord had left it in the smaller room. But nothing in these two rooms struck me as strange. I sensed that I would spend years here.

Our steps echoed on the zigzag pattern of the oak floor. My parents did not see the gaping emptiness. Their mind's eye filled it with our antiques, our carpets, and our pictures on the walls.

Even though the furniture would not arrive for several months, we could not wait to move. "We can sit on our suitcases. We can buy a hot plate. All we have to find are beds."

My mother discovered four beds in a warehouse among the stock that the Reich had provided under their NSV (a program for the bombed-out and refugees). They were raw, unpainted, pine frames that held boards to lie on. Instead of mattresses, the warehouse attendant handed out paper sacks that could be filled with straw. The sacks looked like the ones they had forced people to use for the burials of the multitudes during the last throes of the war. My mother was not in the position to be choosy. She took four bed frames and four paper sacks. She also obtained some felt blankets that were better fit to be cut up into scouring pads than to keep a person warm.

My father and I took the empty paper sacks and went searching for straw. On the morning of the last day of 1945, we found a farm close to the old railroad on the left side of the Pegnitz, where a farmer was willing to sell us the stuffing for our mattresses. He sent us in the barn with a crooked, old woman to help us. She turned out to be deaf-mute. While filling our sacks until they stood up straight, she emitted a mixture of word-like sounds and laughter, indicating her childish delight in creating these curious sculptures. We then carried these paper sausages, one under each arm, across the valley and through town to the castle. The natives shook their heads as we passed on the sidewalks. We could well imagine what they thought.

"Tell me they sleep on that. Live in a castle and have nothing but straw. That's probably what they are used to, those refugees. They all had fancy houses and honorable jobs where they came from. Yah. Would they sleep on straw if that were true?"

We borrowed Frau Kolb's cart to transport our suitcases. It made her realize that we were serious about moving. When she had first gotten wind of our intentions, she had suddenly become aware that her only income was in jeopardy and had tried to persuade us to stay. "You'll be sorry. My husband worked in the surveying office. That building is an ice cellar. You'll all catch pneumonia."

That did not deter us. We were leaving as night fell. What better time to move than New Year's Eve so we could start the new year in the new place? My father gathered our last bags. My mother was about to take down the Christmas tree. It still smelled fresh, and none of the needles had fallen off. "Let's take the tree!" She grabbed the trunk above the stand. Holding it high with its tin-can ornaments jingling, we proceeded down the Amberger Strasse through the Spital Gate and through the old town into the castle. The Hersbruckers dropped their jaws and muttered, "Look, they are not only *Habenichtse*" (have-nothings), "they're also *damisch*" (crazy).

My parents didn't care what people said. They had tried to instill in me the same independence of mind during the previous years of mass delusion; but I was still concerned about what the local children would hear about me from their parents. I was eager to fit into the new surroundings. I hoped, of course in vain, that no one would see my mother carry the Christmas tree through the streets.

My mother put the tree into the corner of the smaller room. As forlorn as it looked in the gaping space, it nevertheless reminded us of the season of gratitude. We were thankful to have escaped from the Kolbs' crammed chamber. We would not bump into each other anymore.

My mother squatted next to the hot plate on the floor in her Arabian posture and prepared some potato soup. My father and I moved the suitcases under the antler lamp to sit on.

A knock came at the door.

My father shouted his resolute "*Herein*" (Come in).

A ruddy, outdoorsy, old man entered and looked bewildered at our seating arrangement. He introduced himself as Slevogt. It was the name we had seen on a brass sign on one of the doors in the hall, which read "Eugen Slevogt, Vermessungsdirektor AD" (survey director in retirement). This sprightly old man had once occupied the whole wing as head official. During the war, he had been required to share his dwelling, first, with an *Ausgebombte* (bombed-out) war widow and her four children and then also with a bombed-out mother and daughter. Now we refugees were moving in on him in two more rooms he had been forced to vacate.

As the gentleman introduced himself, my father echoed, "Slevogt, are you related to the painter, Max Slevogt?"

The landlord looked surprised. No one in this town had ever known enough about art to connect him with this painter of the hunt. While my father talked about the landlord's noted cousin, specifically in which galleries he had seen his paintings, Slevogt's regard for us rose quickly. He started nodding to my father's remarks. He ventured that the love for the hunt was perhaps a family trait.

"I'm a hunter myself. Have been game-warden for many years."

We told him that our furniture was stored in the Black Forest and would be coming soon. At this time, his esteem for us had reached the point where he actually believed us.

"You can use those chairs and the table that are standing in the hall," he offered.

We gladly accepted.

"You'll have to get your water from across the hall in my bathroom," Slevogt went on. "Let me show you."

The tiny room had a toilet that had to serve all occupants and a minuscule washbasin with cold water only. Of course there was neither shower nor bath. Before we could make any comment, Slevogt excused himself with a little bow.

My parents put Monika and me to bed and settled into the borrowed wicker chairs to wait for the New Year. They even had a bottle of wine that they had swiped from Omi's wine cellar. My mother had supported Omi's suspicion that the burglars had taken the bottle. My parents sipped the wine and relived in their minds the earthshaking events of the last year.

I tried in vain to go to sleep. I kept rolling off the overstuffed paper sack until my parents removed most of the straw. After my bed had been made negotiable, the glaring light in the antler lamp kept me awake.

At midnight, my parents opened the window, clinked their glasses, sipped, and cheered *"Prost Neujahr!"* They shouted it into the black and soundless night, as if to appeal to the incoming year to be kind to us.

Not a single New Year's cheer echoed from the town, but the bells from the church just across the moat started tolling in that beautiful, persistent sound that is always the same whether in times of hardship or blessing. After the bells stopped tolling, I fell asleep. The next morning, there was a mountain of straw in the corner of the large room, where my parents had piled their and Monika's excess bedding. I thought how handy it would have been to have Rumpelstilzchen come and spin this straw to gold.

60

I f we had hoped that our landlord would be in some way supportive, we soon buried this expectation. His generosity had exhausted itself with the loan of table and chairs. After our initial encounter, our communications receded to the minimum—the monthly payment of the rent and a "*Grüss Gott*" in passing in the hall or on the stairs.

For two months, we lived in nearly empty rooms. We tried to keep the smaller one at a temperature that would not show our breath. The larger one, in which my parents slept, was unheated and so cold that we could have, as my father said, opened an ice rink. The mountain of mattress stuffing had been burned first. It provided the proverbial straw fire, hot and short. Then my father scrounged some broken furniture from behind the Teehaus, and that somehow tided us over the winter. Fortunately, the winter was mild and brief.

In March, we got a notice from the station that a boxcar full of furniture had arrived and had to be unloaded pronto. The Hersbruckers tried to catch a glimpse when the load was dragged out of the dark of the truck—the grand piano; the huge, polished walnut cupboard; the octagonal coffee table with the carved legs and inlaid star on top; the architect's desk; and the renaissance oak chest that could hide a lover.

While the news of the refugees' riches circulated in town, my parents examined the furniture for damages. Fortunately finding none, they dragged and pushed every piece into its proper place. They rolled out the oriental rugs. As the last steps, they placed the sculptures of Monika and me and the Chinese vases. The hanging of the Hardanger Fjord and the tulip painting took some time to meet my mother's liking. "No, a little lower; a little more to the right; fine."

My parents dressed up a bit by changing into their best old clothes and emerged arm in arm, us children on each side. They proceed through town with their backs straight and heads held high, as if the nobility of old had returned to the castle.

"*Vornehm geht die Welt zu Grunde*" (Nobly the world perishes), my father quoted, hinting at the paradox of our situation. Granted, sounds of culture filled our halls—programs on the NORA from Milan, Paris, and the BBC; arias on the Victrola gramophone sung by Caruso, Gigli, and Schlusnus; and the thundering of my father's piano playing Beethoven's "Madness about the Lost Dime," with the predictable hang-ups. However, while the nourishment of the soul reached peacetime proportions, the feeding of the body became catastrophic.

My father was promoted to a clerical job. The small increase in money was almost meaningless. We could not buy anything. To the contrary, the advancement made our situation more critical. In the process, he had to move from the Oberrealschule to the Stadtbad, the town's bathhouse. It had been occupied by the army for offices. He had his own desk there now, but he was too far from the Teehaus cafeteria to help himself to leftovers. The source that had brought our food to subsistence level dried up. At the same time, during the spring and summer of 1946, the food stamp rations became so small that no one could survive unless they had additional supplies. This meant they either had to depend on the farmers, like most natives, or make some connections to the black market, the only salvation for the refugees. The predominant currency was cigarettes. We tried to get our hands on tobacco any way we could.

Occasionally, my father's employers would ask him to find a local craftsman for repairs. It could be a smoking furnace, a leaky toilet, or broken window. If the soldiers would ask how to compensate him, he always asked for cigarettes. My parents were able to barter enough food for a carton of Camels to keep us alive for weeks. However, by the end of April, we had exhausted the food from these sources. We also ran out of money. We could not even eat at the Adler using the food stamps that we had saved during our black market transactions. My parents responded predictably to the hopeless situation. My father became very quiet and confided his worries to his diary, while my mother expressed her desperation openly.

After the war years, the awareness that our lives were in jeopardy was nothing new to me. Rather than being afraid, I was curious about what solutions my parents would come up with this time. My faith in their resourcefulness had become unshakable.

Our survival depended in large part on my parents' willingness to sacrifice their pride. I can imagine how awkward it was for my mother to ask for help. She had become known at the regular's table as the granddaughter of Erfurt's Blumenschmidt. Pressed to desperation, she finally asked Frau Drieslein, another constant customer. She stammered to ask if the Frau could be so kind as to help us out over the last week of the month and to please decline if it was too much to ask, as it probably really was, and so on and so forth.

Frau Drieslein, remarkably well dressed for the times, with a diamond pendant spelunking her considerable cleavage, had assumed the social leadership of a lady among the women at the table. Even though her husband had fallen in Stalingrad and her clothing store and house had been bombed out in Nürnberg, there was no doubt that she still had money in the bank. She answered my mother's request whispering, "Surely. Glad to do it," and handed her the indicated sum discretely under the table.

On the first of the month, my mother paid the debt promptly. The next month, she ran out again and had to ask once more. After that, Tante Drieslein, as Monika and I called her, asked quietly at the end of each month whether we needed help and followed through on her offer every time my mother cast down her eyes and nodded.

With the rations becoming so meager, money alone was not going to save us. We had to get our hands on tobacco again. Enviously, we saw how the GIs pulled one cigarette after another out of the packs they had stuffed in their shirt pockets, lit them for a few draws, and threw them, half-used, on the sidewalks. At the back of the Hotel Post, this waste was spectacular.

Here, the soldiers had a smoke during reel changes of the Hollywood productions they were seeing inside. When the gong called them back in, they all flicked their cigarettes away, some three-quarters unsmoked. This left a half circle of smoldering litter on the sidewalk. To their surprise and amusement, when they came out for the second reel change, the sidewalk was clean. They had another smoke and threw away another shower of butts. When they left the show, the sidewalk was clean again. What they did not know was that, as soon as they had disappeared in the dark doorway, children, who had been watching from around the corner and across the court, would dart over and, within less than a minute, pick up the butts and stuff them in their pockets. Monika and I observed this scene several times when our parents walked by the Post on our evening spazieren until we sensed that the timing of our passing at the reel changes was intentional. When the children came running from all sides, it only took a questioning look from us at our mother and a little nod from her, and we joined the other children with the excitement of an Easter egg hunt. As fast as I was, I soon captured the best butts, brought them back by the handful, and put them into a brown bag that my father had in his pocket.

At home, my parents took a pair of scissors and cut off the burned end and the other end—not too generously—unfolded the tobacco from the paper, and dropped it into an empty coffee can. I am sure that, when no one was watching, my parents picked up some butts too, since they filled the first can in a short time and moved on to their second. When our supplies of real cigarettes dwindled again, my parents found takers on the market even for this loose tobacco. They did not reveal the origin of the supplies, and the traders did not ask.

And so we subsisted through the spring. I remember the churning in my stomach from constant hunger. When my parents were out of the house at night, invited to see one of the movies at the Post, I would get the bread out of the box and a knife from the drawer. If the bread was at all edible, not stretched with potatoes or sawdust, I would cut a slice and eat it very slowly. Then I could not control myself and cut another and then another. By the time my parents came home, a considerable chunk of the precious bread was gone.

Pretending to be asleep, I heard my father complaining, "What are we going to do now? Shouldn't we tell him not to get the bread out without us?"

And then I heard my mother, "Just let him have it, Papi. The boy is starving."

The Amis at my father's work had no inkling about our precarious state. My father never complained. I'll always remember how horrified my father's boss, Captain Jones, and his wife were when they finally saw our undernourished condition. That was at the villa Rupp, which my father had helped secure for his boss. My father had the difficult task of serving as an interpreter when villas had to be seized from the locals to be occupied by the families of officers. In spite of his charm, sense of fairness, and careful accounting of compensations, those evicted hated him. For his boss, he had requisitioned the prettiest property on the warm south slope of the Michelsberg, a modern, spacious house with a swimming pool in a rose garden. Captain Jones trusted that his wife would love it. He hardly remembered her. He had married her, a nurse, at the military hospital in England after knowing her for only three weeks. Then he'd left to join the fight in France, having recuperated from his wound. When his bride arrived, he was taken aback by how short and pudgy she was. Had his injury clouded his senses? Or was he seeing her in a different light—one that contrasted her to the sprightly and tall Fräulein that he, a handsome, virile, and athletic young man, had picked up in the meantime? Faced with having to drop her, he hired the pretty Fräulein as housekeeper for his spouse. His young wife might have been pudgy, but she was not dumb. She quickly found some pretext to replace her husband's choice with a dried-up, elderly man, a former opera singer from Breslau.

Captain and Mrs. Jones were grateful to my father for providing a dwelling the likes of which they could never afford in the States. During the first warm week in June, they invited us for an afternoon around their pool. When we emerged from their bedroom in our bathing suits, a look of horror appeared on their faces. My mother was sitting in her loose, two-piece bathing suit, dangling her feet into the water. Her collarbones were the most prominent of her visible skeleton. They stuck out so far that water would have collected behind them. My father was a fitting counterpart. One could count all his ribs. However, the total lack of fat was more shocking on my mother's supposedly female body. We children were still not quite as emaciated.

Mrs. Jones, the nurse, immediately summoned the newly hired singer from Breslau. He was weeding around the roses in a worn suit that hung on him. She tried to tell him to prepare six T-bone steaks. After she failed to make him understand, she sent him back to the roses and set out for the task herself.

When we sat down for dinner, steaks like toilet lids covered our plates, displacing potatoes and string beans, and hanging over the edges. We did not know that meat came in such huge cuts, equaling our meat ration for three months. The thought of having to eat all this nauseated us. After five slices of meat, half a potato, and a few string beans, we were stuffed and could not go on. Our hosts looked at our almost-untouched plates. After several unsuccessful encouragements, they concluded that we did not like the American cuisine. This dampened their friendliness visibly. They let us go home and made no further attempts to save us from starvation. Probably, they consoled each other that they had tried.

There were also shortages in fuel and clothing. My mother would work in a cloud of ammonia over the ironing board to rub out spots in pants, skirts, and jackets. She tried to iron flat the knees, seats, and elbows gone baggy in order to make them fit to be worn another week, another month. She dyed some discarded and stripped uniforms that my father had brought home from the Amis. My father, who had looked out of place in his own German uniform, appeared truly pitiful in these black and maroon outfits, but it relieved what was left of his civilian clothes.

The special problem with Monika and me was that we were rapidly growing. Some clothes grew with us, like my blue training suit or Monika's stretchy knit skirt. Some others, particularly shoes, became too small to be forced on any longer. Since there was no meat, there was no leather. The only shoes available for Monika were sandals with wooden soles and cloth straps nailed on crosswise. We called them *Kläpperle* (little clatterers). My mother resorted to similar contraptions during the summer months.

In winter, she wore her riding boots, which, in her energetic marching step, gave her a distinctly military appearance. My father called her "Alter Fritz." With her emaciated aquiline profile, she did indeed resemble the old Prussian king, Friedrich the Great, whom the Berliners had affectionately endowed with this nickname.

As for me, I went barefoot all summer. On my new long walk to school, my soles built up a protective callous. The Oberrealschule had moved from the shared Volkschule on the Schlossplatz to the *Finanzamt* (office of finance), out on the Amberger Strasse. In June and July, my feet became insensitive to the softened blacktop of the road and the glowing concrete sidewalk in the noon heat.

The only article of clothing I wore was a pair of lederhosen that my mother had obtained somewhere from a hidden prewar supply through an incredible stroke of luck. The first summer they were too big. The second summer they fit. The third summer they were too small. I compensated by adjusting the suspenders, which made the horizontal strap with the horn-carved edelweiss descend over the years from my nipples to right above my belly button. The leather of the shorts grew with me and, after years, fit like a second skin. The seat became black and shiny like a mirror. When going to bed, I stood the lederhosen in the corner; in the morning I jumped right back in.

61

In the summer, my father received a disturbing letter from Tante Teddy. My Opa was very ill. He had worked at city hall in Berlin until spring, when Tante Teddy had urged him to leave and join her family in Remels. Churchill had already warned that the Russians were making the border along their zone as impenetrable as an iron curtain. What would that do to the food supply in Berlin, which was already dismal?

"Get out of Berlin while you still can," Teddy had written. "Horsa is trading dental treatments for food. We are doing all right."

And so Georg Tradowsky had left his beloved Berlin after more than fifty years and undertaken the arduous journey to Remels.

Sharing the tight two rooms in the farmhouse, Tante Teddy soon noticed something was ailing her father. He had a continuous, dull ache in his abdomen; she made an appointment for him in the nearby Aurich.

When the doctor informed him that he had cancer of the liver and needed surgery as soon as possible, Georg took it unflinchingly. He was, after all, the son of a war hero.

During Georg's surgery, the doctor found that the cancer had spread toward the spine. It had become inoperable. They did not tell Opa. He believed he would be fine. Tante Teddy's letter closed with the message that my father should try to visit soon if he wanted to see his father one more time.

My father probably had no idea how strenuous such a long trip would be, or he would not have suggested taking me. He swept away my mother's argument by mentioning how much the old man would enjoy seeing his oldest grandson and by my enthusiasm for the adventure.

My parents studied the train schedule. Their hopes of reaching the extreme northwest corner of Germany in a reasonable time were soon discouraged. The distance, which in peacetime could be accomplished in about eight hours, would now take a day, a night, and another day.

My father planned to take the *Bummelzug* (slow train) in Nürnberg at seven in the morning in order to catch the *Eilzug* (semifast train) at Würzburg around noon. Since there was no train leaving Hersbruck early enough to make the connection, my father arranged for us to hitch a ride on a three-quarter ton army truck. My father and I sat backward on the loading deck and looked out of the rear opening of the canvas. How thrilling to see the trees along the road pop into view and recede into the dawning valley, while the unexpected turns threw us from side to side as if the truck were mounted on some kind of capricious turntable.

The ride on the Bummelzug from Nürnberg to Würzburg seemed endless and boring, and the good fortune that we had found two seats was little compensation. My father promised that, if we would get on the Eilzug in Würzburg, we would go faster.

When we came onto the open platform in Würzburg, we found that it could hardly hold the crowd. I would have rather climbed up into the fog-shrouded, terraced vineyards across the tracks than fight these masses awaiting the arrival with silent and frozen determination. When the train pulled in, it was desperately overcrowded. It consisted of ancient cars with continuous doors all along the sides that opened to separate compartments. People battled their way onto the running boards and forced the doors open, only to be met by pressure from people packed inside. The conductor was walking along the wagons thrusting the doors shut. Spotting my father and me standing there not knowing what to do, he opened one of the compartments with a key, shoved us inside, and locked it behind us. I heard a whistle, and the train jerked into motion.

Amazingly, the middle-aged men sitting on the two upholstered benches each had a full seat for themselves. Their relaxed and somewhat droopy postures told me that they had been here for a long time. They'd probably come from Austria and had spent the night in this compartment. Hermetically sealed, the compartment was hot and filled with vapors of damaged lungs and digestive systems. The men on one side moved together a bit and offered me a space at the shut window. I sat down, swallowing my nausea. My father stood, holding on to the overhead luggage net. Who were these men? Why were they locked in this compartment? They looked innocent and relaxed, not like criminals being hauled to jail. They did not talk to each other. I did not find out who they were. However, it dawned on me after a while that they were somehow privileged. The locked door was to protect them from the onslaught of the people on the platforms.

From the vineyards around the Main and the castle-studded hills of the Spessart, our train pushed into the rubble of the destroyed Ruhrgebiet and reached Hagen after night fall. Hagen was the junction where we had to get off. We sat in the waiting hall; boarded doors closed off the ruined parts of the station. My father impressed on me that at midnight, the *D-Zug* (express train) from Köln to Bremen was coming through. We had to get on that train.

We walked on the platform early to get a good position. But as the arrival time approached, people spawned from all openings of the ruins and under the dim emergency lamps, shoving us farther and farther to the edge of the track, and we had to drop back.

When the train finally, carefully pulled past the masses, every door that people forced open from the outside showed a wall of compressed bodies. Those outside clawed into this mass under the screaming and protest from the dark inside.

"We have to climb into a window!" my father shouted.

Many windows were shut tight and contained backs and shoulders pressed against the glass, but some windows were open to keep those inside from fainting. I approached the black square of the nearest open window. I grabbed the bottom of the opening to hoist myself inside, while my father lifted his foot over the edge, gripping the top frame with one hand and holding on to our small suitcase with the other. Instantly, a dozen hands and arms appeared out of the dark, pushing us back with a shattering, "No!"

We tried the next window; again arms and hands and the terrible "No."

A sudden notion that one of us could be left behind frightened me, and then the vision of being half-trapped in the window while the train was starting flashed through my mind.

"Let's go!" my father shouted desperately, pushing me toward a third window. "We've got to get in here."

I escaped his push and stepped back on the platform. "Oh, Papi."

A young man tried to get into that window and fought the rejecting hands. Someone grabbed his tie and shoved it against his chest. He reeled back. "Asshole!" he shouted as he ran along the train for another attempt.

I stood there helplessly and shook my head. I did not have the heart to get on a train full of such rejection and hostility. Time was up. The station master lifted his staff. The train pulled out of the station, and our only chance to get to Remels in a bearable amount of time faded into the dark with the glowing taillight of the last wagon.

"I could have gotten on there. What are we going to do now?" My father pushed into the station to study the schedule. I followed him with my head hung low.

Whenever I hear someone talk about the basic goodness of human nature, the night in Hagen pops into my mind. That night, I saw that a war and its years of constant mortal danger and deprivation will strip people of their humanity and reduce them to a subhuman state. They will become so hungry and desperate that, if a man with five loaves of bread and two fishes were to appear among them, they would trample each other to death trying to get to it.

We spent the rest of the night in the waiting room and boarded another Bummelzug at dawn. The train was so undesirable and slow that we found seats. My father had regained his composure and was calm and resigned. He apportioned our last sandwich over the day and gave me a piece at breakfast, lunch, and dinner. He himself ate nothing.

Since for long stretches only one track had been restored, we spent much time on sidetracks to let the faster trains or opposing trains pass. My father made a valiant attempt to fill the dragging hours. He found some graph paper and two pencils in his pockets and played *Schiffe versenken* (Battleship) with me until we became blurry eyed marking the coordinates of our shots.

Then we played I spy. I searched outside the window along the road and saw something orange. *"Mensch Meyer!"* I shouted. It was a truck on fire. The driver had opened the top lid of the *Holzvergaser*. He must have unwittingly stoked the smoldering wood. It had burst into flames that were shooting out of the top, setting the canvas over the truck bed on fire. The driver beat the flames with his jacket. The train set in motion again and pulled the scene out of my vision. This was the high point of my day, and I spent much time imagining how the story ended and what I would have done if I had been the driver.

We reached Bremen after dark. My father asked where we could find the connecting train to Oldenburg and received disheartening information. "Take the bus to the west side tomorrow morning at six. The tracks through town are kaput."

We had to settle down in the waiting room for another night. It had a high, domed ceiling and a wide arch that used to lead to the main lobby. Now it was filled with a heap of rubble slanting down from the far wall like the scree at the bottom of a mountain chute. The night sky was visible above, and a chalky-smelling air blew over the rubble into the waiting area.

People lay all over on the tile floor. We found an empty spot among them. My father put the suitcase under my head and covered me with his jacket. An old man walked by in socks.

"Don't go to sleep here," he warned. "I fell asleep, and my shoes are gone. They steal everything here, shoes, jackets, suitcases. You can't go to sleep."

My father promised to stay awake. I was too agitated in this creepy place and too overtired to catch more than a short snooze.

The bus ride through the ruins of the city before sunrise was nightmarish. Bizarre remnants of walls stuck out between the heaps of rubble with a whitish light of their own. Once thriving and smooth streets were disrupted and bumpy, eerily devoid of all life.

Another Bummelzug took us to Oldenburg by eleven in the morning. Since we were among the first on the bus to Remels, we had seats. The bus became crowded with workers and farmers.

As we got on the way, a young, burly man with a leather cap reprimanded me. "Aren't you going to offer your seat to this old lady?"

I got up, and the babushka sat down. My father, who had nodded off, woke up and saw me standing. He looked surprised and curiously impressed by my courteous behavior. Far from noble, I felt hungry, overtired, faint, and angry at the man who did not know how far I had come.

Once we reached the Hengstenbergs, I quickly bounced back with the resilience of an eleven-year-old. All it took was a lunch with eggs, bacon, and bread that Tante Teddy had prepared for our arrival, and afterward, a nap. Then I was alert and observed my relatives keenly. Opa had lost much weight. His clothes hung slack. For the first time in his adult life, his enormous belly had shrunk away. The chain of his golden watch, which had spanned his vest in a graceful arch, now dangled.

"Opa endured a lot during the occupation," said Tante Teddy, trying to gloss over his illness and explain his state with what he had suffered in Berlin.

"Yah, those were terrible days—the street fighting. You know that our apartment building was burned out. No? Well, the upper floors to the *Parterre*" (ground floor). "We were all hiding in the cellar, listening to the shooting outside. Then that stopped, and we thought Berlin had surrendered. But then the fighting troops went on a rampage. Every soldier had to get three things for himself—a wristwatch, a bicycle, and a woman.

"We knew they were coming. Somebody called down the cellar stairs. They are in the next block. They are in the front building. Then Russian shouts upstairs. Two soldiers burst into the cellar waving pistols. The women and children shrank back. The one Russian grabbed me by the vest. *'Uri, Uri!'* I reached into my pocket, pulled out my watch, and gave it to him. He looked at it and threw it on the floor. That was not what he wanted. He wanted a wristwatch like all the others. He knew every German had a wristwatch. 'Uri, Uri!' he screamed getting impatient. I shrugged my shoulders. 'Nix Uri, I don't have one.' The soldier pushed me against the wall, his pistol on my chest. 'Uri, Uri.' I thought that was it. I just looked at him and waited. He must have realized he was not going to get his Uri from me. He suddenly ran out of the cellar with the other."

My Opa never dwelled on bad times. "Let's be glad that's over, and you are here all the way from Hersbruck." He held himself bolt upright and became cheerful. With considerable pride, indicated by his pushed-out lower lip, he told how he had upgraded Horsa's barter system. Horsa, as a dentist, was permitted to obtain ethanol from the druggist in Aurich. Being well-informed in all matters pertaining to alcohol, Opa had set to work turning this ethanol into egg liqueur. It proved to be the ultimate trading value with the farmers, far better than Horsa's fillings and extractions. Opa made himself useful in other ways. He took up fishing in earnest again and provided many meals of bass that he caught on little balls kneaded out of flour, butter, and anise.

"Down in the sea there swims a bass, / The water reaches to my knees," he recited to me.

"But, Opa, this doesn't rhyme," I objected.

"Wait for the tide," he twinkled.

In the crammed and primitive quarters, he saw the comical side of all the maneuvers the family had to make to accomplish the chores of daily life. With his rasping laughs from deep in his chest, he told about mishaps—for example, how he had sneezed in the wooden latrine and his dentures had fallen down the hole into the open septic tank, and he had patiently retrieved them using his two bamboo fishing rods like chopsticks. Though it was just an old rubber denture—his golden one was long a thing of the past—it was irreplaceable. Even Onkel Horsa was unable to get the materials. After Tante Teddy boiled the dentures and Horsa sacrificed some alcohol to sterilize them, his choppers were like new!

As I listened to my Opa's jokes and funny stories, I wondered how long it would take him to notice that the pain in his belly was not really gone.

Everyone around him pretended, and it seemed, after a while, that they were honestly forgetting the problem.

For Onkel Horsa it was just one more thing that had to be endured with the stoicism of the Spartans. With a hint of resignation on his saber-scarred, academic face, the handsome, gray-haired doctor shrugged his shoulders. Whenever the conversation turned to the ravages of war, he only said "*Tja*," meaning, What can you do?

Tante Teddy was as bright and animated as always. She superimposed her twittering laughter over Opa's bawdy stories, as if to camouflage them in front of her upper-class husband. The war had taken away much of her concern with appearances and had made her warmer and less constrained.

Christian had recovered little since Bad Dürrheim. While he was out of the stroller now, he limped desperately. He wore a heavy brace with gleaming rods running right and left of his shin. His foot had grown slowly, drooped, and was turning into a club.

I did not get to play with Eva-Maria and Christian for as long as I had hoped. My father had only one week of leave, eight days to be exact, of which six were used up by traveling.

I cannot remember any details of meeting with Eva-Maria other than us playing catch with the neighbor kids in the front yard. Eva-Maria did not run fast and soon disappeared into the house. Then in the evening, it was again Opa who drew everyone's attention upon himself, in part because of his precarious condition and in part because of his entertaining nature, which always let him obtain center stage.

My father and I were soon sitting in the bus to Oldenburg again. I don't recall anything about our trip home except that it seemed shorter, as all return trips do.

During that fall, we looked at mail from Remels with apprehension. We were afraid of getting the letter with the black rim, but it did not come. Opa lived into his eighties.

62

We soon got caught up in our own worries. Winter was approaching. We had no heat, worn-out clothes, and ever-skimpier food rations.

Another problem that arose with the colder weather concerned our hygiene. During the later summer months, the Amis had allowed the Germans into the Strudelbad. On all but the rainiest days, we grasped the opportunity to swim there and use the showers, but the pool closed for the winter. The Stadtbad, the public bathhouse with a dozen tubs, was occupied by army offices. In peacetime, this facility had served those citizens who had no tubs or showers in their ancient houses.

We tried to make do with sponge baths on Saturday evenings. It was a luxury to boil enough water on the hot plate to warm the cold water for the large tin tub. Since we only could heat the smaller of the two rooms, we all had to take our baths there.

My parents had to decide whether to rig some bedsheets around the tub and give the impression that there was something shameful about our nudity or take a bath openly. They chose the latter, and so I came to view our naked bodies as natural and good. Moreover, my father used the opportunity to sketch my mother in his diary, which impressed on me that the female figure was something beautiful and desirable. Applying his artistic license, he omitted her countable ribs and protruding collar bones and drew her more like he remembered her from peacetime.

Washing our clothes was equally difficult and costly. This forced the question, could we wear a shirt or underwear for one more day? Bedsheets were particularly hard to manage. They overfilled the tub and took days to dry when hung in the larger, cold room.

The colder the weather got, the tougher life became. Snow began to fall long before Christmas.

However, my friends and I jumped for joy when we saw the walk from the terrace of the castle down to the river covered with a thick, glittering blanket. When school finally let out for winter break, children from all over town congregated on the terrace slope. We pushed extra snow from the wall and banked the turns. Soon we had changed the walkway into a glistening toboggan run. I regretted not having a toboggan or sled.

Tired of waiting for rides with others, I discovered a novel way of enjoying the hill. My mother had found me a pair of boots for the winter, crude clodhoppers with thick, wooden soles. It was all she could get. The boots were so slick for walking in the snow that I found myself flailing my arms every few steps. That gave me an idea. With the persistence of an inspired youngster, I learned how to ski downhill in those boots. I even performed tricks that I could not do on regular skis, like turning on the way and sliding backward. The other kids became envious. They had just ordinary leather footwear.

Our winter sport was interrupted by our preparation for Christmas. I was expected to make presents for my parents. I often constructed something hurriedly on the last day—a picture or a Christmas ornament, like a violin cut with the fretsaw and painted silver or an angel with a pleated, floor-length skirt folded out of paper. To calm Monika and me, or perhaps to peak our excitement during the last two days before Christmas Eve, my father drew a sheet full of Christmas trees, one for each remaining hour until the celebration. We took turns erasing one for every hour, the last one in the Adler during the meager meal.

Against all odds, we did get a remarkable present. A wooden sled for Monika and me lay under the tree. My father had made several walks through the snow-padded forest to Kleedorf, where a farmer had made the somewhat crude but sturdy sled in exchange for cigarettes.

This year's Christmas and New Year's were the bleakest of all. The candles that my mother had bartered from an obscure source had such large sections of raw suet that they suddenly crackled, flared, and threatened to set the tree on fire. We hardly could finish our "Stille Nacht" before my mother rushed to extinguish them. On New Year's Eve, my parents had nothing to toast with. The last bottle from Omi's wine cellar was long gone. They went to bed early, wrapping themselves so deep into the blankets in their ice-cold room that they hardly heard the bells ringing in the New Year.

As if 1947 had been insulted by not having been greeted properly, it started with a punishing cold spell. The ice ponds at the commons froze thick in a few days. The old codgers who curled there and the Hersbrucker youngsters fortunate enough to have skates were soon displaced by the brewers from Schunk's Mühle. They hacked up the ice into floes and loaded them on wagons. Then they walked next to their steaming draft horses, clicking their tongues and shaking the reins, to transport the icy load to the beer storage room, where they stacked them up to the ceiling. After following them one trip, I returned to the ponds and watched enviously how the boys navigated the remaining floes with poles. I could not trust the traction of my boots enough to hop onto the tipping, half-submerged chunks.

The temperature dropped still further. It became so cold that the Pegnitz froze from bank to bank. Only the old Hersbruckers remembered this ever happening. I stood in the middle of the bridge and stared down on the black ice, trying to see the water flowing underneath. Much of the frozen river was covered with thin streaks of fine, drifting snow. It looked like a street leading up to the Watergate. I could not resist the temptation. I swung over the iron banister and eased myself down on the ice, holding on to the rail. I allowed more and more weight on my feet. The ice did not crack. I freed my hands and carefully started shuffling upstream. I had moved past Schunks living quarters when I felt I had tested the ice enough and should get out onto the road. At this moment, an excited yell came from a high window in the next house. It was the voice of an old man. "Stay in the middle! Don't get out to the side!"

In the icy glare, I could not see the man who was shouting from the dark opening. So much alarm and urgency was in his call that I turned around. Trying to make myself as light as possible, I shuffled back to the bridge and got out of the river without mishap. In later winters, I experienced that the ice hardly ever froze solid close to the warmer banks. I shudder to think how easily I could have gotten onto the thin ice along the bank, broken through, and been pulled under by the swift current. How quickly my life that I had kept through the perils of war could have ended due to my thoughtlessness and inexperience, were it not for the mysterious man at the window.

The next day, I had a slight fever and stayed home from school.

"You must have become chilled yesterday," my mother said.

The following morning, the fever was a little higher. I had a stinging pain in my chest when I breathed deeply and started coughing. My mother had me dress warmly, wrapped a shawl around my neck, pulled my cap deep over my head, and took me across the frozen valley to Doktor Sebert. He practiced in a tiny room in the village of Henfenfeld. He was an older man, tall and vigorous, with kind and concerned eyes under gray, bushy eyebrows. My mother trusted him. He was a refugee also and had been a hospital chief in Sudetenland before he had to flee. Doktor Sebert walked his cold stethoscope over my chest from one specific place to another while he bowed down his head and closed his eyes. "The boy has a *Rippenfellentzündung*" (pleurisy), he exclaimed, with the rolled "r" and high-pitched "i" of his Sudetendeutschen accent. "Keep him in bed and warm for two weeks until he stops coughing and the fever goes down."

After two weeks, Doktor Sebert made a house call. I was not ready to go back to school. I still had a low-grade fever. My cough had become worse, and I was coughing yellowish slime.

"The boy should get an X-ray examination," Doktor Sebert said.

My mother's eyes widened apprehensively. *What could be so wrong with him to require that?*

My mother brought up the doctor's recommendation to Schwester Käte at the Adler's regular's table. She was a nurse at the hospital and got

398

me in for the next free X-ray examination for children that was sponsored by an American charity.

At the appointed time, I stood in line, bare-chested, with the other children, until my turn came. I walked through the light-trapping chamber into a dark room. As my eyes adjusted, the room became slowly illuminated by the greenish glow from a fluorescent screen. Schwester Käte directed me behind it. The doctor on the other side of the screen reached around, grabbed my thin arms, and turned me slowly from front to side. In a monotonous voice, he dictated what he saw. I did not understand his technical terms, something about hilus glands.

After the screening, Schwester Käte called my mother into a private room. On the way home, my mother was very quiet.

"What did Schwester Käte say? What is wrong with me?" I asked.

"The *Rippenfellentzündung* is still there," she said. "You'll have to stay in bed. You'll have to stop coughing before you can go back to school."

My mother put a bucket next to my bed, into which she asked me to spit whatever I coughed up. In the morning, she cleaned the bucket, adding some solution that smelled like chlorine. Whenever I had to go across the hall to the bathroom, she wiped the door handles with a rag with IMMI cleaner. She kept Monika occupied on the other side of the room. She stopped my school buddy at the door when he brought the homework and then called him off altogether because I could not keep the blankets on me when I sat up in bed writing. It did not seem important any more that I kept up in school.

February came with no relief from the cold. My illness became worse. I was coughing up a lot of green pellets now. My mother pleaded with me, "Don't cough, Michael. Please don't cough."

During the day, I tried to suppress my coughing as long as she was in the room. But at night, I would wake up, shaken by spells. My mother would come, put her hand on my forehead, straighten my pillow, and pull the blankets up to my chin. "Please, you must not cough so much."

The days were exceedingly boring. I dozed often. While I lay awake, I started to notice the smallest changes in the room. I watched the sun come around in the afternoon and strike the fern patterns of frost on the window or make the blossoms of the cyclamen on the sill move ever so slightly toward the light. I begged my mother to let me read. After I had promised to stay warm under the blanket with the book, she brought me Storm's short stories.

"I read those in Berlin when I was waiting for Papi to come home from the theater," she said. "I think you're old enough to understand them."

Over the next weeks, I read them all, filling passages I did not grasp with my own fantasies. The harsh Nordic world of this poet from Husum, the "gray city by the sea," easily blended with my cold and austere room. His many tales of romantic love filled my idle and undistracted mind. *Yes*, I thought, *this is how true love is. The lovers know when they meet that they are made for each other. There will be no doubts, no mistakes.* Just as the lovers in the stories, I would recognize the girl. I should wait for this person, for she would unfailingly come. If I recognized places where I was to live for years, how would I miss the person with whom I was destined to share my life?

63

I n the same journal in which my father expressed his deep concern about my illness, he began to record the fate of the Schimmelpfennigs. He reminisced how we had met the couple on the Arzberg observation tower. He recalled how, as refugees from Prussia, they'd had to leave everything—their families; friends; home; and his honorable, lucrative appointment as judge. In spite of all these losses, the Schimmelpfennigs impressed my father with their forward-looking optimism.

He and my mother kept up this acquaintance whenever they would happen to meet in town. The former judge patiently pursued a prolonged and ugly fight with the Bavarian government to get accredited. He took these hurdles without resentment or without losing his optimism. He did not even complain when the state finally awarded him a temporary license as a legal assistant and he started drawing a salary at the courthouse that was insultingly low.

The Schimmelpfennigs moved to the Michelsberg. They lived in a house that must have been so exceedingly small that my father could never find it when he went on his frequent walks up that little mountain.

Considering himself a defender of law, Schimmelpfenning found it inconceivable to live on anything other than what his skimpy pay and food stamps allowed. This incorruptible attitude condemned him and his wife to extreme deprivation. Every few weeks, he would chat with my father when he crossed his path on his way to fulfill his duties at the courthouse.

His air force trousers had become frayed, the heels of his hobnail boots worn crooked, and his hat too big. Yet his brown, intelligent eyes, as sunken as they were, kept sparkling and gazing through the misery of reality into a better world.

His wife maintained the same imperturbable stance. My parents would talk with her now and then when she came down the hill breathlessly to chase through the town after the few things that the stamps provided or should have provided.

Every time my parents would run into them, these lonely people had become a little more miserable and tired and had lost a few more pounds. They still always expressed the belief that things would turn for the better. Perhaps this outlook would keep them going.

In fall, Schimmelpfennig told my father that his wife had fallen ill. He recounted that she had been in the hospital and had to have several ribs shortened as part of an inevitable surgery. She was home now, weak but in good spirits in spite of everything. With a slight smile of triumph, he went on about how he was doing everything himself now. In the morning, while getting dressed, he warmed up the breakfast prepared the night before. Then he quickly straightened up his little household and went to fulfill his legal duties. He went home for lunch and then back to the courthouse. Still, he found time to continue his book about his alpine experiences, which he wanted to finish by the first of November.

All the while his little brown eyes shone. He did not see the emaciated face that must have glared at him at every shave. He did not see the ever more frayed trousers or the threadbare necktie that bunched the unironed collar against his scrawny neck. His mind was with his legal cases and the memories of his hikes in the Alps.

In the cold of January, my mother met Frau Schimmelpfennig again. She was strong enough now to go out. She had to be, for her husband lay in the hospital after an operation. Rather than recuperating, he needed a second surgery. The doctors were hesitant to perform the operation because of his weakened state. She said this in the same accepting way with which she had been meeting all troubles.

My father's last paragraph is full of bitterness as it tells the end of the story and reflects on the state of the times. He had not been surprised when he met Frau Schimmelpfennig all dressed in black with big, overtired eyes that had looked into eternity. She was a "wandering bundle of human misery." He greeted her and left the first words to her. She said her husband had stopped suffering yesterday and that it was a blessing for him. "Yes, it was a blessing," my father nodded. He reflects in his diary that he said this not so much as an expression of customary condolence than out of profound spontaneous agreement:

> What indictment pronounces such an opinion on our present life? How can we count it a blessing that a man who had learned his profession properly and had a claim on a happy and prosperous existence dies at age forty-seven after only three weeks of illness? Do we count it a blessing because his impeccable sense of right and wrong had condemned him to starvation? Has our world become so horrible that we agree without hesitation that it is a blessing to be released from it?

My father's thoughts then turned to the widow. She had to face life completely alone and without the sparse income to pay rent or electricity. She must have been her husband's deepest and last concern. My father concludes:

> I feel we should take care of her somehow. This is the least we can do for Judge Schimmelpfennig +.

Behind the name, he drew the cross that appears behind all those marked deceased in his diaries.

As for the wish to help the widow, it remained a good intention. How could we assist others when we were not sure whether we would make it ourselves?

After drawing the cross, my father went on to other subjects in an attempt to shake the disturbing past and go on. However, this was one of the few times when his diary could not contain all his feelings. Sitting across the room from my bed, he discussed the sad fate of the Schimmelpfennigs with my mother and shared with her his lament about the awful general deprivation.

He put his fountain pen into its cap, closed his diary, and said to my mother, who was mending our socks, "If Schimmelpfennig had not been in such a weakened state, he would still be alive. He sure had the spirit and will to live. How many people die like that these days! The doctors write their cause of death as this infection or that, but in reality, they die from starvation."

My mother winced. Though she nodded an almost-imperceptible agreement, she stooped deeper over her darning as if the weight on her shoulders had suddenly doubled. To me, it was just a theoretical discussion. My realities existed now with the love relationships of Storm's heroes and heroines. I was completely captivated by their bonds that were often tragic, sometimes blissful, but always predestined by fate and for all eternity.

I read unceasingly. All the while, I made a particular effort to suppress my coughing. If my mother would hear me shaken by an irrepressible paroxysm, she would take my book away and tuck me in deep. "You've got to rest, Michael."

In the middle of February, the cold spell continued relentlessly. My temperature started spiking. When I coughed up red, my mother could hardly conceal her desperation. *"Du must nicht husten*, Michael" (You must not cough, Michael), she begged again and again. She left a dim table light next to my bed and came several times during the night to take my temperature.

She got Doktor Sebert to come again. He listened to my chest and looked in the pail. Then he talked to my parents in the next room. Much later, I found out what he said. "You must get some heat into that room and some food into the boy or he will not get better."

My parents started to burn wood from Monika's and my beds. Our straw sacks had since been replaced by regular metal-spring frames and mattresses. This allowed some of the supporting boards to be sacrificed. My father split them with the kitchen knife, and soon a crackling fire filled the tall, green tile stove. For a while, it got so warm that we could not see our breaths anymore, and the ice ferns on the window panes softened and became more transparent. For two days, my parents pulled out board after board until the bedding was barely hanging on the two smallest remaining laths and threatened to collapse. They even imagined that my cough was getting better. Then the cold closed in on us again, crueler than ever.

My father could not contain his worries anymore. His helplessness and sorrow began to show on his face. He dragged through the day at work. His boss, Captain Brooks, asked why he was sighing.

"It's my son," my father came out hesitatingly. "He is lying at home horribly sick. He's getting worse and worse. The doctor said he will not get better unless we get heat into the room. We have no wood."

When my father came home that night, he stared in disbelief at what he found in front of the cellar door—a pile of wood dumped helter-skelter and as tall as he. My mother was stomping up and down the cellar stairs in her old green coat and riding boots, carrying armloads of logs to our storage area.

When she saw my father, she dropped the wood, ran to him, and embraced him. "Oh, Papi," she said, "this will get us through the rest of the winter." She told him how a big army truck had come in the afternoon and dumped the load. "From Captain Brooks," was all the driver had said. The captain had ordered the truck into the next village and simply requisitioned the wood.

A few days later, another surprise was dropped at our doorstep—a big, heavy package that showed by its battered wrappings that it had been in the mail for a long time. My mother dragged it into the room where I lay. It was cozy now in my bedroom. The ice ferns had melted, and I could see the church again standing tall in the pale blue winter sky. The cyclamen that had been bunched small with the cold relaxed and bloomed anew. I was curious about the package.

My mother turned on the antler lamp to decipher the worn name and address of the sender. "Inge Hecht, Shaker Heights, Ohio," she read.

"Who are they?" I asked.

"She is Tante Edith's best friend," she said. "You remember Tante Edith and Onkel Paule, don't you? They visited us in Glienicke once."

A picture of a summer afternoon appeared in my mind—an old man with a walrus beard and a beautiful, dark-eyed lady sitting at the table under the big oak; and then I saw myself bringing a bowl of tomatoes and stumbling over something in the middle of the lawn, flinging the bowl and tomatoes far into the grass. "Yes, I remember," I said.

My mother went on, "Papi gave Inge *Nachhilfestunden*" (tutoring lessons) "when they were in high school. The Aldendorfs and the Hechts were best friends. They all went to America before the war, Inge and Gerhart Hecht first and then Edith and her mother, Muichen, from Norway, after Onkel Paule had died."

We did not open the package until my father came home. What riches did we discover inside! We exclaimed with every treasure we lifted out. The package contained several bars of chocolate, powdered milk, powdered eggs, rice, prunes, raisins, boxes with pudding mix, and even a pack of cigarettes. One item was puzzling. It was a heavy white lump the size of a tennis ball in a transparent covering with an orange-red button in it. My father asked at work about it and learned that it was margarine and that the color button had to be popped and kneaded into the white mass until the lump was homogenous, soft, and without streaks.

The package had taken three months to make the journey. Inge had responded immediately after receiving my father's news that we had survived the war. In the following weeks, a letter arrived from Inge to follow up on the package, another from Muichen, and also one from Edith. She had remarried. Her husband had been assigned to Guadalajara by the state department. What interested me about the letters more than the content were the exotic stamps and the curious, translucent tape with which the letters had been resealed after having been censored in transit.

The package and the firewood slowly halted my decline. For the remainder of February and half of March, my condition stayed unchanged. What eventually tipped the balance toward recovery was my mother's refusal to surrender her son. She surrounded me with her body and soul like an impenetrable force built entirely out of defiant hope. Not once did she dignify my illness by calling it by its name. She wished it out of existence, robbing it of its importance and weight until at last it gave up and receded. My temperature dropped; my cough improved.

64

My parents tried to think of ways to help me recover completely. According to medical knowledge of the time, high altitude with sun rich in ultraviolet rays and air cleaned by pine forests was the best environment for my lungs. They heard of a *Kinderheim* (children's home) in Bad Tölz that lay on the rising plateau at the foot of the Bavarian Alps. This Kinderheim had the pretentious name *Prinz Regent Luitpold Heim*. It was subsidized by foreign charities and took undernourished children from age six to twelve for six-week periods with the sole aim of putting weight on them. A prerequisite was that, other than starvation, they had no other medical problems and were free of infectious diseases.

My mother took me for another free screening at the hospital. Schwester Käte, agreeing with my mother how good this alpine air would be, did some fudging on the application form. Two weeks later, I found myself on a bus to Bad Tölz with children from Nürnberg who were just as skinny as I, but perhaps a little less transparent and less marked with dark circles under their eyes.

The next six weeks were the saddest of my youth. For the first time, I was cut off from my mother, father, and Monika. I was sitting in the gathering room with sixty other boys of all ages who were just as ravaged by homesickness. The tears were running down the younger ones' cheeks, while I, as one of the oldest, managed to mourn inside.

The minutes crawled along while we were waiting for boys from other cities to arrive. Six weeks seemed like a life sentence. Just one night in the dormitory was endless. I was awakened time and again by my coughing and could not go back to sleep, listening to some of the boys snoring and others crying into their pillows.

The next morning, the young women who ran the home (Tante, they asked us to call them) herded us across a scale. They recorded everyone's weight. Then they channeled us through the washrooms, having us do every move together by command. "Put soap on your washcloth. Now wash your face. Now wash your neck. Your chest. Put toothpaste on your toothbrush. Brush your front teeth," and so on.

I could see in the disconnected way the women looked at us that they saw nothing but a large group of children and only reacted to an individual boy if he danced out of line or fell behind. It made me feel exceedingly lonely not to be seen as a person and not even to be known by my name. Being commandeered into the dining hall and assigned a seat somewhere on the two long tables, I had no appetite and hardly touched the massive but repulsive breakfast.

A short walk through the wooded premises—two-by-two, holding hands—followed. I was teamed up with a wiry, dark-haired boy my age from Nürnberg. The boy was as unhappy here as I, and the six weeks were just as insurmountable to him. "What can we do about this?" we asked.

Keeping our voices low, we agreed to escape and walk home. We planned for the next days to secretly put bread into our pockets at meals and hide a cache under our beds. Then, when we had enough provisions, we would sneak out at night pretending to have to go to the bathroom and get on the road.

This fantasy eased our homesickness. After a few days, the women began to learn our names from the daily weighing. Our resolve to escape weakened. If we had made it through one week, we perhaps could make it through the next. We started paying attention to the few entertaining stretches of our long days. A few boys could make things and proudly were willing to teach others—how to make a whistle out of a willow branch, how to fold a napkin into a parachute or a mouse, or how to make a hat or boat out of a piece of newspaper.

After the children had fallen into the routine of the regimentation sufficiently, the women started reading books to us after dinner. We settled on the most exciting one, which was about two boys who lived with their father in a forest fire observation tower.

By the time the second Sunday came around, the women chanced a talent show. Instead of reading the chapter about the forest fire, they asked us to sing or recite something we knew. At first, everyone was waiting for someone else to start. After much coaxing, my friend from Nürnberg stepped forward. He sang a song that every Nürnberger and Hersbrucker knew. It was new and amusing to the boys from other cities, even though they had to strain to understand the franconian dialect.

Wir ham daham an olten Reisbrei.
Mei Mutter hat gsagt den schmeissmer'n Mist nei.
Mei Vadder hat gsagt den demma pholten,
Den Reisbrei, den olten.

We have at home an old rice pudding.
My father said we'll throw it on the dung heap.
My mother said we'll keep it,
The rice pudding, the old one.

This gave a boy from Stuttgart the courage to sing a song. It was in the Swabian dialect, which strikes all Germans from other regions as funny. His song was called "Auf der Schwäb'schen Eisenbahne" (On the Swabian Railroad). It told the story of a little old farmer who bought a goat and tied her on the caboose and only found the rope and the head when he arrived. The success of this performance, measured by loud and long clapping, caused an avalanche of other entertainers ever younger and sillier.

When the show was almost over, I raised my hand.

"Yes, you over there." The Tante pointed.

I stepped to the front, my heart pounding in my throat. There was a pause. The laughing and chattering died down. What is this quiet kid going to do?

"Easter Walk from Faust by Johann Wolfgang von Goethe," I announced. Then I swallowed and went on:

Vom Eise befreit sind Strom und Bäche
Von des Frühlings holden, belebenden Blick
Der alte Winter in seiner Schwäche
Zog sich in rauhe Berge zurück.

Freed from ice are stream and creek
By spring's fair reviving glance.
The old winter, spent and weak,
Retreated to higher, rougher lands.

With more and more confidence, I wound myself through Faust's long monologue. The children were bored but quiet. Everyone had heard of Goethe as the greatest German poet. The women exchanged surprised glances. When I finally got stuck, they clapped loudly. The one in charge put her hand on my shoulder benevolently and escorted me off.

From then on, the women knew me as the one who could recite Goethe. They remembered my name. My mother's insistence that I think for myself and not follow the behavior of my brainwashed classmates had given me the idea that I was somehow special and set apart. When I was pulled out of the dormitory and given a single room, I thought the women were catering to my special status.

Every two weeks, the owner and headmistress of the Kinderheim would examine the children personally. She was a "von," a noblewoman, tall and slim. Occasionally, we would see her walking her two Doberman pinschers on thin black leather leashes. She examined each boy's throat while a Tante read his weight chart and made comments about his health. When it was my turn, the Tante had to report that I had not gained any weight.

"Hmm," said the elegant lady looking at me displeased. "A spoiled brat, I suppose. Is our food good enough for you?"

I did not know whether to nod or shake my head.

"He coughs a lot during the night," added the Tante.

"Keep him in the single room," said the noble lady and moved on to the next child.

Unfortunately, my separation did not save me from an epidemic that started to spread among the children. I developed trouble swallowing, and my neck swelled on both sides. I had contracted mumps.

Precipitated by this infection, or perhaps coincidentally, I started to have an earache in my right ear. For all my short life, my ears had been vulnerable, "my Achilles' heel," as my parents called it. I had learned that I could check these infections at the earliest twinges if I plugged my ear with cotton and put it on a heating pad, but the Tante, who I asked for my customary treatment, did not give me what I knew I needed.

"This is just pain from your mumps," she said. "As you get over the mumps, it will get better."

Two days later, I had a worse middle ear infection than ever before. I was staggering around holding my head. My malaise became so obvious that one of the women took me to Dr. Opitz, the *Ohrenarzt*. His office was on the other side of the Isar River. The young woman led me on a path through low brush and then took a shortcut through the river bed, which was mostly dry and discouragingly wide. We made our way between rounded boulders over blinding river gravel and crossed the receded river at the bridge. As weak as I was and as much as my ear throbbed, my freedom from the confines of the Kinderheim was not lost on me. I followed the view up the sparkling mountain river. There were the Alps, a majestic string of blue peaks in the crisp spring air with the sun gathering the glare of snowfields.

The doctor's office was in his private home. The house was modern, pleasantly furnished, and with big windows overlooking the river and the mountains. I did not see the little treatment area in an alcove until Doktor Opitz, a tall, balding, middle-aged man, asked me to sit down in his examination chair. He was friendly and concerned. I do not hold it against him that he performed my treatment without anesthesia. It was customary in Germany to do minor operations without it. Dentists drilled teeth without it, and otolaryngologists pierced eardrums without it. A certain amount of stoicism was expected from the patients, no matter what age. I did not cry, even though a surprised "Ouch!" escaped me. I felt faint when he flushed the draining pus into the kidney basin, but I did not keel over. He packed a second bandage around my head in addition to the one I wore for the mumps. On the walk home, I hung heavily on the woman's arm. We sat down often on the smooth, round boulders so I could rest. She felt sorry for me. Her name was Tante Trudel. By the time we got back to the gate, my raging pain had subsided.

I was so weak now that I did not mind being confined to my bed. I slept much. The few hours I was awake, I listened to the children's voices from the courtyard. It was warming up enough so the window could be open. The only times I was allowed to leave my room were to take the meals in the dining hall.

Around the middle of my stay, something extraordinary happened. That evening, when I put my dishes on the cart and was ready to return to my room, one of the women came in and asked me to follow her to the office. On the way, she told me, "Your father has come to visit you."

I ran ahead of her and burst into the office. There stood my father, big as life. I rushed up to him and buried myself in his arms. He looked at me and had to sit down.

"Tja, Michael," was all my father said. He had hoped to see me healthier than before with some flesh on my ribs and the red of the mountain air in my cheeks. The information he learned on arrival—that I had the mumps and an earache—had tempered his expectations, but it did not prepare him. Here I was, thinner than ever, my head swollen wider than high and wrapped in a bandage so large that my little pale features must have looked shrunken and forlorn. His first impulse was to take me with him, and my desperate wish was that he would, but we did not talk about that.

"Well, it's only three more weeks," he said.

"Yes, Papi," I nodded.

He had to leave soon. Twenty minutes was all the headmistress had allowed. Besides, his army friend, Antonucci, who had given him a ride, had to get back to Hersbruck. I am quite sure that my father changed the report of my condition to my mother so as not to worry her, but at least it gave her more reliable and tangible information than the two letters I had written. It had been obvious that they had been more or less dictated by the women.

Both started, "Lieber Papi, liebe Mutti, liebe Monika! How are you? I am fine. Today we had pork roast, beans, and dumplings." Above this line, one of the women had edited, "and gravy."

I kept counting the days. The weather was getting milder now. In the evenings, I sat on my windowsill, trying to catch words of the story that the Tante was finishing in the dining hall. I wanted to know how the boys in the forest escaped the fire and caught the arsonist.

The dining hall was surrounded by horse chestnuts. Over the days, I watched with amazement how the buds grew. They opened and released tiny folded bundles of the lightest yellow-green. These bundles stretched out their minuscule folds into delicate five-fingered leaflets, and the white candles of blossoms slowly arose between the foliage. It was the first time I drew strength from the rebirth of nature.

By the time we boarded the bus home, my bandages were off, my cheeks had shrunk to almost normal, and I even had gained a pound or two. The gratitude and wholeness that flooded me when I fell back into the arms of my family did more to restore me than all the meals they had insisted I swallow at the Kinderheim.

65

The mountain air must have been good for me. My cough had stopped, but my general health was still deplorable. Lying in bed for months, I had grown into a grotesque beanpole. The little Hersbrucker boys would shout after me, "Hey, why don't we break you in the middle so we have two people?"

Our food rations had not improved, and the package from Inge Hecht had long been consumed. That May, my father recorded a monthly food allocation for an adult—"400 grams meat, 150 grams butter or fat of some other kind, and 4 to 6 pounds of bread." The number of available eggs fluctuated between one and two from month to month. The ration of milk was proportionate. We supplemented our protein by roasting cow blood when it became available.

In spite of my hunger, being alert and energetic was important to be able to catch up in school. The school year ended in the middle of July. This gave me two months to make up the deficit. Some of my teachers were hinting that it would be best for me to drop back a grade. Neither my parents nor I wanted to accept this. *Sitzenbleiben*, which was to remain seated and repeat the year, was considered the ultimate academic shame. For once, I tried hard. My parents helped me every night, my mother in math and my father in German and English. In class, I had my hand up perpetually. The teachers wondered how this boy could know everything. Part of this amazing participation was a bit of deception. I had discovered that teachers would call on me if I dropped my raised hand, as if suddenly having doubts. It was not so much that they wanted to embarrass me but more that the movement in the forest of raised arms caught their attention. In this way, I got my answers noted when I was most certain of them. After shining once or twice, I could raise my hand whether I knew the answer or not. With fifty-two boys in the class, the likelihood of the teacher calling on me again was remote.

In the written exams, however, the truth came out. I was struggling.

My *Klassenlehrer* (class teacher), Dr. Zeltner, who taught biology and music, was convinced repetition would be beneficial. Two weeks before the final grades, he called my mother in for a conference.

My mother had to admit that Dr. Zeltner was a likable man. He was tall, handsome, and a little older than she, with the high forehead of a thinker. He had the air of upper-class breeding that my mother always responded to. Since he was not really a teacher, he had nothing of the sour stuffiness that many of the professionals assumed after years in the school environment. As a descendent of a wealthy patrician Nürnberg family, he had studied biology more out of pure interest than in consideration of a career or job. He had also studied voice and had developed such a pleasant baritone that he became a soloist for cantatas. During the war, he had been an officer in the army. Having lost his earthly possessions in the raids, he found provisional employment at our school. He had not been in the party and offered considerable scientific knowledge. He had no training in education, and in spite of that, or perhaps because of it, he was a good teacher.

Dr. Zeltner started out the meeting by praising my musical talent. He had noticed that I was the only one in class who could sing all parts of "The Orchestra," which he was rehearsing for the graduation celebration.

"You make him sing the violins, the trumpets, the horns or the clarinets, and he never gets lost. I asked him to sing a song for us. He sang, '*Kommt ein Vogel geflogen*' ('Comes a bird flying'), so pure, wonderful. Does he play an instrument?"

"He wants to take piano lessons," my mother said. "His father plays the piano."

"He should play the violin with an ear like that," Dr. Zeltner suggested.

Having conveyed to my mother that he liked me, Dr. Zeltner came to the point. He tried to explain that it would be in my best interest to repeat the year. He mentioned I had received a 5 (D) on the last written biology exam. He did not make a big deal of it. He emphasized instead that I had missed four months out of the year, that I was the second youngest in the class, and that I would be with students my age if I repeated. I could fill the gaps at leisure, without stress to my health. His points were well founded, but my mother would have nothing of it. She so vehemently opposed the idea that Dr. Zeltner promised to contemplate the matter further.

Coming home, my mother talked to me with those wide-open eyes she made whenever she wanted to impress on me something very important. "Dr. Zeltner has suggested that you should *sitzenbleiben*. Michael, you must try your utmost to change his mind these last two weeks."

We had studied the birds of Germany. Indeed, I had done dismally in the written exam about the classifications—the orders, families, and subfamilies. The mechanics of spelling and writing were so difficult for me that I ran out of time and failed to put to paper the little I knew.

I studied my notes again. I only had detailed notes and drawings about the woodpecker. Its curious behavior had captured my interest. In my frantic studies, I acquired just a smattering of knowledge about the other birds, but I knew the woodpecker cold.

Two days before the grades had to be turned in, Dr. Zeltner called on me for an oral exam in front of the class. He had promised my mother to reconsider. By his stern expression, I sensed he did it to justify his decision to hold me back.

I stepped forward to hear Dr. Zeltner's question. "Can you tell us something about the woodpecker?"

Could I tell them something about the woodpecker!

I lunged into a virtual dissertation about him (*der Specht* [woodpecker] is male gender in German). To Dr. Zeltner's surprise, I was orally fluent and was one of the few students who used High German untainted by any dialect. I knew the woodpecker's anatomy down to the details—the chisel-shaped bill out of bone with special reinforcement for pecking and the covering of feathers on the nostrils to keep the wood chips out. Holding my hands in front of me, I told how the woodpecker grabbed onto the tree with his short legs and two toes pointing forward and two backward and how he propped himself up by his stiff tail feathers against the bark. I was a woodpecker. I went on about how he used his long tongue equipped with barbs and a sticky substance from his salivary glands to get insects out of cracks. Finally, I told how he excavated his nest hole, at first by holding on to the outside of the tree and throwing the chips over his shoulder. Then when the opening got deeper, how he climbed inside and turned around, and carrying the chips in his beak to the opening, scattered them by shaking his head. I went to the blackboard and drew the flasklike nest hole and started to sketch the woodpecker inside. I looked at Dr. Zeltner, wondering whether I should go on.

The same smile appeared on his face that I had seen when I had surprised him with my singing; it was a smile that had a hint of pride. He was on my side. When the teacher's conference came, he had the final word.

On the last day, I ran home to my mother swinging my report card high. I had pecked myself into the next grade.

66

Contrary to Dr. Zeltner's predictions, I performed adequately in the next grade, though the pressure rose markedly. Three repeaters, held back from the upper grade, whose presence weighed on us, were in our midst. If they would not improve this time around, they would be eliminated from the Oberschule and have to return to the Volkschule. We were afraid of falling into the same predicament. We also realized that, out of the sixty students who had enrolled when the school reopened in 1945, only thirty-five were left. By graduation and the coveted Abitur, we would be less than twenty, according to usual statistics.

Up to this grade, we considered our fellow students as playmates and were blissfully unconcerned about their performance in class. Suddenly, we were all competitors. Our rivalry took on all forms. Some kept the well-being of their companions in mind; others succumbed to reckless ambition. Our class began to mirror the adult world. Examples of unfair competition were writing dates on palms for exams, hiding slips with vocabulary or math formulas in sleeves, keeping textbooks hidden under the table, and copying from the neighbor in an unobserved moment.

One of the best forms of healthy competition took place outside—sports. Almost every afternoon, I met with some of my classmates for soccer. We played on a harvested field on a terraced slope east of town. Two pairs of sticks pushed into the ground at each end for goals were all the preparation we needed. Off we went, whacking the leather ball until the evening fog rose from the valley.

Before long I became close friends with the other players. One of the best was Fritz. He was the smallest and the most agile. He could not be persuaded to play anything but offense. He was one of the local boys. His mother, a war widow, owned the Seifen Loos, the soap-and-candle store next to the Adler. "Itzer," the name the natives called him, had been admired in town as the fastest runner. When some of his followers observed me running through the streets, they began debating whether the refugee, that *Zugereister*, could beat their hero. They challenged me to the contest with Itzer, predicting that he would leave me in the dust. They arranged for a race in front of the gym.

I suggested, "Let's run from the bridge to the big horse chestnut in front of the gym and back to the bridge." This course reminded me of the races with my father and Onkel Hans around the big oak in Glienicke.

"Ready! Set! Go!" his friends started us.

We flew toward the tree, our bare feet slapping the clay and the wind whistling in our ears. We were even at the tree. After we had circled it, I had the advantage of half a step, which I defended with fierce determination until we crossed the bridge. The gap was just enough to show clearly who had won. Itzer's friends crowded around him, and they left without saying a word. From then on, Itzer and I respected each other.

Another classmate who became my friend was our goal keeper, "Burre," a handsome refugee with short brown hair and a straight, projecting nose. As best athlete, he had been the leader of the class. He had a knack for imitating teachers. He also had a penchant for inventing nicknames. Usually, they were so fitting that they were adopted by the rest of the class. We rarely objected to these names, knowing that would only encourage their use. For me, he came up with "Duck" because I wore a cap with a long visor sticking out like a beak.

Hamster was the name that Burre bestowed on another of my friends, a stocky boy with a square face and cheeks full enough to suggest the comparison to the rodent. My mother, who disliked Hamster, found the nickname particularly appropriate. She observed how he collected ideas of his talented classmates like a hamster hoards grain in his pouches and offered them to the teachers as his own. "He'll go far in this world," my mother said wryly, implicating him as well as the world. I thought my mother's judgment was harsh. One of the examinations of the Abitur was to draw an assigned object. A few days before the exam, Hamster asked me to draw him an old-fashioned coffee mill. I did not know why, but I drew it and gave it to him. At the examination, the art teacher unveiled the object assigned by the Bavarian state—an old-fashioned coffee mill.

Our best player was an unusual boy, Günther Staudenmeyer. We called him "Staude" for short. He looked different from us, almost exotic. He had browner skin than we. His hair was glossier and wavier. He had larger, darker eyes and wider, more level shoulders. He came to our class as one of the repeaters. Mature for his age, his voice had already changed, which gave him a manly aura. In soccer, it took at least two players to stop him. He was undoubtedly the best athlete, an honor he took from Burre when he dropped to our class.

Burre tried to hide the fact that he suffered under the demotion, but his discontent showed. His nicknames became more demeaning. He changed my nickname from "Duck" to "Watsch" (Waddle).

Why Staude did not react when Burre started calling him "Congo Neger" (Congo Nigger) puzzled me for a long time. Did Staude, like we others, give Burre credit for being the best entertainer in class? Indeed, everyone had to admit that Burre's imitations of teachers and movie stars, which he offered during recess, were worthy of the best stand-up comedian.

Burre was basically a likable fellow. I wondered whether he used the naming to make himself feel superior, particularly after he lost his leadership. I counted it among the subtler of unfair competitions.

Staude was untouched by the rising concern for success or fear of failure. He sat in the last bench next to another repeater and drew cars and houses. When our biology teacher stood rooted in front and only talked to the first and second row, Staude immersed himself in a game of chess with his neighbor. He only looked up when the teacher had one of his occasional fits.

Herr Burkhart, "der Nussknacker" (Nutcracker), did not care whether
the class was paying attention, as long as everyone kept quiet. No one
beyond the second row seemed to exist. Uneasy at not being noticed,
we would start talking more and more. The Nutcracker seemed to have
endless patience. He did not react until, over the course of several weeks,
the din became so loud that suddenly he blew his fuse. The trigger was
usually seeing a student talk at the fringe of his awareness in the second
or third row. He would stop his talk, lift the boy to his feet by the collar,
and address him in an exceptionally sweet and calm voice.

"Why do you want to be here? Wouldn't it be much more sensible
for you to take your books and be *out of here?*" The last words he would
suddenly roar, turning bright red and hitting the boy with his big hand so
hard that the student tumbled out of the bench. When the victim gathered
himself up, Burkhart would lunge into another paragraph of sweet talk,
at the end of which he would scream the words and punch the boy again.
Eventually, he would discharge his anger and regain his senses. To us boys
in the back of the room, this was an awesome spectacle. Burre paid enough
attention that, after a few such performances, he could do the Nutcracker
very well. Even Staude interrupted his game and watched the exploding
teacher incredulously.

Staude was less successful at ignoring our other instructors, particularly
Fräulein Bachmann, our class teacher. The tiny, old spinster, nicknamed
"Wasser Omi," saw everything with her pale blue, watery eyes that were
magnified by round lenses in a thin black wire frame. The Wasser Omi
called on Staude with a question as soon as he lifted a pencil to start
drawing. He then stood up and stuttered a wrong answer. Wasser Omi
flustered him more than any other teacher. In front of her huge, accusing
eyes, all the confidence he showed outside the school evaporated.

His embarrassed self-consciousness had become apparent immediately
on the first school day when Wasser Omi had written down our vital
statistics. "Where were you born?" she asked the students. "Hersbruck,
Hersbruck, Nürnberg, Breslau," came the answers. "Berlin," I said feeling
quite important. When she asked Staudenmeyer, there was a pause.
"Staudenmeyer?"

He cleared his throat. "Honolulu," he said. And everyone turned around and stared.

The more inhibited Staude became, the more the teacher focused the class's attention on him. He stuttered his answers whether or not he knew them. The worst situation was to be forced to recite poetry. We were all required to memorize a poem of our choice and to present it individually in the front of the class. When Staude's turn came, the classmates anticipated his performance with curiosity. He had chosen "The Lorelei." It was painful to hear him clear his throat before every word and then stutter it out. Some students hid their grins behind their hands. Others remained serious. I hoped that Wasser Omi would have a heart and wave him off, but she let him struggle to the end. Then, with the comment, "Well, have you finally finished?" she sent him to his seat. Taking a tiny pencil, she wrote his grade into her little black book. Everyone could discern by her dejected expression that it was not good.

After class, Staude had his fluency back. He overlooked Burre's amusing the class with a rendition of his recitation.

We soccer friends sensed that Staude was self-conscious about his background. We became curious. One day, we got a clue. As usual we had been playing soccer on the eastern slopes, close to the Staudenmeyer's bright, modern house. We had to play near his place because he owned the soccer ball. It was one of those warm Indian summer days, and our ferocious play had made us hot and thirsty. Staude invited us into his house for a drink. His father, who was an engineer at an international company and commuted to Nürnberg, was not home. A woman called from upstairs to check who we were. When we left the kitchen through the hall, I spotted a black-and-white family photo on a dresser that interested me. It showed a man with the handsome, Frankish stature and strong jaw; a little boy; an older sister, dark and beautiful; and a woman who looked strikingly exotic, like Staude. She had the same dark skin and black, full wavy hair; the same big, glowing eyes; and the same squareness in face and shoulders. Palm trees stood tall in the background.

"Hey, Staude," I asked. "Is this little boy in the picture you?"

"Where, where?" the others wanted to know.

Staude pushed through us, took the picture, put it into the top drawer, and shut it.

"Let's go play soccer," was all he said and led us outside.

We were indeed soccer crazy that season. Sunday afternoons, we would walk to the field of the Hersbruck soccer club to watch our team hack it out.

After the games, a bunch of little kids streamed onto the field, kicking rubber balls of all sizes that they had brought in imitation of their heroes. One older boy with protruding, translucent ears got his satisfaction in kicking any ball he could reach off the field, leaving the children screaming. We called him Herr Widerlich (Mr. Obnoxious).

On that particular day, someone had practiced shot putting on the sideline, and the iron ball had somehow found its way onto the playing field.

"Look, someone has thrown his shot put in there," Hamster said.

"Where?"

"That over there. That's not a ball; it's a shot."

We watched with great anticipation how Mr. Obnoxious approached, whacking every ball in sight. The sun shone through his ears. He spotted the ball close to us and, doubling his pace, bore down on it, measuring his strides for the impact. At this instant, Staude stepped over from the sideline and picked up the shot.

"Oh, come on, Staude, why didn't you leave it there?" came a disappointed mumbling from our group when he turned back to us.

The boy with the ears went on without interruption after some other ball.

"Hey, who left this shot on the field?" Staude asked. "All right, if it's yours, hold on to it, will you?"

It puzzled us that Staude acted so oddly sometimes, but in a strange way, it attracted us to him. Through Staude's example, our class generated something the Germans call *Klassengeist* (class spirit)—a sense of camaraderie, of belonging, and of wanting to do things together.

In late fall, a project fell into our laps that drew on our newfound class spirit. The Bavarian *Jugendherbergen* (youth hostels) entered the schools with a fundraiser. The class that would collect the most money would win a one-week trip to a Jugendherberge of their choice. We read through the list of Jugenherbergen and settled on the most remote one, Nattersberg Alm above Reit im Winkl at the Austrian border. That's where we wanted to go.

We talked our parents into donations, giving ardent descriptions of the trip we were going to win. Staude got the drive started, bringing RM50. Itzer brought RM30. Reluctantly, I asked my mother. To my surprise, she found RM5 somewhere. Tante Drieslein gave RM25. By winter break, we had collected RM250 from parents and friends. That seemed a lot, but our parallel class had caught fire from our enthusiasm and had surpassed us.

Unhampered by the mild winter, we took our campaign from door to door. After canvassing Hersbruck, we hiked to the surrounding villages. We found hardly anyone who did not give something. Many had heard a rumor that there would be a *Wehrungsreform* (currency reform) and that the mark would be pulled off the market as worthless. Others somehow fell back into the pattern of the Third Reich, when it was suspicious not to give when boys came soliciting. Every day after school, we collected until dusk.

We accumulated RM500 and then RM600 and then RM750. The competing class made us nervous. We sent spies to track their progress; they reciprocated, planting their own stool pigeons. They pulled ahead. We made up the difference. We decided to keep our numbers secret, but the rival class became just as secretive. From then on, we had to hope that we would be ahead at the deadline. Those of us who had bicycles went farther and farther. I was able to reach almost as far with my inexhaustible jog. On the last day of the campaign, Staude surprised us with an additional RM100.

The cut off was on Friday at four o'clock. In the five minutes between classes, we feverishly emptied the last envelopes and counted the money. Hamster, who was class treasurer, wrote the final result on the board, RM1,045. Itzer sneaked over to the other class to find out our competitor's end result.

We had biology in the last session. The class had just calmed down enough so that the Nutcracker could start lecturing to the first two rows.

Since the campaign had escaped him, he did not know why we were so agitated.

Then Itzer burst into the class. "$\mathcal{RM}$982, we have won!" he screamed, throwing up his hands and dancing forward, where he collided with the one he had not seen in his elation.

Wham! The Nutcracker's big hand hit him so that he tumbled against the blackboard. This time, there had not even been a sweet prologue. Itzer sat down in his bench, held his cheek, and rubbed the tears out of his eyes with his fist. By the time school let out, he had caught himself enough to join the rest of us, slapping each other on the back and boxing each other's shoulders as a matter of mutual congratulation. "Men, we did it!"

A few weeks later, a letter came from the Jugendherberge organization. We had surpassed any other school in Bavaria. As first prize, our trip to Nattersberg Alm had been awarded and scheduled for the second week in June. When Wasser Omi, who as class teacher was entitled to accompany us, asked Dr. Zeltner to take her place, our joy was complete. We were so full of anticipation that the rest of the school year became almost unbearable.

The day of departure finally arrived. Our class, bursting with wanderlust, crowded around Dr. Zeltner on the station platform. When Staude came with his soccer ball tied onto his backpack, our team erupted in ecstatic shouts.

The train was not overcrowded. Tourism did not exist, and no people traveled in the direction of the Alps unless they happened to live there.

After crossing the Donau, we leaned out of the window to compete over who could see the blue, jagged wall on the horizon first.

"It's clouds."

"No it's mountains. See, there are patches of snow."

We were still crossing the southern Bavarian plateau when the light blue surface of a lake caught our attention. During the delay of transfer to a Bummelzug in Prien, we dreamed about hiking down to the flat, grassy bank. We wanted to camp there and swim and perhaps find a boat or raft. Most of us had never seen such a big body of water as this Chiemsee.

But when the Bummelzug jerked into motion and the lake disappeared behind the first rise, the talk of swimming stopped. We were all captured by the dark wall on the horizon. The sun was in our eyes and skidded over the highest peaks, picking out the gleam of the glaciers. Coming closer, the mountains revealed their true structure of massive groups of highlands separated by the hazy blue-green schisms of river portals.

It had been barely over a year since this sight had filled me with awe in Bad Tölz. I had been so weak and pain-ridden that I had hardly been able to put one foot in front of the other. Still, this sweeping view had filled me with longing. Oh, to be up there on those mountains and to be well and strong!

Now my dream was coming true. Was there anyone more excited about the ear-popping turns that the train took through the ever-steeper foothills? Did anyone experience more vividly the ride on the truck deep into the pine-forested gorge? How eagerly I scrambled up the steep trail over rocks, roots, and tumbling creeks! How joyfully I greeted the sun-drenched high meadows with distant cowbells, honey-breathing wildflowers, and the panorama of sharp peaks jutting into the blue! My senses were again as awake and inspired as on the day I emerged from the cellar.

The trail eventually wound over a stretch of little hillocks of grass and moss that covered glacier-polished moraines. The rock penetrated here and there in stern seriousness and made the green carpet around it look even more lush, soft, and delicate. The wavy ground eventually flattened into the only level pasture in sight. On the far end next to the precipice rose our destination, the Nattersberg Alm. The weathered, wooden building had tiny, deep-set, windows with shutters and a low-pitched roof weighted down by rocks. It had not been built as a Jugendherberge but had been converted from a *Sennerhütte* (herdsmen's hut). It used to house the herdsmen and herdswomen during the summer when they would take the cows from the village up to the high meadows. To our delight, nothing had been changed. The kitchen with its primitive woodstove and the living room with its low, wooden ceiling; long, rough table; and worn benches were as they had always been. Upstairs, the bedroom with the four bunk beds did not seem to be altered either. The only two concessions to the house's new function were an electric line brought up from the valley and, in the second bedroom, the placement of an enormous community bed that extended from wall to wall the whole width of the building.

Dr. Zeltner, Hamster, and two other eager students got the bunk beds. We others, all thirty-two of us, packed into the big bed. Naturally, I did not sleep in this wiggling, giggling, joking, laughing, farting, and snoring mass, but I did not mind staying awake. Through the tiny window at my head, I watched the moon wander across the sky and set behind the dark peaks and the dawn slowly illuminate the morning fog that rose from the valleys.

Yes, that week I drank in life in great gulps—the barefoot morning runs through the cool, wet meadows; the climbs to the Fellhorn and Sonntaghorn; the eagle's views across the Tyrolean Mountain chain of the Kitzbühler Alps, the Hohen Tauern, and the Gross Glockner in the far haze. We were thrilled when we got caught in a storm scrambling up the polished, round stones of a creek while, every now and then, a clap of reverberating thunder overpowered the roar of the water.

Returning from the hikes, we should have been tired, but we had energy for a soccer game before dinner. The flat, grassy spot in front of the house was miniscule. We made do. We would have tried to play on a ping-pong table, so possessed were we by the game.

Toward the end of our stay, Dr. Zeltner announced that the Jugendherberge had a drawing contest for the best rendition of the youth hostel. There would be a prize. I thought this prize must be mine, whatever it was. The morning dew had hardly dried when I sat down in the grass with my sketchpad. I worked diligently until I had captured every detail of the house, the valley, and the peaks in the background.

Staude strolled by. He had been drawing not far from me. "Let me see what you've got," he said. He never called me "Watsch." He looked at my drawing. "This is really nice," he said honestly pleased.

"Let me see yours," I said.

He pulled his drawing from behind his back. I looked at it, and my heart sank. His rendering was much better than mine. It had force and certainty. The house stood there as if I could have picked it off the page. My drawing suddenly appeared timid and pale, no matter how loving and painstaking it was. Having seen what a winner's drawing should look like, I submitted my work with little confidence.

While the jury, consisting of Dr. Zeltner, the custodian, and the cook, judged the class's entries, the final soccer battle took place outside. Since there was only room for eight players, four on each team, most of us were sitting on the surrounding hillocks, cheering wildly. Staude was one team captain, Itzer the other. Staude had the weaker players as a handicap. The score was one to one at the final minute. In a last effort, Itzer played around two opponents and fired. Already his fans had jumped up, ready to shout *"Tor!"* when Staude, sprinting from nowhere, whacked the ball off the goal line with tremendous force. It rose to cross the whole field but hit the power line and snapped it. Staude left, embarrassed, to confess to the custodian, while we others cheered for this hilarious climax.

The custodian and Dr. Zeltner looked at the damage. There was nothing to be done except warn everyone not to touch the wire. An electrician had to be summoned from the valley the next morning to reconnect the line.

While the game had raged, the judges had laid out all drawings on the dining table and decided on the winner. When I stepped into the room, I was certain I knew which drawing had been singled out on the winner's table in the far corner. But when Burre and Itzer congratulated me, I had to check. To my surprise, my drawing had won.

"But where is Staude's?" I asked, "I don't see it anywhere."

"It's right over there in the middle," Burre pointed out. I examined it. I did not believe it to be the same drawing I had seen in the morning until I saw Staude's signature. He had traced the outline of the house with an indelible pencil. The purple, metallic lines were dug in mercilessly with help of a ruler and robbed the drawing of any artistic appeal. He had turned it from the best into the worst.

While I was still trying to understand what had happened, the custodian came out with the prize. It was a rucksack. It looked rather small and cheap, as you would expect at that time, but it was new. Much more rewarding was the honor. Someone lifted me up, others joined, and out the door I went on the shoulders of my classmates and around the house in a procession, which was half a mockery, half honest appreciation. I chose to savor the latter as the final highlight of my trip.

By the time the pictures were cleared from the table, it was getting dark. As we all sat down for dinner, the custodian put candles in the center, which spread their mild light over the sunburned arms and faces and projected large, gesticulating shadows onto the whitewashed walls.

Staude was sitting across from me. When I asked why he had changed his drawing, he did not explain. He just laughed in his carefree way and shrugged his broad shoulders.

The next morning, we had to leave. On the train out of the mountains, no one looked out of the window. Some played cards, *Sechsundsechzig*. Staude and Burre played chess. Others watched silently. In Prien, we had one hour of transfer. We lay in the grass above the station and looked across the Chiemsee. No longer was anyone interested in going to the lake. We were saturated with the outdoors. Staude led a small troop into town to check for souvenirs. Impatient with the delay, I was not interested in any diversion. I was eager to go home to my parents and Monika.

Staude returned and showed me what he had bought in the gift store. It was a *Wetterhäuschen* (a little weather house), a wooden Bavarian house with flower boxes under the windows and rocks on the roof and two arched front doors. A farmer in a raincoat came out of the left door to predict rain. His wife in a dirndl came out of the right door to predict sunshine. In between the doors was a thermometer.

"How much was that?" I asked.

"Eighty-three marks. Guys, if you're smart, go and buy something if you have any money left. Tomorrow it will be worthless. We're getting new money."

I had only a five-mark bill and had sworn to myself to bring it back if at all possible. Besides, I was too unsure about this money change to make any drastic decisions in my finances.

When I arrived home, the big news was the *Wehrungsreform* announced for the next day, June 18. Every person could exchange one hundred marks for ten Deutschmarks, the new currency. Any money above that was going to be worthless. That was not a problem. Even with my five marks, we had only twenty-eight marks and had to borrow the rest from Tante Drieslein.

"Why borrow?" she said. "Keep it. It's worthless."

Another change in the economy caused rumors. During spring, I had repeatedly heard my parents discuss something they called "Marshall Plan" with the regulars in the Adler. It always gave them hope, particularly in April when they learned that President Truman had signed it into law. I heard that the Marshall Plan would give billions of dollars to Germany to end hunger, rebuild the cities, and resurrect the economy. I found this hard to believe. It did not agree with my concept of the adult world.

"Why are the Americans doing this?" I asked.

"They want to avoid mistakes that were made after the First World War, and they want an ally against Russian Communism," my father said.

Something about this answer did not satisfy me. It was not because I only had a vague idea about mistakes at the end of the First World War or the danger of Communism. As young as I was, I did not believe that a country could be moved by such reasons alone. I felt I was missing an essential piece of a puzzle, and I kept looking for it.

I gave my parents and Monika a day-by-day report of my trip in the manner my father had recounted his walk home. When I got to the drawing contest and winning the rucksack, I did not give away the story about Staude having changed his drawing. I treasured it too much. I kept searching how to fit this event into my experience of humankind, until it finally dawned on me that there are indeed people in this world who find satisfaction in doing undeserved good for others.

The effects of the currency reform and the promise of the Marshall Plan were immediate and fundamental. Overnight, the store windows were filled with goods like we had not seen in years—shoes, clothes, sewing machines, bicycles, furniture, and, above all, food. There was food in the morning when the stores opened, and there was still food at night when they closed. The lines disappeared. Though my parents lacked the money to buy much of what was suddenly offered, their worries eased. They became hopeful. As supplies of goods and food kept growing month by month, my parents finally dared to accept that they had overcome the big war and that our foursome had indeed survived.

Conclusion

The narrative is limited to my eyewitness account of the war and postwar. Once the memoir reaches its end, it cuts off abruptly, unlike fiction, where the lives of characters and unresolved issues can be spun to conclusion. This may leave the reader wondering and unsatisfied. I, therefore, add information about the fate of my relatives and friends.

When my parents, Monika, and I fled from Erfurt, we left behind Maria Barbara, her mother Ellen, Omi and Martchen, Tante Anneliese, and Jens-Peter. Days after we escaped to Nürnberg, the Russians closed the border of East Germany. The "iron curtain" went down. With time, East Germany was governed by a Communist regime, the DDR. The victorious countries treated the two parts of Germany, commonly called East and West Germany, or "the East" and "the West," fundamentally differently. While West Germany was revived by the Marshall Plan, Russia had rejected any financial assistance to East Germany and had ransacked its industrial machinery as war reparation. The enforced Soviet economy hampered any recovery. In a few years, the difference in work conditions became glaring. Hordes of young men left the East, resulting in attempts of the government to keep the workforce in—the wall in Berlin and deadly impediments and surveillance at the border.

The establishment of the Communist state disrupted Omi's life. The villa she'd inherited from Omi Bauer, her duplex, and her other houses

431

were expropriated. The state permitted her to stay in her apartment with Martchen. Omi implored Martchen not to call her "Gnädige Frau" any more. It had become politically incorrect and suspicious to informers.

Tante Ellen and Maria Barbara were allowed to stay in the villa. Tante Ellen died soon from lung cancer, leaving Maria Barbara orphaned.

Tante Anneliese married a widowed salesman, Bernhard Palme, who brought a son Jens-Peter's age, Siegfried, into the new family. A year later, they had a girl, Steffi. The Palmes escaped across the border at night through the gaps in the patrols, led by a paid guide who knew the woods and the schedule. The greatest danger was that the baby would start crying.

The family settled in Augsburg, where Bernhard worked at Siemens. Ambitious and savvy in financial matters, Bernhard secured Tante Anneliese's and Jens-Peter's claims as heirs of the Schwan pencil firm. He advanced notably in his profession and eventually built a house in the near village, Hainhofen.

My mother told me that Tante Anneliese helped Maria Barbara make ends meet. Maria Barbara had stayed in the East and was now in her early twenties and married. When I heard about her plight, I sent her a part of my very first income as a newly licensed dentist. She responded, thanking me and telling me she had bought a new dress. Neither she nor I referred to our childhood friendship. I'd planned to repeat this act of generosity the following month but kept the money and bought a camera. So ended the only contact I ever had with her.

The Hengstenbergs moved from the hamlet of Remels to the city of Aurich. Onkel Horsa reestablished a modern dental office. They befriended the upper class of this provincial city. When Tante Teddy turned fifty, she and Horsa joined a ballroom dancing class that he, being in his sixties, rarely attended. Tante Teddy became infatuated with a landowner, Franz Dieken. Teddy and Franz divorced their spouses and married. Franz Dieken sold one of his farms, Grossbuschhaus, and built a Guesthaus, named Buschhaus, on the Ostfriesian resort island of Juist for Tante Teddy to manage. Onkel Franz and Tante Teddy planned the guesthouse with the "youth" in mind, their children, nephews and friends, who were sheltered in the finished attic on rows of mats. Prodigious Tante Teddy invited Monika and me every July and August during my dental training and first year of practice, from 1953 to 1958.

Eva-Maria came most of the summers on semester breaks from studying education in Tübingen. Tante Teddy showered us with all-night balls at the luxurious spa hotel; lessons on the red, ashen tennis courts; and riding lessons along the sandy beach. In summer 1957, we had become proficient riders and joined long excursions to the ends of the sandbar island. One afternoon, Tante Teddy gave Eva-Maria a sizable amount of cash to pay for a month of riding for her and me. Eva-Maria stuffed the bills into her breeches; forgot to pay at the stables; and, coming back from the tour, discovered she had lost the money. While Tante Teddy berated her back at the Buschhaus, I, unobserved, went back to the stable. Determined to find the money, I ran, following our tracks through the dunes to the end of the island. The sun was setting when I turned to the strip of wet, packed sandy beach. Here the tracks lengthened. We had chased along the ocean in a wild gallop. The last light hung in the hoofprints, and I got close to completing the loop, when the tracks disappeared in the incoming tide.

I returned to the Buschhaus in the dark. The family was finishing dinner. I explained where I had been and that the North Sea had probably washed away the money. In spite of the disappointment, Eva-Maria gave me a smile worth the effort.

She and I sat on a small bench at meals. Sometimes we touched shoulders, especially when she bent back, amused at Christian's and my contests of wit. Eva-Maria said little, but her emotions played on her face.

"Why do you look at my daughter like this?" Tante Teddy once asked.

"She has an unusual red border in the brown of her eyes."

"Yes, that she has."

At another meal, Tante Teddy talked about Opa's brother. "You know, Onkel Otto Tradowsky. He married his cousin, Ida Tradowsky. They loved each other all their lives, but they never had children—probably too close."

The following year, my parents, Monika, and I visited Juist for the last time on the way to the United States. Eva-Maria had invited a fellow student from Tübingen, Adi, whom people on the island mistook for me. They sat on the bench together and spent most time away from the Buschhaus. Eva-Maria was agitated and disturbed. I, however, was elated about exploring the New World instead of taking over Onkel Horsa's practice. Parting, Eva-Maria said she wished she could come with us.

Three months later in Monterey, we received a letter from Tante Teddy. Eva-Maria was pregnant. Adi offered to marry her, but Tante Teddy advised against it, judging his family as too bourgeois.

Tante Teddy was also pained about Christian, who according to her, had inherited his grandfather's craving for alcohol. "If I would have stayed with Horsa, all this would not have happened," she wrote.

She sold the Buschhaus and built a Haus in the Black Forest in Horben, near Freiburg. Under the same roof, she sheltered Eva-Maria with her son, Philip, and husband, Horst, and her two husbands, Horsa and Franz. Christian and his wife, Anna Maria, were frequent guests. When Horsa and Franz died, Teddy sold the Haus and rented an apartment near Bad Krozingen. Christian and Anna Maria had two girls before they divorced. Christian moved in with Tante Teddy. He tutored and became known for his effectiveness. His polio paralysis returned with age and bound him to a wheelchair. Tante Teddy lived with him until her death at age ninety-two. Eva-Maria taught elementary school in Bayreuth. She and Horst had two boys and eventually got divorced. Eva-Maria built a house in Müllheim in the upper Rhein Valley, near her mother and brother.

Over the years, my wife, Laura, and our five children visited all of the relatives. On the way, we stopped in the Offenburg Sonne and reminisced about Hella with Brigitte and old Frau Schimpf. Hella had married a physician and had borne him a daughter, Petra. Soon after, she had become ill and died from a sarcoma.

In 1982, after the wall had come down, and Germany had been reunited, Laura and I and our younger children, Kirsten and Peter, visited Erfurt. As we drove through the city, the empty lots where bombed buildings were still unrestored should have prepared us for the state of my family's proud possessions. We halted, aghast, in front of Omi Bauer's villa—doors and windows blocked with plywood, the wrought-iron fence and rose gate demolished, the pavilion razed, and the garden a dusty wasteland. Where once my mother had planted roses, weeds choked the filled crater. Across the street at 21B, I pointed to the cellar window of the room where I had lain in the bunk, waiting. I felt dizzy and nauseated. Behind the house, the white picket fence along the water was gone, as was the Walk Mill and its dam. The river had shrunk to a rivulet between muddy banks. We moved on quickly, struggling to understand.

Everyone I knew had died or moved. This new world was less threatening but disheartening. We moved on to Berlin and checked into the Wittelsbacher Hof.

The next morning, I wanted to take my family to Glienicke to see whether the house and garden I left fifty-one years earlier had survived.

"Don't you need a map?" asked Laura.

"No, as long as I get on the Oranienburger Chausee, I'll find it."

I followed the highway north. When the pencil-point tower of the Glienicke church appeared, I turned left into Am Sandkrug.

I found the house. The chain-link fence still ran around the property, but the place showed desperate neglect, the house never painted, the garden bare. The front looked so foreboding that I hesitated to rouse the owner, if there was indeed any life inside. I gave up hope of leading my family through the rooms, of perhaps borrowing a screwdriver and retrieving the Zeppelin coin in the door jamb.

A woman appeared in the neighbor's door. Her blonde, feathery hair; wide face; and large, flat-set eyes reminded me of an owl. She was wondering why we parked here and offered to help us. Hearing my story, she invited us to sit down at her garden table and came with a pitcher of lemonade and glasses. She told us the history of her property. Her parents had owned the house from 1941 to 1945. Glienicke had become part of the Russian Sector. Because of a quirk in zoning, it extended just this one street west, completely surrounded by the French Sector. Berliners called this odd projection "Duck's Beak."

The Communist regime dispossessed the lady's family, and they moved to West Berlin. She had grown up there and worked at the RIAS radio station.

"Do you know Hans Wiegener?" I asked, while she refilled our glasses and waved away a swarm of yellow jackets.

"Oh, yes! I knew him well. He was an announcer there; he did radio plays and dubbing for foreign films."

"He was my father's best friend at acting school. They were at the theater in Straßburg together. Then, of course, he lost the use of his arm in the war. But he had this superb voice."

"Yes, that he had."

"Onkel Hans visited us often here. My father, he, and I used to have races around the house and back around that oak."

I looked across to the oak and, for the first time, glanced consciously into my original garden. The oak was as magnificent as I had remembered. The pine to its left was gone.

I dared a closer look. I saw nothing but sand and weeds from the house to the oak. But what was that? Across the yard where I knew of the crevice, where I had stumbled and spilled the tomatoes, where Jörg had run into the table, where I had ripped the tent, there stood cement posts, a remnant of the wall, and next to it, toward the oak, was a partially overgrown gravel road for patrols. It took me a moment to grasp that the fault line of the tension between East and West that had held the world in fear for four decades had passed directly through my garden.

Three years had passed since the reunification of Germany, and the wall had been torn down everywhere. Was this neighbor leaving it as an icon of his conviction? I could not shake my mind's image—a young man trying to escape to the West over the fence, someone hiding at the bedroom window where I had seen the rainbow, a volley of shots, the young man hanging in the barbed wire, his riddled body dripping blood into the grass. Nothing less could have happened in this cursed place.

———

So much said about my relatives and friends. I will also add how the war shaped my own life.

The trauma of waiting to die in the night of the ultimatum halted my maturation. For much of my adult life, I felt like a nine-year-old in my dealing with others. Though I was taller than most, I looked up to them, tilting my head back. Some thought I looked down my nose at them. Being educated, competent, and creative, they expected a fellow adult. They were puzzled about my disjointed character and mistrusted me. I had no understanding of rank or turf of the adult world and inadvertently offended or amused. Awkward socially, I retreated into solitude and created unceasingly. I wrote books and articles and invented instruments for dentistry. I made sculptures for residences and public places.

Blocked from sharing thoughts, I led my wife, Laura, through a desert of silence. Laura waited for forty years for me to write myself out of the bondage of the war and to mature.

Besides arresting me socially, the war had other lasting effects that changed some of my views from those commonly held. One concerns language.

Observing my parents before I talked, I learned that language can lead to conflict. Six years of war reinforced this impression. My parents refused to read newspapers or listen to the radio, which were full of lies. So was the brainwashing in school that my parents countermanded. I emerged from the war with a deep mistrust of language. I am offended by its constant misuse, like the deliberate misrepresentations in politics, the "spinning" of facts, false claims in advertising, and fearmongering to influence people. I abhor the clashes of ideologies and the inability to see other points of view. They breed endless conflicts and needless suffering.

I do not believe that language can be used to capture truth. Groping for security, people build a mental framework expressed in language and shaped by genetics, culture, education, and life events. The framework differs for everyone and contains individual misconceptions. People believe their framework to be true, needing it for stability like a spider, its net. They will defend their "truth" against any other "truth" with words and, if necessary, by the sword. Persons with similar frameworks unite in groups, political parties, tribes, and religions. They seek the demise of the others, who don't believe their "truth" and consider them enemies. The existence of the others destabilizes their mind.

I cringe at the assumption that language can capture truth. I see language twice removed from reality. How the cosmos is by itself, unobserved, is beyond my understanding. I take in only what my five senses allow, like looking at the outside through five windows. I live in the cosmos, but I am walled from it. My perception is once removed from reality and limited.

Objects I perceive through my limited access are labeled by words. Words are not the thing but an abstraction of it. I understand language as a construct of words, a limited expression of a limited perception of reality, twice removed from the unobserved cosmos.

Another concept altered by war concerns time. During the year of bombardments, I feared being trapped in collapsing buildings. When I entered an unfamiliar house, I tried to fathom how long it would stand. Sitting in my tutor's apartment, I sensed a building in its last days of existence. To know what the future held became a matter of survival. The fearful peering ahead changed my mind. My future became translucent. When I moved to a new city, which happened nine times, I recognized the places where I would stay.

Specific incidences illustrate this knowledge of the future. On a bicycle tour to Rothenburg, a medieval town with hundreds of famous, picturesque houses, I drew a little-known building of massive proportions, the Rossmühle. It was the only sketch I made in this town. I dated it August 16, 1952. The mill burned to the ground three months later on November 23. Later, on a visit to Aurich and a car tour with the Hengstenbergs, I made as my only sketch a moated castle, an ugly brick building emerging out of green water. Something called me to preserve it in a drawing. At my next visit in Aurich, I heard the castle had burned down.

The foreknowledge stays with me. Consequently, my concept of time differs from the common view that the future has not happened yet and is, therefore, unknowable. In my sight, the future is already laid out like the past, a static landscape through which I move, remembering where I have been, living fully where I am, and perceiving where I am going.

We humans live like the inhabitants of a big city. When we are born, we find ourselves on one of the streets. As we grow, we move along that street. We come to an intersection. We look right and left and ahead down the blocks. We have to decide which way to turn, right or left, or whether to walk on straight. We continue on the selected street until we come to the next intersection, where we have to choose again. The sum of our decisions determines our destination, whether we will wind up in the park or the slums.

Seeing life this way, I worry little about the future. I am serious about my decisions at the crossroads. I take advantage of seeing the street in advance. On rare occasions I have yielded to the pressure of others and turned in a different direction than the one foreseen. I soon found myself in a bad district and had to call the builder of the city to guide me back to the point where I had gone wrong.

Now that I am old, I halt at the crossroads in meditation and consult with the builder to direct me.